with a BULLET

A South African paratrooper in Angola

Granger
KORFF

Granger Korff. 1960—Cassius Clay won Olympic gold in Rome, the Beatles made their debut in Germany, apartheid was 'booming' in South Africa and Granger Korff was born on the East Rand near Johannesburg to a realtor father and budding-actress mother. "The apartheid system was sewn tight as a Zulu drum and the country moved to a slow beat," he says of the times. He grew up in the mining town of Benoni, a quiet child initially, before 'enjoying' a colourful school career as a musician and quick-fisted rebel, attending a string of different schools for a string of different reasons. He graduated in 1979—alone from the public library.

In 1980 he volunteered for the crack 1 Parachute Battalion, becoming renowned for being at the forefront of the action in the bush war escalating on South Africa's northern borders. After an action-packed two years fighting in the African bush, Granger took a newfound anger with him to the professional boxing ring where he quickly gained a reputation as one of the most exciting young middleweight fighters in the country.

In 1985, plagued by his demons from the bush war, he travelled to the USA on a six-month boxing/vacation walkabout, haunting the mean streets of Los Angeles, scrapping and boxing to survive. Ike Turner and Mickey Rourke were his drinking buddies and he almost became Jake 'The Raging Bull' LaMotta's son-in-law. Twenty-four years later, Granger still lives in LA, where he runs a small plumbing business.

Published in 2009 by 30° South Publishers (Pty) Ltd.
28, Ninth Street, Newlands
Johannesburg 2092, South Africa
www.30degreessouth.co.za
info@30degreessouth.co.za

Design and origination by 30° South Publishers (Pty) Ltd.
Maps by Genevieve Edwards
Sketches by Murray Korff
Printed and bound by Pinetown Printers, Durban

ISBN 978-1-920143-31-2

For Richard Dawson
and all the paratroopers who served on the border

Victory from above
Ex alto vincimos

Orders issued, kit inspected, waiting patiently
Siren blaring, breath momentary abating
Helicopter gunships locked and loaded, flown to battle
Falcon 3 mounting choppers, blades rotating, dust dissipating
Battle plan explained, maps read, radio comms checked

Loaded to the hilt, licensed to kill
Pressure on Doogy's machine gun guarding open doors
Instinct kicks in, hands check weapons
Camouflaged faces like flint, eyes like fire, fit for battle
Edging closer to war we go

Communications update, enemy sighted
Smelling fear or is that death?
Could the mind defect? Kill or be killed?
Noise, noise and more noise, quiet mind, be still!
Power backs up, target reached

Hovering gunships, effective 20mm cover fire
The flight engineer shouts, "Go boys, go"
Individual determination clambers through the door
Dead-man's ground covered in a sprint
Down on one knee, sighting down the barrel

All-round defence established, eyes wide, alert—searching
Sudden puffs of smoke, cordite burning
Battle shouts, "Contact"—dash, down, crawl, observe, sights—"Fire!"
Confusion reigning, shouts down the line, "Regroup on the move"
The hunt is on, looking for movement, listening for sound
Heart beating, breath rebounding, battle shouts again

Enemy retreating—running—weapons blazing
Charging them down with continuous rapid fire
Victory shouts, advancing Parabats on the move
And Gungie sings his theme song, "I'm nineteen with a bullet,
I've got my finger on the trigger—I'm going to pull it"

John Delaney
Delta Company, 1 Parachute Battalion
1980–1981

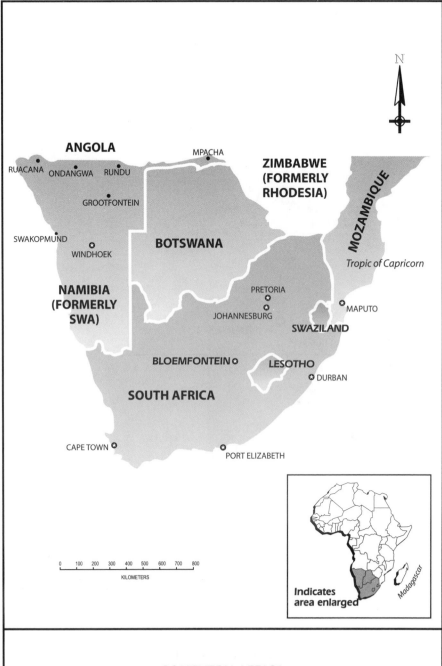

ANGOLA

RUACANA ONDANGWA RUNDU

MPACHA

ZIMBABWE
(FORMERLY
RHODESIA)

MOZAMBIQUE

GROOTFONTEIN

SWAKOPMUND

WINDHOEK

BOTSWANA

Tropic of Capricorn

NAMIBIA
(FORMERLY
SWA)

PRETORIA

JOHANNESBURG

MAPUTO

SWAZILAND

BLOEMFONTEIN

LESOTHO

DURBAN

SOUTH AFRICA

CAPE TOWN

PORT ELIZABETH

0 100 200 300 400 500 600 700 800

KILOMETERS

Indicates
area enlarged

Madagascar

SOUTHERN AFRICA

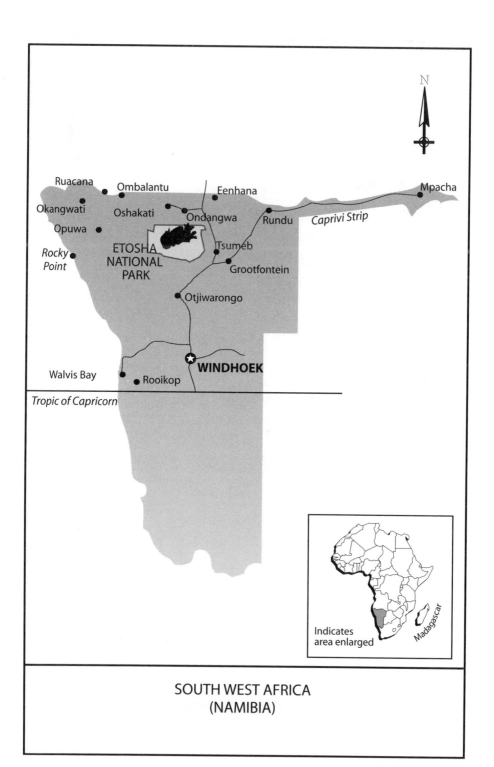

Ruacana
Ombalantu
Eenhana
Mpacha
Okangwati
Oshakati
Ondangwa
Rundu
Caprivi Strip
Opuwa
ETOSHA
NATIONAL
PARK
Tsumeb
*Rocky
Point*
Grootfontein
Otjiwarongo
Walvis Bay
WINDHOEK
Rooikop
Tropic of Capricorn

Indicates
area enlarged
Madagascar

SOUTH WEST AFRICA
(NAMIBIA)

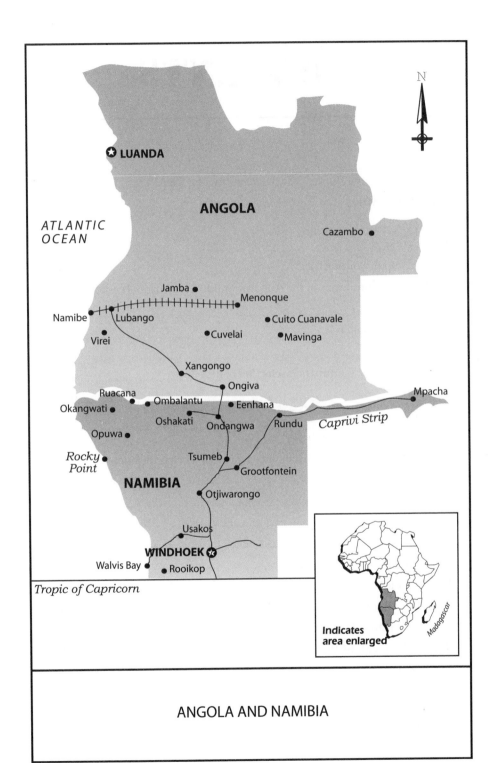

ANGOLA AND NAMIBIA

CONTENTS

Understanding the Border War between Angola, SWAPO and South Africa

Angola

The Portuguese had colonized and been in possession of Angola for some 400 years. Since the early sixties three main Angolan liberation movements/guerrilla groups had formed and commenced operations against the Portuguese in what became a multi-factioned struggle for the control of Angola. This was called the Angolan War of Independence, or the Portuguese Colonial War, which raged from 1961 to 1974. The three liberation movements were:

MPLA—Popular Movement for the Liberation of Angola, headed up by Agostinho Neto and backed by USSR, Cuba and East Germany. The MPLA's military wing was FAPLA—People's Armed Forces for the Liberation of Angola—which in due course became the Angolan defence force when the MPLA took power in 1975.

FNLA—National Liberation Front of Angola, headed up by Holden Roberto and backed by the United States, South Africa and China.

UNITA—National Union for the Total Independence of Angola, headed up by Jonas Savimbi and backed by the United States and South Africa.

In 1974, after 23 years of draining colonial bush wars, a left-wing military coup in Lisbon overthrew Salazar's right-wing goverment. Overnight the new Portuguese government decided to pull out of Africa, handing Angola on a plate to the astonished Marxist MPLA which had been on the verge of military defeat at the hands of the Portuguese army. In 1975 South Africa sent forces in to support FNLA and UNITA, almost taking the capital Luanda, but the Soviet-backed MPLA regained control of the country (only because of the US-motivated South African withdrawal), forcing UNITA and FNLA back to the bush to continue the struggle against MPLA, in what became one of the largest and deadliest Cold War conflicts with well over 500,000 deaths. FNLA soon fell by the wayside as the South Africans shifted their support exclusively to Savimbi's UNITA. With the demise of the apartheid regime in the early nineties, South African support dried up and Savimbi struggled on vainly until he was cornered and killed by FAPLA troops in 2002, which signalled the end of the civil war.

South West Africa/Namibia

South West Africa, now known as Namibia, was a German colony, mandated to South Africa for 99 years by the League of Nations in 1919 after World War I. In the early sixties the nationalist liberation group, SWAPO—the South West Africa People's Organization, led by Sam Nujoma—commenced operations against South Africa for the independence and control of South West Africa. Backed by the Soviet Union and China, SWAPO used guerrilla tactics to fight the South Africans. The Norwegians began giving aid directly to SWAPO in 1974 and in 1976 the newly formed Marxist government of Angola, MPLA, offered SWAPO refuge and bases in Angola from where to launch attacks against the South African military. In 1978, the United Nations passed resolution 435, which called for an immediate ceasefire, South African withdrawal and UN-supervised elections (in other words, a SWAPO assumption of power). However, Soviet imperialism, with its designs on South Africa, assisted by 50,000 Cuban troops and aviators, precluded any settlement as the South Africans and South West Africans slugged it out with FAPLA, SWAPO and their Soviet and Cuban allies. In 1989, the last shots of the conflict were fired as the South Africans withdrew prior to Namibian independence in 1990 under Nujoma's SWAPO.

HOWZIT

I don't like Mondays—Boomtown Rats

It was a beautiful spring afternoon. The bright sun filtered through the long rows of jacaranda trees that lined the main road. The sidewalk was covered in a thick purple blanket of fallen blossoms that spread out into the busy street, crushed into a purple pulp by the wheels of passing cars.

It was a little past noon; the lunch crowd was starting to throng the sidewalks. Cars stood idling in gridlock at the traffic lights, honking their horns at impatient pedestrians who ignored the 'don't walk' lights as they dashed through the slow-moving traffic.

I was on my way to meet my friend Paul at the Wimpy burger joint for lunch. I had left the town library early hoping to beat the lunch crowd to a seat, and was taking a short cut through the small mall. But it seemed like fate had other plans; it began to look as though I would be late anyway. There were three clear reasons for this and they all stood in the entrance of the plaza eyeballing me.

The first one ran about 95 kilograms, with huge hairy forearms and curly blond hair. The other two weren't as big as their friend but all three glared at me as they stood wide-legged, guarding the entrance to the plaza.

It had all gone down in a few seconds without a word being said. The three goons had watched me as I approached the entrance where they were standing, my shoulder-length hair no doubt the object of their conservative technical-college attention. Never one to back down from a challenge or the chance of a quick scrap, I glared back at them and, holding their collective stare for a few seconds too long, raised a macho eyebrow that clearly said: "What the fuck are you looking at, prickhead?"

That's all it took for things to go down.

16

Hairy Arms was clearly the leader of the pack. I watched him crack a little smile as he made a show of passing whatever was in his top pocket to his goon buddy before heading towards me. There was a hectic sparkle in his eye that said this was really going to make his day.

At 77 kilograms I was lean and in pretty good shape. Changing course in mid-stride, I met Hairy Arms head on. It was child's play. I had already judged my timing as he started towards me and closed on him in five or six quick steps.

The moment he was within range I threw a hard, fast straight left to his mid-section, followed by an immediate right to his mouth. I had done it many times before; both punches landed solidly. I had leaned my head into the punch and felt it connect but as I lifted my head I was puzzled to see that Hairy Arms was still standing in front of me.

"What the hell …?"

Quick as a shot, I cocked my right hand. With all my strength I smashed a straight right into his face and, this time, I watched as he went head-over-heels and then down flat on his back. He half sat up on his butt; for a second I thought he might try to get up— but he stayed put, looking dazed and confused.

As I stood poised over him with my fists cocked, daring him to get up, I realized that there were actually two bodies sitting on their asses in front of me, dazed. It mystified me for a second and somehow stole my concentration.

"What the hell's going on here?"

I snapped out of it when the third goon hit me low with a sloppy tackle from the side. He knocked me off balance a little but I could feel there was no conviction in his grip around my waist and I quickly recovered and managed to flip him over in a sort of half-assed Judo throw, using his own momentum to slam him onto the floor. As he fell he grabbed a handful of my newly permed, shoulder-length hair and held on fiercely. I felt my hair tearing out at the roots, so I began bouncing him up and down seriously against the tile floor.

"Let go, you fucking moron!"

I bounced him until he couldn't take any more and let go but not before he had ripped a good chunk of my hair out by the roots. I slammed him once more just for good measure. Just then I looked up to see Paul who had been passing by on his way to meet me at the Wimpy and who was now standing at my side with his fists raised, ready for action. For the first time I was able to look around me and assess the situation.

I let go of the turkey who had tried to scalp me. He rolled away, sprang up like a jack-in-the-box and scuttled off to stand at a safe distance. In a moment of good-buddy-bonding Paul and I stood ready, back-to-back with fists up, but there was no need for the dramatics.

Hairy Arms was yelling withdrawal instructions to his Neanderthal friends who were only now rising groggily from the deck. *"Pas op, pas op! Hy's getrain … los hom uit!"* he shouted. (Watch out, watch out! He's trained … leave him alone!)

A crowd had begun to form around us, gawking stupidly at the action. The three dipshits began to take off, one of them bleeding heavily from his nose and trying to stem the flow of blood that had saturated the front of his white button-down shirt.

It had ended as quickly as it had started. Paul and I turned and headed in the opposite direction, the only evidence of any action a thick handful of my hair that I watched blow across the brown-tiled floor of the plaza on the errant breeze.

I was untouched, except for the burning sensation in my scalp. "Fucking idiots," I mumbled with feeling. We walked fast, in silence, and I glared over my shoulder as we weaved between pedestrians.

I had known easily enough what the outcome of the scrap would be but I was still puzzled how Hairy Arms and his mate had ended up on the floor together. Paul and I walked down the main road past the bus terminal, went into the Wimpy and sat down.

"Damn, you decked all three of those mothers! I saw it go down as I came around the corner but I couldn't get there in time. Not that you needed any help, *broer*. You decked both those *okes*[1] in a nanosecond."

I craned my neck and glanced out of the big plate-glass window to see if there was going to be any follow-up, but didn't see any sign of the unlovely trio. All at once what had happened flashed on the inner eye, so to speak.

---

[1] *broer*: brother; *okes*: guys (Afrikaans coll.)

I had slugged Hairy Arms, but must have closed my eyes for a second as I nailed him and didn't see him go down. As I opened my eyes I thought Hairy Arms was still standing in front of me, so I had slugged him again in double-quick time, but it was his mate I had nailed—the mate who had been standing behind him. Paul cracked up with laughter when I told him about the mystery punch.

"Two birds with one stone, my *boet*,"[2] he hooted, his eyes almost closing with his laughter. He had Chinese eyes and looked stoned again.

No wonder they thought I was trained—I had dropped two of them in one-point-one seconds flat! But they were right. I was trained—backyard trained. For years my brother and I had sparred with each other, using the old black leather boxing gloves my dad had bought us when we were ten. I slammed heavy, rain-soaked bags hanging from a tree in the backyard until my fists were hard as rocks. We even worked on developing our own style of street-fighting that we called 'full force'. It was a pretty useful style; the dynamics of it were that every move you made in the fight, whether it was a shove, a punch or a grip, was to be done with one hundred percent of your force, so that if you shoved a guy he ended up across the room. If you blocked, pushed or pulled, you always used full force and all your strength. It worked but the training was tough.

South Africa, for the most part, is an aggressive country. Growing up on the East Rand of Johannesburg, which has a crime rate that makes New York or Rio look like a walk in the park, it was very easy to end up in a 'situation' if you were that way inclined. So it was wise to learn some tricks of the trade early in life. The East Rand was a string of five or six gold-mining towns that had sprung up in the late 1800s and grown quickly, thriving on the gold mines that expanded and followed the hundreds of miles of gold reef that joined up with Johannesburg and beyond to the West Rand.

Gold!

Our African gold mines were the biggest and deepest in the world, with shafts plunging 6,000 feet into the ground to purge the earth of the precious ore the world hungered for. A century of gold fever brought a flood of fortune seekers from all over South Africa and the world to the gold mines of the

---

[2] brother (Afrikaans)

Transvaal and the East Rand. Black labourers flooded to the mines and cities looking for work. It became almost traditional for young black men from tribes who lived thousands of miles away to flock in droves to the City of Gold to live in cramped single quarters and throw themselves at the rock face every day, miles underground, blasting reluctant Witwatersrand gold out of the earth to get it to the world. Johannesburg itself was built with mined sand that still contained tons of unextracted gold, earning itself the name 'the city built on gold'.

Most of the mines had closed down long since. The straggling reef towns grew to become thriving modern cities and Johannesburg a thriving metropolis. Only the mine dumps towered over the silent old gold mines now—mountains of yellow sand a kilometre or more across, hauled from 6,000 feet below the earth, purged of their gold and left in scattered dumps that stretched as far as the eye could see. Most had now been planted with wild pampas grass and trees; one had a drive-in cinema on the top.

Nevertheless, Johannesburg and the East Rand were good places to grow up ... as long as you were white. An endless sprawl of lovely modern neighbourhoods with clay-tile-roofed houses and well-kept gardens; BMWs in every other driveway; housemaids and gardeners chatting over garden fences as they clacked, chased and reprimanded white babies in Zulu or Tswana as they strapped them, tightly wrapped in blankets, onto their backs and rocked them to sleep.

Johannesburg and South Africa had universities, schools, shopping malls and freeways equal to any in the world—and then some—but they were a city and country suffocating with discontent and torn by strife and racial conflict. Tempers were short and men were quiet and deep.

In my last few years of high school the evidence of this social unrest—the thick smoke of burning car tyres—could be seen in the distance now and then, coming from the sprawling African townships that lay on the outskirts of our towns. Some of these townships housed up to a million black people. These were the workers and families who rose at 04:00 every day and journeyed the 30 or so kilometres to the white world in a stream of taxis and buses, to clean our houses and mow our lawns. A sea of humanity who lived, mostly in squalor, in their own world. A world separate from ours and apart.

A world of apartheid.

The world had damned South Africa, boycotted trade and blackballed any country that broke sanctions and dealt with us. "The evil racist regime," they called us. Personally, I didn't see much wrong with what was going on, and neither did a lot of the Africans I spoke to. It made pretty good sense. We were very different, culturally and economically. After all, this was Africa. The black African people lived over here, the white people lived on that side, and the Indians and Coloureds lived just behind that distant hill over there. It made sense to me.

The world did not see things the same way as me and millions of other South Africans, however, and the world trade boycott that had been imposed on the country for years now was strangling the economy and making life difficult for both black and white.

I wasn't a hundred percent clear on the details, nor did I give a shit. Things were pretty okay as far as I could tell and I didn't really understand what all the fuss was about. The world was claiming that the black Africans were being oppressed because they were Africans. But, as far as I knew, any of the black political parties that were banned at the time had links to communist states that were just waiting to get their claws into our country. That was the reason the blacks weren't given any power even though they were a majority.

Well, it was a good excuse anyway; that's what the newspaper told us. So, like any South African, I just went about my business, not too concerned about world opinion or that we were No. 1 on the world's shit-list.

The scrap at the plaza had lightened my mood; I smoked a cigarette and walked back to the town library. Amazing how cheerful kicking someone's ass can make you feel. I felt in touch again, in control. I felt good. My right cross had not betrayed me, and if 'they' didn't want to see things my way, I would educate them. Whoever it was. But things had not been that easy lately, nor as simple as the ass-kicking of idiots, which was not the source of my frustration. I was 19 and it was the end of 1979—my last year of high school. There were only three months to go before final matric exams and graduation, and I had been 'asked' to leave school. Again. And the school I was at did not expel students lightly.

It was one of the new, very liberal, private college-type schools in an office building downtown where one could do interesting subjects like criminal law, criminology and so on. There were only about 150 students in the whole school. It did not have a uniform like all the other public schools. We could wear our hair long and we could come and go on breaks as we chose. We could also smoke at school, so all in all it was a pretty good thing.

I was just beginning to feel good about myself when word inconveniently leaked out that I was screwing the English teacher, and reached the headmaster. Apparently he had suspected it for a while but could not prove it, while she had denied it with outrage and shock when he had questioned her about it—'she' being the English teacher—a little brunette with freckles, cute as a button and the dream of every schoolboy at the college.

Bev was a doll. All the guys talked about her—the provocative way she stood in front of the class with her tight white slacks riding up her crotch, or how she sat up against the desk with her legs slightly spread as she read from a book. She would pace the classroom, enthusiastically dissecting a sonnet or reading 'The Rubaiyat of Kublai Khan', a poem written hundreds of years ago by a stoned, self-proclaimed opium addict. When she got mad she would pout her lips and flick her short curly brown hair and scowl as she wrote long notes on the blackboard for us to copy, driving the guys wild watching her round backside wiggle up and down the madder she got and the faster she wrote.

One day, urged on by my good friend and constant devil-on-my-shoulder, Darryl, I wrote her a horny letter, marked it 'personal' and handed it to her with a smile as she left the classroom. She took it, also with a smile and stuffed it into her handbag. She probably thought I was having some problem with my poem or sonnet and was too shy to ask for help in class. I spent the whole night deeply regretting what I had done; I was sure she would show her husband the letter, or turn me in to the headmaster the next day or, even worse, pick me out and make a fool of me in class. Who was I to try a hit on her? What was I thinking?

The next morning I crept sheepishly into school, expecting the worst. But, amazingly, my fears were put to rest when she came into the classroom for first-period English beaming from ear to ear, and sent a few provocative looks my way. Jackpot! I had lucked out! I had rolled the dangerous dice of love and landed with huge double-sixes! Since that morning, and for the last five months now, we had been screwing after school any place we could. I would skip classes and meet her at the lake close to her house, or go to her house for 'extra lessons' after school. The black nanny would watch the little tykes and we would disappear into the study. The nanny knew what was going on and would go for obliging strolls in the backyard or around the block.

Bev was 30 years old, married, with two kids; I was 19 and more or less permanently horny. She told me that she had met her husband when she was 13, dated and married him and that she had never experienced another man. She made up for lost time, though, and went wild on me. We became bold and stupid and would even steal quick French kisses in the corridors if the chance arose, or run naked around her car at the lake at 11.30 in the morning.

I was living out every schoolboy's fantasy and she was living out her own. I had unleashed a tigress.

I couldn't brag to the other guys at school about my accomplishment, especially when they would talk and drool over her. I would sit with a ridiculous smirk on my face, and nod.

"Boy—what I wouldn't give to sink a bone in her. See how she was standing just now with those slacks crawling up her bum? She knows what she's doing … I know she does."

"Yeah, cool, eh? I bet she's a tiger in bed too … you can tell."

"Probably loves being slammed from behind," I would say with some authority and a smile a mile wide.

"Yeah, probably," someone would venture.

I would nod my head and crack up.

"What the fuck's wrong with you, laughing like you know something! You wish you knew! Hey, can't I laugh, or what?"

Darryl was the only one who knew; the delicious secrecy of it was killing him more than it was me, but I had sworn him to silence with the threat of bodily harm. He'd agreed, but grilled me endlessly on details. The rumours started to fly soon after a school party at my house when she'd arrived unexpectedly, had a couple too many drinks and was all over me. So, a couple of months later, when the headmaster caught me and a friend red-handed bunking at a café, he saw his chance and delivered a stern ultimatum. "Bring your parents to see me about this matter, or don't come back to school," he said. I couldn't face my parents, either over the issue of bunking or the other small matter of diddling the English teacher, so I chose right there in his office not to go back to school.

GROWING UP IN SOUTH AFRICA

Shine on, you crazy diamond—Pink Floyd

It wasn't the first time I had run into a little trouble at school. I had attended most of the schools in the surrounding towns, and been in a new high school almost every year. To me it was fun—each year I was checking out the scene, and I was the new boy in school.

We lived on a 15-acre plot about 30 kilometres out of town, in a beautiful old farmhouse, built with 40-centimetre-thick brick walls and high Dutch gables on either side of the tin roof. It had huge spacious rooms and creaking yellowwood floors; it was the original farmhouse of the folk who had owned the thousands of surrounding acres that had been subdivided over the years and sold off into smaller plots.

An imposing set of brick-pillared gates led onto a dirt driveway that wound through an orchard of mixed fruit trees and the two acres of garden and immaculate lawn that was my mother's pride, and which she maintained like a park. The garden itself was surrounded by a three-metre thorn hedge that was two metres wide in places. Behind a vine-covered four-car garage was a secondary driveway that led through a wood of tall black wattle trees and a huge woodpile to four acres of fenced paddocks where we had a couple of horses, a few mules, donkeys, cows, pigs, about 30 sheep and a flock of peacocks that roamed free, calling with their unnerving voices and leaving their beautiful feathers scattered around the farm and on my mother's cherished lawns.

All the African staff lived in neat brick houses at the back of the farm. My brother and I would spend hours playing soccer with the black kids on the green grass next to the dam. Afterwards we would sometimes sit at their fires with them and eat *mieliepap*[3] until my mother called us home long after dark. As we grew older and saw that we were all travelling different paths in life, the soccer stopped. I missed it.

When it was high-school time, my brother and I were sent to a private school in Benoni, the town closest to us. It was a Jewish school, as it happened, with a good academic reputation. My brother and I were the only Christian kids in the school for a while, but it was a gas. We rubbed shoulders there with the kids of the local doctors and lawyers. All was going well until, for some reason I can't remember, I broke the nose of an exchange student from Israel. It was my first year in high school and he was a senior. So I changed schools, by popular request.

We were pranksters and would go out of our way to pull cruel and elaborate tricks on each other or on unsuspecting friends, like the time I was kitted out with dark glasses and a white cane and led to a girl's house, where I sat quietly sipping coffee in the living room while Marlon and Darryl told her and her parents how I had tragically lost my sight and my girlfriend in a motorbike accident. The girl fell in love with me and my tragic story, but was furious and in tears when she saw me a week later singing 'Jumping Jack Flash' on stage at a small nightclub without either my white cane or my sunglasses. She never spoke to Marlon again.

It was all rather fun until, at the ripe old age of 15, I got the girl down the road into trouble. Somehow word of it reached the headmaster (who was a world-class prick) so he and his deputies summoned me to his office, called me names and dragged what was left of my good name through the mud.

It turned out that the girl wasn't pregnant after all. That was a good thing for me, as her father was one of the original members of the Hell's Angels in South Africa; he raised fighting dogs and cockerels on their plot; he was one mean cat. Lance and I set a relay-running record over that little business that stood for many years.

My folks decided to send me to a popular private college-type school in the middle of downtown Johannesburg. It occupied an entire office building. We

---

[3] maize porridge (Afrikaans)

could wear our hair long, smoke at breaks, and had no real uniform except a tie. By some great stroke of luck Darryl was sent to a similar establishment a block away from mine. We were having a blast, and would commute the 50 kilometres to Johannesburg by train with the busy morning work crowd. The freedom of the new college was agreeable and we were starting to figure out the downtown girls.

Everything went well for the first four months. Then, on the way home from band practice one night, we stopped for a smoke and were suddenly confronted by a truckload of cops and all arrested for possession of marijuana. At 16, I honestly didn't give a shit—but I did feel bad about letting my folks down.

The next lucky public high school to draw my custom was in Kempton Park. Here I met Taina. She was the drum-majorette leader, and I would watch her leading her troupe of marching girls behind the brass band, dressed in a short-skirted uniform, tossing her mace high into the air and catching it like a circus trick, all without missing a step. She was a doll. All the older guys were trying to date her but I, being the new boy in school, with a bit of a reputation, was the one who snagged her.

I would pick her up at her five-acre plot just outside of town and have to face her father who looked like a ferocious Afrikaans version of Elvis Presley with jet black hair, thick pork-chop whiskers and a thicker waist line. He had beefy forearms covered in a mat of black hair, yellow eyes like a cat and was mean as hell. I understood why nobody was dating her. He would sit at the dining-room table with a bottle of whisky at his elbow and warn me not to bring her home later than eleven. He could be violent but he somehow took a shine to me and soon I was slugging down Johnny Walker with him each time I picked Taina up. I discovered he was a diamond in the rough—as long as you weren't black, that is.

It was an uneasy time in South Africa. The country had been in a declared state of emergency for a couple of years by then; the state of emergency gave the police the power to arrest and detain people at will.

The black political parties—the African National Congress (ANC), the South African Communist Party (SACP) and the Pan Africanist Congress (PAC) had been banned years before because of their communist ties.

27

Powerful bombs were being detonated at shopping malls and bus stops in protest, but it was mostly blacks who were getting killed in these blasts. There were rocket attacks on industrial installations; the appalling murder and rape statistics ranked us among the worst in the world. The riots in the black townships had been going on for a couple of years now, since the 1976 Soweto uprising, and were getting worse. Many times we could see the thick black smoke rising in columns in the townships many miles away as thousands of blacks rioted in the streets, burning and stoning anything in front of them. A lot of blood was being shed in the name of apartheid. The police would not allow reporters into the townships, but the word was that they would cheerfully shoot hundreds of the rioters. The rioters, too, would kill or burn alive any white or—even quicker—any black in their path whom they suspected of collaborating with the apartheid system.

Schoolchildren were often in the front lines of the riots; when police occasionally shot them there would be a global outcry. If you got in their way when they were on the rampage, these 'students' would stone you to death with half-bricks and dance and sing over your body. It made little sense to me, because—besides the rioting in the townships—almost everybody, black and white, seemed to get along and there was a lot of goodwill on both sides, contrary to the simmering hatred portrayed by the world media.

Our black maid on the farm shook her head at the rioters and said that they were *mal,* crazy, and that if the black people ran the country it would be a mess and she would leave.

SWAPO
the bush war on the Angolan/
South West African border

Us and them—Pink Floyd

But this wasn't the only trouble our country was going through. Since the sixties, South Africa had been dealing with an ugly conflict on her northern border. It had started off in a small way with a few isolated landmine incidents and the odd abduction here and there, but over the last six or seven years had erupted into a full-scale little war, sometimes with as many as ten or 15 South African troops being killed in a week.

The objective of the South West African People's Organization, SWAPO, was to try and wrest South West Africa from the control of South Africa and see it become independent. South West Africa, as it was then, had been a German colony until it was taken from her after World War I and given to South Africa to look after on a 99-year mandate as part of the war booty. SWAPO wanted independence for what it called Namibia, which in itself wasn't such a bad idea, considering it wasn't our country to begin with. The only problem was that SWAPO were communists, trained, backed and supplied by Russia, China and half a dozen other communist-bloc countries who, as we saw it, wanted to get their sticky paws on mineral-rich South West Africa, and in particular the uranium that was mined there.

SWAPO spread its communist doctrine by force and propaganda. They would lay landmines on civilian roads, abduct new recruits from villages by force and take them back to be trained in Angolan bush camps. They would often kill the headman of the village and his family, or anyone who crossed their path. They came armed with AK-47s, RPGs and landmines and, by the mid 1970s, were pretty well trained and would not hesitate to stand and fight against South African security forces. The threat to South Africa's security took on a different complexion in 1975 when Portugal, which had controlled Angola (just northwest of South Africa) for over 400 years, threw in the towel and pulled out after 16 years of bitter civil war. The communist-backed MPLA promptly seized control of Angola. The new MPLA government threw its weight behind SWAPO, which had its training camps in Angola, and SWAPO in turn stepped up its intimidatory forays across the border into South West Africa. At the same time, Cuban troops started pouring into Angola as 'advisers', and pretty soon there were 50,000 well-armed Cuban troops in southern Angola, dug in about 160 kilometres north of the South West African border. This was a major threat to the security of South Africa.

My older brother, Murray, had returned from his 12-month stint of national service as an MP, a military policeman, and told us what was happening on the South West African border. He had been in the beautiful Caprivi Strip, a thin finger of South West Africa that drove an 800-kilometre wedge between Zambia and Botswana to the tip of Zimbabwe–Rhodesia. Although Caprivi was not considered a red-hot area, his base had come under 122-millimetre rocket fire from across the Zambian border—the great, muddy Zambezi River. He told us how he had heard the first explosion when the big rockets hit the base and how they had all dived for the bunkers, but he had gone back out when the call went out for a volunteer who knew the area. He volunteered to drive with and direct a Jeep full of ammunition to their mortar pits down by the river. Afterwards, the officer in charge had said that he would be mentioned in dispatches for his action. They had careened the Jeep down a dirt road which was in open ground and taking heavy fire from across the river, so he directed the driver to smash through a fence and a wooden wall and bounce across a field to get to the mortar pits where he spent the rest of the attack.

"It's the sound that scares you," he said. "Shit and dust flying all over the show, bullets sounding like a whip being cracked over your head when they pass over you.

"By the time you do your national service, *boet,* there will probably be a lot more shit going on up there. They're coming in every day."

That was 1978. My folks had moved me from the public high school in Kempton Park to a private college-type school in downtown Benoni. It was great doing the interesting subjects like criminal law, criminology and ethnology.

It was a gas until the eve of my 19th birthday when I was bust once again for weed possession. Some hot-shot undercover narcotics cop was going through the downtown crowd like a jackal in a hen-coop and getting everybody to squeal on one another. Someone must have fingered me because two narcs turned up at the plot at about midnight one night, just as I was going to bed. They were dressed like bikers, with long hair and black leather jackets. They pulled a stash of marijuana out of my desk drawer, having placed it there themselves only moments before and despite my howls of protest and loud protestations of innocence, I spent my 19th birthday in jail. This time the old man flipped and threatened to send me to the big weed party in the sky, but my mom jumped on him in time, stopping him and talking some sense into him.

For a couple of months, life at home was hell again. No one spoke; I sulked around the farm and slept a lot. Mom tried to be her usual cheerful self and walked around the house whistling 'Moon River', but the notes sounded strained and she couldn't reach the high ones. Murray, who was now at university, was the only one who seemed to find my misfortune amusing.

But time healed, as time will do, and soon the family was talking and joking with one another again. One night my dad poured us each a whisky and we talked. He said that he loved me and that I should stop all the drug crap, that I should get on the right track and get on with my life and leave all that sort of stuff behind me. I agreed with him, as I was getting kind of tired of that scene anyway, and had been at it since I was fourteen. I cleaned up my act a bit, stopped hanging around with the downtown crowd and even started dressing a bit better.

It was around this time that I started diddling the English teacher. I was still going out with Taina and had been for a couple of years now, but I was caught up in the forbidden, exciting affair and couldn't give up having Bev on the side. It was simply too easy to meet her after school and screw her brains out in her study, or parked somewhere in her car. It went on for five erotic, fun-filled months, till the end came crashing down surprisingly swiftly when I found myself busted by the headmaster and given the ultimatum: "Tell your parents all of it and bring them in to see me, or don't come back at all."

I made the decision there and then in the principal's office not to return to school.

Paul Jackson would meet me on his breaks sometimes, bringing me the latest extra notes that he had scrounged from class and bringing me up to date on everything that was happening at school. It was during one of these breaks on a windy day that Paul and I were walking down Princess Street, Benoni's main drag. Coming towards us, head on, was a soldier in his stepping-out uniform. It was not unusual to see a soldier in uniform, but this guy looked somehow different.

He was a tall, thin, very tough-looking guy with a small moustache. The deep maroon-coloured beret was set at a rakish angle and seemed almost to glow on his head in the morning sun. The white-and-green cloth wings on the front of the beret jumped out in sharp contrast. His brown uniform was impeccably clean and crisply ironed, with shining brass buttons. He had the two stripes of a corporal on his arm; on his chest were some decorations and a set of gold wings that was burnished to brilliance. He strode confidently towards us and, glancing quickly at our long hair, flashed us a 'Don't even think of fucking with me' look and walked past us, going in the opposite direction.

"That's one tough-looking hombre," said Paul, turning to watch the paratrooper stride down the road.

"Yeah, that's a Parabat. They're supposed to be a mean bunch," I said. I had heard of them, but had never actually seen one before.

"Those guys have pulled some nasty stuff up in Angola," I said. "My brother told me about them. They're always in the action. They jump out of planes."

"Must be fucking mad—you won't catch me jumping out of a plane, especially into the bush," said Paul, lighting a bent Camel cigarette and flicking the still-smoking match in a slow arc to land four metres in front of us.

We cruised around town for a while and then pulled in to a Greek fast-food joint for a bite to eat. There was a lunchtime line and we found ourselves standing near our paratrooper friend who had a far friendlier look on his face—perhaps it was the food, maybe they didn't get to eat much. I immediately took advantage of his friendly demeanour and struck up a conversation with him, asking him about his unit and his opinion on what was happening on the border.

"Fucked up," he said, starting on his burger.

"We shoot the shit out of SWAPO. Track 'em all the way into Angola and go in after them. They bombshell but we chase them and usually kill a few of them," he said, licking his fingers. He had put his beret on the table next to him and it shone deep maroon, reminding me of the colour of a Dinky Toy E-type Jaguar I'd had as a kid.

"We hit their base on an operation in Angola ... jumped right into them. Landed through a tin roof ... hand to hand ... took one of them out with a knife," he said as he popped the last bit of his burger into his mouth.

I told him it was a good thing that he was doing. He wiped his hands slowly, put on his maroon beret at a rakish angle and lit a cigarette. "You should come down; we need guys like you," he said and slipped out the door as fast as if he were exiting a C-130.

I was sold. I wanted to get those wings on my chest and wear that deep maroon beret. I wanted to jump out of a plane, land through a tin roof and fight terrorists hand to hand.

"Boy, sounds like these guys do the real thing," I said, still halfway through my burger.

"Sounds pretty rough."

"Aww ... he's probably bullshitting. That stuff doesn't really even happen up there."

But I knew the Parabat had not been lying. I could see by the look in his eye. I knew that he did jump into terrorist bases and fight hand to hand, and I wanted to do that too. The laughter of girls drew my attention for a moment. They seemed to find something on the menu hilariously funny and were in stitches of laughter. For the moment I forgot about the paratrooper.

INTO THE ARMY

Purple haze—Jimi Hendrix

We stood on a dirt parade ground with tall gum trees lining one side and the camp's tin mess hall and administration offices on the other. Behind us, rising almost immediately from the parade ground, was a large hill covered with scrub and tough thorny bushes. This hill was known as *Kakhuis Koppie*, or Shithouse Hill. I had been in the army for five weeks, having been drafted into the Engineer Corps.

Ours was a field camp—it lay in a long valley with a creek that babbled past the camp and meandered its way past the shooting range at the far end of the valley.

Under different circumstances it would have been a beautiful scene. We were also close to the town of Bethlehem, one of the highest points in South Africa, and in winter the notoriously coldest part of the country with temperatures often below freezing. I had been advised before coming to the army that the Parabats came around to the various camps after a while, looking to enlist volunteers.

When I asked when the parachute battalion might come looking for volunteers my lieutenant, who was a mean, tough-looking guy with a badly pock-marked face and possibly the most sour and unpleasant individual I had met so far in my life, looked at me like I was a piece of shit and told me sarcastically: "The Parabats don't come to field camps looking for fresh victims, so you're here to stay as an engineer. But if you're so eager for extra punishment, I can see that you get some."

I was bummed out, but had kept going on extra runs by myself after PT and worked out on the shooting range, just in case the Bats did come looking for a few good men. I had no intention of staying in this dump for all of my two-year national service. Even by 10:00 it was still freezing cold, with the fog only beginning to lift from the valley. We had to run halfway up a hill to take a crap. On one of these cold winter mornings we had been drilling for an hour, and been chased all the way up *Kakhuis Koppie* a couple of times to fetch a leaf from the tree at the top, only to be told that it was the wrong leaf and to go back again and get the right one. We were wringing with sweat; every troop, every soldier, blew a cloud of cold white mist with every breath.

The camp commandant brought us to attention in our various platoons for his morning instructions for the day. He told us at the end of his rant that anybody wanting to try out for the paratroopers was to stay after parade for some preliminary tests.

Surprisingly, 70 or more guys stayed, and a tall Parabat lieutenant made us line up in front of him as he explained the five tests we had to pass to get 1 Parachute Battalion even to look at us.

He was soft-spoken, with flaming red hair and an easy look in his eye. He told us we would have to run the length of the parade ground and back in 90 seconds—carrying a buddy; do 50 push-ups and a few other tests. The last was to run three and a half kilometres in a specified time. It all sounded easy enough, but right from the first test I began to feel light-headed and out of breath. My heart was pounding and I began getting anxious.

"Don't fuck this up, boy—this is what you've been waiting for," I told myself. My head swam. I had managed all the tests so far, and many of the troops had already dropped out as we set off up the valley towards the shooting range for the three-and-a-half-kilometre run.

Straight away I knew I wasn't going to make the passing time. I was short of breath; my chest felt like it was closing, and by the time we reached the turnaround point I was trailing well behind the others.

I couldn't believe it! I had been betrayed. My body had betrayed me. Why was this happening? This was the very same dirt road that I had run almost every fucking day preparing for this very fucking moment, and now I had fucked it up royally. Halfway back to camp I had to sit on a rock, gulping for breath and watching in disbelief as wheezing troops ran past me. I shook my head and felt weak and useless. I couldn't believe I had fucked up my one-

and-only opportunity to get into the Parachute Battalion. I got up slowly and began walking back along the stony dirt road, feeling totally dejected and mystified by my failure, when my asshole lieutenant drove by in a Jeep and pulled to a halt in front of me in a cloud of dust. He looked back over his shoulder, his one hand on the long gear lever.

"What happened to you?" he hissed. "You're the one who was always asking to go to the Parabats. What's wrong? What happened?"

I shrugged my shoulders and said nothing. I had no explanation for him. He shook his head at my failure, jammed the gear into first and pulled off, spraying me with stones and dust. When I got to camp the troops who had finished the run stood in line, their chests heaving, waiting to give their times.

I was walking dejectedly past them, heading for the bungalow, when someone grabbed my arm roughly and literally shoved me into the front of the line at the desk, barking a passing time to the clerk. I turned to look into the black eyes and pock-marked face of the lieutenant whom I had known as a sarcastic, mean son-of-a-bitch. He held my arm tightly, his fingers digging into my bicep, and glared at the clerk until he was sure the corporal had written down my passing time; then he shoved me in among the crowd of potential paratroopers standing wheezing nearby.

I felt a rush of hope as I stood quietly among the group of passing candidates who were still huffing and puffing. I couldn't believe he had done that. I was eternally grateful to the man. I would meet him later in a similar circumstance and be able to return the favour. Oddly, I didn't feel like a cheat, or that I should not be there. I knew it was through some freak occurrence that I had fucked up on those simple preliminary tests, probably because I wanted to get to the Bats so badly that when they did surprise us by showing up, I was too nervous to get myself together.

Anyway, I didn't give a shit. It was very unlike me, and I vowed to myself that I would push myself with whatever I had and through whatever it took to pass the real paratrooper physical tests that lay ahead.

Later, the group of us which had 'passed' the tests was sent to wait on the lawn outside some admin offices, and told to wait to be individually interviewed by the Parabat lieutenant.

This was the next tricky part, but I had long ago prepared for it. I knew that they would strip us to our underwear and inspect us physically, and I knew the Parabats wouldn't take anybody with tattoos.

Before leaving home, I had bought and carefully kept a jar of skin-coloured theatrical make-up to cover up the butterfly I had tattooed on my shoulder in my early schooldays. As they began interviewing the guys I dashed off to the bungalow on some flimsy excuse, pulled out my special make-up and applied it liberally to my left shoulder and the back of my neck, already pretty badly sunburned after my new no. 4 haircut. I did a good job and dashed back again, full of cream. When my turn came I stripped down to my underwear and walked into the office.

The red-haired Parabat lieutenant was sitting at a desk with papers in front of him. A second lieutenant leaned against the desk, his arms spread wide, supporting him. He was a blond-haired, raw-boned man with thick black eyebrows that met between his eyes.

"Hold your hands straight out in front of you," he barked after glaring at me for a minute. "Now turn around."

I turned around 180 degrees, slowly.

"What's all that shit on your neck and arms?" the fierce blond-haired lieutenant asked in brisk Afrikaans.

"It's for my sunburn on my neck, lieutenant," I answered quickly and confidently.

He stared at me for a moment with fiery green eyes. "Why do you want to join the Parachute Battalion, and why should we let you try?" he demanded, still leaning against the wooden desk.

"I want to see action, lieutenant. I also want to learn how to jump from a plane," I replied quickly.

He stared at me for a long second, as if trying to look into my mind, then bent and mumbled something into the ear of the red-haired lieutenant sitting next to him. It seemed that he was in charge, even though he was the lower-ranking lieutenant of the two. It was cold as I stood in my underwear and bare feet on the cold tile floor. As he broke his stare I looked quickly at his name patch. Lieutenant Taylor wrote something brief on a notepad in front of him and dismissed me.

About 40 of us waited outside the offices while everybody was interviewed.

We were told that the Parabats would only take nine volunteers out of the 40 so of us from the Engineers' camp. The make-up covering my tattoo was beginning to melt in the midday sun, and I was thinking about making an excuse to go back to the bungalow and get some more when the two paratrooper lieutenants came out the office, brought us to attention and quickly started to read out a list of names.

I got a cold feeling in my gut when, by the time he got to the sixth or seventh name, mine still hadn't been called. Then, on the ninth and last name, he paused for a second, unable to pronounce the next name. With the usual difficulty he coughed out my name: "Korff." I quickly went to stand with the other—chosen—eight. They were only taking nine of us from the whole camp, and technically I shouldn't have been there. I smiled. I smiled, but I didn't feel bad; I knew I was supposed to be there. By hook or by crook or good luck.

Two of the guys they had chosen were from my bungalow. Hans Kunz was a tall, strong, good-looking German Afrikaner with intense blue eyes and a strong square jaw, and looked like a fine example of the 'master race'. The other guy was Anders, who was one of the toughest-looking blokes I had ever seen. He was short, with curly black hair, olive-brown skin and eyes with an almost unreal white and blue brightness to them, like a Husky dog. He had veins that bulged on the front of his short, thick forearms, and I don't think he had trained with a weight in his life.

We were to *klaar* out immediately and start handing some of our kit back to the stores. I had to take my routing form to my platoon lieutenant to be signed and released. He looked at me with his pock-scarred face and the same look of bored hatred, and gave absolutely no indication or acknowledgment of the incident on the parade ground when he had shoved me in among the chosen, with a passing time. He signed my papers and thrust them at me as though I was a piece of shit.

'Signing out' took the rest of the day, running around the camp—but it was a great feeling. I was getting out of this dump and going to a real fighting unit.

The truck took us to Bethlehem station, where we were met by the red-haired lieutenant. He turned out to be a pleasant fellow and he told us what to expect when we reached 1 Parachute Battalion in Bloemfontein, a few hundred kilometres away. There we—together with hundreds of troops selected from dozens of other units—would undergo basic training. Only after basic training would we move on to the notorious PT-based paratrooper selection course, designed to "fuck you up", as he put it, and to weed out most of the original 700 candidates and leave about 200 troops for paratroop training. The troops who didn't make it would be RTU'd—the dreaded 'returned to unit'.

I had already fucked up once. By luck or fate I had got this far, and vowed to myself right there and then that I would not be among those returned to unit.

The Bedford truck lurched as it drove over the speed bump at the big wrought-iron gates of 1 Parachute Battalion in Bloemfontein. Smartly dressed guards with maroon berets and full webbing stood solemnly on each side of the big black gates. Behind them stood the yellow-brick guardhouse with old ivy covering the walls, while on the other side was a busy-looking duty office with sliding glass doors. As we drove up to the parade ground, a huge brown and white fish eagle in a ten-metre-high dome cage whooped loudly at the passing trucks.

"This looks like the real thing," said Hans Kunz in his thick Afrikaans accent with a touch of German. "This is where we belong … this is good."

He was even more excited to be there than I was.

"Yeah, this is it … Airborne … Parabats. Let's go," I answered with a bravado I didn't altogether feel at that moment. Hans spoke of the nine of us as a team; we had already established a kinship, coming from the same shithole Engineers' camp. James Anders had said perhaps ten words in the last two days; he just surveyed the scene quietly as we pulled onto the parade ground, his hands gripping his kit tightly. The camp lay along the side of a long hill. A couple of tar roads led up the hill between rows of long white bungalows with red tin roofs. At the top of the hill was a huge, three-storey parachute hangar. From behind it poked out tall aircraft 'mock-ups' and the 'ape cage', from which we were told we would jump if we passed the dreaded two-week PT course.

1 PARACHUTE BATTALION

Welcome, my son. Welcome to the machine—Pink Floyd

There was a huge modern mess hall and recreational area, not like those at the corrugated tin dump we had just come from. There were small flowerbeds around the long, low-roofed administration buildings and all the tarred streets were named after legendary paratrooper battles in Angola, such as 'Vietnam', Moscow' and 'Cassinga', where the Bats had done a dawn drop, landed right next to the SWAPO base and fought a hard battle, successfully taking the base by midday. The whole camp radiated a feeling of energy and professionalism and a sense that one was lucky just to be allowed through the gates. Wherever I looked troops were being led, drilled or chased at double-quick time by gimlet-eyed instructors wearing maroon berets and sporting huge handlebar moustaches.

Any illusions of glamour soon disappeared, however, and we realized that we were in hell. We were sorted into platoons and chased mercilessly from 04:30 till 17:00. Everywhere we went, we had to run. Pulling equipment from stores on the run. To the chow hall on the run. To the shitter on the run. And, of course, around the infamous *pakhuis*—the parachute hangar—where all the parachutes were prepared, packed and stored. It was a high building set back from the barracks next to the jump-training hangar, about a 400-metre sprint up the tar road, along a dusty, rocky, well-trodden path, around the huge hangar and back to the front steps outside the bungalow. It had to be done in 70 seconds by the whole platoon or company, or we had to do it again. We ran it hundreds of times, as did every paratrooper who passed through 1 Parachute Battalion. And we hadn't even started the basic training yet.

Basic training—no sleep, inspections, running 35 kilometres to the

41

shooting range, and sleeping overnight with ice-cold winter winds blowing down the huge, flat, stony shooting range. We were instructed on rifles, LMGs (light machine guns), radio procedure, patrol formation and—of course— drill. We drilled for a couple of hours daily, until we moved like a well-oiled machine—fast, tight and moving as one. I sat on the bungalow steps at night and smoked a cigarette with Hans. My feet were starting to give me trouble and were getting rubbed raw.

The feet were the worst. For the first time in my life, I felt the cold breath of mortality. I had always thought that nothing could hurt me; the invincibility of youth—that I was untouchable, that my body was like a machine that I could push on and on. I had always felt like Superman, with unlimited youthful energy and strength. For the first time I began to understand how easily a body can just stop working; how something can go wrong and that you could get sick and maybe die.

"You should tell the lieutenant that you want to change your boots," Hans said, checking out the blisters on my feet.

"Yeah—the staff sergeant said they only do exchanges on Thursdays. That's five days away. By that time I'll have no toenails left!" I answered, still picking moodily at my wounds.

"I heard that the PT course is going to be extra tough for us, because they got to many troops," said Hans, blowing a cloud of smoke into the night. "They've got to lose more troops than usual. There's almost 700 here. They only need two companies. Most of these guys are going to be RTU'd back where they came from. You'll never make the course if your feet are in bad shape. Boom! — RTU!"

"Bullshit. I'll make it," I said quickly. I felt a surge of anger through me. I was angry at always having to be controlled by others. I was angry with the stupid fucking army for only doing boot exchange on Thursdays, probably costing me the chance to get into the Bats.

"Bureaucratic bullshit," I mumbled.

The notorious paratrooper PT course started under bright floodlights early one dark, cold Monday morning on the frozen-hard parade ground. It consisted of two weeks of non-stop PT, all day long, from 05:30 till 17:00. The day was broken up into hour-long PT classes with a few minutes in between for a break, and was designed to "fuck you up" and to send 70 percent of us back to where we came from. Each instructor took pride in the number of troops who would quit his class and drop off the course to be RTU'd.

One class was to run carrying your buddy across the parade ground without him touching the ground. It was impossible after the tenth time. In another class we would have to carry a 30-kilogram concrete block, called a 'marble', for an hour. We would have to run around the damn *pakhuis*, which was a 400-metre run, carrying this wretched marble, and do various horrible exercises with it, never letting it touch the ground. Another fun class involved an hour on the obstacle course, telephone-pole PT, or knocking each other's lights out wearing boxing gloves.

Getting up in the mornings was the worst, and the time most troops thought of quitting. Should I get up for a day of pure hell, or just lie here in bed and legally quit? It wasn't that the PT in itself was so hard, but day after day of it with no let-up made the body weak and limp and you moved forward on pure willpower, with zero energy. Each day would end with a nine-to-15-kilometre run in boots, webbing and rifle with an ambulance driving slowly behind to pick up that day's crop of new RTUs who'd cracked and sat down on the side of the road, beaten.

My feet were killing me. Every step I took I could feel new skin being torn from my feet. I had tried to exchange my boots, but the hairy-faced son-of-a-bitch staff sergeant at the stores told me with a smirk that I had already made an exchange, and that we were only allowed one swop. I was too green to make a fuss and thought that I would just make do with the second pair of boots, which weren't quite as bad as the first. I had made this mistake before. My feet had always been flat, like a SWAPO, and an odd, non-standard size between 12 and 13. Whenever I bought shoes I made the mistake of taking the smaller size 12 because they felt snug and okay. The same with the boots, which seemed to fit for the first couple of days. But after the first 15-kilometre run I started having problems again.

By the end of the first week, my feet were one open wound. I had lost all the skin on my toes right down to the flesh. I pulled a couple of my toenails out like old rotten teeth, showing them to the guys in the bungalow and tossing them in the trash. I rose half an hour earlier than everybody else, when it was still pitch dark, and dressed my feet, wrapping each toe in gauze and Band-Aids, with a thin bandage around my heel. I smeared thick Vaseline on the inside of my hard boots, all the way down to the toe. After that it would take five minutes to push each foot into the cold, hard boot. By the time I'd done that, it was time, and I would shuffle to the bungalow door and down the tar road to the parade ground looking as if I was skiing down a black tar slope. I found that by sliding my feet and not lifting them I could get through the first hour of PT, until the intense pain was replaced by a comfortably numb, deep ache.

I was determined to carry on. I had screwed up once at the preliminary tests at Engineers, and if it wasn't for the Engineers' lieutenant who had plucked me from failure and pushed me into line I would not be here. I wasn't going screw up again. I was going to get my wings if I had to lose all my fucking toes for them. I gritted my teeth and pressed on.

"C'mon ... do it! This is what it takes ... don't stop now!" I found that one of the tricks to ease the pain was to keep moving. I wouldn't stop moving during the short smoke breaks between PT classes, and would shuffle around or walk on the spot as if doing a rain-dance while I quickly smoked a cigarette. Every day the instructors would encourage us to report sick or sit out for a while if we couldn't carry on, and then laugh as they wrote those who did so off the course. I knew that if I made one word of complaint about my feet I would be off the course and RTU'd

"Just think to the next second ... no further."

Every morning at 05:00 roll call, under the big parade-ground floodlights, there were always a couple of guys missing who just couldn't get out of bed to carry on. Already our class had shrunk from 50-odd men to less than twenty. Every full day of PT ended with a 15-kilometre run and every night I pulled out another toenail and tossed it in the trash.

My feet had became a conversation piece in the bungalow at night, with guys crowding around to see the injury and wondering how much longer I could hack it.

"Your feet are pretty fucked up, mate," said John Delaney, a cocky, John Travolta lookalike from the south of Jo'burg, who would later become a good friend.

"We've still got a week to go and they say that it's going to be even tougher—you'd better get some painkillers or something, or you wont make it with those feet," he said matter-of-factly.

"Yeah, if I sick-report for pain pills even once I'm off anyway, so I might as well carry on."

John nodded in support.

"It's only five more days. If I drop off I'll regret it for years," I said with false bravado.

"Well, I have to tell you ..." said a blond-haired troop a couple of beds down from me, "when I see you get up early in the morning and bandage your feet it helps me go on, because if you can carry on with those feet, then I can also push on."

Another troop laughed from across the bungalow and agreed with him.

One afternoon we were split into eight-man teams and each team was assigned one of the steel 200-kilogram vehicle parachute pallets that stood in a pile next to the hangar. We were told to carry it for 21 kilometres without the big pallet touching the ground. We thought they must surely be joking, because we could barely pick the thing up and carry it past the camp gates without wincing in pain, never mind carry it for 21 kilometres. It wasn't a joke. The pallets were not only very heavy— so much so, in fact, that six men could just about shuffle with one on their shoulders—but they weren't designed to be carried and had sharp edges that cut into your shoulder, no matter how you tried to carry them, making the whole business almost unbearable after just a few minutes .

Six guys would be carrying the pallet while the other two took a 'sanity-keeping break' of about a minute. We alternated almost continually, with the front guys eventually ending up at the back resting for a minute before they started at the front again. If you were the two guys at the back who were next in line for a break, your mind would almost be at breaking point from having carried the thing for something like five minutes and having moved from the front to the middle, and then to the back position. The men who were resting had to keep running to stay up with the team. Nevertheless, we got it past the gate and ran like this for 21 blood-and-sweat-soaked, non-stop kilometres across long open fields and endless dusty sand roads, with our instructor behind us, carrying a long switch. One of the guys on our team, a 'Dutchman', an Afrikaner, nicknamed Cheese, lost his mind at some point. He screamed and sobbed and had to be slapped repeatedly across the face to get him to get a grip on himself, because if one man cracked and gave up the team was sunk.

JUMP COURSE

Comfortably numb—Roger Waters

Cheese thanked us afterwards for the face-slappings and said that was what snapped him out of the hell. By this time my feet were numb, but I knew the damage that was being done with each step. So we bit the proverbial bullet and somehow our class came in first. It was the first and last time that they used the steel pallets. When the top brass heard about it they banned the pallets from being used on future PT courses because they were too gruelling for the troops. Some guys really broke down after that run. They went back to using telephone poles and tyres.

Suddenly, one afternoon at 16:00, it was all over. Two hundred of us stood on the parade ground; all that was left from the 700 hopefuls. Two companies of paratroopers. We had made it through the PT course. Two weeks of non-stop PT. I smiled stupidly, shook my head and swore with sheer relief.

After a week's break to recover, the next step for everybody was the three-week jump course. For me, it was hobbling straight to the hospital in sandals, where a horrified doctor looked at me strangely after checking my feet and immediately gave me enough antibiotics to kill a horse and three weeks' light duty, also in sandals. I had lost all my toenails. He could not believe that I had gone for two weeks with feet in that condition. He shook his head as if disgusted with the army and muttered something in Afrikaans. I said nothing. I spent that day—and the next few weeks— once again comfortably numb from double doses of the strong painkillers he had given me.

My feet would take years to fully recover and were to give me trouble throughout my whole military service. The rest of the guys from the newly formed D Company went off to do the three-week jump course while I worked in the stores on light duty. I would do the jump course a month later with H Company. I found myself side by side with the shit-head staff sergeant who wouldn't change my boots in the first place. He was a real prick, oblivious to the suffering and pain he had caused me, but needless to say I got the perfect size boots for myself. I also picked up some old, faded uniforms, which was cool because all of us had stiff, brand-new brown uniforms. Only after a long time and many washes would they fade to a light khaki colour, the symbol of an *ou man*, an 'old man', a veteran.

One crisp winter morning we were all standing stiffly on the parade ground as usual when the fish eagles in the huge aviary at the battalion gates whooped loudly. Eight large trucks, billowing black smoke, came roaring through the gates, past the admin offices and pulled up to a stop on the parade ground, sending a cloud of brown dust drifting over us. The open trucks were piled high with brown kit bags. Wild-eyed troops with long hair bleached blond from the sun and uniforms faded almost to white leaped out from the backs of the closed trucks.

They were all tanned a deep brown, while well-used R4 rifles hung loosely from their shoulders and long bush knives hung from their web belts. Some had monkeys sitting on their shoulders or clutched under their arms as they passed bulging kit bags down from the trucks. They all jabbered excitedly to one another, hardly taking notice of us and giving the distinct impression of a group of men that had been very close for a very long time. They were one of the senior operational paratrooper companies, just arrived from the hot, dry South West African/Angolan border, which was a four-hour flight from the northwest in a C-130.

It was the first time that we had seen a proper operational paratrooper company who had been doing the real thing—fighting in Angola—and not just running around the base camp singing and shitting off.

The following morning there was a parade with everybody present, where the battalion commander, Archie Moore, warmly welcomed the seniors home and congratulated them on a successful Operation *Sceptic* in Angola, and on one apparently particularly successful ambush . The seniors stood at ease in their faded uniforms, long hair and maroon berets at rakish angles on their heads. It was a breath of fresh air for me and a light at the end of the tunnel. The excitement that had faded in the face of all that cruel PT came back to me as I looked at them and I saw what we were was going to be. Fighting soldiers! After lengthy congratulations and a patriotic welcome home, Moore, beaming from ear to ear, waved the company off on a two-week pass, like a happy father seeing off his favourite children.

The seniors came back to camp two weeks later, this time all sporting short, new, regulation haircuts. After a couple days of harassing us, making us drop for 50 push-ups and stealing our kit and cigarettes, they sat down and told us about Operation *Septic*. They had attacked a SWAPO base, code-named 'Smokeshell', deep in Angola. The base was difficult to hit, because it consisted of 13 smaller bases spread over an area of about three by 15 kilometres, surrounded by thick sand and dense bush with deep, well-concealed trenches and bunkers. They told us how 18 Mirage jets had attacked the base first at around 08:00, dropping like arrows from high in the sky and throwing 250-pound bombs to try and take out the anti-aircraft guns that were filling the sky with white cottonwool bursts of flak. After the Mirages had left there was apparently some sort of fuck-up and a two-hour delay before the paratroopers moved in with armoured troop-carrier support, fighting from trench to trench, but they had a hell of a time of it because the element of surprise was now lost and SWAPO was ready, angry and waiting. Some of the anti-aircraft guns hidden in the brush had been cranked down and were now firing at ground level, wreaking havoc. Early in the battle they took out two Ratel troop-carriers, killing 12 infantry troops inside the big armoured vehicles. The Bats also lost one man on the ground as they advanced through the initial defences; he was shot by a wounded terrorist lying under a bush he happened to be passing. SWAPO fought doggedly, holding their ground, and only after vicious trench-to-trench fighting that lasted the whole day did the fighting finally die down. Seventy-six SWAPO terrorists had been killed and 14 South Africans had lost their lives. It had been a high price to pay.

"It was fucking heavy," said Richard Dawson.

I had known Richard since first grade, and had gone to Sunday school with him as a kid in my home town. He was sitting on the edge of my bed, his eyes burning with an emotion that I was yet to feel. His face was serious as he described the operation. Richard did not have a 'senior-junior' attitude like most of the others in the senior company; he had no trouble sitting in our bungalow and talking to us, and I knew he wasn't bullshitting.

"We were crawling on our bellies with anti-aircraft guns shooting two metres over our heads, with branches falling on us. You can't believe the sound of an anti-aircraft shell going a couple of feet over your head. You shit yourself." He looked around, deadpan, at the rest of my platoon standing bunched around him, listening eagerly, trying to not miss a word.

"We shat ourselves when SWAPO took out the two Ratels. The fuckers killed 12 infantry ... I thought we were going to get it right there. Then the Mirages came in again and they abandoned their guns. We had to flush out each bunker with machine-gun fire and white phosphorus grenades," he said, shaking his head.

I spoke to an infantry troop later who was involved in the operation, and he told me how one second his section was advancing slowly through the scrub, and the next it was obliterated by 23-millimetre anti-aircraft fire. His section leader's head was blown off and the guy next to him cut in half. He dropped everything and crawled away, bleeding from shrapnel wounds, and flagged down an armoured Ratel troop-carrier that stopped to pick him up; but then the Ratel too was taken out by the anti-aircraft guns. He was blinded in one eye but survived to tell the tale and drank a beer with me full of goose bumps as he told me his story. Oh, yes—he told me that he also had to do a cutaway on his first solo skydive as his main parachute had malfunctioned. He had a lot of bad luck.

The South African fighting group ended up spending a few more weeks in Angola when more bases were found from new intelligence gathered during sweeps of the area. These smaller bases were easier targets than the first and were quickly overrun by the South African fighting group, which got a lot of kills. A lot of these kills apparently came when SWAPO troops ran wildly into the Bats' stopper groups hidden in the bush a mile or so behind the small bases. The Bats even wound up having a punch-up with the Angolan army, FAPLA, when they tried to intervene to help SWAPO and the South Africans killed about 90 of them. A South African Impala jet was shot down, as well as an Alouette gunship, killing the flight engineer. Overall, some 380 terrorists had been killed, with a total loss of 17 South African troops.

"That's what it's all about, *broer*!" exclaimed John Delaney after we came back from the full military funeral in Bloemfontein of the paratrooper who had been killed in Operation *Sceptic*. We had hurriedly practised the slow funeral march on the parade ground until late at night with legendary Parabat RSM 'Sakkie' roaring at us until we got it right, shooting our legs out stiffly in unison like a slow mini-goose-step.

"That's what it takes to get SWAPO. Sometimes you lose men. It could happen to any one of us when we get up there—it could happen to you or me, my *broer*, but someone has to kill them, and it's going to be us."

"Hey—we're always going to go in first, I can tell you that." John stared at us with his blue John Travolta eyes as if he was shocked. He always looked as though he was startled and lost for words. "That's why we're here; trained to kill and wreak havoc," he said, taking off his step-out trousers and putting on his shorts.

"They're communists, and they want to take over South West Africa— the next step will be South Africa. Until they run into us, the Bats," Hans laughed, emphasizing his point by pounding on his locker so hard with his fist that the doors fell off.

Because of my fucked-up feet I had waited a month and done the jump course with H Company, not my own D Company. I still had a week to go to finish the jump course. I had already made five jumps and had four to go before getting my wings and maroon beret like Hans, Johnny and the others. Perhaps after I got my wings I would also be full of piss and vinegar.

After my first jump I was surprised when they called my name out, giving me the highest score of the whole company. I sat on a high mock-up and the company clapped as the jump course commander praised my perfect exit and landing.

"Good exit, knees together, perfect drills and a good sideways-right landing," said Kieser, the legendary jumpmaster and one of the small nucleus of men who had founded 1 Parachute Battalion back in the 1960s. I think they only noticed me because I was first in my stick and first one out the door of the C-130 at 1,000 feet.

The night jump was exciting; this time we jumped from an old DC-3 Dakota, which wallowed round the night sky like an old ship. We were cramped beside each other and were jumping with PWCs (personal weapons containers), substituted in this case by the 30-kilogram concrete 'marble' of ill repute that we'd had to carry and sweat with on the PT course. It would be wrapped in canvas and strapped to our sides, to be released on a four-metre rope when our parachutes deployed.

Everything was bathed in the soft red of the 'no jump' light with only the full moon sending soft white flashes through the windows as the plane rolled up and down, lighting the face of the man opposite you.

"Stand up, hook up!"

We heaved to our feet and fought to keep our balance as the plane lurched and the tail swung to one side, pushing the plane into the wide final turn to the drop zone. A quick kit-check of the man in front of you, and then:

"Stand in the door!"

It was difficult to maintain balance as the old Dakota struggled to slow down to the ideal jumping speed, making us lurch forward with little to hold onto except the man in front. Then the green light came on and there was the long-ringing buzzer, like a smoke alarm, a mad shuffle-run to get to the door and the hard slap on the rump from the dispatcher. Then down into the night, upside down, head over heels through the aircraft's cold slipstream to be tossed up behind the plane and start falling; all the time trying to maintain a good exit position with knees and feet together and arms over the emergency parachute. Suddenly—and thankfully—the *pop* as the parachute canopy snaps open, filling with air. Breathlessly you try and do your drills: look up to check if the canopy is fully deployed or whether the guide lines are entwined around each other, or perhaps over the canopy. Everything looks okay—now look down and kick your legs out, pulling the leg straps to a better position, and then jettison the heavy PWC at your hip. With a jerk it drops away, four metres beneath you, as you hold knees and feet together in a good parachute position.

Only then can you relax for a second and look around at the floating canopies around you, or do a Red Indian whoop into the night. Then there's barely time to get ready as the moon-tanned ground comes rushing up at about forty feet with ground rush, and to roll on good Mother Earth with a crash. It was a training jump, but for a while I was a World War II paratrooper jumping over Normandy on the night of June 6, 1944 … D-Day.

On the day of our last jump, our families were allowed to come and watch the jump and we were all, unceremoniously, handed our maroon berets and fabric wings to sew on the berets. And that was that. I was finally a paratrooper.

I felt great, and we headed home for a long-weekend pass. It was only my second pass in 16 weeks, and it was great to be back in Civvy Street again. The farm was winter-dry and brown; the tall trees stood nakedly against the cold winter sky. It was great to have mom's home-cooked stew again and to chat and joke with the black workers and hear what had been going on with them, and in the area generally.

My father was pleased that I had got my wings. We had a few whiskies together as I told him what I had been up to. He told me that they had all heard about Operation *Sceptic* on the news, that it had been a big operation and a great success. He also gave me the latest news on what was going on in South Africa. He said there had been quite a few bomb blasts in downtown Johannesburg, and that the ANC was to blame. They were stepping up their campaign against the apartheid government.

We all vaguely knew that the apartheid system in South Africa was wrong and would have to change one day; but likewise, everybody also knew that to accede to majority rule, then the banned African National Congress would surely rule. They and their jailed leader Mandela had direct communist links. Their small band of 'freedom fighters', or terrorists—or whatever you wanted to call them—were being trained and supplied by a host of communist countries that backed the whole anti-apartheid struggle. Red stars and hammer-and-sickle flags were waved openly and enthusiastically at large rallies in the townships for the whole world to see. The world saw it as a black-versus-white thing, South Africa as an evil white empire, trying to keep the noble black man down. We saw a party, the ANC, with strong communist ties that would take over the country if there was the much-clamoured-for 'one-man-one-vote'.

"If the ANC gets control of the government the country is fucked!" my father said with feeling as he cleaned his FN rifle, his Sunday-morning ritual. He was one of the best shots in his reserve regiment, with a stack of trophies.

"These guys want to nationalize all the gold mines and big industry in the country. Next minute we'll be communist."

"But we can't keep them down forever, pa," I argued, playing devil's advocate. "The blacks live better here than anywhere else in Africa; we bend over backwards to help them with jobs and housing, and they just fuck everything up ... but they are the majority."

"I say ... tell the world to mind their own business, and let us look after ours. If it wasn't for the whites, this country would be like Zambia or bloody Ghana." He ran the rod through the barrel, sipped on his Hansa lager, and gave Taina a smile as she walked onto the verandah.

"Free Mandela ...free Mandela. Mandela belongs where he is, in jail. He's the one that's connected to these communist countries."

I looked out over the large well-kept garden with its sweeping lawns and beautiful flowerbeds. The huge hedge was brown with the winter dust from the dirt roads, the birds were chattering in the tall bushes and doves cooed in the high trees that surrounded the park-like garden. The winter morning sun was weak but warm on my forearms and made Taina's large green eyes twinkle as she held up her hand to shield the rays and squint at me in the way that wrinkled up her pretty nose.

"And that's not counting what's going on at the border with you guys," my dad carried on. "There are 40,000 or more Cuban troops on our doorstep, helping SWAPO and the MPLA. We're surrounded by communists and the world wants us to hand over the country to the 'people'." He shook his head.

I wasn't thinking about communists anymore, and looked at Taina, thinking how she had filled out in the last couple of months. It seemed that she had matured a lot; she sat in the chair and gazed at me flirtatiously. I knew that look and the way that her lips puckered. I couldn't wait for my mother to serve up brunch out on the garden table so that Taina and I could disappear for a while and catch up on four lost months.

1 RECONNAISSANCE COMMANDO SELECTION COURSE

Walk like a man—Grand Funk Railroad

Walking in the thick, white Caprivi Strip sand was hard, and the mortar case filled with cement on my back made it all the harder. I had eaten two meals in the last ten days and had walked almost 150 kilometres. The three weeks before that, we'd had the luxury of a meal every third day. So, in a month, we had had 12 small meals and walked about 500 kilometres.

It had been Hans's idea that we volunteer for 1 Reconnaissance Commando when they came around looking for a few good men. These were the elite—the guys who dropped hundreds of kilometres inside Angola or Mozambique in four-man teams for months at a time, observing the enemy and blowing up bridges and installations. These boys were the real thing, legendary in South Africa and around the world. We where impressed with the movies they showed us of camouflaged soldiers doing HALO drops from 20,000 feet in the middle of the night; small sticks of men sneaking around the bush watching every enemy movement. It sounded pretty exciting, so John Delaney, Hans and I casually put our names down and were surprised when a month later, after we had almost forgotten about it, we were told that the three of us were among six who had been selected from around 30 applicants from 1 Parachute Battalion to undertake the fearsome Recce selection course, and that we were to leave the next day.

So here we were—a group of sweating, skinny, filthy men trudging through the harsh bush and thick sand of the Caprivi Strip and trying to hold on to the very tiny part of our brain that pushed us on, one step after another, to the next rendezvous point 25 kilometres away, knowing that we would simply be sent back again when we arrived. It was one of the toughest selection courses in the world. (Recces' equivalent would perhaps be the United States Navy SEALs who, as far as I understood, did not spend seven weeks of their selection course walking 700 kilometres with next to no food.) The first phase of the selection process was a nine-week PT course, which we were spared because we had already gone through the gruelling PT course at 1 Parachute Battalion.

When the six of us paratroopers arrived at the infamous Bluff in Durban (1 Reconnaissance Commando's base was on a large bluff, concealed by trees overlooking the sea), it was at the end of the nine-week PT course. We watched as straggling lines of dead-beat troops came in from kayaking around the bay and were now running with their kayaks on their shoulders. We climbed down from the trucks and felt awed standing in the legendary 1 Recce base camp, but were quickly hustled off to our quarters overlooking the sea. We had arrived just in time to be shipped off in trucks to Zululand for the second phase of the selection course, bush orientation.

It began with not being fed throughout the day-long drive to Zululand—a wilderness area a day's ride north of Durban. When we arrived in the middle of the night, we immediately set out on a 25-kilometre route march. This sort of thing went on for two weeks.

Zululand is humid and subtropical. It was beautiful and lush on the coast, so we were able to get an occasional green wild banana or some maize meal from the local people who lived in scattered villages. We had to cross high mountains on our route marches, and would walk for miles on the long, deserted beaches carrying telephone poles. It was fun at the beginning to get away from 1 Parachute Battalion and all the bullshit. At least we were in the bush, sleeping in the dirt and walking all day covered with 'Black is Beautiful', a thick black grease that is used as camouflage cream—but after two weeks of marching 15 to 25 kilometres a day with little or no food, the adventure began to pall. One of the paratroopers, a senior bloke we didn't know well, got lost. They had to send a spotter plane to find him.

The two weeks in Zululand weren't that bad; only when all 200 of us volunteers left Zululand in a C-130 and flew thousands of miles north up to the Caprivi Strip for the third phase, did the shit really start.

The Caprivi is a piece of beautiful South West African bush that stretches in a long finger between Zambia and Botswana. It has tall trees and scattered evergreen scrub grows everywhere. At the start of the border war it had been a hot spot for SWAPO infiltration from Zambia but when Zambia lost interest in the 'cause' it became inactive, but it was still a 'red area'—ideal for a Recce selection course. It is usually very hot and dry but it was the rainy season and the tough thorn and big mopane trees were thick with green leaves while the bush teemed with game.

Sightings, spoor and brushes with buffalo, wild dog, hyena, elephant and lion would be fairly common, as we were to find out in our hundreds of kilometres of meandering. Rainy season or not, when we climbed off the C-130 onto a small landing strip in the bush, the heat hit us like a wall. The glare from the white sand was intense and we were greeted by rough-looking black and white Reconnaissance troops dressed in terrorist camo and holding strange machine guns.

"This looks menacing," I thought. "These guys look like they live in the bush."

We were strip-searched and all hidden watches, cigarettes or anything that could make life easier in the bush was taken away. We were then divided into six- or seven-man teams, given a compass and a compass bearing and told to start walking through the bush to the rendezvous 20 'clicks' (kilometres) away.

We walked and walked and walked. Then we walked some more. Day in and day out. Through nights, days, and nights again. We walked for five more weeks, 20 to 30 clicks every day, through the African bush.

No mad PT to fuck you up like there had been at 1 Parachute Battalion, just trudging through the Caprivi bush day after day, week after week, for 500 kilometres, until my brain screamed "No more!"

I pushed on.

My stomach shrunk to nothing, so did my body fat. We now had one meal every five days. We were given three cans of food and a loaf of bread to share between two guys every five days. And, every day, relentlessly, without flagging, another 20 or 30 kilometres. No nutrients; zero energy. Day after day. I had no idea that walking could be such prolonged torture. And now they gave us 60-millimetre mortar cases filled with cement to carry in our kit.

My mind started to play games with me. Some days I felt okay, gripped my mind and pushed on, step by step, but the next day I was depleted and could hardly move or think properly.

"Fuck this … I can't carry on … no, carry on, you can do it … I can't go on. I'm stopping at the tree! Carry on, boy … go past the tree and keep on … don't stop now!"

It became a second-by-second mind-fuck.

We were a mixed bunch, but most of our course mates were older Permanent Force personnel with rank. Their rank was meaningless on this course and we spoke on an equal basis to sergeants, lieutenants and captains. Some were civilians who had finished their military service and had come back to try out for the Recces, like the skinny blond-haired bus driver who ended up coming first out of everybody on the course. There was Jan Muis, a huge bull of a man with bright blue eyes and a big walrus moustache, whose quiet manner kept us going. He had come from Civvy Street after his brother, a Recce apparently equally as big, was killed on a mission deep in Angola. The story was that he had taken 12 AK-47 rounds before he went down, taking a handful of SWAPO with him. Everyone had their own reasons for wanting to become a Recce. I was running out of reasons.

We had all lost weight dramatically; our filthy, torn uniforms hung on our skinny bodies. We had not shaved, washed or had a change of clothes since we had left the Bluff, which had been almost seven weeks before. We were filthy from the black camouflage grease that we had to put on every so often.

My stomach had long since shrunk so much that I wasn't even that hungry any more, and had passed fantasizing about juicy hamburgers and huge, sizzling steaks. But the longing for an ice-cold Coke was ever present.

After well over a month now of constant walking and little food, I was having a hard time holding onto my mind and had lost the ability to judge distance and time. We had stopped quarrelling among ourselves over teamwork and now just walked in long silence, a line of six men spread over the space of half a kilometre, walking on each other's spoor.

Hyenas constantly followed us in the distance; at night they would come right up among us hoping to take a chance bite of a carelessly exposed limb or skull. We slept like the spokes of a wagon-wheel, around a tree with our heads against the tree and our feet sticking out. Wild dogs would also be yapping in hunting packs close by, but they never bothered us.

We had reached a rendezvous point; it was feeding day and John Delaney and I were sitting under a large tree wolfing down our weekly three cans of beans. The instructors told us that 'another paratrooper' had been attacked and mauled by a lioness but was alright, and was continuing on the course with a few scratches. The lioness had crept up to him as he settled down to sleep. She had jumped him but quickly took fright and ran off when the other troops yelled at her in unison. We laughed, because it was Hans, and we knew that he would have a long story to tell when we met up with him again.

John and I were scooping the remains of the beans juice from the can with bread. We had no food left for the next five days.

"Fuck this—I've had it with this horseshit. Fuck this! I'm not going on," said John suddenly.

It was the first time we had openly said what we had both been wrestling with every second of the day for the last two weeks. I needed no more persuasion. I didn't even look up from soaking my bread with bean juice.

"Ja, me too, I've had it. I don't want to go on."

An elated, blissful feeling flooded through me now that I had quickly and finally given up. All in all we had walked close to 700 kilometres with a handful of small meals, and it had taken its toll. My body was far beyond just being bone-weary: my brain was fatigued and drained of nutrients and chemical reactions were taking place over which I had no control. I suddenly felt that I couldn't walk another step.

John and I walked over to the instructor who was sitting in the Jeep, smoking. They called him 'Bones'. He was thin and dark-skinned with penetrating brown eyes. He glared at us and took a deep drag of his cigarette, holding the smoke in for a while. He rested his right arm, which had been disfigured by AK-47 rounds in some cocked-up reconnaissance operation, on the steering wheel of the Jeep. His forearm seemed to jut out at an angle just before the wrist, giving it a broken look, and the scars looked like thin plastic, hollow and concave. They did not look very old.

He exhaled smoke into our faces.

"Bullshit. You can't get off the course on this phase; it's not allowed. You have to complete it. Fill your canteens. Tonight you do 30 clicks. You guys are paratroopers—I thought you were supposed to be tough."

We walked most of the night and the next day. Now that I had no will to carry on, every step was pure hell and we dragged behind the rest of the stick.

I felt I had betrayed myself to have gone through six weeks of hell only to give up now. This self-condemnation only made it worse. I comforted myself by saying that I had not really wanted to be a Recce in the first place. All I had wanted was to be a paratrooper. I contemplated just sitting down and sleeping, but the constant presence of the hyenas not far behind spurred me on. We walked for a few more days before they mercifully took John and me and about 12 other dropouts from other teams and left us at a large tree until the course ended. When that would be, nobody knew.

We sat and rested under that big tree for five more days before the course came to an end. We dug a two-metre-deep waterhole with branches; some had even used their rifles as spades, not caring a damn. We got enough water out of it to wet our clothes in a crude wash. Instructors picked us up in a Buffel and we drove for about 50 kilometres until we finally came to Fort Doppies, the Recce bush base in the operational area.

The showers felt glorious after so long. We laughed at how much weight we had lost. We looked like the prisoners of war in photos I had seen in history books. Hans's once-muscular 1.94-metre body was now skin and bone. He had lost at least 12 kilograms, and had lost all his buttock cheeks. His ever-intense stare, with bulging eyes in his thin face, made him look like a mad man

After the showers we had peanut butter and honey sandwiches on fresh bread with lots of butter. For many years afterward, I could still taste that sandwich every time I thought of it. There was an air of relief as we lay around the camp, all cleaned up and in torn —but washed—clothes, smoking and drinking ice-cold Cokes. The following day the instructors shot a huge buffalo and we had a *braai*, a barbecue, with buffalo steaks bigger than even our bellies could think of eating.

Out of the 200 hopefuls, only 17 troops had made the course to become Reconnaissance operators and who would get to wear the springbok head on the maroon beret; to do HALO oxygen jumps hundreds of miles inside Angola. Hans was one of them. John and I were told we should not have quit because we had been really close to the end of the course and had come in 27th out of the two hundred. So about 170 had quit before us. Some consolation!

"At least one paratrooper made it," I said, patting Hans on his once-muscular shoulder. John and I hadn't done that badly. Most of the 200, we found out, had long since been RTU'd, dropping out in the first couple of weeks.

"I suppose it's back to 1 Para for us," I said, staring at Hans, who seemed to have changed and didn't have much to say. Perhaps the last week was the one that really killed you, I thought. We had got to rest under the big tree for five days and we were already feeling better.

NOW WHAT?

Last train to London—Electric Light Orchestra

It was the first time I had thought in terms of going back to 1 Parachute Battalion since I had started the Recce course, and it caught me by surprise. Now we were probably going to be shipped back—ignominiously RTU'd.

In my fatigued and depleted state it made me sick to think of going back to the battalion and being a *roofie* again—to run all over the base singing bullshit songs, hair shaven in #4 style, corporals and stupid fucking lieutenants shouting at the tops of their voices. Since we had been on the Reconnaissance course we had been walking side by side with majors, lieutenants and captains. We had slept and suffered together and all been treated as equals and as men—not as raw green recruits, which is what we were going back to at 1 Para. Nothing worse than being a a *roofie*, a scab

The thought was not a good one. John and I asked around if anyone knew where we would be sent and they told us that we would perhaps be sent to 32 Battalion reconnaissance that was also based on the border and with a good reputation as a fighting unit. We were relieved that we might not have to return to 1 Para and saw ourselves staying in the bush. We hung around the base for a couple of days getting our meagre kit together and listening to the Recce instructors' war stories.

The reason they were instructors on the selection course was that they were all no longer fit for operational duty, and they all eagerly showed us the bullet wounds they had received on Recce missions-gone-wrong in Angola. I came across an acquaintance I knew from back home; he too had a pretty recent AK-47 bullet hole in him. He enthusiastically told me to come back on the next course; he said a lot of guys made it the second time around because they knew what they were going to be dealing with. I agreed with him and said that I would, but inside I felt mentally numb and had no inclination to do it all again. Actually I had no inclination for anything much and just wanted to rest. I was deep in thought when John came walking across the small grassway.

"Bones just told me we're all going back to the Bluff tomorrow and you and I are going back to 1 Para."

We packed our kit onto the C-130 cargo plane and took off, leaving the Caprivi Strip and its endless vistas of bush and its idiotic laughing hyenas. I looked out of the window at the vastness of the terrain we had walked across, and at how the bush stretched featureless and ended in a white haze far on the horizon. I wondered why the sky was white—not blue like at home, but just a white haze every day. It was strange. Was it the reflection of the white sand? I pondered this for a while, then quickly fell asleep like everyone else. I still felt drained and detached from the rest of the world, like my mind was working in slow motion. I had had enough of this soldier bullshit. My desire to be a fighting soldier was gone. I didn't care anymore. I had got my wings at 1 Para and that was going to have to be good enough.

I spent the rest of the trip scheming how I could get transferred to a service unit close to home, where the guys got to go home every weekend. I would be close to Taina and there'd be no more walking, heavy kit, shouting instructors or sleeping in the dirt. I would drive a food truck or work as an office clerk and maybe even get to go home during the week. My dad was quite a big knob in the Reserves and could possibly pull some strings.

We landed at Durban just in time to see the sun slip away and darkness envelop the high-rise holiday city. We were quickly piled into Bedford trucks and peered out as we drove through the city with its flashing neon lights, rushing cars and busy sidewalks. At the Bluff we dragged our kit upstairs to the empty two-storey barracks overlooking the sea and wolfed down the sandwiches and strong hot coffee that were waiting for us in the kitchen. The Recce camp seemed deserted. We were casually told that we were free to go to town if we felt like it. Eagerly we pulled our borrowed, wrinkled civvy clothes that we had arrived in from the bottom of the kit we had left at the Bluff. John, Hans and I wasted no time scooting out the base and catching the ferry that took us across the bay to the twinkling lights of downtown

Durban. It was the eve of my 20th birthday, so there was added cause for celebration.

"Hey, here, this one looks good," said Johnny as we dodged cars crossing the busy main road and headed toward the little pub squashed in between two restaurants.

He looked hilarious, dressed in too-short borrowed jeans with a belt pulled tight around his skinny waist.

It was great to sit at a bar and taste a beer again. I had dreamed of this moment countless times while walking in the sun.

Hans was guzzling his third Castle lager and getting feisty.

"Ever tried walking 700 kilometres with no food?" Hans was loudly challenging the few patrons around us. Sensing trouble, I suggested that we move on. Pretty soon we were walking down Marine Parade, loaded to the gills, wild-eyed and looking for some girls to talk to. But with our looks we had no chance. We crossed the busy road to the beach and ran into a kid who said he had some marijuana to sell, and did we want to buy some? Loaded as we were, we said "Why not?", bought enough for a couple of joints and started walking, looking for a place down at the beach to smoke the stuff.

But Lady Luck had other ideas.

Just before the beach, I saw a car driving past us with its lights off.

"Hey, your lights are off!" Johnny yelled without hesitation, and I walked up to the car as it pulled to a stop. Inside were five burly men who any street kid even a mile away would instantly have known were cops—but perhaps my judgment was off, just coming out of the bush.

"Where's the action around here?" I inquired, leaning into the car window.

They looked at me and casually told me that they were on their way to pick up a load of marijuana, and did I want to come along?

I replied that we had already scored our own and opened my fingers to show them the small quantity I had in my right hand. I realized too late that it was the wrong answer and that they were cops. The doors swung open and they sprang out of the car like a Natal rugby forward front row and tried to grab me. In a split second I realized that it was the same time, almost to the hour, that I had been arrested the year before, on the eve of my birthday, and

I had no intention of it happening again.

I stood my ground and started throwing punches as hard and fast as I could. I caught a beefy, fat-faced cop full in the mouth and he staggered. The others tried to grab my clothes and pull me down, but I kept moving, trying to break up the weed and toss it away at the same time. One tall cop got a good hold of my collar, tearing my T-shirt to the sleeve. I turned and slammed my fist into his ear, hurting my knuckle. They weren't having much luck; I was catching them with combinations that still came easily to me, even after being in the bush with no food!

I was just starting to think that I was going to get away with fighting them off.

"Get on the fucking ground or I'll shoot you," one of them finally yelled desperately in Afrikaans. It was the chubby one I had caught in the mouth. He was standing a couple of yards back with his gun drawn. He was standing, legs apart, breathing hard with both hands holding his revolver and pointing it directly at me.

I had no choice but to sit on the ground. John and Hans had wisely split during the fight, so I was alone. It was a bad situation. I couldn't believe I had been arrested again. I had only been back in Civvy Street for three hours and already I was busted and on my way to jail.

In the cell I pulled up an old grey blanket and fell into a deep untroubled sleep. I woke in the morning feeling like puking, with a dull headache and a blue eye from where I'd taken a knock the night before. I was moved to a holding cell with about 20 other unfortunates, and waited my turn to see the judge, who was in the same building but on a different floor.

I kept to myself and sat quietly on the floor, thinking over the recent events in my life and weighing up my situation. I had received a two-year sentence the year before, which had been suspended. Those two years were not yet up, so I was probably going to be in the shit; I would get a jail sentence. I wondered how they would react at 1 Reconnaissance and if I did time whether it would be in a civilian jail or in Detention Barracks, DB.

I also wondered what kind of jinx was on me that I was in jail on my birthday, twice in a row. In court I had no counsel; I stood abjectly in the dock and pleaded guilty to possession. I was fully expecting the full brunt of the law and thought I would probably be in the right frame of mind for jail after living like a dog for the last month and more.

"Are you the guy from 1 Reconnaissance Commando?" the judge said, shuffling through a stack of papers on the bench in front of him.

"Yes, sir," I said, standing at ease with my hands behind my back and looking straight ahead with my best Special Forces look. I told him that I had just come from the operational area and had been in the bush for seven weeks straight, that I had got carried away buying the marijuana—a thing that I did not usually do and would certainly never do again.

He shuffled his notes again and told me that I could end up in serious trouble, that a man of my calibre from 1 Recce should know better. He seemed impressed by my serious demeanour and clearly thought I was a Special Forces operator.

"And how are things going up at the border?" he asked by the way, without lifting his head.

"Where I've just come from it's been pretty busy, sir," I answered in an over-serious voice.

He wrote for a minute, then looked at me and paused. "Well, Mr Korff, from your record it looks like you are always looking for trouble—and in this case, it looks like you have found it. However, I'm informed that you have important work to do and that you need to get back to your unit as soon as possible. You'll receive four strokes of the cane, and let's not see you here again."

Four strokes! What luck!

I walked out of the dock and was led downstairs down two long corridors, to a small room. I was chuffed. Someone must have pulled some strings for me to get off with just a caning. I was no stranger to a good caning; although I had heard about these police canings—they were supposed to be pretty harsh. A stocky constable pulled two benches together and indicated that I should lie on my belly. He then put two grey jail blankets over me, one across the small of my back and the other across the back of my thighs, leaving my arse exposed for the cane.

He pulled out a cylinder of long plastic canes, made a show of selecting one and bent it, touching it from tip to tip, testing its flexibility. At high school the headmaster or teacher was only allowed to use a rigid cane, and could not lift the cane above the level of his shoulder. This was a little different. This guy pulled the 'whip' back as far as he could and brought it slamming down on my arse with all his might as if he was trying to cut me in half. I was determined not to show any pain. The first two were so hard that I did not feel anything. It was too much pain too quickly for my brain to register. Only when he brought the third and fourth ones slamming down on the same spot did the pain shoot waves through me like an electric current, and I felt as though the top of my head would blow off.

There was a pretty little policewoman who had poked her head around the door to watch the caning. Even though the pain was excruciating, almost overwhelming, I was poker-faced and showed no reaction to the pain that was going through me like 1,000 volts. The only clue I gave was slamming my fist as hard as I could into the wooden bench as I calmly got up.

In measured words I asked the cop where I could get a taxi back to the Bluff, and whether he could perhaps lend me a couple of bucks for a taxi. He could scarcely hide his surprise at my cheek, and had a stupid smile on his face as he packed away the plastic whip. I really felt like bellowing at the top of my voice and could hardly contain the impulse to jump up and down and rub my burning arse as hard as I could, but with a supreme effort I calmly walked out of the room and the building with my hands at my side, as if I had not felt a damn thing.

He declined to lend me money for a taxi.

GATVOL

Stones in my passway—Robert Johnson

Walking into the quiet 1 Reconnaissance base, on the way to the bathrooms, I met John Delaney at the bottom of the stairs. He was all cleaned up and in uniform. He told me I had to pack my kit immediately and sign out right now if I was to catch the truck taking us to the train station. It was leaving in about half an hour. After a quick change from dirty civvies into my browns I hastily inspected my still-throbbing arse, revealing huge, thick, black-and-blue welts across my buttocks. The skin had not been split, but it was very close as pinpoints of reddish plasma oozed from the swollen black pores. The whole of my skinny rump looked like a technicolour sunset—it was inflamed cherry-red all the way from my back to my thighs. The whip had also curled around the far side of my hip and reached the hip bone, which hurt the most. I felt it for many weeks.

I double-timed down to the dark administration block and walked to the only office that still had a light on. Behind the desk sat a black-haired major with an aide standing at his side. The major's face was terribly scarred. It appeared too that he was blind. It also seemed as if most of his fingers and part of his hand were missing.

"Stand easy," he said after I had saluted him.

I wondered how he had seen me. He seemed a nice fellow.

"What the hell happened to you last night?" he asked unassumingly.

"I got in to some trouble, sir ..." I answered.

"I know, I got you out!" he said loudly and quickly. He asked me why I hadn't made the course because I had been doing well. That was news to me and I answered something about having a beautiful girl waiting for me at home and not wanting to sign up for another four years.

We chatted casually for a while on a one-to-one level that impressed me; he rubbed his slits-for-eyes with his stumps-for-fingers as he did so. (I later found out that he had been maimed in an accident while setting an explosive charge.) He invited me back to try the selection course again, saying that my chances of success would be far greater next time and that a lot of guys only made it on their third or fourth try. He then had his aide walk me through some 'class' photos that were hanging on the wall and point out the operators who had been killed in action. Every class photo of 15 to 20 men featured three or four who were now 'operating in the big bush above'. I thanked the major for his help; he signed my release papers and I walked away, down the now dark, echoing, deserted halls of 1 Reconnaissance Commando.

John and I sat deep in conversation on the two-day train ride from Durban to Bloemfontein. As we were in no hurry to get back to 1 Parachute Battalion, we decided to jump the train, go AWOL and hitchhike home to Johannesburg for a couple days of R&R. To hell with everybody, the Parabats included. We deserved it after what we had been through. We spent a cold, wet night under a freeway bridge, which was a walk in the park after spending all that time in the bush in the Caprivi. The next day we were cruising past the yellow mine-dumps of Johannesburg.

I sat quietly sipping my Johnny Walker and savouring the pleasure of normal life. Taina sat next to me with her legs squeezed tightly against mine under the table; her big green eyes sparkled. This was life. To hell with the army—I had had enough.

A few days later I drove up to one of my favorite spots where my brother and I used to go horseback riding. We would gallop recklessly down the long, uneven, potholed dirt road that was lined with old 30-metre-high black wattle trees until it petered out and came to an end in the never-ending veld. Standing there, I could look down across the miles of long shallow valley which the old farmhouse overlooked. On the far crest of the valley I could see the busy road that led to town, 25-or-so kilometres away. In between was a patchwork of long, ploughed fields of vegetables that belonged to the Portuguese farmer and fields of long dry grass around the small houses of the black farm workers, bunched together in a row and from which fragrant wood smoke drifted lazily and hung heavily at the bottom of the valley.

I was contemplating not going back at all. Fuck them—I'll go AWOL for good this time and leave the country if I have to. The Transkei, a popular fishing and holiday spot for South Africans, was a black 'homeland'. It was also called the Wild Coast, and was a loosely-run independent black 'state' wholly within South Africa. It had the feel of Jamaica or some other seaside banana republic, with little ragged black children holding up huge crayfish for sale at the roadside. The terrain was thick, lush and tropical, with rolling mountains that rose into the low layer of clouds and canyons that were dense with high trees and covered with moss and long Tarzan vines. It was a favourite place for 'heads'—some of the best pot in the world grew in abundance here, high in the misty mountains, and you could buy sacks of the stuff for next-to-nothing.

I thought I would find a job in one of the many resorts or just live and fish on one of the many long deserted beaches until the heat was off. I even thought of going overseas. Fuck this—I could get a ticket and just go to America. I had enough from my army payroll for an air ticket. I had an uncle who lived in Colorado; he could probably help me out. Or I'll plead for political asylum; the Yanks will go for that—I'll say that I didn't want to fight for the white racist regime.

I had been in the army for only seven months and all I had achieved was to shit off in a big way. Straight from the tough Bats to one of the toughest courses in the world at Special Forces selection. I needed some time off. I needed to relax for a while and replenish myself. Screw everybody and everything. America?

It was a thought—but what the hell would I do there? All my family and friends were here. I loved Africa. I loved the open bushveld and the big thorn trees, the smell of wood smoke from the kraals in the winter and the high brown grass. I had no personal quarrel with the black people; I never had. I loved the people of South Africa. The *ousies*, the old mamas, who could walk for many kilometres on the side of the road with improbably large bundles balanced on their heads; the snot-nose *piccanins* who ran around steering cars fashioned from wire and with bottle caps as the wheels. These were the people, black and white, that I loved. My family had been here for generations. My grandfather, at the age of 12, had ridden out with his father to fight against the British in the Boer War in 1899. They had fought not far from this same ground where I now stood smelling the wood fires. They had suffered terribly in the winter after years of fighting as commandos and living off the land. They were finally ground down after the Brits launched a scorched-earth policy, destroying the farms and incarcerating Boer families in concentration camps, where they had died in their thousands. It had taken more than 400,000 British troops from all the corners of the mighty British Empire three years to subdue 87,000 Boers.

Now there was a different threat. South Africa was surrounded by communist countries. Russia was real, still a great threat and, as far as I had been told, was trying to get a grasp on southern Africa from within by supporting the ANC, the PAC and the anti-apartheid movement, and sending 'freedom fighters', better known to us as terrorists, from across the border to try and accomplish it.

I read a newspaper for the first time in months; it told how the Angolan army was aiding SWAPO and had helped repel a South African attack against a SWAPO base camp in Angola. Also that Soviet-supplied and Cuban-flown MiGs had been seen flying menacingly close to the border.

I couldn't go AWOL. What was I thinking? I would just have to go back and bite the bullet. Before you knew it I'd be on the border and all this training bullshit would be over. It sounded like it was getting serious up there, with all those Cubans in Angola. They said that 40,000 Cuban troops had already arrived and were operational. I felt ashamed that I had even thought of going AWOL and drove home quickly in the fading light as the setting sun shot a magnificent volley of red and orange against the enormous rolling wall of black storm clouds advancing from the north.

I called John right away and told him that it would not be worth the trouble to go AWOL. He agreed. We booked a train the following evening to Bloemfontein.

BACK TO 1 PARACHUTE BATTALION

Hold the line—Toto

We arrived at 1 Para early the next morning, walked through the big wrought-iron gates, past the guards. The big fish eagle whooped us a greeting as we strode up the tar road past the parade ground with our heavy kit bags on our shoulders. We hadn't had a haircut in months, our hair hung well over our collars and we both sported big moustaches and a dark brown border tan. The rank that we passed ignored us, not knowing what or who we were on our last stroll of freedom as we neared our bungalow and saw the sight I had been dreading, but had known could be no different.

The whole *Valk* 4, Platoon 4, was standing clean-shaven outside the bungalow in open order, blowing hard in the cool early-morning air after completing a couple of laps around the *pakhuis*. Corporal Berger and the new lieutenant were yelling at the tops of their voices at the same time, and did not notice us as we walked casually past the platoon towards the bungalow door.

After a moment of silence and a long stare the lieutenant recognized us, broke into a big sarcastic grin and shouted: "Well, I'll be damned! Korff and Delaney! What—you guys didn't make the Recce course and you came back to us? How special of you!"

I found this lieutenant particularly irksome and could easily have knocked him onto his stupid arrogant arse, but instead I came to attention and threw a smart salute. All attention was on us now and I could see the guys in the platoon grinning and sniggering among themselves. John the Fox and

Stander stood next to each other in the front row, blowing white mist into the morning air and trying to hold back their laughter.

"And what the hell is this shit? Get inside and shave those moustaches off, and have your hair cut tonight!"

"Yes, lieutenant."

The next couple of days weren't much fun. Although it was good to see John Fox, Stander and the platoon again it was really hard to get back into the swing of things. It was business as usual, just as we had expected. Run here, run there, inspections, hurry up and eat, hurry up and wait … shouting, asshole rank all over the place. After a week I still felt unnaturally low and decided to sick-report to the military hospital across the road from the battalion, where I told the same doctor who had treated my torn feet months before that I was really feeling pretty low and couldn't shake the feeling. The stutter that had troubled me since I was a kid had also returned in full force; I stuttered on every other word. I told him about the last couple months on the Recce selection course and of walking many hundreds of kilometres with next to no food. He listened and finally said, "No problem; you need some good rest," and booked me into the hospital for a week of observation.

It was a good move. I was taken to the small psychiatric ward at the far end of the hospital, where they gave me a bed and I changed into pyjamas. I took some sort of liquid medication and disappeared into a glorious, restful, deep sleep from which I surfaced two days later, half-waking for one blurred meal a day and more medication. The white sheets felt soft and smelled clean; I was oblivious to the world around me.

I eventually woke up, medicated and drowsy, but feeling a lot more relaxed and chirpy. I walked around the ward starting conversations with a couple of the flaming queens who were in the psychiatric ward waiting for their discharge papers to come through. They would sit in their gowns in groups on each others' beds and cackle with laughter as they told stories of Civvy Street and how they would go out cross-dressing for nights on the town. Each had a couple of photographs of themselves dressed in drag from the good old days.

Some guys, I had heard, acted homosexual to get out of military duty, but this bunch of 'girls' was definitely no act. One evening just after dinner the night nurse came screaming out of the bathroom, where one of the flamers had cut his wrists after hearing that his discharge had been denied, or something to that effect. I never did hear the full story. I felt sorry for them. Military service was hard enough for anybody, but for these poor guys it was like being in hell.

After a week in hospital I was discharged and walked out feeling great. No one had given me any explanation of what I had been through, but I figured it must have been that I was drained of electrolytes or vitamins from the lack of food and the hundreds of clicks of walking. I wondered what drugs they had given me. It must have been powerful stuff because I felt like a different man and was ready to take on the world again.

I was very glad I had sick-reported.

The first night back at 1 Para, John the Fox and I walked back from the canteen. Fox sipped on his Coke and handed me a cigarette as we sat down on a low wall and watched as a platoon of juniors came running through the main gate in a squad, singing and covered in mud from head to toe. They were coming to camp after an *opfok*, fuck-up session at the *kooikamp*, which was a large, open, muddy area about ten clicks from camp, with which we were only too well acquainted. John started to fill me in on what they had been up to since we had been gone.

"You guys are lucky—you missed all the worst training. Company attacks and conventional attacks. We had to sleep out on the shooting range for a week, doing attacks every night with live ammunition."

I laughed and told him that he was the lucky one. I told him about the selection course and how we had walked hundreds of kilometres with so few meals. I told him about how Hans had been attacked by a lion, but had made the course and looked like a bag of bones. I told him how we had decided to quit but had stuck out the course almost to the end and that we were the last 27 out of 200 to quit. I also told him how impressed I had been by the Recces, that they were really sharp individuals, that they treated soldiering like a business and that there was none of the bullshit that we had at 1 Para.

John knew that I felt bad about dropping off the course and was quick to fill me in on the news. "Well, don't worry, Gungie. We're going to see more action here than any Recce. They are not supposed to make contact with the enemy. Our job is going to be to seek them and destroy them. Just have four more months of training down here and then it's up to the border, *boet*. There's lots of shit going on up there. A Company made contact with FAPLA in Angola and got the shit shot out of them, and SWAPO is all over southern Angola and coming across the border every day. Our guys are making contact every day!"

John was excited. He was a stocky, neat Englishman with a red English complexion, a pointy nose and sharp, alert blue eyes that never missed a trick, hence the nickname, 'John the Fox'. John the Fox didn't have to do military service as he was a British citizen. His father had left England to come and run a large tea plantation in the Tzaneen area. John said he volunteered for service so he could shoot some kaffirs before they took over the country.

"Don't worry, Gungie—this is where the action is going to be. We are South African paratroopers and we're the ones who are going to go into Angola and find these kaffirs. We're going to be attacking their bases in Angola and there's 40,000 Cubans in the area there now too! You watch, bro—you just wait and see."

Fox carefully stubbed out his cigarette against the wall, put the butt into his empty Coke can and lit up another. I flicked my butt into the bushes, knowing that the juniors would probably do chicken parade tomorrow and would need some work. John the Fox was right. That was all I wanted to be in the first place—a paratrooper, not a Recce—and this was where the action was going to be.

ONDANGWA
1 Parachute Battalion's
operational base on the border

Broken English—Marianne Faithfull

"There are many more of these out there, men. You've done a lot of training, and it's going to be our job to go in and find Boy and bring them in."

'Boy', I'd learned, was army slang for SWAPO. It had a ring to it.

Our OC looked like a Marabou stalk with his tall frame, stooped over with his hands thrust into his pants pockets and his boot on one of the four dead SWAPO terrorists laid out in front of him. He rocked the terr back and forth a couple of times, then slowly took his boot off the bloodied corpse and rubbed it in the white sand. The four SWAPO had been shot to pieces—they looked small and broken, clad in dirty, blood-soaked Chinese tiger-stripe uniforms that had been pulled around their necks and knees from being dragged. Their faces were caked with blood and white sand; one of them had a bullet hole square between the eyes with a huge exit hole in the back of his head. An execution wound. The other one's skull had been shot clean off and its contents lay spilled around. By now someone had stuck a Marlboro cigarette between his lips and so he lay there, brainless, smoking a cigarette.

They looked thin and miserable, I thought to myself as I inspected the four cadres, before quickly changing my mind when I looked over to the pile of weapons lying in the sand nearby. Their arsenal included an RPG rocket launcher, an RPD machine gun and a couple of AK-47s. No; this bunch was definitely not out for a walk in the park. On their feet they all had worn black ankle-high boots with chevron-pattern treads on the soles. I had listened to many an instructor during training telling us that the distinctive chevron-pattern spoor left in the soft border sand would be our key to following up and making contact with SWAPO.

D Company had finally arrived on the Angolan/South West African border. The Operational Area. We had started out as not much more than a group of school kids. For one solid year we had been drilled, trained, hammered, moulded, taught, kicked and forged into to a company of tough, fighting paratroopers. We had learned to live close to each other like brothers, to work as a team, to push ourselves and our minds way past the point of quitting and into a newfound mental no-man's-land. Most other infantry units were on the border after only six months of training. But then they were not going to be used as we were. We were going to be the tip of the spear in the fight against the common enemy. Well, at least that's what they told us. We had arrived in the operational area on the Angolan border only three hours ago for our first 'bush trip' as an operational paratroop company; we had come to relieve E Company, the senior company who had done their time and were now going back to South Africa to *klaar* out, sign out. We had disembarked from the C-130 and carried our heavy kit across the concrete runway, past the helicopter pads and 100 metres into a square of dusty brown four-man tents that housed a company and was to be our home base for the next four months in the operational area. This was the 'Fireforce', or reaction force base where a Parabat *valk*[4] was always on standby to react to any contact made with the enemy within a couple of hundred kilometres or so and all the way to the Angolan border 130 kilometres away. The seniors came out of their tents to give the new troops stare-downs and to jeer as we walked into the tent square and leaned our kit against the canteen wall. We were going to spend the night under the stars until E Company flew out the following day.

No sooner had we put our kit down and bought a cold Coke at the canteen than a siren high on a pole next to the operations room slowly started to whine and then hold its pitch at a loud howl for a full minute.

"What the hell's going on?"

The seniors reacted immediately. They dropped their darts, suntan lotion

---

[4] paratrooper platoon, lit. falcon (Afrikaans)

and pool cues and raced to their tents, from which they quickly emerged, some still shirtless, carrying their R4 rifles and fumbling with their light webbing and Fireforce vests as they charged across the tent square to where the two Puma helicopters stood 100 metres away, turbines already whining. We watched in stunned silence as the Pumas lifted off after each other with our guys still dressing and shuffling about in the doorways. Just then two Alouette gunship choppers lifted off close by like dragonflies and disappeared after them with their long 20mm cannons poking out the side doors.

"Fucking hell!" exclaimed John Delaney as he came trotting around the canteen. "Did you see those *okes* sprinting to the choppers? They're going into a contact. That's what Fireforce is all about!"

John was right. Two hours later the Pumas returned; the seniors unloaded the shattered bodies of the SWAPO cadres and pulled them into the tent square to show us greenhorn juniors how it was done. If they were trying to impress us they succeeded; we were all respectfully silent as we watched them hang up their rifles and webbing and go casually back to their dart and pool games as though killing SWAPO was just another day's work.

"Hey, Gungie, they said these gooks were part of a bigger group spotted near the base. These four were walking casually along, close to the main road."

"I wonder why they were doing that?"

"Because they're stupid, like I said," exclaimed John Delaney. "They get orders to mix with the local population when they get this far into South West Africa. These guys tried to mingle but forgot to take their uniforms off."

"How the hell do you know so much on your first day with the A team?" Stander quizzed Delaney.

"I spoke to one of the E Company guys—he says you don't usually find them this deep and this close to Ondangwa, and these four are just part of a bigger group who have probably already dressed in civvy clothes and stashed their weapons, waiting for the 'call'."

"Oh, so they started the offensive when they heard that D Company had arrived?" I quipped.

Commandant James Lindsay was the CO of the 1 Para companies in the operational area. He was nothing like Commandant Archie Moore, who had been our CO back at 1 Para in Bloemfontein, who had a reputation, true or false, of being a bit of a playboy and a glamour boy. Lindsay wanted nothing to do with Civvy Street. He loved to stay in the bush and make war. We knew, because he told us this himself. He had been involved in the Angolan conflict right from the start in 1975 when the Portuguese, after 400 years of control and 16 years of civil war, had finally pulled out of Angola.

South African troops had swept all the way up Angola, almost as far as Luanda, with the backing of the United States, to try and 'stabilize' the country and oversee elections between the factions that had been fighting for political control for those same 16 years. The communist-backed MPLA had quickly seized power in the midst of the chaos and the remaining parties, FNLA and UNITA, had fled back into the bush to continue the struggle against a different opponent—the MPLA instead of the Portuguese. The United States had withdrawn its support, which forced South Africa to retreat and to plunge the region back into a conflict that would last for another 15 years.

Commandant Lindsay was a short, energetic man. He had dark olive skin with black hair that sprouted from his arms, neck, ears and which even grew on his cheek bones under his eyes. He called us to a loose parade after we had settled in and explained to us that he ran things differently up here to how they did "back in the States".

"We are up here to find and kill Boy for the security of our country," he said matter of factly in Afrikaans.

"We are the A team and our goal is to bring in as many heads as we can and to put SWAPO out of business." He told us that the Parabats' reputation had already reached SWAPO's ears. He also emphasized how well the senior C and E companies had done in their time on the border; they had jointly racked up hundreds of kills. He ended his pep-talk by breaking into a crooked smile, exposing a set of long white teeth, saying that the busier we kept ourselves shooting Boy, the faster we would get back to the 'States'. (Bloemfontein was the city where 1 Para was domiciled, in the province of the Orange Free State.)

He struck me as a capable man who knew his business. He was also definitely not like the rank that we had just endured in Bloemfontein. The seniors had told us that as long as we brought in kills he was a great guy, but that he could get very upset when you let Boy slip through your fingers. We were going to spend most of the four months at Ondangwa on Fireforce, while our sister H Company, who we hardly ever saw, would be doing patrols in another part of Owamboland. This is a section of Namibia (or South West Africa, whatever you want to call it) named after the Owambo tribe who lived in the roughly 600-square-kilometre area. It is a dry and sandy area, like the rest of South West Africa, which is basically desert, but the terrain can change in a few kilometres from open sparse bush to thick bush with high brown grass that is impenetrable by man or vehicle. But always the ground beneath you is white sand. Always sand.

They said you couldn't find a rock or stone in Owamboland, and they were right. There were no stones to be found; maybe hard-packed clod but no stones. The sand was sometimes as hard as rock and sometimes as loose as a beach, but there was always sand—hence the nickname of our base, 'the white sands of Ondangs'. But things change in the rainy season when the dry sandy ground springs to life, as it does in Africa when the rain falls on the thirsty earth. Small flowers of every imaginable colour bloom thickly. In the place of long dead grass rises thin, new green grass and the long flat *chanas* and sandy areas sprout fine, thick, short green grass that gives the area the look of a well-kept lawn or a golf driving range.

Chanas, or *shonas,* are clearings in the dry Owamboland bush with no trees or brush. They come in all shapes and sizes. Some are long clearings hundreds of metres wide that meander through the bush like a fat dry snake for many kilometres until they fade out and blend into the bush. Others are just a wide clearing in the middle of the bush that are sometimes 400 metres and sometimes 20 metres across. These *chanas* are as sure as the sand—they are all over Owamboland and southern Angola.

We soon all got settled into our new home and John Delaney, John the Fox, Stander and I ended up together in a tent that was a lot closer to the crappers than we would have liked. At night when a slow breeze blew, we got the sickly smell of a full cesspool wafting through our tent flaps. Besides the unfortunate location of the tent, it was quite a cozy set-up. The tents were semi-permanent; they had a little table and chairs in the centre and four beds in the four corners. Brown mosquito nets hung from the roof of the tent and draped over each bed, giving it a snug bushveld feel, with a bit more privacy when you were lying in your bed at night. John Delaney bitched and moaned about being the one closest to the crappers but he had been the first to throw his kit on the back bed when we were assigned the tent, only realizeing his folly a couple of hours later.

"That will teach him," smiled John Fox as he pulled his gear from his *balsak*, his kitbag, and packed his drawers, placing his clothes in impeccably neat squares on the first shelf and folding all his brown pants in the same way on the middle shelf. "He's always quick to claim what he wants ... let him enjoy what he's got this time!"

We found it amusing how Delaney tried to con and bribe his way out of his situation, to no avail.

Later that afternoon we were brought out and told how Fireforce worked. There would always be at least one platoon on standby with light kit packed for three days in the bush in case of any follow-up after contacts or hot-pursuits across the border. If any infantry or any other unit made contact we would immediately be flown and dropped into the contact area or on the spoor. The platoons on Fireforce were not allowed to leave the tent area and had to keep their long pants and boots on. All we would do was lounge around the small plastic-lined swimming pool and suntan, sleep or play pool in the recreation room at the canteen until the siren wailed, signalling us to 'kit up' and move to the choppers in double-quick time.

Each platoon would spend a week at a time doing Fireforce. The platoons not on Fireforce would be doing foot patrols or vehicle patrols in Owamboland or along the Angolan border. It went without saying that Fireforce quickly became the preferred activity. *Valk* 2 got the first week of Fireforce, while the rest of the company pulled the old hard and torn sandbags off the bunkers outside each tent, filling hundreds of new bags and packing them into place. Even *Valk* 2 got to do their share of it, as the 'activity' was inside the tent square. So we were all pleased when Lieutenant du Plessis brought *Valk* 4 together and announced that we must draw rat packs[5] for a four-day patrol.

---

[5] C rations

We would be patrolling an area of Owamboland just south of the *kaplyn*, the cut-line, that he said was a well-used infiltration route. He added that we had better buck up because this was the real thing and there was to be no more goofing off. We lined up eagerly to draw our rats and went to the tent to pack. We handed in our old, thick, green canvas backpacks in exchange for the newest type of thin H-frame backpack that looked the same as a civvy hiker's Bergen pack, with a thin metal tube for the frame and a big back-pouch that sat high on the back with a thick band that tightened around your waist for extra support.

We had also been issued a Fireforce vest—a sleeveless, light canvas-type vest, almost like a waistcoat—that was worn over your shirt. It had pouches in the front against the chest for six long 30-round magazines and other pouches on the side for smoke grenades or M27 fragmentation grenades.

"This is where we reap the rewards of a year of shitting off," I announced as I excitedly checked out the new kit.

"Nobody else has got kit like this—probably just the Recces and 32 Battalion."

32 Battalion was a black fighting unit made up of tough ex-Angolan FNLA and Bushmen soldiers who had spent years fighting in Angola. They were veterans, battle-hardened by countless clashes against the Portuguese during the long Angolan liberation war and later against the MPLA. South Africa had backed them in the race for Luanda in 1975, a race that was lost to the communist-backed MPLA. After South Africa pulled out of Angola in 1975 they had brought many of them over to our side, forming them into a tough fighting unit that became legendary in the bush war.

"Yeah," added Stan, "most of these infantry units are up at the border after six or seven months' training and probably see only four kills in their whole year of service. We've had a whole year of hell but we've already seen four kills in our first two hours up here."

"You guys need to take it a bit easy. You're too eager to get into a fight. When it comes, then it comes," said Doogy in a slow voice. He had mooched over from the next tent to try and swop his rat-pack corned beef for steak and onions, but found no takers.

"Yeah ... when a fucking cheese mine blows your arse into the sky then you'll wish we got them in an ambush a little earlier," Stan snickered.

"Well, when you run headlong into a fucking L-shape company ambush then you'll wish you had taken things little bit slower," said Doogy, leaving with his corned beef.

It was a strange feeling finally being out in what we called Indian Country. We had spent the previous night in a small TB[6] and had dug in for the night. Nobody slept very well the first night out and, sure enough, around one in the morning, what sounded like a fire fight broke out a couple of kilometres away. Green tracers could be seen arching lazily and haphazardly into the black night. It lasted for about 30 seconds, then stopped. We all sat tight and no one said a word until daybreak, when a security patrol was sent out to scout the area around our TB.

Lieutenant du Plessis called in on the radio and reported what we had seen and heard the night before, saying that we should head into the area and check it out.

"No contact has been reported," he said in a hushed voice, "and we're the only troops in the area, so it must have been a SWAPO patrol that got spooked by something and let fly with everything they had." It was the first time Lieutenant du Plessis had seen live enemy fire; he seemed just as jumpy as we were and snapped at us too readily.

I had done my jump course with Lieutenant du Plessis; he was probably about three years older than us. He was tall, with very blond hair and a pale complexion that would colour very quickly at the first sign of exertion. He had an angular, shark-like face with very thin lips and deep brown eyes that shone like those of a Great white when he got excited, which was often. He was a little lumbering and unco-ordinated, quick to shoot his mouth off without thinking what he was saying. He had been assigned to our platoon about four months before our bush trip and was to be our permanent lieutenant. No one was too happy about this because he had not really built any kind of relationship with us and still spoke to us as though he had just arrived in the platoon. Now he rushed us to get our kit packed and said that we could have breakfast later … after we had investigated the area where we had seen the shooting.

---

[6] temporary base, a rest area or an overnight sleeping position while patrolling in the bush

The terrain had changed; we moved cautiously through the thickening trees, trying to peer into the bush for any sign of movement. We had been trained at Bloemfontein to look for any unnatural impressions in the bush like a rifle barrel or the shape of a cap. SWAPO always wore small peaked caps. They would be dressed in a plain thick khaki uniform or the Chinese tiger-stripe camo. Even blue jeans were popular among the cadres but they weren't well known for doing themselves up in full camouflage with leaves.

They would be carrying AK-47 assault rifles, RPD machine guns, which had a belt drum and were excellent machine guns that experienced few jams, and RPG-2 and -7 rocket launchers—actually anti-tank weapons, but in Africa RPGs, or rocket-propelled grenades, had become an effective anti-personnel weapon. They would also usually have a big backpack as they invariably carried landmines to plant on the long deserted dirt roads. They could be, the instructors had told us, walking in company strength before splitting up into smaller parties, or they could be in a small eight-man squad. We had been told earlier by some black South West African troops that it was important that we should learn to look *through* the bush and not *at* the bush. This in itself was an art that none of us had yet mastered and we stared blankly at the bush as we moved warily along in V-shaped formation.

Somehow I could not picture seeing a live SWAPO terrorist walking or sneaking around in the bush. I had seen dead ones and a hundred pictures of them during training, but in my mind I could not imagine looking through the bush and spotting one sitting or walking in front of me. I was troubled that I could be looking right at one and not register what I was seeing. Or perhaps look right past him and not even see him. He would see me first and blast me with an RPG. It was stupid, but I couldn't get the mental picture.

We slowly and cautiously scouted the area where we thought the shots had been fired. It was pretty thick bush, with a lot of short sturdy thorn bushes which made it hard going. We found no spoor or explanation for the shooting we'd heard in the night. After a couple of hours we stopped for a cold breakfast. I mixed up a powdered milkshake in a plastic bag with water and condensed milk, shook it up till it was thoroughly mixed, then bit a small corner off the bag.

"This milkshake tastes great!" I said, sucking the plastic bag like a tit. "It's just as good as any milkshake I've had in Civvy Street."

"Yeah … these rats aren't bad. These are the new ones that just came out this year. I heard the old ones were horrible." Stan was chowing down a cold corned beef hash. We shared a smoke and discussed why we hadn't found any tracks and came to the conclusion that it was probably a lot farther than it had looked at night and that we were far off the mark. I said that we should move about five more clicks in a southwesterly direction.

"Nah … it was more west … three or four clicks," Stan said, squatting on his haunches like a Bushman and trying to follow my milkshake recipe.

It was a strange feeling knowing that someone else was in the bush with you who would kill you if they got half a chance. I looked around in a full circle and stared hard into the high trees and thick shrubs that surrounded our TB.

"This is how those seniors get that crazy look," I thought, "from staring into the fucking bush all day looking for terrs."

For some reason Lieutenant du Plessis called off the search, as we headed north and spent the next three days walking stealthily near the Angolan border. The only excitement came on our last day when we found a huge unlit night flare which had apparently been jettisoned from one of our fighter jets. Lieutenant du Plessis got permission from Ondangwa and we lined up and shot at it. The flare ignited with a huge blinding flash of light that lasted for at least a minute. I had found a metre-long parachute that had been connected to the flare and I managed to grab the parachute before anyone could get near it.

We met our four Buffels at a prearranged spot and drove the 50 clicks back to Ondangs, winding through the bush and then down the infamous *Oom Willie se pad,* a long straight road of white sand that was well known for its landmines and ambushes. We arrived at base, still 'cherries', back from our first patrol. That night we had a *braai* of huge army pork chops over long concrete fire pits with iron grids that were burned black by the many paratroopers' *braais* before us.

We told the *Valk* 2 guys what it was like out in the bush and that we had seen SWAPO shooting their green tracers in the night pretty close to us, but never found any spoor. At least we had seen enemy fire first time out. The chops were just getting done and I was just opening my second Castle lager when Lieutenant du Plessis came running out the ops room and shouted for *Valk* 4 to get kitted up in double time. We piled into the Buffels and careened out of Ondangwa base, heading out on the main tar road that ran past Ondangs all the way to the Etosha National Park, about 350 kilometres away.

There had been a shooting at one of the kraals near the base. The black South West African troop who was guiding us took us quickly off the tar road and down a long narrow dusty road that wound about five clicks into the bush, ending at a small village. The village had about 30 well-kept square, little mud-brick houses with corrugated-tin roofs. The path leading to the huts was swept clean; I could smell the pigs that were squealing and snorting in an enclosure to one side of the huts. A strong-looking Owambo man, dressed smartly in his weekend best, came running to meet us and started telling us in a calm voice that "We have him, we have him," pointing towards the pigsty. I followed his hand motion and saw a small black man lying on his side with his hands tied behind his back. He looked anguished and was crying, his face shoved into the dirt.

We walked into the kraal with our rifles held nervously at the ready, not really knowing what was going on. Stan and I came into the centre of the village. At my feet I saw the body of a big, strapping man lying dead, with his arms outstretched. As I looked I saw another man dead in the doorway of a hut and an old, lighter-skinned and wrinkled woman still sitting in her chair—dead—her chin resting on her chest, her arms hanging loosely at her side, with her legs pushed out in front of her. Her beer mug lay at her feet.

I walked into a house and saw three bodies, one lying across a small table that had been pushed on its side and two more—a man and a woman—lying on the floor, also dead. We walked around the little village and counted 15 dead civilians who had been shot by the man they had tied up at the pigsty. He was a member of the local 'home guard' unit, formed among the local population around the area close to the air force base of Ondangwa and Oshakati, a civilian town about 60 kilometres from Ondangwa on the main tar road.

We never discovered why, but the shooter had clearly lost his mind, taken his G3 military rifle and walked through the village calmly blasting everybody he saw. The scene looked prearranged, like a movie set, with bodies everywhere … propped up against walls, dead in chairs, sprawled in doorways. Some had tried to run and had been shot in the back; they lay face-down on the outskirts of the huts. I noticed that they were all clean and well; it seemed like a Saturday afternoon party that had gone horribly wrong. I also figured that this guy must have been quite a good shot because everyone he had shot was dead and looked as if they had died quickly, on the spot.

I saw no wounded; everybody had been hit in the body. His weapon, as all the home guard used, was a G3. The G3 fires a 7.62-millimetre NATO round—a big bullet, the same as the FN, with awesome killing power.

In the middle of the open area between the huts lay a pretty teenage girl in a clean white dress. The top half of her dress was completely soaked with blood from a shot through her chest. The black South West African troop who had guided us to the kraal suddenly broke down, sobbing and wailing, as he recognized that the girl was a relative of his. Lieutenant du Plessis led the begrimed man away towards the Buffels, trying to console him, but not very successfully. The black troop was howling.

It was beginning to get dark as a Jeep arrived with a trailer hitched to the back. We began loading the bodies into the trailer. It was a small trailer, the kind you would use behind a *bakkie*, a pick-up truck, if you were going camping for the weekend. Pretty soon the 15 bodies lay piled on top of each other, almost to the point of sliding over the edge. A black South West African troop produced some rope and began lashing the bodies down, as if he was tying down a heap of firewood. He pulled the rope through the tie-eyes on the side of the trailer and finally had the load secured to his liking.

"Fuck—why don't they just send another trailer, or at least a truck to put them on?" asked Kevin McKee, a small and thuggish-looking ex-professional boxer with a thick scar that ran across his face, but a man with a heart of gold.

"They're going to drive all the way to Oshakati on the main road with these people piled high like this? They hit one bump and they'll all go flying off onto the road. They haven't even got a canvas tarp to cover them with!"

We all stood around and inspected the gruesome pile of bodies and tugged on the ropes, testing the strength and tension.

"It's getting dark anyway—who's going to see them?" Stan said smugly, seeing an opportunity to antagonize McKee. Stan and McKee were both Capetonians who had known each other on the rougher side of the Cape Town streets and were always at each another. Anthony Stander, aka Stan, although he could hold his own, was not a rough and tough physical fighter. His main weapon was his mind and a cold, piercing stare that could bend spoons. He was slender, with curly blond hair and hard blue eyes which he would use to glare menacingly at whomever needed to be glared at. He fancied himself as a throwback to the tough German infantrymen of the Third Reich. Stan was a hard case who was emotionally as cold as ice. He had grown up in an orphanage in Cape Town and had reached 1 Parachute Battalion via a spell in a reformatory. Stan's favorite trick was to find the chink in one's armour and then exploit that chink retentlessly until the victim either exploded or imploded. This time the chosen prey was his old street buddy, Kevin McKee, from the mean, ultra-tough slum suburb of Woodstock in Cape Town. McKee was a fighter, no doubt about it, and had been a professional boxer at an early age—before he even joined the army—but he had a very soft heart and a long fuse. Stan knew just how far he could push his luck with Kevin McKee.

"It's only 50 kilometres to Oshakati and the roads are pretty smooth," Stan said. He smiled, lit another cigarette and glanced at me, urging me to join in the fun. Stan had got the reaction he wanted.

"Only 50 fucking clicks! Your *poes*![7] How would you like to have *your* family piled like that and carried in a trailer for only 50 kilometres?"

McKee glared, dropped his neck instinctively into his chest and stood ready to deck Stan, who knew his limits and had taken a couple of steps back, but still smirking at McKee.

Lieutenant du Plessis broke up the tension and we got a couple of blankets from the village to cover the heap of bodies, securing them so that they would not blow off on the journey to Oshakati, 50 kilometres past our base at Ondangwa. Some MPs arrived and took the culprit away, who now looked composed and relaxed as he climbed into the Jeep. We rode back the short

---

[7] cunt (Afrikaans)

distance to Ondangs with the Buffels' headlights piercing the moonless night and smoked more cigarettes. The Jeep with the trailer followed slowly behind. I couldn't wait to get back to base and wash my hands.

I had never touched a dead person before and I could still feel the cold, stiff feeling on my hands where I had grabbed them by their ankles and heaved them onto the heap on the trailer. Especially, I could still feel the rough material of the pretty teenage girl's clean, embroidered short white socks on my hands. Back at the base the other platoons had finished the *braai* and were in their tents playing darts. They were all loaded because it was the first time we had been allowed to drink beer. We were told that if we wanted to get some more pork chops from the kitchen we could start the fires up again to finish our *braai*. I had lost my appetite for greasy pork chops however, even though it was our first night back after patrol and four days' eating rat packs.

I washed my hands thoroughly, grabbed a couple of beers and a pack of cigarettes, went to the tent and flipped on the tape recorder. Marianne Faithfull spat out 'Broken English' in her disturbed voice. It sounded like fitting music for the moment.

INTO ANGOLA

The tide is high—Blondie

"We're going to attack a base?"

"That's what I hear—there's a terr base in Angola and we're going in to hit it!"

Danny, our section leader, was a sturdily built native South West African with a deceptive, sleepy way about him. He was gathering the company for orders in the middle of the tent square next to the pool. The whole company sat chatting excitedly when Commandant Lindsay came walking briskly onto the square, followed by the four lieutenants and our company commander, Captain Verwey

Lindsay was smiling happily (for him, anyway), and stood on the little sandy mound next to the pool. "Men," he said in Afrikaans, and looked around with satisfaction. "Our reconnaissance planes have identified a SWAPO base about 100 clicks over the border into Angola."

He paused, looking around smiling. I got the distinct feeling he had done this many times before. "They've seen a lot of activity around there lately. It's probably a jump-off base for infiltrations into Owamboland and is responsible for the increased SWAPO movement and landmine incidents in this area lately.

"We're going to go in tomorrow and will take these people out! D Company will fly in and be dropped by Pumas on a *chana* next to the terr base after the air force has bombed the target for ten minutes. H Company will be on standby from Ondangwa if there are any problems."

He carried on talking and gave more details, saying that there were possibly 150 SWAPO in the base and that they were probably new recruits in training before their usual big push into Owamboland during the rainy season that would be coming up in a few months.

There were apparently five buildings: three of them were barracks for the troops, one was the officers' quarters and the other some sort of ops room. Lindsay spoke easily, as if he was planning a picnic and then handed over to Captain Verwey and the platoon lieutenants.

"This is what it's all about," I thought and moved excitedly to the front of the company as we all crowded around to get a better look at the little model that Lieutenant du Plessis was drawing in the sand with the back of a pen. He drew the three buildings that were close to each other, then two larger ones that were about 50 metres from the main buildings and which were supposedly the troops' barracks. Captain Verwey showed us on the model where the choppers would land and how we would advance from the *chana* into the small base.

Lieutenant Doep, as we'd taken to calling him, then took our platoon aside, as did the other lieutenants theirs, and told us that we would be dropped in the *chana* 500 metres from the base, would spread out in a battle line and advance on the base until we started to draw fire, then we would do fire and movement into the base. Lieutenant Doep stared around at the platoon with a frown. It would be his first action too. He wore his feelings on his sleeve, unable to hide his nervousness. "*Valk* 4 will be in the last two Pumas. We will exit last and be at the end of the battle line. There are some shallow trenches on the southern side of the base that we will have to deal with. When we take fire, we take cover and start our fire and movement into the base, just as though we were training this afternoon."

"Will we have any armour support?" questioned Dan Pienaar, our newly appointed section leader, trying to sound important.

"Well, the last time we checked, a Ratel troop-carrier with a 90mm cannon didn't fit into a Puma," snapped Lieutenant Doep sarcastically.

Dan shuffled his boots in the sand in embarrassment as the platoon laughed at this slap-down. I felt it had been a good question and thought that you should usually have armour support when you hit a base. That afternoon we drew white phosphorus smoke grenades from the locked armour store. Each platoon went to the small shooting range at the side of the base to 'sight in' their rifles.

I had been carrying an LMG, a light machine gun, for a couple of months. It was a Belgian-made 7.62 MAG that was belt-fed. I had fancied myself standing up and mowing down sections of the enemy like corn as they advanced or retreated, but had found it more work than it was worth. It was a good machine gun, but you had to keep the damn thing scrupulously clean or it would jam on you. I, not being the tidiest or most conscientious troop around, had many jams and now didn't trust the thing if I had to jump up suddenly and my life depended on the weapon. Although, it was a thing of pure beauty when it did fire without a jam as nothing could beat the feeling of blasting out a belt of 50 rounds in a rapid four or more bursts. It was a heavy gun but I had become used to it and for months I had been doing exercises with it—using the whole machine gun as a barbell to do curls and soldier presses until I was so used to the weight that it felt like an R4 rifle in my hands.

That afternoon, in an open field next to the chopper pads, we dressed in full fighting kit, with helmets, and huddled together as if we were flying in choppers. Then, on command, we 'exited' and formed a spread-out battle line, advancing as a company in a long line until Verwey shouted "Taking fire!" and we dived into the sand and began moving forward. Doing this fire and movement with the MAG and 500 rounds was tough.

Later we all sat under a small tree trying to avoid 'Spikes'—the sun—relentlessly nailing everyone with its burning afternoon rays.

Captain Verwey spoke calmly to us in the relaxed way he had. "Be sharp, men, and only shoot when you see a target. Aim for the belt buckle and, if you hit Boy, make sure you put another shot in his head as you walk past, because you don't want him getting up behind you and surprising you. That's what happened to A Company and they lost a troop. If everybody is sharp, we'll all get to go home together after this bush trip."

He motioned casually toward the tents with his chin. "Now get some rest and get your kit ready, because *môre gaan die poppe dans*." (... tomorrow the puppets are going to dance.)

That night I filled my water bottles, took the MAG, stripped it clean and oiled all the moving parts. Then I pulled out all my ammo belts, laid them out on my bed and carefully checked all the rounds, making sure they were snug and there were no breaks or chips in the belt. I made sure that my second, Aaron 'Doogy' Green, checked his belts too. It was the first time we had been issued white phosphorus grenades and I laid them out in a line on my pillow like favorite toys. We would be wearing our jump helmets and not our regular floppy bush hats. We had also been given DayGlo, a bright orange sticker to put on top of our helmets so that the gunships would be able to see us from the air and not mistake us for terrs and take us out with their 20-millimere explosive-head cannon shells.

"What did I tell you? It's only our third week on the border and we're flying into Angola to hit a terr base!" John the Fox had stripped his rifle to pieces on his bed and sat polishing every moving part until it shone.

"Yeah, but I thought there'd be some armour to go in with us!"

"That's what the fucking bombs are for! We're going in as the bombing stops to clean up what's left!"

I didn't say anything. I sat carefully cleaning out the firing mechanism on the MAG and slammed the top cover-plate closed. I sat and worked quietly and smoked a couple of cigarettes. I felt a twinge of nervousness but nothing too bad. I was sort of puzzled why it was such a quick and simple plan to attack a base. I thought there would be more detailed planning, with some armour for support and a couple of days to go through the drills. Some sort of emergency plan if things went wrong … and what if a company wasn't enough to take them, or we were outgunned? But I was learning how the military worked and that they didn't seem too preoccupied with such details.

Stan walked into the smoky tent and sat down at his kit. He seemed excited. "Lieutenant du Plessis said there's a chance that these guys aren't just raw recruits, that there could be some old hands who'll put up a hell of a fight." He looked around the tent for some reaction.

My emotions were carefully veiled and I stood calmly in the middle of the tent and started to do some curls, using my heavy LMG as a barbell. "Well, all the better for us to cut our teeth on," I snapped, feeling a flash of anger. I was getting a bit tired of the stupid little mind games that Stan always played. I finished the rep, put the LMG gently down on its bipods and went outside to get some air and have another smoke. The high bush sky was inky black and filled with a million stars. The hot day had changed abruptly and a cool night breeze brought the pleasant pepper-bush smell of sand and sweet crushed leaves.

All the tents had their lights on; the place was a hive of activity. I could hear music from half a dozen different cassette recorders mingling outside the tents. Troops were bent over, cleaning their weapons and readying their kit, or going from tent to tent to borrow this or that and have a nervous chat. Even the ops room across the square was active which, as far as we had ever had anything to do with it, was unusual. I had never been shot at before and wondered what it was going to be like. How I would react under live fire. Would I shit myself? I started thinking stupid thoughts like putting myself in SWAPO's place … I wondered what they were doing now and whether they knew that tomorrow their world was going to be blown apart. It was like knowing someone's future—what was going to happen to them; secrets they did not share—like sitting facing forward in a train and seeing the guy facing the future backwards.

I snapped out of it and walked to the tent next door to see what else Doogy had heard about the 'old hands' we might get to face the following day.

★★★★★

I sat cross-legged in the open door of the Puma with my LMG poking out and the 500 rounds of ammo weighing heavily in my kit. The taste and smell of the Aftur fuel was thick in my throat and gave me an instant headache. Thankfully the noise ruled out any conversation. I looked around the chopper. Everyone looked solemm and grim with their rifles pointing down at the chopper floor, the men avoiding eye contact with each other. Each man concentrated on his own thoughts, hypnotized by the bush flashing by beneath us. This was to be our first action. We flew low and fast over Owamboland in a formation of eight Pumas and a couple of gunships. Small kraals, skinny cattle and tatty *muhangu* fields flashed past in a backward-disappearing blur. We skimmed the patchy bush and it seemed that I could almost reach down and touch the treetops. Within minutes we reached the Angolan border and the cut-line, the kilometre-wide no-man's-land separating South West Africa and Angola, and the terrain immediately changed.

Inside the cut-line it looked like an overgrown, lost Garden of Eden, untouched for years by human hands, hungry cattle or goats. The zone between Angola and South West Africa was strictly enforced; any cattle or person crossing it was open game to be shot. As our chopper hurtled across the border into Angola I immediately felt my excitement rise. This was the real thing. We were raiders flying into another country on a cross-border operation. We were paratroopers hitting a terrorist base in Angola.

Suddenly the bush was a lot thicker and wilder, with no sign of any kraals or cultivation like there were in Owamboland. Our chopper veered and changed course slightly and seemed to accelerate as we straightened out again. It flashed through my mind that if this craft went down it would be all over for us in a second, at this speed and 30 metres off the ground! (A fate that awaited our juniors in E Company when they were shot down by anti-aircraft fire as they flew an operation on their first bush trip, killing 12 paratroops and three crew.)

After what seemed like five minutes' fast flying the Puma veered aggressively upward, then turned at a slight angle, which it held. I looked out the door and saw that the eight Pumas were now flying in a big circle in a follow-the-leader. As the machine gunner, sitting cross-legged at the door, I found myself looking straight down at the bush as we flew in a wide orbit—but I was held perfectly in place by the strong centrifugal force of the chopper. It felt like I should be sliding out the open door.

Something caught my eye on the horizon. As the chopper came around again, I saw that it was the target that was being bombed. A couple of big clouds of dirty brown smoke billowed up in columns from the target area in the bush kilometres away. I saw the jet that had just delivered them streaking away at low level.

"Shit, look at that!" I nudged John Delaney and pointed, but he had already seen it and in turn was showing it to the troop next to him. The strafing must have been going on for quite a while; already a couple of the big dirty grey-brown clouds of smoke and dust had wafted a couple of kilometres downwind of the target and hung lazily over the treetops. I looked back, just in time to see another Buccaneer shoot in low, like an arrow above the treetops, drop its load and veer off, a silver streak. The 500-pound bombs blasted dust and smoke hundreds of feet into the air.

The guys all strained to get a look out the door at the show, but everyone was pretty well stuffed in and could not move without upsetting the applecart. The whine of the big Puma turbines drowned out any words as we watched the bombs silently exploding for a few more minutes. I felt as if I was watching some Vietnam war documentary or TV footage; it seemed surreal. I felt calm. My previous night's nervousness was well under control and I had decided that if I was going to die here today, then let's get on with it!

Suddenly the explosions stopped with just the great clouds of smoke lingering, thick and grey, hanging over the target area. One Puma broke out of the orbit and headed low and fast towards the clouds of smoke, the other choppers following like ducks in a row, with us the last in line. This is it! Let's go! I would be the first one out of our chopper because I was sitting at the door with the LMG. I got up onto my knees and shouldered the strap of the heavy machine gun. I held onto John the Fox's shoulder for support and felt like a spring ready to uncoil. I saw that the lead choppers had landed at the far end of the long *chana* and that our guys were already out on the ground and starting to form a ragged-looking sweep line. The target was still smoky and about 400 metres ahead of them.

Our Puma was last to land; it seemed that there was no more room on the long *chana* where the other Pumas had landed to drop their troops. I saw that we were coming down right on the end of the *chana* and there was some pretty thick foliage underneath us. I sat undecided at the door as I watched our approach, not sure what was going on. The Puma stopped about 20 feet from the ground and shuddered as the pilot pulled the collective up and we hovered. The prop wash bounced off the ground, creating a windstorm that blew sand right back into our faces. I heard a muffled shout, looked back and saw the helmeted flight engineer frantically waving his hand, gesturing for me to exit the Puma.

Being in the middle of the door, with the LMG and Delaney next to me, we were the only ones privy to the fact that we were still some way from the ground. I looked around at Lieutenant Doep who was unaware of the

The author as a child, playing soldiers.

Soon to lose his 'bonnie'. The author savours his long hair, the day before his enlistment.

Valk 4 (Platoon 4) outside their bungalow during training.

The author on a weekend pass flanked by brother Murray and his mother.

The whole gang back in base after a night out AWOL and drinking in Bloemfontein. *From left*: Anthony Stander, John Delaney, Granger Korff, Dan Pienaar, Aaron 'Doogy' Green, Kevin Green in front.

'The Jollers': Lance (*on the bike*), the author (*right*) and Darryl (*front*)— old high-school mates enjoying a rare weekend off at the same time. Lance was an infantry lieutenant and Darryl a medic.

Kurt Barnes feeding one of the base's feral cats.

John 'The Fox' Glover fools around on a patrol in Owamboland.

Back from an operation, the author jams on his guitar with his mates. Section leader Dan Pienaar is on the left while John 'The Fox' Glover and Louwtjie Nel look on glassily.

The author poses with a UNITA soldier prior to a raid on a SWAPO base in Angola.

D Company troops on the South West African–Angolan border, returning from a month-long search-and-destroy operation in Angola. D Company was involved in several running battles with FAPLA and SWAPO.

The canteen and pool area at the Ondangwa para base. This is where Baba drowned, having made it unscathed through numerous ops and fire fights, two weeks before the end of his national service.

Centre and right: The Angolan town of Ongiva burns after a day of fighting during Op *Protea*, August 1981.

Operation *Protea*.

Captured Soviet-built FAPLA tanks (*above*), vehicles (*right*) and artillery and anti-aircraft pieces (*below*)—a massive haul. FAPLA became the SADF's supplier of preference.

Mirage 1,000lb bombs soften up Ongiva's defences during the opening of Operation *Protea*.

Operation *Protea*. Captured Soviet BTRs and tanks.

A captured Soviet Gaz truck inside the FAPLA military base of Ongiva.

D Company was later returned to Ongiva to occupy the deserted town. In the initial operation the infantry had taken the town and the paras the air and military bases. Ongiva was to remain in South African hands until near the end of the war in 1989.

situation sitting deep in the chopper with a stony mask of determination on his face. Once again the helmeted figure waved me out urgently. I looked out hesitantly and saw that we were still at least ten to 15 feet from the ground, but that we had at least moved away from the foliage. I finally got the message that he wanted me to leave his craft, so I took a deep breath and leaped out into the dust storm with my LMG at my chest, like I had seen in the movies.

"This is how you do it—jump out like it's fucking D-Day, man!"

I fell through the air as if in slow motion and felt all my battle webbing and 500 rounds of ammunition come flying up around my neck as my body fell and struck the ground.

I had badly underestimated my extra weight and hit the ground hard, losing my breath and rolling onto my side. Immediately I felt a sharp pain shoot through my ankle. With nowhere else to land, the rest of the ten-man stick came crashing down on and around me and we all ended up lying in a pile, dazed and disorientated. I lay at the bottom of the heap and waited as the rest of the stick scrambled to pick themselves up. I dragged myself up and, as I took a step, I immediately felt that I had hurt my ankle. I could still walk but sharp pain shot up my leg and I could feel the warm tingling sensation of swelling.

I limped and skipped, trying to keep up with the stick and retrieve the heavy bag of ammo that had hooked up on my back water bottle which was half strangling me. I couldn't do it and with a vicious curse I yanked it free and advanced forward with the stick at a breathless hobbled trot to catch up with the other platoons. They were about 30 metres ahead of us and had already linked up and formed a long, jagged sweep line that was advancing on the smoking target that looked a lot closer now that we were on the ground.

Our end of the sweep line was still lagging behind as we got clear of the long *chana* and started crashing through high dry grass and bushes that had not looked so thick from the sky. I was holding my LMG thrust forward as if doing a bayonet charge, with a 50-round belt hanging and swinging underneath it.

It had become very quiet after the helicopters had left and the only thing to be heard was my own rapid breathing and our boots crashing through dry brush, with a surprising amount of shouted battle-talk going up and down the line as we crunched across the last 100 metres.

"Easy, boys ... don't bunch ... spread out!"

It looked like the bombs had started a fire in the grass somewhere to our left; brown smoke rose up from the veld. The grey smoke from the bombs had wafted in several directions now and it was hard to tell exactly where the target was. We came up to some trees and I braced myself but still there was no enemy fire. After a few more metres a shout came down the line.

"Turn around, everybody ... Left wheel! ... Left wheel!"

"Goddamnit ... what's going on?"

"We missed the base ... turn, head this way!"

The whole sweep line started to turn in a more northerly direction and, being at the bottom of the sweep line, we had to move at double-time to keep up with the wheeling line. Personally, I was not doing well. Like everybody else, I was wound up like a spring, ready to uncoil, but having to try and run on a twisted ankle and catch up at the same time was taking its toll. I was breathing hard and sweat was pouring down my face into my eyes, blinding me with the sting of it.

I tried to wipe my eyes with my forearm but this just made it worse because my forearm itself was drenched with sweat. My hands had formed sandy, sweaty grease all over the MAG and I had to readjust my grip every few seconds. To top it, my right ankle was forcing me to kind of roll and skip as I walked, using up twice the amount of energy.

Regardless of everything I kept my burning and blinking eyes firmly fixed on the surrounding grass and bush as best I could. I was determined to nail any SWAPO terrorist bastard—recruit or veteran—before he nailed me. Strangely, I was still unable to visualize a live terr moving in the bush before my eyes. It was a mental block. What *did* a live terr look like? Would I recognize one?

We had crashed through about 50 metres of high brown grass in the new direction and soon came on another thicket of trees—and then, suddenly, there was the target. There was a huge tree on the edge of the thicket whose thick limbs had been blasted off by the bombing, which now showed big white patches of flesh. Behind the tree, in the shadows and bush, I saw the remains of what looked like two long huts that had been made of branches tied together.

One looked like it had taken a direct hit and had been blown to pieces; only part of one wall remained standing. Behind it stood another hut that seemed untouched but the whole hut was leaning to one side. I realized we were right in the target. No AK-47 shots! No RPGs! Quickly it became very obvious that the base was deserted. We moved forward slowly. My finger was poised around the MAG trigger, ready to let off a 20-shot volley at anything that fucking moved.

"Check that one out!" barked Lieutenant du Plessis, pointing quickly at the hut that had been destroyed by the bombs. Kevin Green and I moved cautiously towards the destroyed hut.

The acrid stench of high explosive was still thick in the air as we walked across a green carpet of leaves and small branches that had been blown off by the powerful bomb blasts. Around the hut were a couple of bomb craters about five metres wide by a metre or so deep, with big clods of earth burned white and grey by the blast. The hut itself was a tangle of twisted and broken branches. It had not taken a direct hit but there was a crater about three metres from the hut and this had been enough to completely destroy it. Kevin Green and I moved through the mess and found nothing.

We discovered a couple of well-trodden paths leading from the hut into the bush behind. I made quick eye contact with Kevin and we gingerly started to walk around a small sprout of bush, our fingers on the triggers—ready. We crept on and came across a small clearing under some high trees that was untouched by the bombing. In the middle of the clearing stood a long, rough but sturdy four-legged table made of branches tied together and about five rows of benches behind each other, made in the same way. It seemed to be some kind of classroom. The ground around this 'bush furniture' was well used and even seemed to have been swept. On one side was a long rack that stood at an angle—what looked to be a weapons rack where SWAPO would lean their weapons while they learned new ways to 'kill the racist *boere*'. By the looks of it, it seemed that the camp had probably been deserted for a couple of days.

By this time the company had gone through all of the five buildings—or what was left of them—and all found the same thing ... nothing. Not even a scrap of paper.

"The bastards are gone," Lieutenant du Plessis observed with feeling.

We stood in the clearing. Doep spoke briefly into the radio that had quickly been set up. We got a minute to relax and get our breath. I leaned against the table and peered around into the bush, trying to will a terr to come walking out from behind a dusty bush. I examined the way the branches on the table had been tightly tied together with long strips of green bark.

"They were right here, sitting on these benches," I thought. Standing in their classroom broke the spell and in a second I imagined the bush class of SWAPO sitting on the benches, dressed in tiger-stripe uniform and the little peaked caps. Their faces were coal black and their eyes were bloodshot red— they were sweating. Against the rack they had their AK-47s and RPGs lined up, ready for action. Funny ... whenever I thought of SWAPO, I imagined them red-eyed and sweating.

"Back to the *chana*. Go to the same helicopter that dropped you!" came the urgent shout from one of the other *valk*'s lieutenant, Dudley Grant.

We hurriedly turned and moved out the deserted little base and made our way back to the *chana*. The Pumas were already coming in a long formation over the treetops and landing like ducks in a row down the length of the *chana*. Being 'cherries', the sound of the Pumas' loud chopping turbines biting the air spurred us on and we double-timed it for a couple of hundred metres.

I was limping and having a hard time keeping up but finally we got to the last Puma at the end of the *chana* that should have been ours, but *Valk 2* was boarding it and the flight engineer pointed with a gloved finger to the next chopper. We all turned and rushed off through the dust storm to the next Puma but it too was full, and we were told to move on again. Heaving for breath we carried on running to the next chopper in line. Before we got there we could see it was full and bypassed it to the next.

We had been double-timing for about 500 metres from the deserted base all the way up the *chana*. My lungs felt like they were going to burst and my eyes were blinded by the dust. My legs felt like lead and my shoulders burned from the weight of the MAG and 500 rounds of ammo. I cursed as we ran. Lieutenant Doep turned to wave us on, his shirt filled like a balloon by the prop wash. He looked like a fat little man running on the spot and waving. I gritted my teeth and thought back to running the 3.4 kilometres with full kit on the PT course. It did not make it any easier.

We eventually ran the entire length of the *chana*, past seven Pumas and arrived at the last one that was empty. It turned out to be our Puma, which had moved to the top of the *chana* because there had been no space for him at the bottom where he had first dropped us.

"Idiot! Stupid idiot!"

I could hardly lift the MAG onto the chopper but somehow managed to heave it up with two hands. Stan grabbed my shirt collar and heaved me up into the chopper and then fell flat on his back, heaving for breath. I was still cursing and swore I would never again let the sound of a chopper or a frantic idiot flight engineer force me into unwarranted urgency. My lungs burned and my chest felt like bursting. I leaned my head on the LMG I was cradling in my lap as the Puma lifted off. I had thick phlegm in my throat; I felt like retching and had the same kind of breathlessness I had experienced when I did the first selection run for the Bats at the Engineers', when I couldn't carry on. I made a mental note to cut down on the cigarettes because I felt I was going to die. I would find out later that this was in fact an athletically-induced form of asthma that would, indeed, almost kill me.

BASE NIGHTS

All along the watchtower—Jimi Hendrix

I sat at the wobbly fold-out table in middle of the tent. It was midday and I was concentrating without success on getting the beads of sweat dropping from my forehead not to fall on the Red Cross writing paper. Even my writing hand left wet smudges on the small pad. I was telling my brother about the ops, but in a rough slang code to fool the army censors. I told him how we had flown into Angola to hit the base and that it had turned out to be a lemon with the terrs gone before we got there. But still, I told him, we had flown a cross-border operation which not everybody in the army got to do. I stopped and wondered just how they had known we would be coming, or whether it was pure luck that made them move on before we arrived.

Dan Pienaar, our section leader, sat in the tent doorway, leaning back on a plastic chair. He had the usual dreamy, half-asleep look on his face that was his claim to fame and the reason for his nickname *Vaak Seun*, literally 'Dim Boy'. He was a rather philosophical South-Wester. I had grown to like him over the months; we had spent a couple of hours chatting about various things. He was a native South West African from a farm near Windhoek; all his family were in the military, so he too had earned his one stripe and was trying his best to be a good leader and work his way up.

I gave up writing, closed the pad and leaned back to adjust the small electric fan that we had scored from an air force 'tiffy', a mechanic. "Hey, Dan—how do you think those terrs knew that we were going to come, 'cause it sure looked like they cleaned up and cleared out just before we got there."

"They probably picked it up on the bush telegraph … they've got their spies all around these parts. Some of them have probably even got family living around here and heard about the op before we did."

"Nawww, c'mon … what spies?"

Danny spoke in his slow South West African way. As he stared out of the tent with his droopy eyes he reminded me of a Red Indian in a Western movie who had insight and wisdom as he spoke a slow warning to the white man. "Half the SWAPO've probably got family in this area; you'd be surprised how fast word can spread here in the bush. They could even have someone in this base who saw us training."

I paused and listened, even though I doubted there was a spy in Ondangwa. Ondangwa was a big 20-square-kilometre air force base. There were hardly any troops here except for the Airborne and 5 Recce sections down at the far end of the base that was shrouded in secrecy and barbed wire—the story was that they had live anti-personnel mines around their enclosure, even though it was inside Ondangwa air force base. Although there was also a black South West African infantry company, 101 Battalion, which had moved in two weeks ago and were staying in some tents behind the air force admin block.

Who knows; Dan might be right—one of these troops could spill the beans if they saw unusual activity. Local black Owambos were also employed at the base. Maybe Dan wasn't full of shit after all and had a point. At 20 years of age, I didn't know very much of the history of South West Africa. All I knew was that communist-trained forces were trying to take over South West Africa, and they were the vanguard for other communist countries such as the Soviet Union, Cuba and East Germany to move into the area and grab South West Africa's vast mineral wealth, which included uranium, and then move on to South Africa. Or so I had always been led to believe, and never having heard an alternative point of view, I did believe it.

Dan spoke slowly and gave me a half-hour lesson on the history of South West Africa. He reckoned that 80 percent of the SWAPO troops were probably from Owamboland. I listened with interest when he told me that the fight for South West African independence had actually started in Cape Town in 1956 by one Herman Toivo, who was a World War II veteran and railway policeman. Dan even hinted that perhaps it was their land anyway. I found myself agreeing with him that it probably was the people's land. It had been a German colony and was now run by South Africa. They wanted to break free from the chains just as South Africa had broken free from Britain and most African colonies from their respective European masters.

"The trouble is that they are backed by fucking communists who will want more than independence. They want the whole shooting match."

"That's a crock. Do you think that the Yanks and the West will sit back and allow Russia or China to just move in and take over South Africa if South West Africa got independence? No way; it's not that simple. They're feeding us bullshit again."

"Bullshit? You think having 40,000 Cubans and a communist country as our new neighbours is bullshit!" I was getting a bit upset at Dan's weird point of view.

"Zimbabwe's so-called freedom fighters were communist-backed and they've just won their independence. They are just north of us. I don't see them trying to take over South Africa or building freeways to Moscow."

Our conversation was interrupted by a bellow from RSM Louw who had recently arrived on the border from 1 Parachute Battalion and thought that he was still in Bloemfontein. He was known as a first-class prick who seemed to have a genuine chip on his shoulder and a fierce hatred for us troops. Rumour had it that a troop had run off with his wife a couple of years ago, but of course we had no proof. We could hardly believe it when, for the second day in a row, he had us fetch rakes and shovels and walk around the tent square doing a chicken parade for butts and looking for weeds.

The terrain was all pure white sand. He was being fucking ridiculous because there was not one single weed in the camp! It crossed my mind to use my week-old twisted ankle as an excuse to get out of this futile exercise but decided against it, not wanting to take the chance of being left behind on light duty if the siren wailed and we had to fly out on Fireforce. I picked up a rake and joined the seek-and-destroy mission that ambled about in small groups, chuckling among themselves at the stupidity of the action.

"This is almost as futile as finding and shooting a real live SWAPO."

"Yeah—we're on the border fighting a war and he thinks we're raw recruits in 1 Para!"

That night in the tent square we relaxed as the burning South West African sun sunk red behind the sand banks that surrounded us and threw a beautiful pink against the sky. As soon as it was dark Stan and I shuffled down, heads low, past the ops room and down through the air force tents to the prefab air force offices on the far side of the big brown hangars, where twenty Mirage fighters were kept. The place was crawling with blue; our brown army uniforms stood out like SWAPO tiger-stripe in the blue air force world that we were in.

We stood in the shadows like insurgents and listened to The Police's 'Walking on the Moon' as it drifted softly from the cassette player in the bar. Stan and I peeked through the flap into the bar. There was a tall air force sergeant with a walrus moustache, talking loudly about all the bullshit he had to go through to get his mail and complaining that he'd had to personally go and check at the postal unit for his parcels.

We stood in the shadows a full half an hour before he finally left and Stan quickly slipped into the long bar and bought two bottles of good South African brandy. The barman was a happy, chubby lad who was also doing his two years' national service. He sold us booze even though he knew he could lose his cushy job if he was caught.

"When are they going to allow you meat bombs to have a drink?" I heard him ask Stan mockingly.

"After the next contact, or when we get ten kills a week," Stan answered, trying to sound like an old bush war veteran and glaring at the barman with his well-known 'I'll kill you' Waffen SS stormtrooper look.

"You know, you guys must be the only unit in the whole damn South African Defence Force that's not allowed to have a cold beer at night—why?"

"Because we're always on standby looking after you guys' arses. We're like Squad Cars—on duty 24 out of 24, you know. We've got no time for daily drinking like the rest of you."

"Probably won't let you because you can't handle your drink. Look at us … easy, relaxed … making the best out of a bad thing. Here, I know nothing about it if you're caught."

Stan quickly passed me the bottles through the tent flap, walked calmly out the bar empty-handed and slipped past two lieutenants who were just walking in and luckily seemed too deep in conversation to notice him.

The chubby air force barman was right. The Parabats were the only unit I knew of that was not allowed to drink. Nobody knew what the real reason was. Every other unit in the SADF was allowed two beers a night, starting from after basic training. The Bats weren't allowed to drink at all; not throughout training back at Bloemfontein, or even up here on the border. It was a pretty low rule for a tough paratrooper outfit—not allowed to have a cold frosty after a long, hard day—but we had all sort of got used to it and just made the most of it when we got the chance. The result of this was that when we did get the chance to drink, we would all binge, go overboard and get fucked up. This binge-drinking would result in a sad loss to us later on. One of the stories as to why this rule was in place was that, years ago, some drunken paratroopers had walked into the officers' mess in Bloemfontein, fucked everyone up and torn the place apart; hence no drinking for any paratrooper any more, except now and then at *braais* when we returned from patrol or ops. So far this had only happened twice.

We walked quickly and purposefully through the rows of air force tents, sticking to the shadows. I was hunched over to try and keep the brandy tucked in the front of my pants and from sliding down my trousers. We looked like two fat hunchback paratroopers going for a pleasant evening stroll among the tents.

At night, the big air force base of Ondangwa took on the cozy feeling of a summer camp. Yellow, naked light bulbs shone through the flaps of the long rows of tents occupied by the air force and the paratroopers. The untarred roads that ran between the tents also had the occasional light that shone on camo netting … the occasional roar of laughter or strum of a guitar mingled with a dozen cassette players blasting out a variety of music, all backed by the constant, gentle but insistent hum of half a dozen big electric generators. I enjoyed the nights at Ondangs.

Reaching our tent undetected, we triumphantly pulled out the two bottles of brown gold and disappeared down into the underground bunker next to the tent. John the Fox and Doogy had already made preparations and had some warm Coke, canned sausages and cigarettes at the ready. I was in a great mood, full of energy. We had borrowed a guitar and pretty soon I was hammering out Hendrix's 'All along the watchtower' and some smoky, hazy blues. Dan had come in and soon we were all tanked up and trying to speak louder than the next. I tried to coax Danny into airing his views on South West Africa as he had that afternoon, but with a crowd he was not too eager and made a point of drinking a toast: "May all SWAPO leave clear spoor under the full moon for us to follow!"

We were having a whale of a time when suddenly we had to move the party upstairs in double-quick time after a jealous neighbour tossed a red smoke grenade into the bunker, instantly filling the bunker with thick, acrid smoke and sending us scurrying to the top, coughing and cursing. The red smoke soon enveloped the bunker and wafted up into the tent which we had to evacuate and dangerously take the party out into the open air, in the line of sight of any wandering corporal. I had the presence of mind to unscrew the light bulb on the way out so that the dense red cloud billowing from the tent would not be seen and which now looked like a dark, spooky form rising from the tent.

The grenade had stained the guitar with red dye that would not come off, which made the owner mad as hell when I later returned it.

FIRST BLOOD

Bad moon rising—Creedence Clearwater Revival

I had always loved the bush and was starting to get the feel of Owamboland. I was getting used to the wild, perfumed smells that wafted in from the vast bush and the faint peppery smell of sand that was on everything you touched. I was even getting used to the baking hot sun that had us sweating at seven o'clock in the morning, and the inky-black cold nights that fell so suddenly.

The only thing that I could not get used to was the squadrons of mosquitoes that would rise, seemingly from nowhere, as soon as the sun dipped under the horizon to strafe and torment us till daybreak. At Ondangwa we had nets over our beds that were a blessed protection, but out in the bush we were easy pickings for the marauding squadrons. They would send out a scout to recce the area for targets and once they found exposed white paratrooper skin, it was mere minutes before a 'Fireforce' mozzie platoon was called in to relentlessly attack the hapless target. Military insect repellent seemed useless; the only relief was to retreat into your sleeping bag like a cocoon and breathe stale air and vile rat-pack gas and smelly feet. It was a tough choice.

We had been in the bush for three days doing vehicle patrols. We were driving in Buffels, South African-made anti-landmine troop-carriers that carried ten men. The Buffels were high with an open top, allowing us to enjoy the weather, and had a V-shaped underbelly to help deflect the mine blast to protect us from the landmines that were SWAPO's weapon of choice. I had seen a Buffel that hit a big 'cheese' mine just a week before; it had merely lost a wheel and been blown over onto its side. (Cheese mines from their shape, much like a big Dutch cheese.) All the troops were unharmed, except for ruptured eardrums and a few bumps and bruises. They were great vehicles; we could crash through the bush with their big tyres and make our own path, staying far off the dirt roads to avoid the landmines on the established roads that were there, as sure as Monday.

We had been split up; half our *valk* was patrolling with the ruthless Koevoet[8] battalion who were stationed at nearby Oshakati. Koevoet were well known for their high kill rate and tracking abilities. Koevoet, much feared by SWAPO, was a special police unit that was very active on the border and had achieved astonishing successes. Many of their troops were ex terrs who had been 'turned' and who now fought with vigour on our side against their old comrades. Our half of the platoon had the misfortune to ride with 101 Battalion who were noisy, undisciplined and rowdy. I sat and watched them chattering among themselves, oblivious to their surroundings, their rifles hanging and pointing in all directions.

I was not too eager to go into our first contact with this bunch at my side. To have come through all that training and bullshit just to get shot by a 101 Battalion troop! Our five Buffels were patrolling the cut-line, the no-man's-land between Angola and South West Africa. We had seen the cut-line from the air but this was the first time we had patrolled through it. It was lush, with old buildings long ago destroyed in an earlier war that now stood silent and ghostly, overrun with wild flowers and long vines that seemed to thrive in reclaiming the ruins. The grass and weeds were lush and long from being spared the destructive grazing of cattle and goats.

We rode in the Buffels, winding through the bush, standing up and relaxed, stopping often to sit awhile and make lunch or brew coffee under tall, shady trees. I wondered why it was so lush here when 80 kilometres away it was so sandy and dry. This sector had once been a main SWAPO infiltration route and many a contact and hot pursuit had taken place in this very area. However, now, we were told, SWAPO chose to cross the border in the bushier region around Oshikango, 120 kilometres east of our position. That was where the rest of our platoon was patrolling with Koevoet. We bumped slowly along a green *chana*, while Stan was rambling on about how hot these Koevoet guys were.

"Once these guys get on a spoor, that's it ... they're like dogs. They stick to it for days. Boy has had his chips if Koevoet gets on his trail. Their troops are

---

[8] crowbar (Afrikaans)

ex terrs and know this bush inside out and they don't do foot patrols like us; they're always in vehicles, driving right into the contact ... that's their MO."

We had all heard stories about how, once they had identified a SWAPO spoor, they would chase it for days until they got the terrs. One of their legendary top kill-scorers was a Lieutenant Frans Conradie who, over a ten-year span of fighting in Rhodesia and then in South West Africa, had been in over 180 contacts and had personally dispatched something like 1,000 guerrillas to the happy hunting grounds. This must be some sort of all-time record, in any war anywhere. One man in the bush, with a thousand kills!

The story went that Conradie was one of the finest trackers in the operational area and would often follow spoor for three days at a time. He would start at daybreak and follow it at a run until sunset, or until he made contact. He would run on the spoor for 50 kilometres at a stretch, leaving his comrades far behind. One recent story went that he was tracking three SWAPO on the run. For three days Conradie, on foot and running, followed their trail, heading steadily for the Angolan border. When they bombshelled—split up—he followed one spoor at a time until he killed the man at the end of it. Then he returned to the original point of the spoor and started again on the next terr, and so on until all three were dead. He would run on the spoor far ahead of his support vehicles, bare-chested and clad only in shorts and running shoes, rifle in hand. He had mounted a 20-millimetre cannon from a Vampire jet fighter on his Casspir, and apparently this feared weapon had accounted for many of his kills.

"This guy's a fucking legend; he goes into a contact with music playing at full volume like in *Apocalypse Now*—'Bad moon rising' or 'Another one bites the dust'!" Stan found this intriguing and went on and on about how we should have big speakers rigged on the choppers and gunships and play loud rock and roll when we went into a contact.

"That's the kind of stuff that we've got to do ... the Yanks did that in Vietnam ... it freaks them out as you attack."

I agreed with him that it was a good idea. It sounded right up my alley.

We had just stopped under the shade of a couple of big thorn trees for another afternoon break, about six clicks outside the cut-line. Someone tossed a wire tied to a stone into the tree to get the antenna up high and the radio crackled and hummed to life as we sat down in the sand and fired up a fuel tablet to brew a bucket of coffee. I was sitting with my back against one of the tall Buffel tyres and had started to prepare my small meal and a cup of Java.

After a couple of minutes the 101 Battalion lieutenant, who was preparing his own meal with the radio at his side, quickly turned to our little group and called out excitedly. "Hey! Your guys are making contact right now ... they walked into an ambush!"

I put down the small can of steak and onions that I had just started to warm up. We all stopped what we were doing and moved towards the radio to listen to the contact being broadcast live over the airwaves. The lieutenant told us to go back to our positions and not to bunch up. We sat in the shade eagerly grinning at each other and looking at Dan, our section leader, who was now sitting with the 101 Battalion lieutenant listening to the contact and passing down reports.

"They charged the ambush and are in among the terrs now."

"It's close quarters ... they're calling for gunships. Shit! ... at last!"

It was hard to imagine our guys in contact at that very moment; I wondered quickly what Johnny Delaney and Kevin Green and Doogy were doing right this second and hoped that they would be all right. It sounded like a pretty chaotic situation. Now and again we could pick up an excited voice among the static, blurting co-ordinates to the gunships or giving directions to the Casspir drivers—I couldn't tell which.

We all sat dead still for several minutes, quietly grinning at each other, all our attention on the crackling radio a couple of metres away, passing along information as it came. Even the black 101 troops had shut up for a change, which was no easy task for them. After about five minutes the urgency in the radioman's voice had toned down, but it still seemed that there was fighting going on. A calm voice was still giving instructions to the gunships that seemed to have just arrived on the scene.

What we could gather was that Koevoet and the platoon of Parabats had found spoor and had been chasing it and ran into to an ambush, which was always the downside of following up on spoor but as it was Koevoet's trademark action, they had charged and driven right through the ambush

111

with their Casspirs. From the sound of it, they had come out tops. Everyone's mood had been lightened by the news of the contact; we were chatting and laughing and trying to imagine what it must have been like. We were jealous but also thankful that someone had finally made contact with the ever-elusive SWAPO. Ten minutes later, the lieutenant yelled again.

"They're making contact again with a second group of terrs!"

We were ready to mount up, so this time we all stood around the radio and listened. The voice was now calmly directing the gunships to the positions, telling them they should look for the red smoke and to watch out, because our troops were almost hand to hand with the terrs who were making a stand.

"A second contact ... fucking hell, way to go!"

I could not contain my excitement and was now really pissed off that I had not been with the other group. Well, at least our platoon got to have the first contact out of both H and D companies. We listened silently and intently for about five minutes to what sounded like some fierce fighting and then, by the sound of the communication, it died down as the gunships picked off fleeing SWAPO. We sullenly boarded the Buffels and headed slowly back into the cut-line to continue our fruitless patrol.

It was getting late in the afternoon and the lieutenant, sensing our frustration at days of riding around in a dead area, called a halt as we came across a herd of black and brown cattle lazily grazing not quite in the forbidden green grass of the cut-line. He shouldered his South West African-issue G3 7.62-millimetre rifle, took a slow aim and loosed a shot that shattered the stillness and collapsed a young bull to his knees in the long grass, 150 metres away.

The black 101 troops whooped and yelled in excitement and anticipation of fresh meat. They jumped off the Buffel and ran to the young bull that was still in his death throes. The usually surly lieutenant grinned like a schoolboy and quickly told us all to say nothing. His action would be safe with us.

The gunshot was a release for everyone's energy. We were thankful for the change in activity and watched as the 101 troops expertly and quickly skinned and gutted the young bull. They happily chatted with each other as they cut prime slabs of meat from the loins, neck and rump and fought over the liver and kidneys. They hooted with laughter when the lieutenant, who was a white South West African, told them in fluent Owambo not to forget that we also wanted some good pieces.

They danced a jig which I took as the 'fresh meat' jig and rolled the skinless carcass off the hide and onto the grass for the hyenas and jackals. Then they piled the heaps of cut meat into the soft hide of the bull and wrapped it closed in a neat bundle, which we hoisted onto the Buffel. The rest of the herd of cattle had gathered around and stood and watched us dumbly. As we rode off they slowly assembled around their fallen comrade, but bolted when they got too close and caught the smell of his slaughter.

We would also have a celebration tonight. We rode off in the direction of Charlie water tower about 20 clicks away, close to *Oom Willie se Pad*. Charlie water tower was a big concrete water reservoir that was enclosed by a high fence. It had a small, constant guard of infantry who lived in tents behind a mountain of sandbags with twin MAGs pointing out from behind a tall watchtower.

The sun was dipping behind the thorn trees when we pulled into the area. It had once been a small border post but now only the big reservoir stood surrounded by a dozen empty and broken-down small buildings. Old political slogans in Portuguese were faded and barely visible on the crumbling walls that were riddled with hundreds of bullet holes.

That night, safe in the compound, we lit big fires and feasted on fresh steak which we shared with the infantry who were happy to have some company and fresh meat. They told us that there had been no action in this area for many months and confirmed that the new infiltration point was farther east in the thick bush. We casually bragged about our company who had made two contacts that afternoon. They were impressed and we put on our 'paratrooper bush fighter' act, even though all we had shot was a poor young bull who had been grazing away peacefully.

At dawn the following morning we received a radio dispatch to join the rest of the platoon as soon as we could at Oshikango, a base camp that was smack in the middle of the dense, high-treed bush close to where the previous day's contacts had been made. We wasted no time and loaded the Buffels, bade our infantry buddies goodbye and headed east, shivering in the chilly dawn. We reached Oshikango that afternoon. Kevin Green and John Delaney were sitting with the others in the shade of their Buffels on the far side of the camp. They could not stop talking about the contact. They quickly took Stan and I over to the chopper pad, where they gleefully pointed out 13 green body bags that lay propped up against the sand embankment. Kevin unceremoniously unzipped the first bag a few centimetres and revealed a two-day-dead, grey-faced SWAPO who had had his half his jaw shot away, the corpse now crawling with maggots. John had his wide-eyed John Travolta look and took over the story.

"Lieutenant Doep and I were running dog with some Koevoet on the spoor of about 30 terrs. We had been on them the whole morning; fresh spoor. All of a sudden, as we come out of a *chana* and cross a *muhangu* field, boom! boom! Fucking RPGs just over our heads; just miss the vehicles behind us." John bopped up and down, as was his fashion. "All fucking hell breaks loose. We hit the dirt and I start shooting fast as I can pull the trigger. Couldn't see what I was shooting at."

John Delaney put his arm up and moved his finger as if he was shooting in rapid fire and keeping his head down.

Kevin took over. "Yeah the moment they started shooting the Koevoet charged the ambush with their Casspirs and we followed them. We crashed right into their ambush positions and were right in on top of them and shooting down at them. Bardie, the driver, rode right over one guy laying on the ground with an RPD machine gun." He demonstrated how the unfortunate terr had curled up and died under the huge tyres of the Buffel.

John Delaney was now hopping and dancing, his blue eyes wide with excitement as he took up the story. "Soon as the Buffels rushed past us into the ambush, we went in after them and were the only ones on the ground. This terr turns around and makes a run for it through our Buffels and runs straight into us. All of us open up on him from ten metres. He had no chance!"

They described how, 20 minutes later, while giving chase to the surviving terrs who had bombshelled from the failed ambush, they ran into a group of 20 terrs on the run, heading for thick bush, who stopped to make a fight of it when they saw that they were trapped. Because of the terrain our troops had to disembark and were almost hand-to-hand combat, shooting from ten metres apart, and less. Point-blank stuff.

"They stood to fight," John repeated uncharacteristically, looking solemnly down at the dead terr's grey face who, despite his missing chin, looked relaxed in death and almost at peace. Then, back again to the John we knew as he grinned broadly: "You should have seen them dance when those gunship cannons ripped them up!"

That night we had a small party, with free access to the infantry pub and Castle lager. We sat in the recreational area and hooted with laughter at the ten-year-old black piccanin who was mimicking South African troops shooting SWAPO. He would charge into an imaginary contact, taking giant steps and look from side to side with his eyes bulging wide. When he spotted his enemy he would stop suddenly, hunch over and creep up on them and then jump up, pointing and shouting loudly, "Hey ... hey!" Chasing his enemy he would close one eye, cock his head to the side and shoot a volley of shots from his outstretched finger. He would then become the dying SWAPO, push his tongue out and roll his eyes in his head and collapse in a heap. He wore a brown army shirt that had been cut to size, sleeves rolled up and old worn—but clean—grey flannel school shorts. His parents, as well as almost everybody in his small village, had been cold-bloodedly gunned down in front of his eyes by a SWAPO patrol which had wandered into the kraal. He had been adopted by infantry and had been living in the camp ever since, doing small chores for his keep. He had a wide, mischievous face that would light up with a big grin, but a scowl would cross his young brow when we asked him about SWAPO.

"SWAPO ... *maak dood. Maak dood!*"[9] He spat on the ground in disgust, and then stomped in the sand like he was squashing a bug. *"Maak dood ... maak dood!"*

After he had done his SWAPO routine the deep scowl changed back to a broad thick grin, as he hustled us for some spare change. He then sat quietly and watched us drinking and laughing, his eyes darting from person to person, not missing a thing.

"He is going to make one good soldier," I thought.

---

[9] kill (Afrikaans)

CONTACT

Fixin' to die—Bob Dylan

Dark ominous rain clouds loomed high in the distance and a low thunder that sounded like far-off artillery rumbled in the west, signalling the beginning of the rainy season. A fresh breeze had sprung up, blowing in cool air that tasted like iron and left a tangy taste in the back of your mouth. It was about four days since the contact and we had been conducting a fruitless vehicle patrol of the area, this time as a full paratroop platoon with only a few black troops from 101 Battalion to act as interpreters and trackers. We were all tired after manning a couple of all-night ambushes on a likely crossing point, but to no avail.

We pulled into a small infantry camp 30 clicks west of Oshikango for the night to wash and rest, but were not allowed in and had to sit in the Buffels for half an hour before the camp CO begrudgingly let us spend the night in his camp. Rumour was that he disliked paratroopers, calling us "glamour boys". This just made us strut our newly acquired 'bad ass' paratrooper pose all the more, now that we could rightfully do so, since our platoon now had 13 kills to its name. We were told not to mix with the troops or to roam the small camp and could only shower and sit tight in the tents provided for us at the entrance under a sandbagged watchtower.

We eyed the infantry troops with venom from our tents, but later that night got out to talk to some of them; they said their CO was a real prick. They turned out to be okay and even gave us some cans of sausages and fruit from the kitchen.

The next morning, just as we were preparing to 'shoot in' our rifles on the small shooting range, Lieutenant Doep came charging over from the ops room shouting that we were to mount up immediately, as some helicopters

116

had sighted a group of about 20 terrs just north of us. We ran to get our gear and, still shirtless, piled into the Buffels that had fired into life. We pulled out like police cars, with half the troops still hanging onto the sides.

The infantry troops scampered to give way as our five Buffels threw some tight U-turns on the small parade ground, spraying them full of fine red dust. We careened out of the camp gates and headed north up the straight dirt road, sending clouds of dust billowing into the air.

"Put on your safety belts; we're going to be driving on the road," barked Doep in a hoarse voice, his small brown eyes shining with excitement.

I squeezed on my Fireforce vest and fumbled with the safety belt which I was not used to wearing. We didn't usually buckle up as we hardly ever used the road when we drove patrol. We stuck to the bush because of the reduced risk of landmines. After I finally got buckled in tight I shifted around trying to get into a comfortable position.

Lieutenant Doep was rasping on the radio in his strange new confident voice, trying to fix co-ordinates, but was apparently unsuccessful because he yelled to us to watch for a chopper that was coming to look for us so that we could follow him to the terrs which the other choppers had trapped in some thick bush. I felt cold with excitement and, contrary to the lemon ops we flew a few weeks ago when I had felt all hyped up, I now felt emotionless, numb and eager. I checked my rifle, took out the magazine, pushed the top bullet snugly against the back of the clip and clicked it back into my R4 clamped between my knees.

"There! There's the chopper!"

We all followed Kevin Green's finger; a small spot on the horizon was following the road and coming towards us low and fast. We quickly met the Alouette gunship and his rotor blades hammered as he turned and headed into the bush at a 45-degree angle from the course he'd followed coming in. We turned off after him with a bump and crashed through the small thorn trees, zigzagging to avoid the clumps of tall, thick trees that made SWAPO choose this area. The Buffel bounced and flew over old stumps and swerved at right angles to go around the trees.

"Thank God we're strapped in," I cussed.

The Buffel lifted at such an angle I thought we would surely topple over,

117

but bounced back onto all four wheels. Bits of branches and leaves showered down on our heads and shoulders from crashing through low-hanging foliage. It would be pure suicide to try and stand up.

"Here we go ... here we go ... fucking SWAPO ... here we go!"

We crashed onward on the haywire ride for about another five clicks, when suddenly I could hear the hammering of the gunships' 20-millimetre explosive rounds not far away.

Lieutenant Doep was at the radio with an authority I had not seen before. His hair blew in the wind as he barked orders to the helicopter, which had to return several times to find us because we lost sight of him when we got caught up in the trees. John Delaney, too, seemed confident and ready. He had his peaked bush hat turned around back-to-front for better vision, and was talking to no one in particular.

"Here we go ... here we go ..."

I could hear the gunships' cannon shells exploding in bursts of two and three, close by now. *Doof doof ... doof doof doof.*

I risked a knockout shot from a passing branch and raised my head but could see nothing except thick high bush. We rode over a long *chana* and at the thick tree line could see an Alouette gunship orbiting and pounding away with its cannon.

"This is it!"

John had undone his safety belt, was hopping around and had already shouldered his rifle. We all followed suit and unbuckled. We came off the *chana* and into the thick tree line where the SWAPO were trapped.

"Go around! The last two Buffels break right! Go around the trees as stopper groups," Lieutenant Doep shouted into the radio. We were under the canopy of trees now and couldn't see the gunship, but it sounded as if he was just above us—the explosive heads hammered down, hidden by foliage, just 20 metres to our right. I loosened my chest webbing for a quick magazine change and flipped the safety off as I shoved the rifle tightly into my shoulder. Thorns scraped my forearms as we edged further into the thicket. The gunship was directly above us now and had stopped shooting.

"They're here, they're here!" Doep shouted hoarsely in Afrikaans.

I peered into the bush. I had my cap turned backwards as well. All I could see was the thick, dry, tangled bush and scrub that formed a solid wall in front of me. Once again the thought flashed through me that I might not recognize a terr if he was standing right in front of me. All of a sudden John Delaney started to shoot into the thicket.

"Come on ... come on ... come on!"

"What the fuck is he shooting at?"

For a split second I thought John had lost his mind as he blasted into the trees. Maybe he's trying to show us how it's done, seeing he and Lieutenant Doep were the only ones on the Buffel who had already been in a contact. I held my fire and tried to stay calm. I looked to see what John was shooting at. I could see nothing. What the fuck's he shooting at, then? He could hit one of our guys on the other side of the thicket!

The other Buffels were somewhere abreast of us, riding into the thicket, but we could not see them. There was the crackle of rifle fire about 30 metres away to our right. Suddenly, right in front of us and coming out the dry bush, was a small figure wearing a dirty brown uniform. He didn't even see us, his arms flaying at the thorn bushes that cluthced at him. He had an AK-47 grasped in his right hand. I started shooting at him, as did Fourie and John next to me, not even aiming. It seemed to be happening in slow motion; the only reality was the kick of the R4 rifle against my shoulder. I fired about five or six rapid shots, then everyone opened up. The small figure fell back into the thorns but kept thrashing about wildly. The earth around him came alive as our bullets kicked up sand in high spurts and I could see his clothes tug as they struck him.

He rolled over onto his belly and lay still, half-concealed by the thick thorn bush. Instantly I looked around for more targets. I flinched as bullets cracked and buzzed over our heads, probably from our own guys in the Buffel opposite us, who sounded like they were having a party. Then there was a shout from the other side of the Buffel and they all opened up at a target that we couldn't see. I scanned the wall of bush in front of me. The veil had been lifted from my eyes now that I knew exactly what I was looking for. C'mon ... bring on some more!

The shooting came to a ragged halt and the other Buffel came into view through a clearing in the bush. We had driven through the thicket. The whole thing had lasted about five minutes, if that. I became aware again of the gunship still circling above and looked up.

I could see the door-gunner with his big visor and helmet, like a big one-eyed bug sitting behind his long 20-millimetre sting. *Valk* 2 went in and swept the small thicket on foot, dragging the dead SWAPO and putting them in a line on the *chana* floor next to where we had parked the Buffels. We had killed four of them; the gunships, for all their shooting, had apparently not got any. If they did, we didn't find them. The gunship crew must have felt safe with us around, because they landed in the *chana* and waltzed over to look at our handiwork.

"The bush was too thick to see them here, but we got some further back when we first saw them ... back over there."

The pale-eyed, blond door-gunner smoked a cigarette and pointed with his big bug-helmet into the bush to our right. He was tall and lanky; his flight suit seemed too small for him and his trouser-legs showed his ankles. Doep sent a section to scout for more bodies but they soon returned empty-handed and we gave up the search.

We all lit cigarettes and relaxed for a minute. My mouth was as dry as a bone and my body felt clammy with sweat. I found myself glaring around with an intense stare and a frown, but apart from that I felt completely cold and calm. It was my first action—I felt no emotion at all. It had not been as much a fire fight as a plain, simple killing. I felt like some old colonial hunter riding high on the back of a elephant in the bush and shooting down at tigers that were trapped and tangled in the bush.

I felt no exhilaration or discomfort. I felt nothing. *Valk* 2 had come back from sweeping the area and reported it clean. This had probably been part of the group that had ambushed our guys five days earlier and had bombshelled into smaller groups. I looked at them lying in a row, dead. Three of them wore torn tiger-stripe uniforms, they had makeshift webbing with small round Chinese water bottles. One, who looked about 16 years old, wore a plain khaki tunic and pants and chest webbing stuffed with shiny, worn AK-47 magazines. We dragged them to the Buffels and trussed them to the bumpers at the back and front of the vehicle like deer after a hunt.

I noticed some kind of fuss going on at the second Buffel. When I walked over, I wasn't surprised to see a couple of our platoon struggling to cut a finger from one of the dead terrs with a big Bowie knife. They were having a hard time, because when they kicked the knife that was held against the middle knuckle of the finger, the terr's hand slipped into the soft sand. Finally they put the finger against the wheel rim while one troop held the knife in place on the joint of the finger and the other gave it a hard stomp with his boot, which cut right through the joint, leaving half a finger hanging by a thread of skin. I also noticed that there was a white bloodless patch that stood out against the black skin where the terr's ear used to be. I knew what they were doing was wrong but the only thing I could think of saying was a stupid rhetorical question.

"What the fuck are you doing?"

"Dries up like old biltong ... show the folks at home what we're doing up here."

The troop smiled and popped the finger into his side pouch and then proceeded to truss the terr up against the bumper. I said nothing and turned and walked back to the Buffel. I had heard that it was a popular pastime to take ears and fingers but as far as I was concerned it was bad karma. Not good. What happens if you get zapped and have to explain at the Pearly Gates why you have a string of ears around your neck? "I was going to return them but no one could hear me!"

As we drove away the only thing that was left at the scene of the killing was the small, almost intact brain that had plopped out of the 16-year-old's broken skull as we tied him to the Buffel and which now lay in the dust of the small *chana* among the tyre marks and boot prints, the only evidence of what had happened here today for anybody who might happen to walk by.

I wondered where this kid's mother was right now. Did she perhaps feel his death? What was she doing now and how long, if ever, would it take for her to find out what had happened to her young son out here in the bush? *I knew what happened. I* could tell her exactly what happened and even show her the only thing that was left at the scene. Her son's intact brain, lying in the dust among the spoor of big army boots and truck tyres.

We drove back into the infantry camp like deer hunters and the infantry troops gathered around to look at the dead SWAPO, whose faces and

121

wounds were coated in thick dust from hanging from the bumpers. The bodies would be picked up sometime later by chopper and taken to Oshakati. All terrs killed inside the South West African border had to be brought back to base and then taken to Admin HQ at Oshakati to be photographed and fingerprinted. Many more times in the future this requirement would have us riding into a camp with bodies hanging from the sides of our vehicles, sometimes a couple of days old.

That night we had a rowdy celebration with cold sodas, chocolate bars and cigarettes. The next morning, bright and early, just before breakfast, the shit hit the fan. The camp commandant came to inspect the dead terrs and found them missing half their fingers, all their ears and one of them minus a scrotum. We took it lightly and joked but Lieutenant Doep warned us that the infantry commandant was furious and rightly so.

We were told to unpack all our kit from the Buffels. We were supposed to leave that morning to continue with our vehicle bush patrol and then head in a roundabout way back to Ondangwa about 70 clicks away, but the commandant had blocked us from moving out, determined to find out who was responsible for the mutilations.

"Maybe someone heard something," Stan sniggered.

"Or maybe they should look for some fingerprints!" the guys laughed. No one took the problem—or the infantry commandant—seriously. We soon got to realize his commitment when we spent the morning confined to our hot tents at the entrance of the camp and bored as hell. The hours dragged by slowly; we sat shoulder to shoulder, smoking and sweating and wondering what was going on. Thankfully a cool breeze from the pending rain sprang up and came billowing through the tent flaps, bringing relief after Spike's mid-morning assault had turned the tents into saunas.

I took a deep breath, sucking in the sweet air that always smelled of iron and pepper. I looked out at the sky. The high clouds shone brilliant white at the edges but were a dull grey in the centre. Everybody kept mum. Blame for the missing digits quickly fell on the jealous infantry troops who had snuck in under cover of darkness and clipped off some trophies to toss around at home like bush fighters and brag about their fire fights.

Later in the morning everyone who had been directly involved with the contact was called into the commandant's office in the middle of the camp and given the third degree. When my turn came, the commandant said it was a serious crime to mutilate bodies in any way and was punishable with a year in DB and that if I knew anything about what had happened it would be wise for me to come forward, or I would be held as an accomplice. Standing to attention in the small hot tin office I explained what I had seen from when we had dragged the terrs out of the bush into a line on the edge of the *chana* after the contact. I told him how we had searched the dead terrs for documents and that we had relaxed for ten minutes, smoked a cigarette and spoken to the chopper pilots before loading the dead terrs onto the Buffels. I told him, respectfully, that I did not know anything about any missing ears, that it might equally well have been some of his own troops right here in the base who took them and that he should check his men too. His eyes darkened and looked like they might explode. His straight black hair bounced as he jumped up from behind his wooden desk and rushed me like a bull, stopping right in front of me. I blinked instinctively and braced myself for what was surely going to be a punch or a shove, but he surprised me and stopped inches from my face, glaring at me. I could see the sweat running down his forehead, I could smell his breath as he yelled, spitting, into my face in Afrikaans.

"Fuck off out of my office!"

With a hasty salute I turned around and almost fell through the narrow doorway and through the short, dark hallway into the bright morning light.

Stupid fucking idiot. What gave him the right to charge at me like he's going to do something and to talk to me like that? The prick! The guy's obviously got some serious personal problems. I gave him the benefit of my psychiatric evaluation as I walked out of the small tin admin area in a hurry, headed back to the tent at the camp entrance and squeezed my way back to my kit. Nobody can have such deep-rooted anger without a serious hang-up, I decided.

In the tent I lay back on an old foam mattress and bummed a cigarette from Stan. The guys laughed when I told them what I had said and how he had reacted.

"You should have told him our trackers followed a spoor to his cook's tent, and that he should check his steak and onions for bits of terrorist." Kurt

123

Barnes roared at his own joke.

After the attention had shifted from me, Smitty sidled nervously up to me and spoke quietly as he puffed on a butt. "Was that all you said?" he asked quietly, trying to sound casual and by the way. He looked searchingly into my eyes to see if he could catch me lying.

"Of course ... what did you think I was going to tell him? That I saw exactly who did it?" I said out the corner of my mouth.

He was visibly relieved and gave an empty chuckle. Kevin, who was in earshot, gave me a grin.

"But you know it's a fucking crime to mutilate bodies! A fucking year in DB! Haven't you ever heard of the Geneva Convention?" I said forcefully, as if I had a good grasp of military law.

Smitty nodded his head slowly, saying that he had recently heard this.

"Just be cool when you go in there ... don't freak out ... tell him we found them like that."

Smitty grinned at my joke, lit up another smoke and prepared himself for his grilling by the commandant.

I sat pondering the situation. I felt relieved that my good sense had kept me from getting involved in this trophy-cutting business when I saw it happening back at the contact. This commandant seemed determined to have somebody's balls for the incident and it appeared it was going to be paratrooper balls. If Smitty and Kevin were our only guys to take a couple of ears and fingers, it must have been the infantry fucks who took the rest—and it seemed like this prick of a commandant thought his men were beyond doing such a thing! I knew this wasn't going to go away and that someone was going to have to go down for it, or we wouldn't be leaving the camp for a while.

I mentally washed my hands of the whole situation and picked up my rifle that was lying on my kit. I inspected the new inscription: one dead. I'd scratched it in English next to the *drie dood*, three dead, that was already scratched deep into the chipped green-and-brown camo paint above the handgrip. I felt that I was entitled to put the notch there, although all four of us had shot the poor bastard. I asked myself if it was altogether the right thing to mark the poor skinny terr's death with a notch on my rifle. I fantasized morbidly whether my name would end up as a notch on the side of a worn AK-47 somewhere in Luanda. I pushed the thought out of my mind.

"Fuck 'em."

At least I had got to see my first contact. Most SADF, South African Defence Force, troops go through their entire service without seeing any action. I thought back to the cold excitement of the contact and the small brown-clad figure flailing desperately, crashing through the bush only to run into our hail of bullets. I was surprised at my cold emotion. I had shot somebody. Aren't you supposed to feel something? I thought perhaps it would sink in later.

That afternoon we packed all our gear onto the Buffels. Smitty and Kevin, after going back and forth to the commandant's office a couple of times, had confessed to taking an ear and a finger. The pair of them were charged with corpse mutilation, a punishable offence under the international rules of war laid down by the Geneva Convention many years before. The charged pair would be allowed to leave with us to complete the patrol and return to Ondangwa where their case would be handed over to the proper level of authority. We never found out who else was to blame for the rest of the missing fingers and ears. We drove out of the base, glaring at the infantry troops who looked away as we openly challenged them, jeering at them.

I was glad just to get moving again. The cool breeze blew through our hair and with it came the smell of the coming rain. We were in the bush again, where we belonged, where we were in control and not some dipshit infantry commandant. Our four Buffels immediately left the dirt road and made their own path, winding through the dry bush and heading west. I sat relaxed. After nearly a month of vehicle patrols the Buffels had become our home. We were quite comfortable squashed shoulder to shoulder, kit knee-high, bouncing through the thick bush. This was where we belonged—in the bush, hunting!

Our senses had adapted and sharpened in the last weeks, becoming accustomed to the sights, sounds and mood of the bush. We were bush fighters. We had all lost weight from living on rat packs. We slept in sand holes under the moon and lay awake at night, waiting for SWAPO to walk into our ambushes.

Late that afternoon, when the sun started to cast long shadows, we crossed a long flat *chana* and entered a most quaint, almost magical forest of tall, flat-topped thorn trees. We drove under this long avenue of trees, whose intertwining crowns totally blocked out the sky above. All the trees grew at almost the same angle and, if you did not know better, you might easily think that the entire scene had been landscaped and maintained by the local parks department. Suddenly the lead Buffel came to an abrupt stop, forcing the four following to brake quickly, sending us tumbling into each other at the front of the vehicle.

We watched the front troops get out and walk around, looking at the ground. They seemed to be chattering excitedly, so after a few minutes we also hopped down and walked over to see what was going on. In front of the Buffel's front tyres was a patch of churned-up sand about a metre and a half wide and about 20 centimetres deep. I didn't understand what it was for a while, until I saw a lone, clear, chevron-shaped boot spoor on the side of the path … and then another … and another. This was a huge fucking terr spoor! There must be hundreds of them!

"SWAPO!" said the black tracker, chewing a green stick to clean his teeth. "*Indji*! Many!"

Lieutenant Doep was on the radio. His voice crackled with excitement as he reported that we were on the spoor of somewhere between 100 and 150 SWAPO, walking in single file. The tracker with the stick said that it was about a day old; he indicated happily that we must start to run on it fast and leave immediately. I bent down to inspect the trail. There were so many walking in single file that they had actually ploughed a small furrow in the soft Owamboland sand. It looked like a giant snake winding through the bush. The only trouble was that it was heading north, back to Angola.

"They've already been in here for weeks—probably planted hundreds of mines. They regrouped and they're high-tailing it back to Angola," John said, looking down at the thick snake.

Everyone spoke slowly and softly as if in a dream. I ran my fingers through the sand that was riven by hundreds of SWAPO boots and felt a strange feeling run through me. For a long time SWAPO hadn't really meant much more than situation reports in the morning and elusive ghosts in the bush, the only sign of their presence being the bent and burned-out wreckage of a vehicle that had fallen victim to a 'double cheese' landmine or a murdered village headman. Now we were starting to see them and no ghost left a spoor this wide!

These fuckers were heading for Angola—we would have to move fast to get them. I tried to imagine 150 SWAPO walking in single file, all wearing tiger stripes, carrying AK-47s and RPG rocket launchers. Fuck! We wouldn't be able to handle them!

I felt a twinge of panic but quickly relaxed when I realized that we would surely get some aerial support on such a clear spoor. I looked around. The one black tracker was stealing the show, so happy to find the spoor that he was smiling and lying on the spoor, making as if he was fucking it. Our troops laughed. He was beside himself and got up and danced a jig on the spoor. We would joke about this display of glee for a long time to come.

Then, without warning, as if the bush gods were looking down on the hundreds of SWAPO fleeing back to safety across the border, the grey clouds that had been building for a week finally opened up, first a drizzle patting down on the leaves and then a soft, steady rain that came falling through the trees. It was the first fall of the rainy season and SWAPO's most active time of the year.

"We're on our own ... let's chase it." Lieutenant Doep came from the radio. He had a deep frown on his brow and seemed pissed off.

He chose the front Buffel to run dog, with two men on the ground. One man to run looking down and staying next to the spoor; the second running behind him looking ahead into the bush, with the support Buffel keeping up behind. Many times the vehicles would get hung up in bush and the guys running dog would find themselves far ahead of the support vehicles. The running dogs always ran the risk of an ambush, or a POMZ anti-personnel mine laid on or next to the spoor, or an anti-tank 'cheese' mine laid on a likely vehicle route next to the spoor ... or all three at the same time. All of us being around 20 and gung-ho, these seemed like minor details. We whooped like hunting dogs as our Buffels turned onto the spoor and crashed through the undergrowth, following the thick snake that wound silently through the bush, heading steadily north. We were in the rear Buffel, so for the time being did

127

not have to run. We just sat strapped in, bouncing in our seats, trying to keep dry by covering ourselves with our plastic liners. Every time we bumped or clipped a tree, water would come pouring down on us from the wet foliage.

There were only a couple of hours of daylight left. I sat, quite content, under my plastic liner and opened a can of corned beef that I ate cold and then mixed up one of my powdered milkshakes with water and condensed milk. This was it. What more did I need? I was driving in a vehicle, not walking, dry, I had food and a milkshake and cigarettes and was driving on the biggest terr spoor in fucking history. My needs had become very simple in the last couple of months. Shit, you don't need all that bullshit back in Civvy Street. The army takes good care of you; you don't even need to think.

My brief spell of contentment was broken by a flutter of panic. Lieutenant Doep had said that we were on our own. Did that mean no support? We were not much more than a platoon; the enemy had more than a company, maybe two. It didn't make sense.

"Hey ... you think we'll catch them before they go over?"

John Delaney, who had become the Buffel's new bush expert, paused and looked around thoughtfully before answering. "Ja, I dunno. They don't seem to be headed directly north. Maybe they want to hook up with another group before they cross back into Angola."

We had about an hour left until sundown, made premature by the low ominous clouds that had enveloped the world. Just before the light faded, Lieutenant Doep called a halt to the chase and we built lean-tos around the Buffels with our plastic liners and settled down. It was a long, cold, miserable wet night. Then, to top it all, early in the morning the heavens opened with a bombardment of thunder, sheet lightning and an hour of driving rain that rendered our lean-tos useless, sending us scurrying under the Buffels, wrapped in our plastic liners, shivering and waiting for daylight.

First light revealed a miserable grey, overcast dawn. We packed up and a scowling Lieutenant Doep put our Buffel second in the chase. We set off on the spoor in the dawn light, our teeth chattering from the cold and wet. The night's rain had destroyed much of the spoor but the deep furrow remained—smudged but clear—winding like a snake in and out of thickets, through *muhangu* fields and straight across long open *chanas*. These terrs weren't worrying about trying to hide. They were pushing hard and probably felt they were home and dry, almost back in Angola. We found dozens of large blue and white cans of sardines and a sort of corned beef discarded next to the spoor with 'Product of Denmark' on the labels. We also found a number of broken glass vials scattered around the spoor.

"Hey, look at this! They're shooting it up. That's why they're moving so fast!" I picked up one of the smoky brown vials, sniffed at it and looked to see if there was a lable on it. There wasn't.

We had been told that SWAPO would sometimes inject themselves with adrenaline when on long speed-marches or hot pursuits and were capable of covering incredible distances. I had thought that half the things we had heard were bullshit but here was the proof right before my eyes. These guys were probably as high as kites and moving at twice the speed of normal marching men. By mid-morning the sun had broken through the clouds and we ran shirtless, drenched in sweat. By noon they had started to bombshell.

Here and there a group of ten or 15 would break off on their own, disappear into thick bush, then break off again in ones or twos. Somehow they either knew we were on them, or it was just a standard precautionary tactic. This was a proven last-line defence tactic that had saved many a guerrilla's life in South West Africa, the former Portuguese territories and Rhodesia. After splitting up into ones or twos each man would fend for himself, making his own way, then regroup when they reached their prearranged rendezvous point.

The only way to combat this would be to leapfrog ahead onto the main spoor with helicopters to stop them before they all disappeared into the bush but—for some reason I could never find out—we could not get choppers to come to our assistance. The main spoor was a lot thinner now but also a lot fresher. We had been chasing it hard since first light and even I didn't need a tracker to tell me that these terrs were not far ahead.

Our Buffel was now in front. John Delaney was running on the spoor and I was behind him, scanning the bush for any sign. I had taped two 35-round magazines together for a quick change and stuffed a white phosphorus grenade in my pocket for easy access. I never did like the clip-type chest pouches that we had in our Fireforce vests. They were tricky to clip open quickly with one hand; you had to hold down the vest with one hand and tug on the clip pouch with the other. Sometimes it would get caught on the water bottles at your side.

We had found some huge terr shit next to the spoor that was very fresh. I was nervous. I did not like the idea of running straight into a 50-man ambush.

"Where the fuck are the gunships?"

Doep told us that H Company was on Fireforce standby to come to our aid if we needed it, when we made contact. What would that help us if we ran into an ambush and they took 15 minutes to get here? I was starting to see the great foresight and logic of the men who ran our little war. They did not seem detail-orientated and clearly favoured a brand of impenetrably hidden logic that we were yet to figure out. I had always heard that you wanted to attack your enemy at three-to-one odds but I was quickly learning that this was not how the SADF was run. They seemed to believe in one-to-three, with us being the one!

The still-thick spoor led into a low thicket of thorn bush that grew up a small incline. It was a perfect place for an ambush. John and the tracker in front waved their hands and stopped running; we followed suit and went down onto one knee. The Buffels came to a stop 20 metres behind us. Lieutenant Doep motioned for us to advance into the thicket, then waved us on, annoyed when we hesitated for a minute and none of us moved. No one wanted to be the first to enter the eerie thicket of bush that reeked of ambush. The five of us who were running dog and the two trackers looked at each other as we steeled ourselves to go in.

We slowly stalked into the bush and disappeared in the shadows of the overhead canopy of leaves. I had my R4 rifle on full automatic and held it up high in an odd way, with the handgrip almost next to my temple and with my head pulled into my shoulders, trying to protect my face behind the metal part of my rifle. I was walking in a curious crouch, almost like a duck-walk, in an effort to make myself a smaller target. In this peculiar manner, I scanned the bush with hard eyes.

My stomach had been up in my throat with fear, but now it disappeared and that strange, dead-calm feeling took over over once again. I felt a cold and reckless resignation to get it over with, whichever way it went. I tightened my torso muscles as tight as I could in an involuntary effort to deflect the hail of AK-47 bullets that I expected to come at any second. I was just behind John Delaney, the platoon 'veteran' who, along with Lieutenant Doep, had already walked into an ambush like this while running dog and had survived to tell the tale. John, too, was walking in the same strange duck-walk that seemed to be a natural instinct. We had pulled ahead of the others who seemed to be shuffling on the spot and not keeping up.

The tracker was at my side; his eyes were huge and white against his tar-black face. He was in a crouch and stopped in mid-stride with his mouth hanging open as if tasting the air, like a snake, or perhaps just plain scared shitless. We stopped soundlessly in our tracks. He crouched in this position for a second or two and then motioned to us with his wide eyes and pointed with his chin that he thought something was in front of us. I saw then that he was in complete control of himself, but the other tracker—a skinny troop with an oversized uniform—had dropped ten yards behind us.

Bam!

A staccato rifle shot close by shattered the tense stillness like a small bomb. Instantly I dropped like a dead man and rolled into some foliage next to the natural path that led into the thicket. I held my rifle tight into my shoulder and glared with both eyes down the barrel, waiting to see any movement in front of us, my finger tight on the trigger. There were no more shots and, after long seconds, I looked around and saw that all five of us were in the same position, except that one tracker had his rifle pointing forward and his eyes tightly closed.

"They're behind us," I hissed to myself. It had sounded as though the shot had come from somewhere behind.

I quickly scanned the bush to the side and saw nothing—no gun smoke or movement. I signalled to John who was staring stone-faced into the bush. I was puzzled, because it now dawned on me that it had sounded more like an R4 than an AK-47. We lay still for a few minutes and then we heard relaxed voices coming from the Buffels some 30 metres back.

"What the fuck?"

I was still intently scanning the bush in front of me, not convinced that it was all clear. So was the black tracker who had not lost his concentration. We both lay flat with our rifles pointing straight ahead into the dark thicket. John was looking back, as he was in a position to see what was happening by the Buffels. After a minute he motioned for us to move back. We slowly backed up out of the thicket. Had there been an ambush waiting for us in that thicket, where the 50-man SWAPO spoor led? We would never know. Maybe now the bush gods were looking with favour on us as they had done on SWAPO when they brought the season's first rain to wash out their spoor as we had come upon it. Maybe we too had now been saved from walking into an ambush by something that had happened behind us. We slowly backed away from the thicket, back to the vehicles.

When we got to the parked Buffels we found that Kurt Barnes, who had had his R4 on 'fire', had accidentally let off a round that had ricocheted into Kevin Green sitting next to him. I never did find out what really went down. As far as I could gather, everyone in the Buffel was ready to open fire into the thicket when Kurt had let a round off that ricocheted off the inside of the Buffel, narrowly missing Greef's head and ploughing through Kevin Green's hand.

Kevin's eyes were clenched with pain; he was holding his hand that was bleeding profusely as Kurt, who also happened to be the platoon medic, tried to apply pressure and put on a field dressing. Kurt was an enormous ex-company cook who had grown tired of cooking and, after a couple of failed attempts at the PT course, had finally pulled through, got his wings and had recently been assigned to our platoon. He was a big lumbering fellow with fists like hams and ice-blue eyes.

Kevin, a feisty little guy from the south of Johannesburg, who had chipped teeth and was one of the company's handful of amateur boxers, was squeezing his eyes, telling Kurt that he was going to fuck him up. Kurt, who was three times Kevin's size, grunted and told him to put a sock in it as he turned and fumbled in his medic bag for the morphine. But he, and most of us standing around, suddenly all seemed to realize at the same moment that he was not going to find any morphine. The reason being that recently, at a small but wild 'invite only' party in Ondangwa, just before we had left on the vehicle patrol, the regulation two shots of morphine per medic bag had been liberated and used as the highlight of the party.

"Give him some Sosagon!" Lieutenant Doep barked as we all watched Kevin closing his eyes, grimacing in agony. Kurt's voice was barely audible as he said he couldn't seem to find any.

We all looked at each other sheepishly and Kevin, who was the last to remember the party, let out a loud groan of pain and anger when he realized there would be no quick relief. Doep began grilling Kurt on the missing Sosagon. Kurt in his low innocent voice was acting dumb and saying he was sure the vials had been there when he did his full check on the medical supplies at the beginning of the patrol, but which had probably fallen out of his medic bag somewhere in the bush.

We moved the Buffels back to a more open *chana* and secured the area. If there had been any ambushers, they were long gone now after this shot-in-the-hand episode. The medevac helicopter that Doep had radioed for took about 30 minutes to arrive. In the stillness of the bush we heard his blades chopping the air for fully five minutes before he spotted our third orange smoke grenade and the little civilian-looking chopper zoomed over us at treetop level.

I could see the burly pilot clearly as he hovered and expertly brought his little craft down in the small LZ we had quickly cleared, his rotors clipping small branches on the way down with loud cracks that sounded like gunshots. I was impressed with how they could find us so quickly in this vast and featureless bush. It gave me a feeling of confidence knowing that in no time at all we could be located and medevaced. It had always been boasted to us in training that if you were seriously wounded out in the middle of the Angolan bush, and if need be, they could have you back in Pretoria, thousands of miles away, in a state-of-the-art military hospital inside six hours. That made us feel good, and this quick response time for Kevin seemed to back the claim.

We went back to the chase.

The medevac pilot had told Doep that we were only 20 clicks from the Angolan border so it seemed we had lost the race, especially after the unfortunate delay. We threw caution to the wind and everyone rode on the Buffels, driving fast on the now-thinning spoor, sometimes losing it in our haste. By late afternoon we came to a small village of about eight grass huts. The old black headman told us that about 30 SWAPO had been there about two hours before and had commandeered the village's horses and bicycles. We followed the horse spoor for a while but they soon bombshelled again into different but largely northerly directions. These fucking terrs were good; they had given us the slip for close to 40 clicks and had bombshelled into nothing. We hung on for dear life as our Buffels bounced around, evading the scrubby trees, staying on the spoor of a small group of about ten boot tracks and a couple of bicycles that had stayed together. The boot prints were far apart with the front toe print deep and broken. The tracker said that they were running fast. The terrain had changed a lot too and we were now in tall dark trees that looked almost like a forest, unusual for the countryside.

"That's the border, right there."

I stared at the couple of strands of rusty wire hanging loosely from old crooked wooden posts that stretched through the trees. We came to a stop at the broken-down border line and all stared at the thick foliage on the other side. It seemed that almost right at the border there was a drastic change in the type of bush. This was a phenomenon that I would come to notice many more times; there seemed no real explanation for it because both sides of the border here were uninhabited and wild.

"So what's the stop? Let's carry on after them! I bet they're going to slow down pretty soon after crossing; they think they're home dry. We might even catch them sleeping!"

I was caught up in the chase. I agreed with the sentiment and was also pushing the issue. I sensed I was right and that if we stayed hard on them we would catch them regrouping or taking it easy just across the border.

Stan, for once, agreed with me. "Ja … we got to keep on. We've come this far and they're probably only half an hour in front of us, if that."

"That's Angola across there; we could meet more than SWAPO in there, my man. What if we run into a company of FAPLA with a couple of BTR armoured cars, or a couple of T-55 tanks. Then what you going to do?"

"Aah, bullshit … what's wrong, scared of a few Soviet tanks?"

Fox and Stander were at each other again. I sat quiet now, staring over the border into the trees. They might even be looking at us right now, wanting us to follow them over. There was an even bigger chance of an ambush when they were in their own backyard and felt safe.

Maybe it wouldn't be such a good idea.

Lieutenant Doep was deep in thought, barely listening to Stan mouthing off about FAPLA who had shot the hell out of A Company a few months before. A troop tied a stone to the long antenna wire and tossed it high in a tree and the radio crackled and hissed to life as we lit up cigarettes. After 15 minutes of going back and forth, Doep put the receiver down, shook his head and said we had been denied permission to cross the border in hot pursuit. There was a chorus of disappointed jeers and cusses. Doep said that the infantry commandant in charge of this section had said *no way* were we to cross over. Once again the infantry had screwed us over. If it had been our Commandant Lindsay, he would surely have given the go-ahead. It was clear that infantry and paratroopers did not share the same philosophy. Thinking back, I never could figure out why we hadn't had some sort of support to help make contact with this big group of SWAPO. It would surely have been a worthwhile effort as there were so many of them. At least get some choppers to leapfrog ahead to cut them off?

We moved back a few clicks and cooked up a lunch from our dwindling supply of rat packs, then started the slow trek back to Ondangwa. We had spent three weeks doing vehicle patrol, winding through the vast bush. We were tired.

We could have kept going for another year and still only have covered a very small portion of the endless terrain, but at least we had made contact three times and brought in 16 kills without any of us getting a scratch (except Kevin's unfortunate shot-in-the-hand incident), so it was not too bad. It was time to head back to Ondangwa, which suddenly seemed like a well-deserved rest.

We were all getting a bit too used to sitting shoulder to shoulder bouncing through the Owambo bush. We looked and smelled like terrorists ourselves with our three weeks' growth and dirty, torn-up bush browns.

32 BATTALION

Too much time on my hands—Styx

In response to allegations of atrocities, South Africa has furnished information about a battalion made up mainly of foreigners that it has been using for raids into Angola against the guerrillas of the South West Africa People's Organization. The battalion, made up of black refugees from Angola and a few Europeans who would normally be described as mercenaries, is a unit of the South African Army. New York Times, 27 May 1981

"You men are off to a good start—you made your mark on SWAPO and the news will spread that there's a new bunch of paratroopers up here. You're going to be just like old D Company!"

Commandant Lindsay stood near the fire that crackled in the long chipped concrete fire-pit. He stood in his usual confident stance—legs wide apart, which exaggerated his shortness—beaming like an extremely happy, hairy gnome. His teeth flashed red from the firelight. He was holding a plate and biting into a huge army pork chop, laughing as he listened to the different versions of the contacts from various troops who, after a couple of beers and some fresh meat, had plucked up the courage to take mild liberties with the commandant.

He smiled broadly, but even the dancing firelight could not hide his eyes, eyes as black as coal pits. He knotted his forehead when someone brought up the pursuit that had been stopped at the border and nodded his head but smiled again as he shook his pork chop in a defiant gesture.

"You'll get your turn; don't worry. Soon enough we will go looking for Boy in his own backyard and show him just what it's like making war with the *Boere!*"[10]

There was a chorus of whoops from around the fire. We knew that if Lindsay said we were going in after them, then that's what was going to happen.

He was a born warrior and had been up here making war since Operation *Savannah* in 1975 when the South Africans almost reached Luanda. The story was that Lindsay only went back to South Africa for two months each year and had been doing so for the last five or six years. After a shit, shave and shampoo we chatted like happy school kids and wolfed down the huge chops with thickly buttered bread, followed by cans of ice-cold Castle lager and slabs of refrigerated Cadbury's chocolate. It felt great to look like a white man again after washing off weeks of dry layers of Black is Beautiful camo grease.

Later that night, after a foray to the air force bar for additional supplies, we partied late into the night without any sign of the leadership element who, by the sound of it, seemed to be having a party of their own. The next morning we were told that *Valk* 2, while we had been partying the night away, had made contact while doing foot patrols near Beacon 10, about 80 clicks east of where we had been, and had got four kills in a night ambush at a waterhole.

Apparently the SWAPO had been on a long-range patrol, heavily laden with landmines, heading deep across the border for the mining town of Tsumeb, a few hundred kilometres south of Beacon 10. It seemed that SWAPO was doing a big push which was apparently normal in the rainy season.

We settled into Fireforce, which was a pleasure. A short parade at 07:00, followed by morning situation reports and a few menial chores like cleaning ablutions and storerooms, then lying around the pool the rest of the day writing long-overdue letters and just generally bullshitting.

Luck was with us; RSM Louw, for some reason, had been shipped back to South Africa and life on the border was like it was supposed to be—no bullshit and let's concentrate on killing terrs, not pulling up fucking weeds. It wasn't so blazing hot these days and I began going for a run in the afternoons. I felt weak after almost a month in the bush, living on rat packs and cigarettes, and started slowly at first, but I was soon running halfway around the big air

---

[10] Afrikaners, der. farmers

force base, a distance of 13 kilometres. I would then go to the small home-made weight gym next to the hangar, which consisted of a pull-up bar and a few paint cans filled with cement with poles in them that served as barbells. I even began shadow-boxing when I was alone, working my right cross and left hook but it felt useless—boxing seemed so far away and irrelevant to where I was in the middle of Owamboland.

I also got to see how the PF, the Permanent Force, lived. Their accommodation, surprisingly, was just as sparse as ours, except for their well-stocked bar, snack canteen and new swimming pool—it was strange to see Commandant Lindsay and company relaxing at the pool, because somehow I could never picture him relaxing anywhere.

It was here that I first saw a group of about nine American dogs of war who had sauntered into the HQ to report their arrival. Their spokesman was a tall captain, with dark aviator sunglasses, who wore a maroon airborne beret at a rakish angle on his clean-shaven head. They wore South African browns. A couple of them were shaved bald with eagles and parachutes tattooed on their forearms. They had R4s slung over their shoulders but a few had old, well-used M16s hanging on their shoulders and pistols at their sides. They were part of 44 Brigade, a newly formed outfit that had moved into some tents next to us behind the kitchens. They seemed to be mostly made up of ex-Rhodesian soldiers who had come over to South Africa. Now that their war in Rhodesia had been lost for them by the politicians, they had come to join our little war in Angola.

The Rhodesians looked like a tough bunch, having fought a long brutal bush war for the last however many years. Their kill rate against ZANLA and ZIPRA[11] was sometimes a thousand to one. I had read somewhere that their paratroops would often do three combat jumps in a day. I had read that between 1950 and 1952 the French Colonial paras had boasted of 50-odd combat jumps, while in Vietnam the French had made 100 major jumps and the Americans only one. These Rhodesian troopies beat them all with hundreds and hundreds of jumps. Most of them had probably grown up in the bush and had been exposed to their bush war from a young age. Some of

[11] ZANLA: Zimbabwe African National Liberation Army; ZIPRA: Zimbabwe People's Revolutionary Army

them looked not much older than us, but had years of bush-fighting behind them in the hot Rhodesian sticks.

After the Yanks left the HQ, I overheard Commandant Lindsay and his staff laughingly saying that the Americans were a bunch of cowboys and boozers who thought they were in the movies. His words would later prove true when one of them was killed by SWAPO in a contact while he performed moves that belonged in Hollywood and not in the Angolan bush war. When Stan mentioned that the Yanks' airborne tattoos looked cool, I told him I could easily do a tattoo of an eagle and a parachute on his shoulder. He hesitated at first, but was soon enthusiastic about it and wanted me to start right away.

I had done a couple of tattoos on my brother and a friend at home, so I found two needles and glued them together between two matchsticks like a small harpoon, broke open a pen for ink and we had an instant tattoo-parlour in our tent. Stan was cheerful once he had made his mind up and sat in the chair with a pillow under his arm and smoked as I drew the swooping fish eagle and parachute, our battalion emblem, on his shoulder.

"The fucking 101st Airborne was a crack outfit in Vietnam. Over there they were called the Screaming Eagles. They were the ones who fought that battle at Hamburger Hill. They got the shit shot out of them, but kept on going for two days until they took the hill. They also took that bridge, didn't they?"

"You got your wars mixed up— that's in the Second World War, and I think that was the British Airborne. Stop moving around! Keep still, for fuck's sake!"

"Huh? ... hey, that hurts!"

I had read a book about the 101st Airborne during basic training and was familiar with their actions in the Second World War. They had dropped into France on D-Day and had fought gallantly against the Germans but, as was usual with paratroopers, their drop zone had somehow been fucked up and they landed in separate pockets and fought for days in small groups with no communications with their HQ.

"They shaved their hair like Mohicans, with a strip down the middle and painted their faces like fucking Red Indians on D-Day."

In the meantime the tattoo that I was needling on his shoulder was taking on a different dimension as I began to ink it in. By the end of the sitting the aggressive, fluid swooping eagle I had drawn with the pen had come out as a motionless lame chicken with its stiff wings in the air and its head bowed as if scratching in the dirt for worms.

I wiped the bird clean of the blood, hoping I was seeing it wrong but it jumped right out at me, plain to see. It was a fuck-up, plain and simple. Stan stared at it in the small hand-mirror and was quiet for a very long while as he contemplated his inflamed, smudged right shoulder.

"What's wrong with the wings? ... They're kind of ... too high up ... and stiff." He laughed a bit with everyone else but by the time he returned from looking at it in the bathroom mirrors he was fuming.

"It looks like a fucking kaffir chicken pecking mielies! You better fix it up, or take it off! I'm not going to walk around with this fuck-up on my arm!"

He was seriously upset and was threatening to burn it out with a hot knife. I told him that there wasn't much that I could do to improve it, but consoled him by saying that he shouldn't worry about it too much because it would probably look better when it healed and, if not, he could get a professional to go over it back in South Africa and he would never be able to see that it had even existed.

"But in the meanwhile I look like I belong to the Scratching fucking Chickens!" He was really upset and stormed out the tent and disappeared towards the cooks' tents. He was fuming; if he could have decked me, I think he would have.

I decided it was also time to disappear and went visiting some other tents just to get out of his sight. I came back much later when the lights of the tent were out and everyone seemed asleep. Nevertheless, the story of the tattooing got around and soon I had customers lining up in my tent at night for tattoos. Needless to say I stayed away from the more difficult swooping fish eagle and stuck to a basic parachute and wings which I could do quite well. I had no more dissatisfied customers.

The stars twinkled like a thick milky blanket high in the clear black winter sky. A cold chill had settled over Owamboland. We were lying wrapped up and sound asleep in our tents when Lieutenant Doep hurriedly woke us at about two in the morning and told us to kit up, pull fragmentation grenades and some extra rations as quickly as we could and meet at the chopper pad in ten minutes. Half asleep, we lined up in the dark at the small armoury shed and stuffed grenades into our kit as the turbines of the three Pumas cranked up on the dark pad 50 metres away, identifiable only by their winking green and red lights.

All we were told was that 32 Battalion was in deep shit in Angola. It was pitch dark inside the chopper, except for the soft green glow of the instrument panel that illuminated the troops closest to the front in a soft green haze. The Pumas were flying faster than we had ever flown before. The side door was closed this time, and the fuselage shuddered as we reached almost full speed, hurtling north into the blackness of Angola.

I peered out of the window and was taken aback by the vast blackness of the Angolan bush below, with not a light to be seen as far as the eye could see and probably not for hundreds of kilometres farther. We were all fully awake now. No one said a word, but we all knew that if 32 Battalion was in the shit then we were going to be in the shit too. 32 Battalion were all battle-hardened veterans of the Angolan civil war. They were called the 'Terrible Ones', and their war cry 'Advance!' was legendary on the border, as were their countless victories that spanned more than ten years of bush-fighting. Readying myself for the worst, I fidgeted with my rifle and tightened my bootlaces, expecting to be to be dropped right into a night-time fire fight.

We flew at breakneck speed for about half an hour and finally slowed down, circled and landed in a small clearing in the bush where there were a few huge rubber bladders of Aftur and Avgas for the choppers surrounded by light vehicles with groups of black troops hanging around. We disembarked in the dark and were told to sit and wait near the choppers. We lit cigarettes and sat with our teeth chattering in the early morning cold and checked the scene. In the black stillness we could hear the faint thump of mortar fire far off to the west.

I nudged John Fox. "Listen ... mortars."

He said nothing and pulled deeply on his cigarette as Lieutenant Doep came over to tell us what was going on.

"Three Two is doing a night attack on a SWAPO base. Boy is dug in and

141

Three Two are getting revved. We are going in as support from the north to flush Boy out. Put up your night sights and stand by!" That's what I loved about the army—they didn't bother us troops with boring details like what the enemy's strength was or how they were dug in.

Usually we only wore our floppy bush hats on patrol, but this time we had our the new fibreglass jump helmets, with chinstraps, which we had used only once—on the operation that had turned out to be a lemon. After about 40 minutes the mortar fire seemed to quieten down; we sat in the stillness of the bush smoking and hugging our knees for warmth. We waited and waited and soon the soft, cold blue light of dawn started to line the horizon. Doep came and told us we were not going in, as 32 Battalion had broken through—most of the SWAPOs had fled into the bush and we would be joining a 32 stopper group to sweep for stragglers. We flew in at 06:00 and were dropped in the bush where we were met by a platoon of 32 boys.

It was the first time I had seen the 'Terrible Ones' face to face and they looked the part. They were all older black troops with hard, worn faces. They were heavily laden with kit and firepower, but they moved easily with an animal stealth that only came from spending many months at a time in the thick bush. Their leader was a young, tough-looking white sergeant with curly blond hair and angry blue eyes; he made no bones about showing his distaste for us being there. He snubbed Lieutenant Doep when Doep asked him what had happened the night before, only saying that SWAPO was dug in; he gave no further explanation.

"Well, we know that much—that's why we were woken from a good night's sleep to come and help you, you stupid cunt!" I muttered.

We walked silently the whole day, sweeping through the bush with no sign of SWAPO and spent a miserably cold night shivering in our light inner sleeping bags. We had been caught off guard by the cold weather and had not brought along our full sleeping bags. Early the next morning after a quick breakfast the 32 Battalion sergeant's shit attitude boiled over; he snapped at Lieutenant Doep over something and there was a heated exchange of words. Doep came back, clearly mad as hell, and sat fidgeting with his chest webbing until he barked at us to kit up. The sergeant clearly had no respect for us and thought that we were not fit to even be walking with his fucking

32 Battalion. The ill-feeling quickly spread through both sets of troops and pretty soon there was a noticeable gap in the patrol formation as we walked slowly through the bush. Our attitude had become 'Fuck 32 Battalion'. At midday we sat and had a cold lunch in a thicket of trees and swapped thoughts on the situation.

"Fuck them—let them fight their own battles. If they're so good, why did they need any help? We could still be relaxing at Ondangs. They didn't seem so sure of themselves the other night when they sent an SOS for help, did they?"

I sat chewing on a hard energy bar, keeping an eye on the 32 Battalion TB about 50 metres away. I had heard stories of these guys getting into shootouts among themselves over women and really petty arguments, so I was taking no chances. They spent their lives in the bush as a Lost Legion, refugees from the Angolan civil war who had been employed by the South African army, that didn't want them either but had formed them into a battalion, keeping them on condition that they fought until they were too old or too wounded. They were a legion that lived and died by the sword and its rules.

Stan was getting into it as usual and was standing there glaring at them, saying that we should take them on and show them who was who. "If we make contact they might try to put a few bullets our way. I tell you … I'll start shooting back if I even suspect it's coming from them. I don t give a shit!"

Lieutenant Doep told us to stop talking shit and concentrate on finding SWAPO, which we did for the whole day, finding a few cold, lone tracks that weren't worth chasing.

My mind was drifting to the few short weeks that we still had on the border before we headed back to South Africa for a month back at home base in Bloemfontein. I had been missing Taina a lot lately and although I was enjoying it in the boonies I couldn't wait to see her and to squeeze her as tight as I could and tell her about what we had been up to. She had been writing regularly and I had a pile of steamy 'I miss you stacks' letters describing what she was going to do with me when she saw me. Others were more mundane, telling me what she had been up to. There was even the occasional tear mark on the paper that was circled in pen, just in case I missed them.

I had the habit of carrying her latest letter in my top-left shirt pocket, so that she could be close to my heart ... and that if I caught a bullet she would be right there with me, and for the convenience of pulling it out in the bush and reading it for the tenth time, just to see her handwriting which, I felt sure, I would be able to recognize out of a pile of a 1,000 letters. We had been going together for five years now, since she was 14 and I 16 and she was more than a girlfriend—she was my best friend, too. I was missing the ordinary things that we would do together, like driving around or sitting at a roadhouse after a night out, chomping on cheese dogs and sipping Cokes. I had recently come to realize that I surely did love her, even though some times I didn't appreciate quite what I had. But I did know that lately I had been longing to see her again.

After a third fruitless day of scouring the bush for SWAPO, Lieutenant Doep told us to get ready for the choppers that were coming in to take us back to Ondangwa. About fucking time. I was thankful; because of the tension with 32 it had not been an enjoyable patrol. They too seemed happy when the big Pumas landed on the small *chana* and we piled in to be lifted away.

"Fuck the Terrible Ones!" shouted Stan as we lifted off.

FREE NELSON MANDELA

Give me the night—George Benson

It was like a dream—sleeping in my own bed between crisp white sheets that smelled of sweet soap and waking to my mother's cheerful voice. That evening the family, as always, sat at the long, polished, antique oak dinner table as my mother served up huge helpings of yellow pumpkin and my favorite stew, which I could not finish, having lived on a couple of small cans of corned beef and a few biscuits a day for the last few months. My father was as proud as punch and took me to his offices when I had to go into town to get a few things, telling his staff that I had just returned from a bush trip in Angola. I knew most of them and they pumped my arm vigorously, asking me if I had run into any SWAPO or FAPLA. I told them that we had, but that SWAPO was no match and usually ran away.

Taina had grown lovelier than ever and insisted that I pick her up from college in my uniform. At her request I wore my faded bush browns with my spit-and-polished jump boots and my maroon airborne beret at a rakish angle on my head. I prayed that no one from 1 Para would see me because, apart from being strictly forbidden to go out in browns, we would laugh and scoff at any troop who walked around in his jump boots to try and impress the civvies and yet, here I was, guilty of this mock-worthy sin. Anyway, it did feel great to walk down the street in my bush browns and jumpers with a gorgeous girl at my side. All her college mates' heads turned; she got the effect she was looking for and almost crushed my hand as we crossed the busy campus to her car.

I told her what we had been doing up on the border, how it felt being deep in the bush with the enemy walking around the same area, and about the operation in Angola with the jets dropping bombs and us rushing in to find that it was a lemon. I told her about the contact that we'd had and how the SWAPO we had shot seemed so young.

"It will all be over before you know it, Gray, and you'll be back, and we could maybe move somewhere on our own. You know, we've been going out for five years … we could even perhaps … you know … get married."

I was quiet. Even though I knew that I loved her, marriage still seemed a thing that you did much later on—not at twenty-one.

"Yeah, maybe," I said slowly.

"You don't sound too enthusiastic," she said disappointedly.

"Well, it's not that, Tains … let's just wait and see when the time comes. Perhaps we could go off and do something exciting together."

"You always want to go off chasing excitement." She was sullen for a few minutes and stared up at the night sky, but soon bounced back to her usual bubbly self. "See those three stars in a row up there?"

"The three kings?"

"Yes. Whenever you look at those stars, think of me and I'll think of you … that way we might be looking at them at the same time and be together."

I laughed at her, and looked up at the stars. "Okay, Tains—those will be our stars forever."

I saw on television how South Africa had become the whipping boy of the world and how tough new trade sanctions had been imposed by the USA. I felt angry whenever they showed groups of protesters outside the South African Consulate in Washington, with signs saying things like 'Down with racist South Africa' and 'Bomb South Africa'. I wondered whether all Americans were that stupid, or whether it was only some. I shook my head. Stupid shits—didn't they know that the ANC and Mandela had communist ties and that if the blacks took over they would welcome the Soviets into our backyard? I felt contempt for the US and their do-gooding naïveté, thinking that they could dictate what another country should and should not do. The chanting morons with the signs knew nothing about the 40,000 Cuban troops who were spread across our border, or that our country was surrounded by communist countries and that Mandela's ANC 'soldiers of liberation' were being trained in Libya and the USSR.

Back at 1 Para base camp in Bloemfontein, life was a little easier. We swung a little more clout now and got a little more respect from the rank who roamed the base like walruses. When they did chase us, there was always a new lot of juniors for us to take it out on. The new juniors seemed petrified of us and came to attention whenever they ran past us, just as we used to do to our seniors. Some of the guys were hard on them, ragging them and having them drop for 50 push-ups, and then making them fetch photographs of their girlfriends for us to pervertedly drool over. I did not get into it because I knew how I had hated it when I was a junior and had got ragged on and humiliated, wanting nothing more than to slug an ugly fucking senior in the mouth.

Commandant Archie Moore, for some reason, was not his usual cheerful self. He proclaimed that the morale and attitude of the whole battalion stank, and that we were all to go on a 50-kilometre route march in boots, just to pull the battalion together and give us a quick, much-needed attitude adjustment. Everyone in the base was to march. Cooks, clerks, drivers and even fat storemen who hadn't done PT for years turned up in browns and boots early one Saturday morning. We took off on the long dirt roads that crisscrossed the open farmlands behind the base. It took us the whole day; we came back into base around 15:00. At 19:00 the last small groups of clerks and stragglers were still coming in.

The following morning at parade Archie Moore told us that he wasn't satisfied, that we would march again the following Saturday and that this time we would all stick together as a battalion. My feet, which had never really recovered from the obscene beating I had given them on PT course so many months before, had started to tear up again—so once again I was smiling, on light duty and in sandals, as I watched the whole battalion set off again on another 50-kilometre march.

BACK INTO ANGOLA
Operation Ceiling, June 1981

Moontan—Golden Earring

The month back in South Africa had flown by and before long the C-130 delivered us to the white sand and dusty bush of Owamboland once again. This time our sister company, H Company, would have the pleasure of being based at Ondangwa as Fireforce, while we were to be based at Ombalantu, an old *berede* base, mounted unit base, about 100 clicks from Ondangwa.

There was one long, straight, white sand road that led into Ombalantu. For security reasons the small camp was situated in the middle of a wide, white *chana*, with open ground for 200 metres around the camp in all directions. The camp itself was about ten clicks from the Angolan border, and consisted simply of a 400 x 400-metre tent square enclosed by high sand embankments with a couple of lookout towers and old steel-fenced horse corrals. The only interesting feature was that on one side of the base, near the HQ, there stood a massive baobab tree wide enough to drive an army truck through, which had been hollowed out and had a small chapel inside it, complete with chairs and a pulpit.

Being so close to the border we were told to be on extra alert because the camp had come under mortar attack from SWAPO in the past. Stan, Johnny Fox, John Delaney and I surveyed the scene. There was no air force bar, just a small canteen that sold basic supplies such as shoelaces, soap and sweets. Once again, no beer for the paratroopers.

"This place is a dump," declared Stan with feeling, after a quick recce of the situation. He glared as though he had just smelled shit.

148

"Well at least its peaceful—listen to the birds."

"It's like a French Foreign Legion outpost in the fucking Sahara desert— look at those palm trees—all you need are some camels and ragheads to come across the *chana*."

Stan scowled with his usual look of distaste and disgust. I sat on my kit bag and looked at the sun-bleached tents and high sand embankments that surrounded the small empty base. He was right. The wide, white *chana* and tall palm did give the appearance of a French Foreign Legion outpost and, to boot, it seemed as though the cool season had forgotten about spring and had moved straight into summer. Or perhaps this *was* spring, and summer would be twice as bad. Our old friend Spike was blazing away happily and once again would turn our tents into ovens. Stan, John Fox, Kurt (the giant ex-cook) and I bunked together in a tent and we soon got back into the ways of life on the border.

There were two stray kittens that we had coaxed into our tent and adopted. They were wretched little things at first, but we fed them up with raw meat and scraps that they wolfed down and held onto so fiercely that you could lift them head-high as they held onto the meat with their jaws locked, growling. They soon became our mascots and would not wander far from our tent. They took turns sleeping on each of our beds at night, happily purring and tramping their feet in pleasure. One of the kittens was a fiery ginger colour, with a great bush of a tail like a squirrel. He was a fiercely tough little character who would swagger around as though he owned the place. He normally slept with me, purring away happily like a little hairy generator at the bottom of my bed.

It seemed we were set for a peaceful bush trip. There was no deafening roar of Mirage jets taking off next to out tents, or the constant *boom boom boom* of the gunships practising with their 20-millimetre cannons, which was the daily background at Ondangwa. The only drag was that we had to stand guard at night, which the air force had kindly taken care of for us at Ondangs, what with it being an air force base. We also started doing daily dawn mine-sweeping patrols of the long sand road that cut through the bush like an endless, straight white knife and led to our camp here at Ombalantu. The group of field engineers whom we escorted could walk faster with their detection wands and earphones than we could run and it amazed me to watch them scoot down the endless road like speed-walkers in a race, with their legs shooting out in front of them.

These early-morning patrols turned out to be pretty enjoyable, especially because those going on the five-hour mine-sweep patrol did not have to stand guard the night before and would have time off when they returned to camp.

We pulled a four-day patrol around the area but it was quiet with no sign of any activity. It was a relaxed patrol with long breaks; all we ran into were some smiling locals with herds of goats and skinny brown cattle. We relaxed in the shade to eat, the only excitement being when the two top boxers in the company got into a short but vicious fist fight in the middle of a small rural *cuca*, a shop, and smashed up all the flimsy shelves of tinned foods, literally tearing the small tin shack down.

"That Louw needs to get fucked up one of these days. Why don't you take him out?"

"He's never messed with me," I said as we watched Lieutenant Doep talking and waving his finger at McKee and Louw. Kevin, an ex-professional boxer, had recently rejoined the company after serving 60 days in DB over the missing-fingers-and-ears incident of our last bush trip. He had a large welt under his eye; it looked like he'd got the worst of the scrap. Louw swaggered away with a smirk on his face and rejoined his little clique under a tree. Kevin came to us shaking with anger and told us that Louw had just slugged him out of the blue when he'd had some words with another troop over some cans of warm Coke.

The tension broken, we continued on an easy patrol through some enchanting terrain that was a montage of thin bush and many small *chanas* that interlocked with each other and looked like small secret clearings, like the magical ones we used to play in when we were kids.

It actually became enjoyable as it seemed such a quiet, undisturbed area, even though it was so close to the border. The only shit came when I puked after drinking too much Johnny Walker in the middle of the day on patrol. I caught up with the platoon after hurling and ceremoniously poured the rest of the Red Label bottle out onto the sand.

★★★★★

"Hey, we got to get down to the HQ—the whole company is *treeing aan*.[12] There's something going on!"

I took my time finishing the last sentence of a letter to Taina and was one of the last to get to the small white-brick HQ at the side of the tent square where the whole company was assembled, sitting crouched in front of Commandant Lindsay who had already begun his orders.

"I told you we would be looking for Boy, and that is what we are going to do. Enough of this waiting to run into a SWAPO patrol; we are going to go into Angola and find him!"

He paused for effect, looked around and grinned. There was a chorus of whoops from the company.

"We will be going in in company strength, but splitting up into four *valks*, eight kilometres apart, crossing the border to do a zigzag *kak soek*[13] patrol into Angola."

Lindsay was in his element as he drew out a rough sketch of how the operation was to go. His short hairy arms moved quickly on the large sheet of paper stuck to a folding table lying on its side; he was surprisingly artistic. He drew the four platoons as arrows that would move parallel to each other, yet kilometres apart, in a wide sweep. He loved making war and could hardly contain his delight. "We will cross the border right here and patrol in a zigzag fashion north into Angola. We will spend four to six weeks in Angola, and cover about 15 to 20 kilometres a day, getting resupplies dropped in every five days."

"I tuned you it was going to happen. It's what we've been waiting for," John Delaney whispered and nudged me with an elbow. I nodded my head in agreement, grinning.

"This is not a *jollie patrollie*," Lindsay carried on, looking around slowly. "You're going deep into Angola. It's SWAPO's backyard and he will be there, make no mistake about that. SWAPO has been getting too comfortable, moving around too freely close to the border—they seem to have forgotten about the last time we gave them a hiding. You will be going in to find and

---

[12] assemble, form up (Afrikaans)
[13] looking for shit (Afrikaans)

make contact with these small patrols, to establish a presence and a buffer zone in this section between these beacons."

He tapped the layout with his pointer, indicating the bushy area across the border north of Ombalantu. "We want to take control of this area. You will have gunship support on standby and Mirage fighter jets if it becomes necessary."

Lindsay beamed as he told us that there had been a build-up of FAPLA activity closer to the border and that we might even run into FAPLA patrols the deeper we went. (He failed to mention that FAPLA would be a lot more heavily armed, with tanks and troop-carriers armed with 14.5-millimetre anti-aircraft guns.) We would also be carrying RPG-7s and claymores; in addition each man would carry four 60-millimetre mortar bombs as well as full kit with five-days' rations.

His explanation of the operation was short and sweet and simple. We were part of a larger operation with 32 Battalion, hitting smaller SWAPO bases throughout southern Angola. Our plan was to cross the border into Angola in a long-range sweep lasting four weeks, or longer if necessary, to look for and make contact with SWAPO. Sounded easy enough!

"The name of this operation is *Ceiling*," he added as an afterthought and then dismissed us to immediately pack and draw supplies to leave the next day.

Full of surprises, I thought. Just as I was getting set for a relaxing bush trip, we get a six-week cross-border patrol hundreds of kilometres into Indian country!

That night there was a merry, excited buzz over the camp. The tent lights burned late into the night as we readied our weapons and packed our kit for a long stay in the bush. I nipped off to the kitchen on a search-and-seize recce for any cans of decent chow and came away loaded with canned peaches and vienna sausages, or *wambo piele*.[14] I also gave instructions to the cooks to leave scraps out for the two kittens and they said they would happily do so.

*****

[14] Owambo penises (Afrikaans)

152

A feeling of excited vulnerability was evident in the platoon, which suddenly seemed very small and under-armed as we stepped over the old collapsed barbed-wire fence into Angola. We crossed the lush cut-line. We patrolled slowly in a V formation, heavily laden with kit, mortar bombs, full line ammo and water. I scanned the bush continuously. I had been cured of my inability to visualize SWAPO; now that I had shot one I had a clear picture in my mind of what a terrorist lurking in the bush looked like. I almost expected to suddenly come across a group of SWAPO sitting relaxed under a tree, at ease in their backyard, planning their next insurgency raid across the border. I was almost disappointed when we stopped uneventfully in a small thicket for a late lunch-break.

I sat with John Fox, who was my partner for the operation. I had chosen John as my partner for a couple of reasons. He and I had become pretty good buddies on this bush trip, bullshitting about girls all the time. He would tell me about his girlfriends' figures, going into great detail about their anatomy, and I would describe a few of my own conquests. I admired his outlook. He was always as neat as a pin and kept a low-key but upbeat and positive attitude which was the opposite of mine, as I occasionally suffered from spells of depression and was quite probably the most untidy troop in the platoon.

"They're here, I can feel it," he said in a hushed tone as he brewed a fire bucket of tea on a heating tablet.

I looked around at the bush as he spoke. I, too, had the feeling that we were not alone. I brewed up some tea and sat quietly scanning the bush and sipping the refreshing sweet brew.

We carried on and walked hard, covering about 15 clicks, hard-humping with our heavy kit. Late that afternoon we dug into a small TB for our first night in Angola.

We stood a watch of two at a time, while the others slept uneasily. Even the night sounds seemed different in Angola and no one got a good night's sleep—me especially, as from first-hand experience I didn't trust our platoon to be conscientious on night watch. One of my fears, besides landmines, was to be shot in my foxhole at night while I slept. It had happened to a patrol of South African reservists a couple of years back, when some of them had had their throats cut as they lay snoring, sound asleep. Or so the story went.

The next morning our security patrol rose at daybreak to scout the area before the whole platoon rose from its foxholes and—sure enough—found some chevron-pattern SWAPO boot spoor not far from our TB. It spooked everyone and we moved out very cautiously at a right angle to the way we were heading in order to avoid an ambush, before gradually wheeling north again.

Lieutenant Doep was second in command for this operation. A first lieutenant we didn't know, who was on leave from a military college, was in charge. He was a small, good-looking guy with collar-length blond hair, who was friendly and smiled easily. He explained that we could not follow up on every SWAPO spoor we found but had to keep heading north and stay alongside the other platoons moving parallel to us and see what we ran into.

The following night we dug in early once again and had chow, but after darkness fell we quietly moved out and made another TB about 100 metres away in a small, odd-looking thicket of tall trees. No one could really sleep and at around midnight we were all jolted out of our half-sleep by the unholy shouting and chanting of a man not more than 50 metres from our TB. We lay quietly in our holes, our rifles ready as the babbling and chanting rose steadily like an evangelical preacher building up to a fiery crescendo. But it did not stop; it carried on to a fever-pitch. Now, like a man possessed, he screeched and shrilled into the night like an animal, then went into warlike chants, repeating the same chant dozens of times over. We all lay as still as death, listening for more than half an hour to the maniacal voice whose intensity never faltered as it shrilled its crazy message—and then, as suddenly as it had started, it stopped, so that all that was left was the night stillness that seemed to ring in our ears.

No one moved a muscle. I lay with my finger on the trigger, hardly breathing, straining my ears to an almost painful point, willing them to pick up any sound approaching us in the dark. I lay like this for at least an hour as I peered into the darkness, ready to shoot, but hearing only the night sounds that had now started up again.

"What the yellow rubbery fuck was that?' I hissed to myself. It sounded like some lunatic preacher, or possibly some nut-job giving some sort of crazy suicidal orders to some equally crazy suicidal troops.

In the morning the security patrol rose cautiously and returned with a report that about a dozen, what looked like non-military spoor, were visible not 40 metres from our TB.

What was going on? Was it SWAPO playing games with us and trying to scare us, or was it a bunch of civilians who just happened to have a very special inspirational speaker at their midnight mass, considerately held just 40 metres from our TB?

We moved out ever so cautiously, deeper into Angola, our eyes scanning the bush constantly. The terrain had suddenly changed again, becoming even more dense. It was now impossible to move silently as we had to crash through brittle dry brush packed under the larger trees and which snapped with a loud crack if you pushed it aside too far or got hooked up on your webbing. The new lieutenant changed course; we turned and circled in a wide horseshoe to try and get out of the 'petrified woods' which seemed endless. Finally, after a few hours the terrain dissolved back into the more familiar solid bush and clearings.

We turned north again, walking alongside a long *chana* that gave us protection from one side. We stopped for lunch with a clear view over the *chana*.

"The kaffirs are all around us," Stan sneered. "I can smell a kaffir and I tell you they're watching us right now."

I could not argue with this, lying propped up against a tree smoking after a cold lunch of bully and potatoes and a can of the peaches. I was deep in thought about the events. We had found spoor around our TB every morning and that crazy babbling had got us all a bit spooked. I thought of the movie *Apocalypse Now* and of the crazy scenario of us running into some strange, lost SWAPO outfit in Angola who were possessed with the wills of African madmen. I snapped back to reality.

"Maybe they don't want to make contact and they're just trying to fuck with us until they can get a stronger force together," I said after a pause, with a lot more confidence than I felt. I was convinced we were going to be attacked at night in our TB. I nipped my cigarette and put the half-burn back into the box. It would still be a couple of days before the resupply chopper dropped us rations, water and cigarettes.

My feet were killing me again, so I asked Lieutenant Doep for permission to wear my blue sneakers which I had brought along just in case. My feet problems were legendary in the platoon; he quickly agreed after I showed him the bruised and blue tender scar-tissue that covered my toes, which for some reason refused to fully heal. Delaney and the others looked on in envy as I tucked my hard, sand-scuffed boots into my H-frame backpack and slipped on my comfortable old Adidas sneakers ... with a big grin. I walked around in a circle for a few paces to drive home the point and test the feel of them.

"What bullshit! If your feet are so fucked, you should be flying back for light duty with the resupply chopper," John Delaney grumbled, genuinely put out by my little show.

I let his envious remark wash over me and smiled as I readjusted the laces to a snug fit. "Doep seems to think I'm okay as long as I've got the sneakers on ... why don't you take it up with him?" I laughed.

We hugged a long winding *chana*, which gave us a sense of protection and a bit of time to relax. Later that afternoon, nestled in a wooded area of tall trees, we came upon the trenches and bunkers of the old SWAPO base, code-named 'Vietnam', which had been one of the bases attacked by the Parabats in Operation *Reindeer* three years before. SWAPO had lost 859 troops in that operation. The Bats had jumped in after heavy bombing by the Mirages, and in the best airborne tradition the jump did not go as planned. Smoke from the burning camp and strong winds fouled up the DZ and gave SWAPO time to regroup and put up a fierce fight, but with armour support it was over by 14:00. The Bats lost four troops. Or at least, that's what I heard.

We walked through the collapsed trenches and bunkers and kicked around in the sand awhile at bits of metal and old AK-47 shell cases. I stood and looked at what seemed to be a collapsed underground bunker. The half-filled trenches stretched into the tree line and seemed like a good defensive position. A hell of a fight had taken place here between SWAPO and the Parabats. I thought back to the chance meeting I'd had with the paratrooper walking down the street when I was in high school. He was the one who had first got me interested in becoming a paratrooper when he told me about the Bats jumping into a terrorist base and how he had taken out a terr with his knife. This could have been the operation that he was talking about, because as far as I knew the Bats hadn't jumped into a base since then because that drop had been such a fuck-up.

The story was that SWAPO fought determinedly in the trenches till the end and that scores of them had died with their hands clasped with the thumb pushed through the two forefingers in the well-known 'Fuck you' gesture. A fuck-you sign on their chest as they died? I never did believe this story ... but would soon be able to check its authenticity first-hand.

We dug a TB in some thick trees about a mile from the old Vietnam base and bedded down for another long night. As the darkness closed in my imagination took off and I imagined the sounds of the battle that had taken place here in 1978 when some two thousand men faced off against each other early one morning. I could hear the big 450-kilogram bombs from the Mirage jets exploding, the *crump* of mortars and the clatter of AK-47s, overlaid with the loud crack of the paratroopers' folding-stock 7.62-millimetre FNs. (The old Bats did not have the 5.56-calibre R4 that we now used.) I dozed off into a light sleep.

It was almost full moon when I was woken a few hours later for my watch. The moon bathed the bush in a 'moon tan' that was almost as clear as day. I tried sleepily to stay awake, peering into the bush over the white sand that shone like a beach. I was nodding off when I heard the faint *thump, thump* of what sounded like mortars in the distance. For a second or two thought I was still imagining the old sounds of the Vietnam battle but quickly realized that this was real, that there was a battle going on somewhere to the east of us. The radio in the centre of our TB crackled softly to life and was quickly turned down to a low, broken hiss. Quickly the word was whispered from hole to hole that *Valk* 3 was getting the shit revved out of them five clicks to the east and that mortars were landing in their TB.

We lay silent as we listened to the continuous barrage that was muffled by distance, but clear in the still bush.

"This is it. I told you they would hit us at night. Ja, this is when the fucking fun starts." I lay quiet, listening to the almost continuous boom of 82-millimetre bombs falling so fast that they sounded like a single, rolling barrage.

"Roll up your kit," Lieutenant Doep hissed in the darkness.

Instantly my kit was rolled and I was ready to move.

I quickly got back in the hole while I waited for the rest of the platoon to kit up. The hole suddenly felt very shallow and small and I swore to myself that from now on I would take the time to dig a decent fucking hole!

The mortars had stopped for a while but were now starting up again. It seemed that the attack hadn't been going for more than five minutes when the welcome sound of a fighter jet could be heard high in the night sky, coming from the south and tearing through the blackness towards us. It was hard to pinpoint exactly where the sound came from. It seemed to bounce around the sky, but within two minutes the horizon east of us lit up like a small sunrise as the jet dropped its bombs on the SWAPO mortar flashes. Instantly the mortar fire stopped.

We could hear the jet roaring high in the dark sky above us, patrolling like an avenging angel from the south. After ten minutes or so the roar disappeared into the distance, the jet heading back to Ondangwa, its mission accomplished and leaving us only with the night and its bush sounds. The mortars did not start up again but not a lot of sleeping got done for the rest of that night.

We did not move but stayed in the same TB. In the morning we heard that *Valk* 3 had had no choice but to break ranks and run like hell in all directions when the mortars began landing right in the middle of their TB. Luckily SWAPO did not have any stopper groups set up waiting for them, with the result that only two troops had been slightly wounded. Later on I would speak to my buddy Willy Bray in *Valk* 3, who explained that they had all shat themselves but sat tight in their holes, shooting back. He said that SWAPO had started to do a full-on attack into their TB, even doing fire and movement forward. When SWAPO's mortars began landing accurately and heavily in among their holes they retreated, because there was nothing else they could do.

(This, much later on, led to a few punch-ups with the infantry who, on finding out what had happened, called the Bats, and *Valk* 3 in particular, 'chicken' because they had run away.)

It was our fifth day in Angola. We had probably covered about 35 clicks so far and were advancing cautiously north, deeper into Indian country. Our eyes scanned the bush continually as we walked. Even while taking a dump or opening a can of bully, you scanned the bush.

As anyone who has gone on a seek-and-destroy mission into a foreign country on foot in only platoon strength would know, it has a distinctive, unusual and very dangerous feel to it. It felt clearly as though we should not be there. Like 'trespassers will be shot'. It felt that if we were caught, 'they' had every right to kill us. Now I knew how a SWAPO patrol felt when they crossed the border into South West Africa. In the last few days my R4 rifle had started to feel very small and inconsequential in my hands.

Our first five-day resupply was scheduled for today. I still had some water and chow, but was out of smokes and had been bumming Camels off my partner, Johnny the Fox. While making our way through a dry, lightly bushed area next to a *chana* on our way to rendezvous with the resupply chopper, we crossed paths with a herd of goats. Before you could say "Tickle my balls with a feather", the black trackers had grabbed a goat ... then another ... and another. One minute the goats were walking past us, eyeing us with suspicion; the next they'd had their throats cut, head in the fork of a tree and were gutted, partially skinned and missing all four legs up to the hip and shoulder joints. The deceased goats were later to be shared between those who had helped capture the unfortunate beasts. John and I were among them. Lieutenant Doep, who had been walking near the head of the formation, did not even know it had happened—and the only way he bust us was when he smelled the appetizing aroma of meat cooking as we sat down next to a small *chana* and waited for the resupply chopper. Our punishment was to give him a fair portion of goats' meat.

"This is going to taste better than the steakhouse back home," I said, eyeing the strips of goat meat that I held over the miniature fire. I licked my fingers, wet with fat, as I slowly turned the sizzling strips directly in the flame. I held the meat between two green sticks, like chopsticks. I had extra-green sticks to take over when the first ones got too burned. I had to pick the two shrinking pieces of meat out of the fire a couple of times, having a hard time flicking off the ash that had stuck to the meat. I finally figured out just to leave the ash and brush it off when the meat was cooked.

"See how fast they gutted that goat?" remarked Stan, who was also one of the chosen few and was cooking next to us. "That's how fast one of these terrs can gut you if you give them the chance."

He was frying his meat in his dixie can, sitting seriously as he watched it cook and stick to the bottom of the pan.

I sat equally seriously, watching my chopsticks burn and weighed his comment. Stan and I had recently been getting on each other's nerves and I took his comment without much humour.

"Stan, do you really think I would allow myself to be cut up by SWAPO like a fucking goat? I've got a rifle with 35 rounds in the magazine and another 35 strapped to that one—no one's going to cut me up like a fucking goat. If they do, I'll be long dead and so will all of us because you guys will be there to help me, right?"

He was a bit taken aback by my uncalled-for response and so was I, but I was getting tired of his constant cynical remarks and bullshit comments. He smiled a big shit-eating grin but didn't answer, sensing that we were getting near the end of our tethers with each other. And he knew that although he could out-mouth me any day, he would be no match if we came to blows.

"Hey, calm down, both of you," said Kurt the ex-cook. I knew he didn't really mean it, because he too was getting tired of Stan's bullshit and I'm sure he was secretly hoping for a confrontation.

I finally took my blackened goat meat off the fire and ate it slowly with salt from my rat pack but had lost some of the joy of the meal. Then all at once the tension and silence of the Angolan bush was broken by the distant hammer of the resupply chopper's rotor blades. Lieutenant Doep shouted for someone to get ready with an orange-smoke grenade. Someone popped one and tossed it into the *chana*. The orange smoke seemed to hug the *chana* floor, not wanting to rise above treetop level, but finally a breeze took it and it wafted high above the trees. The chopper landed close to the tree line, blowing up a storm of dust, as some of us ran to help unload a mountain of rat packs and jerry cans of water, taking it in turns by section to fill our seven water bottles and pull five days' dry rations.

As we reached the chopper I had noticed a ragged, skinny African in SADF browns miles to big for him, jump out of the chopper. He was led over to

Lieutenant Doep by our own Company Staff Sergeant Greyling who had flown along to personally deliver the resupply and was full of cheer and bullshit. Thinking that the black man was just another tracker joining us, I thought nothing further of him.

There was about three hours of daylight left as we formed up, heavily laden with our new supplies and headed in a northeasterly direction for about three clicks before we sat down to eat and make a false TB in some trees.

DAWN AMBUSH
'Take no prisoners; kill them all'

Gimme shelter—Rolling Stones

Before we could break out some new cans of rations and a can of warm
Coke that had been brought with the supplies, Lieutenant Doep called us all
together. He had the skinny black man standing next to him. Doep's forehead
was knotted in a deep frown and he had a serious look in his brown eyes as
he stood waiting for us to form in a group around him.

"Listen up, this here is a SWAPO turncoat," he said in Afrikaans and
indicated the shrivelled-looking figure next to him. All eyes fell on the
thin black man at Doep's side who seemed to shrink further into his new,
oversized SADF uniform.

"Tonight he is going to lead us tonight to a platoon of his friends who have
a small base camp not far from here. Apparently it's some kind of SWAPO
Navy HQ, believe it or not. There are 15 of them. They're not dug in and have
no bunkers or heavy weapons—just AKs, RPG-7s and a few Tokarev pistols.
This character was with them until a few days ago, so the information is fresh
and confirmed. It looks like we might get some luck here. They're believed
to have a pile of documentation, maps and information that's important to
retrieve as they act as some sort of roving administration HQ. Not all of us
are going to go—it will be too noisy. So I'm going to choose a group of 16 of
you. We'll leave at about 21:00."

He continued, looking around at us all as he spoke in the deep monotone
that seemed so out of place with his rosy cheeks, smooth baby face and blond
curls.

"He is going to draw us a sketch of how they are laid out, where they sleep and who has what weapons." Lieutenant Doep stopped talking, his eyes darting around. The night-attack plan was simple.

"When we reach the target, we will form a spread-out formation and go through their TB."

He paused momentarily, looking around at us, making eye contact, and coldly emphasizing his next order. "The orders are to take no prisoners. Kill them all."

The words echoed in my ears: 'Take no prisoners ... kill them all'.

I always wondered later why it had been so important that we kill them all, why we were to take no prisoners. Doep stood up and immediately started walking along the group of eager faces, pointing out individuals as he went.

"Kleingeld ... Greef ... Green ..."

I stood energized, as though a bolt of energy was shooting up from my toes and through my spine as I stared directly into Doep's eyes, daring him to leave me behind.

Without hesitation he pointed: "Korff ..." and then also to John the Fox standing next to me. I was relieved that I would not be left behind on this one! The others, who were not picked, moved away, either disappointed or relieved, and quietly went back to preparing their dinner.

The sixteen of us who had been chosen stood in a circle as the skinny SWAPO turncoat crouched on his haunches and began drawing marks in the dirt. He drew trees by poking his finger into the sand a dozen times and smoothed out the sand with the palm of his hand to indicate a *chana*. Then he drew short lines in the sand indicating how his comrades slept in a sort of triangle. He talked quickly and with new vigour, sensing his moment of importance to the *Boere*, all attention fixed on him.

The black tracker from 101 Battalion interpreted equally as quickly in Afrikaans. "This one has the RPG-7 and the other one on this side has an RPD machine gun. This one is an officer. The documents are hidden in the trees all around here ... and here."

"Ask him if they stand watch at night," snapped Lieutenant Doep at the tracker, who rattled off in Owambo to the skinny figure still crouching, staring up at us with wide eyes.

"He says that they do not stand good watch; they feel safe so far in Angola."

163

We were told to eat and get ready to leave by 21:00. We went back to our kit, and John and I cooked up a small meal and brewed some tea. I was getting into the tea habit from John Glover who drank tea avidly, good Englishman that he was. We said little, helping each other completely cover our faces and arms with the ghastly camo grease, until all that could be seen was our eyes; not a speck of our tell-tale white skin could give us away under the almost full moon that would bathe the bush.

Then we tried to catch some sleep before the long walk ahead of us but sleep was elusive and my mind raced through a hundred scenarios. Why a night attack? Why not just surround them, wait until morning and then hit them? How will we see who is who in the dark … might end up shooting ourselves! What if this fucker is leading us into an ambush … sacrificing himself for the cause and there are actually 50 of them waiting for us … or perhaps he could just run for it at the last minute. Has anybody checked out this information of his?

I lay on my back, looking at the bright three-quarter moon that was just breaking over the treetops. It looked clean, clear and friendly; it seemed to have an extra shine this evening. I had always wondered about the moon, ever since I was a child. I was fascinated that every living soul who has walked the earth since the beginning of time had looked up at this very same moon and wondered. This is the very same moon that Jesus Christ looked at. Julius Caesar, Napoleon Bonaparte … how many men have lain unable to sleep on the eve of battle and looked at this same moon, wondering if it might be their last night alive? I thought I might write a poem about it one day. I wondered if the moon was going to be our ally tonight and reveal our targets for us, or would she be on the side of the terrorists and betray us?

I told myself to stop thinking such bullshit and to try and get some sleep. After some forced deep breathing I actually dozed for what seemed like a minute, before the rustling of kit woke me and I quickly rose and kitted up.

There were hushed calls of "Good luck" from the others as we moved out in single file, with only water bottles and battle webbing. The moon shone bright as a torch as we picked our way through the quiet bush, handing each branch to the guy behind so as not to cause a rustle.

Presently we got into some lighter brush; we were able to move quite quickly for a few clicks and dashed across the *chanas* in twos and threes, regrouping on the other side. We passed a couple of dark kraals, the neighbourhood mongrels picking up our faint noise and letting go with a barrage of barking that in this war-torn countryside the locals knew better than to investigate. I was about third or fourth from the front behind Lieutenant Doep. We stopped a couple of times for a rest. Doep inquired through the 101 Battalion interpreter how much farther it was, and the SWAPO would indicate with a hand motion as if to say "Just a little". We walked and walked and walked, till way past midnight. There were grumbles and hushed curses from behind me, as the slow and careful pace started to take its toll on our energy. A cold midnight chill had set in and we had only our shirts and webbing.

Two hours later Lieutenant Doep, cursing in hushed Afrikaans, grabbed our worthy guide murderously by the throat and slammed him into the dirt, putting his full weight behind his grip. After prising him off, the interpreter said that the SWAPO said he had got lost but that now he knew where he was again and that we were very close.

The line had grown noisy behind. We passed the word down to shut up and that we were close. Suddenly, after about another half an hour, the SWAPO sat down and frantically motioned with his hand just ahead. Doep looked at him viciously but the skinny figure pointed, more precisely now, at a tree line to our front, nodding his head furiously. He whispered something in the interpreter's ear and the interpreter indicated to Doep that SWAPO were in the trees just ahead.

Doep shoved the skinny traitor aside, indicating that he should 'fuck off', then turned to us and pointed to the trees. The moon seemed to blaze like a living thing. It bathed the small open *chana* between us and the tree line that was our target in a silver light, illuminating it like an open beach. The leaves on the trees of the target 40 metres ahead were bathed in silver—just the shadows under the trees were as black as tar. We grouped together in the shadows at the edge of our trees and looked across. We would have to cross about 40 metres of completely open, moonlit *chana* to get to the other side. Then we had to enter the black tree line.

My mind thought uncomfortably what a perfect fucking ambush this was. There could be 50 AKs trained on us right now, waiting for us to start across that *chana*. I pushed the thought aside and replaced it with the now-familiar cold numbness. Let's get it over with. Let's just do it.

Doep hurriedly signalled for us to form up in a line and to start moving forward across the *chana*. No one reacted right away; it all seemed too fast and unplanned. No one had discussed any details or come up with a clever plan; we had just been told that we were going to hit them in a night attack and to take no prisoners. Everything hung on the word of the skinny SWAPO deserter who looked like a cunning bastard to me.

Sixteen of us unenthusiastically formed up into a close line that was more like a group. I was one of the first to start moving across the *chana*, with John Glover a step behind me, our rifles pressed hard into our shoulders and trained on the shadows of the tree line now 30 metres ahead of us. I just wanted to get it over with, either way. Halfway across the *chana* our line had become a V, with me at the apex. Not that I was braver in any way, but I was gripped by a strong and single-mindedly emotionless feeling of 'we have to do this, so let's get on with it'.

We moved like ghosts. I was now ten metres from the tree line and still expecting a volley of AK-47 bullets to rip through me at any second. When I reached the trees and the shadows I hesitated for a second, surprised that I had made it to the other side. I paused, moved into the shadows and then froze immediately as I saw the soft glow of an almost-burned-out fire just two metres in front of me. I turned to the sweep line that was now in a bunch behind me, held my hand very precisely above my head and pointed up and down in front of me, silently mouthing "They're here! They're here!" at the same time.

I moved completely into the shadows, expecting my head to be blown off at any second. My eyes got accustomed to the light and a whole world jumped out at me. There was a dug-out with bedding to my right, with cans of food stacked next to it. Ahead of me were more remains of a fire, whose coals were glowing brightly now, brought back to life by the cold pre-dawn breeze that had suddenly come up. There were racks made from cut branches and what looked like benches made in the same way.

We moved farther into the shadows, all 16 of us now in the black shadows of the trees.

"Where are they?"

We spread out now, creeping like killers through the shadows, rifles pointed at weird angles as we did the duck-walk thing, trying to shrink as low as possible, but still walking and ready. Nothing! They're gone! It *is* a fucking ambush! Why don't they fire?

I stood still in my crouched duck-walk position with my rifle tight in my shoulder, straining my eyes, staring into the shadows and willing my eyes to pick up any human form sleeping or hiding in the dark. I was holding my breath to hear better and to pick up any tell-tale sound that would save my life and make me quicker than him, the enemy. Up to now we had crept in on the soft sand, as still as death, and so they might still be soundly sleeping right under our noses. Seconds went by, then minutes, and still no bullets cracked. I breathed deeper again. After a couple more minutes of moving through the dark thicket and finding more bedding and more glowing embers it became clear that our terrs were not here—they had flown the coop. We had now passed through about 30 metres of their deserted base.

We looked at each other. Lieutenant Doep signalled with his hand for us to go forward to the next tree line and then get down and wait. John Fox and I sank quietly down next to each other. I was suddenly very cold and tired; I had a flash of feeling human again. I shoved my rifle disappointedly into the sand next to me and wrapped my arms around myself in an effort to keep warm from the cold, pre-dawn chill that was blowing in pretty strong and cutting through my thin shirt.

No one paratrooper made a sound. No one said "Aw fuck ... we walked 20 clicks and missed them!" No one said "Aww ... another fucking lemon!"

We lay just as quiet as we had crept in and waited for the sun to rise so that we could go back and get some hot coffee. The sky was just starting to get a blue tinge as the dawn started to creep in. Suddenly out of the darkness there came a short burst of laughter about 30 metres to our left. Then the sound of a can being kicked and a longer bout of laughter. John and I looked at each other wide-eyed and pointed in unison. All 16 of us had heard the laugh and we all rose as one man. I picked up the rifle that I had carelessly thrown down and shook the sand off it. Without instructions we moved forward as one, our eyes trained in the direction of the sound, moving quiet as assassins through the trees—each man on his own, yet together. The thicket of bush we were in came to an end after about 15 metres where there was a natural rise in the ground. Behind this mound was a small, flat *chana* and right there, right at the end of the *chana*, under a few trees not more than 30 metres in front of us, was SWAPO. They had lit a small fire and were joking with each other. I could make out about five figures under the tree. No, six or seven.

A couple of dark figures moved around calisthenically, maybe trying to keep warm, while others were joking and concentrating on the fire. All 16 of us Parabats crept to the edge of the mound at the tree line. It could not have been a more perfect ambush if it had come out of the army textbook from Pretoria. We lay with our rifles trained on the scene unfolding in front of us, not believing our luck. No one had said a word. John Glover was to my right. Horn with his RPG-7 was on my left. We lay for maybe ten minutes, maybe twenty. We watched as three more terrs came walking in down a path and joined them. It was almost light enough now to see details. Four or five of them sat around the now-blazing fire. I could smell porridge cooking. Their AKs were leaning against the tree behind them. Two now had a bicycle turned over on its handle bars and were fixing the chain. A group stood on the opposite side of the fire. I traversed my sights from figure to figure a dozen times, unable to settle on a target. I then decided it was between the group standing behind the fire rubbing their hands together and the man sitting at the fire cooking, with his back to me.

They were all bathed in the light blue-pink of the dawn. I had just changed my sights and had them trained on the two standing by the fire when Horn, next to me, with an almighty bang let loose with an RPG-7 rocket that exploded in a blinding white light right smack-bang into the cooking fire. With a deafening noise, all 16 of us opened up simultaneously. Instantly the breakfast party was covered in a cloud of smoke and dust. I was up on one knee. I shot as fast as my finger could pull the trigger, got a jam with a double-feed and cleared it, shooting into the sand a foot from my boot, and kept on shooting. I thought I was empty, flipped the magazine over and put in the one taped to it, pulled back the bolt and kept on shooting. I could hardly see through the cloud of smoke. Hot, ejected shells were hitting me in the face and leaves showered down on us.

"Are they shooting back?" I heard a shout as everybody stood up and charged across the *chana* through the thick clouds of dust and smoke into the killing zone. The three at the fire lay dead where they sat, killed by the RPG-7 or the dozens of bullets that had ripped through them. A terrorist in camo was lying on his belly a metre or two to my right, trying to get up. He looked for all the world as though he was doing a push-up. I shot him high, between the shoulder blades and he collapsed on his face, dead. On the other side of the fire a SWAPO sat on his backside motionless and dazed, like a bear sitting in a pool at the zoo. John Glover shot him through the head from a metre and a half as he too fell forward on his face. John, in an amazing combination of good soldiering and looting, scooped up the unfortunate SWAPO's peaked camo cap and tossed it at me. I snatched it in mid-air feeling a messy goo still on the cap. I stuffed it into my pocket. All this was done in seconds.

John and I, almost choking on the dust and smoke, moved quickly to our immediate right into clearer air. Most of the Parabats had moved left looking for stragglers, or had stayed in the killing zone. John and I seemed alone. We moved fast and purposefully, rifles in our shoulders. About 20 metres away from the fire we came upon a SWAPO in camo uniform lying on his back with a gaping, bloody bullet wound through his throat. Critically wounded, he had managed to run a short distance from the kill zone but had collapsed just as we reached him. Somehow his torso was still raised off the ground and on his chest was something I had heard about but had not believed. His fist was clenched in a defiant 'fuck you' sign, his thumb between his fore and middle fingers.

I stopped, pulled my rifle into my shoulder, held my breath, aimed and fired twice. The first one missed and I saw the dust jump just under him, spraying him with sand but the second hit him somewhere low and he faltered, but amazingly still managing to keep his upper body raised, propped up on his elbows. I ran forward and stopped about five metres from him, took a wide stance, aimed at his head and pulled the trigger.

Click! Click, Click!

My mind froze. Empty.

I pulled at the Fireforce vest I had on, but it had become twisted around me and I would have had to use both hands to get at another magazine that was now twisted under my armpit. The terr turned and looked at me. I froze for a split second and, seemingly in slow motion, I thought of the knife at my side that I had discarded days before because it had been chafing me. Then, sensing that John was close by, I shouted. It all seemed in slow motion but was actually happening in seconds

"Johnny!" I barked out urgently. I looked quickly to see John Glover bursting from some bush to my right, his bright blue eyes locked on the wounded terrorist like a serpent. He flung the US-designed M79 'snot ball' grenade launcher that he had in his hand over his shoulder, pulled his R4 off the other and slammed it into his shoulder as he walked in small, quick steps up to me and the terr. The SWAPO, still supporting his upper body with his arms, turned his head and looked at John for a moment. Knowing his fate, he let out a long, low moan that sounded like he was calling out someone's name. It sounded like 'Ma'.

John put six or seven shots through his head. The bullets almost decapitated him. John and I stood quiet for a second or two. In the early morning chill, the hot contents of his head sent up a thick white cloud of steam as if someone had emptied a bucket of hot water onto the cold sandy ground. The vision would stay with me for many years. We quickly went through his pockets and found some propaganda booklets and about R400 in South African money.

"The bastard probably killed someone for this money."

Then and there we split the cash and without a second glance moved farther into the bush looking for more stragglers. Single and double shots banged around us as troops found and finished off wounded terrs, as per our orders to take no prisoners. Then, slowly, the shooting stopped. After about five minutes John and I moved back. When we passed the old bush soldier, he still held his 'fuck you' sign as mute witness to the cause, but his hateful expression had changed and, except for his gaping neck wound, he looked peacefully asleep, albeit without the top of his skull. His war was over.

The sun was just breaking over the horizon. Back at the kill zone the university lieutenant was smiling as the radio crackled to life. "We got a count of nine confirmed," he spoke into the mouthpiece with a broad grin.

"We got two more over here, lieutenant," I said, indicating with my thumb over my back.

"No, correction," he told the radio. "We have eleven, maybe more." He was as pleased as punch. What a story to tell his mates when he got back to university. Dan Pienaar arrived and reported a further two dead down a path to our right.

"Make that thirteen."

We stood around for a while. The SWAPO deserter who had led us to his comrades had come out of whichever woodwork he'd been hiding in and now stood gleefully looking down at the bodies of his former comrades lying in the killing zone. He scoffed, swearing at them in Owambo with a smirk on his face. I felt like ramming my rifle butt into his teeth as I watched him.

"Fucking bastard."

I swore loudly at him in English. He seemed to think I was congratulating or thanking him and he grinned at me, baring rotten teeth. I made a small feint as if hitting him with my rifle butt, then turned and walked away. He looked confused.

We spent about an hour searching the surrounding trees, finding about 30 satchels, bags and suitcases. It was like hunting for Easter eggs—finding them stashed high in the forks of trees and stuffed in bushes. They contained maps, documents, books, propaganda, civvy clothes, soap, uniforms, medicine and food. I found a web belt that had been carefully stitched and completely covered in what looked like python skin. I also took a few items of clothing and a FAPLA tracksuit top which I immediately put on against the morning cold. We had now formed a defensive circle around the sandy killing ground and waited while the radio crackled as the lieutenant tried to get a chopper to come and pick up the small mountain of AKs, RPDs, RPGs, bags and satchels we had stacked in a pile close to the campfire.

It dawned on me that it was Sunday morning. I wondered what my family would be doing now? On the farm, mom and dad would be getting up. Mom would soon be rustling up a breakfast of eggs, sausage and coffee which they would probably eat outside at the round cement garden table. The old man would be reading the paper and my brother probably sleeping in after a night on the town. And here I and my merry band had slaughtered 13 SWAPO in a textbook ambush.

"Let's get the hell out of here; we shouldn't stay at a scene this long."

Some of the guys had got the bad idea of hanging some of the dead SWAPO in the trees to leave a terrifying message for their comrades who found them. Pretty soon there were two or three terrs, with parachutes cut into their chests, strung up from the branches, swinging in the breeze above the smouldering fire.

I was not happy; and the scene was quickly becoming even more gruesome. A small herd of domestic, or perhaps feral, pigs had moved in. They were totally unafraid of us as they snorted with glee and actually started snuffling at the open head wounds of the dead terrs, eating the spilled contents.

"C'mon, now ... fuck off, pig," I swore, as I tried to shoo them off. I picked up a clod of earth and threw it at the big mother pig but she hardly budged. John got up and chased them and they broke away squealing, but were soon back again. John got up again to chase them. I turned to look the other way.

"I don't fucking believe this."

We had now been here for about three hours. We waited for a chopper to pick up the mountain of weapons and kit. The morning sun was already blazing down, the bodies on the ground and in the trees already stiff, with arms sticking out at grotesque angles.

"This is bullshit, we've got to move! There could be a another bunch of terrs here at any minute."

"Hey, more kills for us if they do."

John and I shared a last cigarette and sat eyeing the bush. I did not agree with his sentiment. There were only 16 of us and we had blown out half our ammo.

Dan Pienaar sauntered towards us; he too had a terr's peaked camo cap stuffed in his pocket. His blue eyes looked weary. He sat down and scanned the bush. "Hey ... they can't get a chopper. Three Two Battalion is in contact right now and all the choppers are taken up. They're talking about us carrying all this shit back with us."

"Oh, that's cool ... we have to walk back with all that crap?" I looked at the pile of captured loot and intelligence.

Sure enough, after half an hour we loaded up with suitcases, weapons and satchels, and we began legging it all the way back to the TB, sticking to open *chanas*. It did not take us nearly as long as it had taken us to walk in the night before. Now, in the daylight, it was only about a two-hour walk. The rest of the platoon at our TB popped a red smoke grenade as we got close to them. They congratulated us excitedly and said that they had heard the sound of the gunshots early that morning and it had sounded like "a hell of a battle". They gathered around as we told them about it and brewed a hot fire bucket of coffee.

Often, over the years, I have wondered how that SWAPO turncoat had been able to lead us through the bush at night over such a long distance to the exact spot where his comrades were dug in.

And I never forgot the pigs ...

DEADLY CLASH WITH FAPLA

Brothers in arms—Dire Straits

The official Angola press agency reported today that Angolan forces shot down three South African helicopters and one fighter-bomber in fighting along the southern border with South West Africa. It quoted a Defence Ministry statement that said fighting was continuing around the border town of Kuamato 10 days after South African Army units crossed the frontier into Angola. The statement said Angolan anti-aircraft batteries shot down the three helicopters as they prepared to open fire on Angolan ground units last Saturday. One of four Impala fighter-bombers sent to the rescue of the helicopters was also shot down, it added. New York Times, 22 January 1981

After nearly two weeks in the bush and a successful ambush under our belts we began to feel and look like real bush fighters. Old sleeves were torn off, army T-shirts were worn out and the only piece of regulation SADF uniform I had on were my ripped browns trousers. I was wearing my dirty blue sneakers and the FAPLA zip-up sweatshirt that I had taken from the ambush. On my head I wore the SWAPO peaked cap, complete with its prized SWAPO pin-on badge, which had a clenched fist that supposedly proclaimed solidarity, freedom and justice. Looking like a bunch of terrorists ourselves, dirty and covered with old camo grease, we headed farther north into Angola looking for more trouble.

It had been three days since the ambush. We heard that *Valk* 1 had had a rough contact with some SWAPO cadres they had surprised at a waterhole. It had been close fighting, almost hand to hand and had been quite a battle. Swanepoel, a tall quiet chap from a farming area near Cape Town, had been shot through the groin but had still managed to kill a terr who apparently was just about to pull another troop who had been slightly wounded. Their lieutenant had been scheduled to go back to South Africa but had pleaded to stay on in the bush for a few days. He had been shot through the hand for his trouble and had also picked up a scalp wound. Both Swanepoel and the lieutenant had to be evacuated by chopper, but they had killed six or seven terrs. We learned all the details later back at base camp.

The sun blazed as it reached its zenith. We sat relaxed, the platoon spread out among some long dry grass under some crooked thorn trees that gave us just enough shade. We were pretty far into Angola, probably about 60 clicks, and for some reason our platoon was too far ahead of the others. We were told to sit tight for a day or two till the other platoons caught up.

We were all feeling confident after the textbook ambush two days ago. I had let bygones be bygones with Stan. He had been quiet for the last two days. I felt bad for him, knowing that he had wanted to come with us on the ambush; he seemed quiet and disappointed not to have taken part. But today he bounced back and chatted on about how 12 months of hard training had turned us into machines and how we would be able to handle a SWAPO force three times our size because of the quality of soldier that we were.

"Well, I wouldn't be too sure. Look what happened to *Valk* 3 ... they were hit good, mortars landing in their TB ... if SWAPO had a stopper group waiting for them when they ran, we would all be singing a different tune now. Even *Valk* 1 had a fight that could have turned out different."

John Delaney, who was in one of his morose moods, lay against his kit chewing a long piece of dry grass. He wasn't his usual cocky self. He and Stan were still at it.

"You think these guys haven't been trained? Some of these guys have been trained in Russia and China! We're just lucky we got them in an ambush. Wait till we hit a base that they can defend! Plus, they think they're winning this war!" John Delaney said, referring to the propaganda leaflets we had found that told of countless South African soldiers walking the steeets of Pretoria, Johannesburg and Cape Town legless and armless as a result of encounters with SWAPO mines. They also said that the morale of our troops was so low that we just smoked dagga, marijuana, all day to escape the hopelessness of

175

the situation and the harsh treatment we received from our rank.

We lazed in the shade, chatting and joking, feeling totally at home in the bush. John the Fox was going on about life on his dad's huge tea plantation in the beautifully lush area of Tzaneen and how they would ride dirt-bikes around the plantation, when I noticed an old black man casually walking along the small footpath that ran about 20 metres past us.

"Hey, look here!"

I pointed to the old man who appeared to have seen us but walked on, seemingly unconcerned. John Delaney and I jumped up and waved to him to come to us and he casually complied, approaching us with a little smile on his aged face, toying with a long blade of grass in his fingers. He was a short, grey-haired, pleasant-looking fellow who appeared to be a local. But I quickly noticed that he was wearing the same pale olive green zip-up sweatshirt that I was wearing, the one I had got from the ambush. This did not strike me as too odd, because I figured it was probably easy for locals to buy and trade from troops around the area.

We asked the old man if he knew where SWAPO was. He did not understand what we were saying but obviously understood the word 'SWAPO'. After eyeballing us for a minute he casually signalled with the bit of grass in his hand that SWAPO was not far away, in fact just ahead of us. We thought he had misunderstood us and asked him again.

This time he smiled, pointed more emphatically ahead and repeated as he pointed. "SWAPO ... SWAPO!"

John and I excitedly led him to Lieutenant Doep, who was now in charge again since both the university lieutenants had been flown back to South Africa (one with half his hand). Doep was resting on the other side of our TB. He stood up under his tree, eyed the old man suspiciously and then called the 101 Battalion tracker to interpret. We stood by as they spoke; it quickly emerged that there was a SWAPO group or base just ahead of us but the old boy didn't know how many there were. He didn't think too many.

"Ask him if they have trenches dug into the ground," Lieutenant Doep instructed the interpreter, making a digging motion with his hands.

"He says no, he has not seen these."

"Does he know if they have many weapons with them?" Doep indicated his R4 rifle as he spoke. The old man just smiled sincerely and did not answer but when questioned again the interpreter replied: "He says he thinks they do."

The interpreter and the old man jabbered back and forth while John and I stood around, not wanting to be left out, feeling protective towards our captive. The receiver crackled as the lieutenant sat on his haunches and tried to get comms with Commandant Lindsay back in base camp, but he had been having trouble with the radio the last couple of days and was unable to get through.

"Tango Lima, do you read me, over? Tango Lima, do you read, over?"

The radio crackled and squelched for 15 minutes with no response. Finally, a decision had to be made. We could not let this old man go, because he would almost certainly compromise our position to the SWAPO whom he said were so close by. We had no comms and did not know what we'd be walking into by just taking this smiling old man's word. It did not feel right and I was not for it. It did not make sense; even if there weren't many of them, if one of us got hit we could not get casevaced[15] out because there were no communications. Who knew what this old fucker meant by "did not think there were too many"?

I voiced my opinion. "I don't think it's a good idea to go into something where we don't know how many there are, without gunship support or comms. It's not good planning."

There was muttered agreement from some of the other troops who had joined the small conference under the tree. Stan, however, seeing a chance to make up for missing the ambush, egged Lieutenant Doep on, saying that we wouldn't need gunships if we caught them by surprise like at the ambush. This was not a game of cowboys and fucking Indians, I countered. Some of us might get killed because of a wrong decision. Even our two-line corporal didn't want to go without at least comms with the operations room for back-up.

Finally Lieutenant Doep, like a schoolteacher in a class debate, listening to both sides, said we should have a vote. There were more ayes than nays, so the decision was made to immediately follow the old man. We kitted up and

---

[15] casualty evacuation, in this case by helicopter

checked our weapons. I had used almost two 35-round magazines in the ambush three days before but had five more that were full. I filled up the two mags that I had taped together with medical tape for a quick change. This time I put my knife back on my belt, took the SWAPO cap off my head and changed back into my dirty, torn brown skin. If I died, I didn't want to go in a SWAPO uniform with their cap and badge on my head.

At about 15:00, with the sun halfway down the western sky, we moved out in a V formation, with the old man leading the way up the small footpath. We walked for about 30 minutes and the bush thinned out. We came upon what seemed like the beginnings of a populated area, with our path leading into a bigger, well-used track that had smaller paths breaking off in a crisscross spiderweb leading to a few scattered kraals. A handful of locals in threadbare clothes came out and stared at us with curious and not-so-friendly faces.

I felt in my gut that this was not good, but the little excursion seemed to have taken a life of its own and could not be stopped now. I had a horrible feeling we were walking into something deadly. Pretty soon there were a few distinctive chevron-shaped SWAPO boot spoor clearly imprinted on the sandy path, which were soon joined by many more with different spoors. Suddenly, up ahead, we came to a group of small, well-kept white brick buildings with tin roofs. We were entering a small town. A few locals standing in the shade of the *stoeps*, the verandahs, looked at us in amazement as we strode through their little town with false bravado, still in our formation which was gradually becoming more and more ragged.

We rounded some tall old trees and to our surprise in front of us stood a huge old white Portuguese church, the size of a small cathedral. Its square steeple, extending 20 metres or more and its high-pitched roof covered in old, cracked orange tiles seemed bizarrely out of place. We stopped outside the church. The doors were open. We cautiously walked in. It seemed that it was still in use, with pews and an old metre-high carving of Christ on the cross next to the the pulpit. I thought how out of place it all looked, then it slowly dawned on me that, to us, Angola might be one big war zone, but to these people it was their home. There were some remarks of astonishment at our find; someone said the big carved figure of Christ would make fine war booty but there were bigger concerns and we quickly moved out. (I understand that later some South African troops did in fact take this fine piece as plunder but that it was later returned in a small ceremony at the end of the war.)

It seemed that the old man had, wisely, gapped it while we were in the church and we were now on our own. Just past the church were more small brick buildings and a low cement reservoir where a group of young women were scrubbing heaps of brightly coloured clothes. They stopped to stare at us in astonishment as we approached. None of us waited for the interpreter. "Where's SWAPO? SWAPO! SWAPO!"

I confronted a pretty young African girl with her hair teased up into a small untidy afro, and shouted at her in English. "Where's SWAPO?"

She stared at me, silent, her eyes burning with something that seemed to be both shock and anger. She had probably, her whole life, heard about the racist South African *boere* and how they would eat her—and now here she stood, face to face with the white devils. They all stood dumbly staring at us, not hiding their contempt.

"Don't waste time ... we're already in it." My mind was racing ahead.

We briskly moved on, leaving the little town behind us and I sensed that this was it, that we were now truly walking into the shit. The track quickly became a white sand road. There were now all sorts of boot tracks, with large vehicle tracks turning onto the road.

Our platoon was falling apart. Half the guys were languishing some 40 metres behind. I turned and frantically waved them on, mouthing a silent "Come on! Come on." I looked at Doogy, walking long metres back, carrying the MAG.

He silently shook his head at me in a unmistakable message: "This is not good!"

I was shocked to turn again and see that some of the guys had stopped altogether and were mumbling among themselves. To my amazement our corporal, who had been with us since basic training and who had chased us unmercifully, saying that we had to be tough to be a paratrooper, was sitting on his haunches, muttering in Afrikaans, "This is *kak*. This is shit! I'm not going any further."

I looked at him in disbelief and felt something rise in me. "We're in it! It's too late, we're in it! Let's go," I mimed to no one in particular and turned again to wave on the rest of the platoon, still dragging far behind on the sand road. Once again I was filled with the numb feeling of 'let's get this over with', knowing it was already too late to turn back and that our best bet was to go forward—hard! I was right, because seconds later the shit hit the fan.

Shots rang out from the tree line in front of us. Isolated at first, but then furiously, kicking up sand around us and whip-cracking overhead.

I bolted across ten metres of open ground, with spurts of AK bullets kicking at my heels, to a two-metre-high anthill and found cover with three others as sand and dust flew up around us. It was a pretty open area with only scattered bushes alongside the road. The platoon had scattered and taken cover where they could, but most lay flat ... out in the open.

No one was returning fire! I could not see exactly where the firing was coming from and did not particularly want to put my head around the antheap, as rounds were cracking all around us. We sat huddled in cover for half a minute or so, before there came a lull in the firing. I took the chance to peep around, as did the other three. Puffs of drifting white smoke hung in the tree line 30 or 40 metres to our front left. A tall figure made a mad dash, with elbows pumping, across some open ground into bushy cover.

"There!" I shouted, and fired off six or seven quick shots at the bush where the figure had just disappeared.

Now we began to pour fire at the tree line. I heard Doogy's MAG open up with a welcome sound, in one long salvo of about 30 rounds. We were all up now, moving forward and shouting encouragement to each other. Back in training I had not realized how important battletalk was ... now we were all shouting to each other to "C'mon, let's go, c'mon, c'mon!" as we ran spread out across the open *chana* towards what seemed to be a retreating enemy, firing at fleeting glimpses of running figures in the trees. Suddenly an RPD machine gun opened up from the other side, to the right of the *chana*. We all dived into the dirt in the open. He was shooting high but corrected himself as sand spurted yards in front of us, spraying us. By now we had the hang of it and all opened fire at the tree line and the tell-tale smoke. The RPD stopped.

Away to our left somewhere a heavy fire fight broke out at the far end of our broken sweep line, I could see four or five of our guys lying on their bellies in the *chana*, blasting away into the tree line. I recognized Lukie Nel who was calmly kneeling and slowly being enveloped in a cloud of white smoke as he laid down a barrage of fire. Still on the ground after the RPD fire, I turned to see if I should shoot across the sweep line to help, but decided against it because I couldn't see the target and from my angle it was too close to our guys. I looked for Johnny Fox and my surrounding troops who all had their heads turned, momentarily caught up in the fire fight that was building to a fever-pitch, but they held their fire and it seemed that they too had decided that the angle was not good, with no visual targets.

Just then, literally out of the clear blue sky, and with the timing of a Hollywood movie and unbelievable navigation, two South African Air Force Alouette gunships came swooping over our heads like the fucking cavalry. With blades hammering, they turned in a tight orbit above the fleeing terrs 60 or so metres ahead of us. Doep must have got through on the radio, the very obvious thought struck me.

"DayGlo ... DayGlo!" the shout came up and down the line. I quickly turned on my side and punched my bush hat inside-out to show the bright neon-orange sticker stuck to the inside of my cap, putting it back on my head back-to-front, for better vision. The DayGlo had saved many a troop in the bush from being blasted to hell by the gunships above mistaking him for a terr. I forced myself to my feet as we all rose and charged across the *chana* with a new feeling of courage and invincibility.

The gunships' big 20-millimetre cannons opened up, like music to our ears. The second gunship was orbiting and shooting almost behind us to our left, where the other fire fight had taken place. We charged forward toward the fight in front of us, into bush and trees. I flipped over my magazine before it was empty, paranoid about the empty 'click' of two days before in the ambush. A terr dashed from cover 30 metres in front of us like a bat out of hell, tearing across our field of fire with long strides. He seemed to have forgotten about us while making a break from the gunship whose blades hammered and guns boomed all about him. He stumbled and fell as nine rifles opened up on him almost simultaneously.

I saw a huge white explosion that looked like one of Horn's RPG-7s going off in some trees. It had become a running battle and we had to dive for cover a few more times as we took fire and moved away from the gunship, which seemed to be having its own party. We ran farther into the trees, alive with figures dashing about like rabbits, but still stopping to take occasional pot-shots. The running fire fight had been going on now for about five minutes. I reached a mound and a thicket and was breathing hard, with sweat stinging my eyes, making it almost impossible to see. I had become the end troop at the far right of the sweep line and had strayed a bit on my own. (It was a position I had grown accustomed to from the days when I'd carried the MAG. I usually sought it as it gave me opportunity to flank around the side if the shit hit the fan.) I searched the trees ahead of me as best I could but saw nothing.

For the last couple of minutes I had been fighting back a retching, tightening sensation in my chest. Now it was building into dry heaves. This time, too powerful to control, I bent over as my stomach and chest convulsed in a spasm. My chest had closed up completely and long globs of saliva drooled from my mouth as I retched and heaved and my eyes filled with water and sweat.

What the fuck's going on?

I was bent over, paralyzed by convulsions. I had always had trouble with my lungs and on and off for years had been plagued with these dry convulsions that sometimes came on if I suddenly overexerted myself. I blamed it on too many cigarettes and smoking pot. I could not believe it was nailing me in the middle of a fucking fire fight. I stood bent, fighting for control for what must have been a minute but seemed like an age, trying to get my vision and breath.

In the middle of a heave I heard "Gungie! Gungie!"

Voices on my left were shouting my nickname in a tone that meant unmistakable and imminent danger! Blindly, with my mouth still open and holding my rifle at my hip, dripping with puke and saliva, I shot seven or eight rapid shots in a half circle in front of me. A dozen bullets cracked past me, so close I could feel them. When my eyes cleared I could just make out a terr rolling over, dead, not more than six metres away from my right, his head coming to rest on his outstretched arm and his old, worn AK-47 lying untidily next to him.

182

"Jy moet wakker word, Gungie … hy het jou amper uitgevat!"[16] Paul Greef shouted, pointing to the figure lying in camo on the ground in front of me. Paul's eyes were wide. John Glover, a few yards past Paul, was also glaring at me, his eyes ablaze with reprimand. He shook his head at me, a small white cloud of smoke still hanging above him.

I could not explain to them what had happened. I stared foolishly at them, blinking my eyes which were now clearing of tears and sweat. We carried on into the trees but I hung back, still recovering from my attack and trying to calm the occasional spasm that racked my chest.

"These are FAPLA! Not SWAPO! Can't you see?"

We had slowly returned to the open *chana* and were still sweating and catching our breath while we dragged seven or so dead bodies in camouflage uniform and laid them in a row close to the tree line, leaving the ones that the gunships had got deeper in the bush. SWAPO had a khaki or tiger stripe uniform—*not camo!* It was obvious now that no one had even noticed the different uniform in the fire fight.

The one gunship landed on the *chana* and the blades swung lazily in idle as the flight crew in their green coveralls came over to inspect the kills. They confirmed that these were indeed FAPLA soldiers.

We stood around looking at the seven camouflaged bodies lying in a row. It didn't make much difference to us that they were FAPLA. No consequences really sank in because we were still high on adrenaline from the contact.

FAPLA, SWAPO … same thing, I thought, They've got uniforms and they've got AKs.

The pilot, an older, beefy man with thinning hair and a walrus moustache, took off his helmet off, indicating the bodies. "This is a fuck-up of note … we knew as we flew over you, but it was too late. You guys were already into them. There's a FAPLA base camp, complete with BTRs and tanks about ten clicks north of here. This is probably some sort of OP that you hit. I don't know … but I think you better get the hell out of here very quickly before they come running down here after you … in battalion strength. What are you doing so far north, anyway?"

The lieutenant quickly told him about the old man we had shanghaied

---

[16] Wake up, Gungie … he almost took you out! (Afrikaans)

who had said that there were SWAPO close by and about the radio that was not working properly.

"Well, he led you right into a hornet's nest, lieutenant. You had better get your troops out of here ... and quickly. This might start a fucking war. We don't have a beef with FAPLA at this time and they sure aren't going to appreciate us killing half a platoon of their finest."

It still did not fully sink in. We stood around, had a smoke and took some photographs. I posed like a deer hunter with my rifle, kneeling in front of the nine dead FAPLA, my bush cap pushed high on my head.

Lieutenant Doep told the chopper crew to let Commandant Lindsay know what had happened, that we were having radio trouble and were heading south right away at *stink spoed*, at high speed. They agreed and turbines whined as they took off, blowing a small hurricane of dust down the *chana* that covered us and the dead FAPLA cadres.

"We have to move out of here and fast. We shot the wrong people. These are FAPLA ... kit up and let's go!" Doep spoke in an almost panicky voice that could not hide his concern.

We had all heard bits of the conversation and needed no second urging. We kitted up and took off in single file, heading immediately south into bush across the way that we had come, leaving the nine dead FAPLA lying on the far side of the *chana*.

"Put on a *draffie*, a trot," Doep shouted. "Do anti-tracking!"

The black tracker ran last, trying to do a quick job of clearing out our spoor with a branch of leaves but he wasn't having much success. We switched to a slow run that was too taxing to maintain with our full kit. We were still exhausted from the running battle we had just fought and soon slowed to a fast, purposeful walk, crashing through the bush in single file.

The sun was dipping into the trees, casting long welcome shadows when the reality of our position struck me as *Valk* 4 crashed hastily south.

FAPLA was regular army, not some SWAPO terrorist outfit with only AKs and RPG-7s. These guys had big Soviet-built T-55 tanks and BTR armoured troop carriers with mounted 14.5-millimetre guns. There was probably a battalion of them heading our way right this fucking minute!

Each man held grimly to his own thoughts as we trudged on. I had taken up

CERTIFICATE OF
PARACHUTE TRAINING

It is hereby certified that

Rfn Granger N. Korff

SUCCESSFULLY COMPLETED

A BASIC PARACHUTE JUMPING COURSE

OVER THE PERIOD 31 Mar 80 TO 2 May 80

AND IS NOW A QUALIFIED PARACHUTIST

INSTRUCTOR _(signature)_

TRAINING WING COMMANDER _(signature)_

COMMANDING OFFICER _(signature)_

Vlak 4 takes five.

Training jump over the Caprivi.

The author with Paul Greef (*left*) prior to a training jump in Bloemfontein.

Dispatchers check paras prior to a training jump in the Caprivi Strip. The author is on the left with the MAG machine gun plus 500 rounds of ammunition.

Paras emplane for a training jump.

Paras en route to the training jump DZ.

Paras jumping into the Caprivi at M'pacha.

MAG gunner, Aaron 'Doogy' Green, takes a break during a patrol.

Valk 4 refill their water bottles from a muddy waterhole in Angola.

The author poses at the Angolan border fence. He is wearing a SWAPO cap and pin-on badge, a FAPLA sweat shirt, blue civvy sneakers and carries a SWAPO bag.

Valk 4 practise-fire their mortars in Owamboland.

A civilian truck becomes yet another SWAPO landmine victim in Owamboland. Most casualties were local black civilians.

A SWAPO-sympathetic kraal in Owamboland is torched by SADF troops.

The big grin from John Delaney signifies the end of an operation in Angola. The author is centre, looking out, with Aaron 'Doogy' Green on the right.

The author poses outside his tent at Ondangwa para base.

A captured anti-aircraft gun at Ongiva. The FAPLA gunners put up a brave and stubborn resistance, firstly against the Mirage aerial bombardment before lowering their barrels against the advancing paras.

Operation *Protea*. This Soviet-built tank didn't even get the chance to leave its moorings inside the FAPLA military base of Ongiva. Paras can be seen inspecting the tank from above.

Paratroopers leaving Ongiva on their way to attack the big FAPLA base at Xangongo. A captured T-34 tank is on the right; sundry captured red lorries and buses can also be seen.

A T-34 tank burns at Ongiva. The brave, or foolish, tank commander had decided to attack the paras single-handedly when an SADF 'Noddy' car (Eland armoured car) brazenly careened through the scattered Parabat lines and took out the tank with one well-aimed shot.

A Buffel armoured troop-carrier destroyed by a SWAPO 'cheese mine'. Fortunately for the paras, casualties were minor.

A 44 Brigade Q-Kar, or Sabre, well camouflaged during Operation *Protea*. At the time 44 Brigade was comprised mainly of Rhodesians and Americans.

The author en route to R&R, showing clear signs of strain.

D Company returning to base in Angola after a combined assault with UNITA troops on a SWAPO camp.

Valk 4 troops watch as an SADF Buffel troop carrier burns during Operation *Daisy*. The troops were loading captured ammo onto the Buffel when a booby-trapped case of SWAPO ammo exploded. A quick-thinking major jumped into the Buffel and drove it off to a safe distance. He was awarded the Honoris Crux for his action. Half an hour later a lieutenant was killed by a booby trap when he entered a SWAPO bunker.

Stan and Granger Korff take five.

Blackened up!

Chopper dropping off troops in Angola.

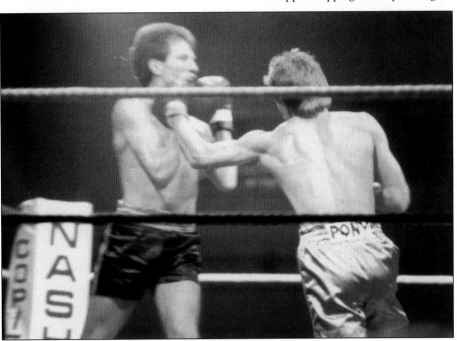

The author knocking out an opponent in the fourth round.

The author fighting in Los Angeles. This particular opponent had just come off a split-decision loss to James 'The Heat' Kitchener, a world-renowned 'bad ass'.

near the back of the line. I was still rushing from adrenaline. I had completely recovered from the weird asthma attack. Once again my mind had flipped into some primal one-track high gear and I felt like an animal running on immediate, basic instinct. My mind was clear and sharp with no thought, no clutter, no bullshit. I felt neither fear or courage. I felt an almost animal absence of emotion. I kept turning to look back, expecting to see runners on our trail, but the only thing to be seen was our African tracker (who had now abandoned his efforts at anti-tracking) and Doogy, whose face was contorted and focused as he concentrated on the business of carrying the heavy LMG at such a furious pace.

I noticed by the body language of the troops ahead that the bravado had left them. They hurried along and suddenly looked every bit as young as they were. We had walked south for about 20 minutes when the first 82-millimetre mortar boomed behind us and, after a long minute, another exploded a kilometre or so away to our right. More of them came quickly, exploding loudly in the still dusk, closer and haphazardly around us, but never closer than about 300 metres.

"They don't know where we are! They're throwing a circle of mortar bombs and hoping for the best!" I said to myself. The realization struck me with a gush of hope. We pushed on into the fading twilight that enveloped us like a mother's arms.

And we crashed on.

"Put on some speed!" the word came down the line and we hitched our heavy kit higher on our backs and put our heads down, unconcerned about the thorn trees and dry branches that ripped at our forearms and faces as we plunged forward. The *crump* of mortars had stopped and started again a couple of times but now, after 30 minutes, they were still and all that could be heard was our boots crunching, heavy breathing and the occasional sick hushed joke that was tossed down the line and quickly followed by a chorus of *ssshhhh*!

We began to breathe a little more easily as it became clear that they didn't know exactly where we were and may have even run out of mortar bombs. After about an hour of hard walking we stopped, bumping into each other in the dark.

"Make a TB and dig in," Lieutenant Doep whispered loudly.

Doep, for some stupid reason, had decided to TB. The 'herd instinct' made us dig a tight circle far too close to one another and we sat down wearily. The radio crackled and hissed in the dark as Doep, calmly but desperately, tried again to reach South Africa.

"Tango Lima, Tango Lima, do you read me?" Nothing. Then again: "Tango Lima, Tango Lima, do you read?"

The radio had fucked us again. We quietly handed all our 60-millimetre mortar bombs, of which we were still well stocked, to Kleingeld, who set up his pipe and laid all the bombs neatly in a row next to his hole. I took my two M27 grenades out of my Fireforce vest, stuffed them into my pants pockets and lay on my stomach, staring into the dark and taking stock of the position we were in. I had blown out two magazines at the ambush three days ago and two and a half in this contact. I had one and a half magazines left. That was about 40 rounds and at least half the platoon was in the same boat. If we had any contact now, we would literally run out of ammunition.

Horn had blown away most of his RPG-7 rockets shooting at who-the-fuck-knows-what and now all of a sudden tells us that he has just the one rocket left! I felt the first flutter of real fear. This was a fuck-up of the first order, standing alone as a prince among complete and utter cock-ups! We lay in our holes and listened to Doep trying to make contact on the radio.

"He's trying to get some choppers to pull us out," John Glover said, staring quietly into the dark.

"We shouldn't stop ... we should keep moving," I whispered slowly.

"Yeah ... it's a fuck-up."

We lay quiet for a couple more hours in the still darkness. A light reckless mood had swept through the platoon and we were whispering and grinning to each other in the dark, making stupid comments and jokes.

The almost full moon broke dramatically above the trees as if gleeful to see us and shone with a luminous, malignant brilliance that exposed us at once, lighting up our dark hideaway in a silver bath.

"I love these full-moon nights," some idiot piped up and was greeted by nervous, muffled sniggers. I looked around at the still night and started to relax a bit. It looked as if we might have got away ... once again victorious.

The night birds shrilled in the trees and a chorus of bugs and insects kept up a constant hum.

We could not move our TB and dig in again, so we sat in the moonlight with our TB partially lit and waited as Lieutenant Doep whispered into the radio. "Tango Lima, do you read ... over?"

At about midnight a sound broke through the still bush that made my blood run cold. It sounded like a huge beast roaring in the night but it was the roar of a huge diesel engine that suddenly seemed very close, gunning its engine as if it was stuck in something and trying to get out. Shock ran through the platoon; everyone was up and looking at each other.

"What the fuck? This is it ... they've been tracking us in the dark and are nearly on us. How the fuck did they get so close without us hearing?"

The small TB became a newly disturbed ants' nest of troops standing bolt upright, looking at each other in shock, not knowing what to do next. I stood up too and hurriedly joined one of the small groups huddled together in urgent discussion.

"Maybe they've just sent a vehicle to come and pick up the bodies and it's back at the *chana*. Sound travels far at night."

"No way, man, we've walked pretty far. There's no way that BTR or T-55, or whatever the fuck it is, is that far away, believe me!"

I agreed. "No way is it at the *chana*. They're tracking us and they're close."

"This is it, boys— *nou gaan ons kak*," Paul Greef said in a low voice.

I smiled a sick smile. We were indeed going to shit.

The engine bellowed again and then tapered off to a low rumble that was barely audible. We all stood quiet and looked at Lieutenant Doep who was on one knee, desperately and hoarsely calling on the radio but to no avail. He got up. "Horn, get ready with that RPG! Move your kit to that hole," he said, pointing at the closest hole facing our retreat.

Horn, who looked more like a sad office clerk than a paratrooper, slowly picked up his kit and moved into position. All eyes were on him as he moved deliberately, lay down in the shallow hole, loaded the RPG rocket into the launcher and pulled the silver safety pin from the rocket, arming it. He braced his loaded weapon against his kit bag and pointed it towards the sound of the growling engine. He had a little crooked smile on his face as he acknowledged that he held the fate of the platoon in his hands. If that BTR or tank came breaking through the moonlit bush it was up to him to stop it ... or we would all piss blood.

"Horn, you had better make sure of that rocket, boy," I said with a nervous laugh. A string of warped humour and encouragement followed as we watched Horn slowly settle in on his belly and fiddle with his sights in a slow ritual.

"If that T-55 comes through those bushes, I'll have him," he looked back and assured us in his slow Cape way, still smiling his wry half-smile. "But you better clear the way for back-blast behind me!"

"Get to your holes!" Doep barked, and went back to the radio in the centre of the small circle.

I lay in my shallow hole, fidgeting with my rifle, checking my one-and-only full magazine and placing the half-used one next to me in the hole. I pulled the two M27 grenades from my pants pocket and laid them next to me too.

I too had a weird little smile on my face that I couldn't seem to wipe off. Stan's words came back to me about being gutted like the goat. I thought of the dead SWAPO we had left hanging in the trees, stiff and bloated, with parachutes cut into their chests. In my mind, I could clearly see FAPLA soldiers laughing and cutting us up for trophies, then pissing on our corpses in retribution. What goes around comes around. I could see the headlines in South Africa: *SA troops massacred in Angola; no survivors or prisoners taken; bodies mutilated.* I thought of my family and of Taina. What would they say when they heard about it? I couldn't stop smiling my sick grin. I noticed that I wasn't the only one; quite a few guys had stupid smiles on their faces.

The engine had gone quiet as we lay listening into the night ... silent now, not even the sounds of the night animals, just the sound of Doep's radio ... but it sounded now as though he was talking quietly on the radio? He was! He had got through! They'll send choppers to get us out in an extraction, or Mirage jets to blow these fucking FAPLA laddies to the dark side of the moon! All heads turned to hear his hoarse, low voice rattling off in Afrikaans in a serious monologue and then a long inaudible response.

After a minute he jumped up. "Kit up, let's move, and fast. FAPLA is on our trail and they've radioed a warning to South Africa. They are following up and have said they will wipe out any SADF troops within 15 kilometres of their base. Kit up now! let's move … *loop pas*, let's jog. Come on!"

We were standing, strapping our kit to our backs before he'd finished his sentence. We struck out at a slow run, heading south once more. It was the obvious direction of retreat, the safest way to get as far from the FAPLA base as we could. I held my chest strap with one hand, pulling it tight to try and stop the heavy backpack thumping on my back. I held my rifle low with an outstretched arm, at the trail.

Blowing caution to the wind, Doep chose to run along *chanas* whenever we came to them, making us easy targets for any sharpshooters lurking in the trees. In the red operational area there was a strict night curfew on everybody—SADF and civilians alike. That's why Lieutenant Doep had TB'd in the first place—probably scared to move at night as we could have been shot by our own troops in the area. This being a secondary worry right now, we ran stop-start through the bush … and this time there were no sick jokes.

My arms were ripped by thorns and low branches again and again. I did not even feel it. I got a good rhythm going and breathed evenly, like a long-distance runner. My earlier almost deadly, asthma-type attack had been and gone. I thought about how, back in training, one of the qualifying tests at the end of the gruelling PT course was to run 3.5 kilometres with full kit in a certain time. I had become pretty good at it and recalled the arduous route we used to take. Out the gates of 1 Parachute Battalion, along the tar road and over into the big sports complex, down to the turnaround point under the big trees and back again, this time uphill all the way. It was tough to make it in the required time, although I had always done okay but would, like everyone else, almost drop from exhaustion at the end of it. Now our big H-frames weren't packed with five days' rations and my magazines were empty.

Tomorrow was a scheduled resupply day … that is, if there was going to *be* a tomorrow. When we stopped and walked, we walked like speed-walkers, zigzagging south, choosing the easiest way through the bush. All that could be heard was our laboured breathing and the occasional curse as a thorn tugged out a chunk of bloody skin. We moved like this for about two hours before we had our first rest by the white sand walls of a large old Portuguese water reservoir and collapsed onto our kit, sweating in the cold night.

Doep said we were probably long past the 15-kilometre 'death perimeter' set by FAPLA and that they were unlikely to follow us this far south, because FAPLA did not want to get tangled up fighting SWAPO's war and didn't want to fuck with South Africa.

Stan came over as I sat leaning on my kit, smoking a cigarette that burned my lungs after the exertion. He too was wet with sweat in the dwindling full moon that had lost its eerie brilliance and was starting to dip behind the trees. He looked excited as he sat down next too me. "Why didn't they just come and pull us out or send a Mirage to bomb them? They said we had support for this op, so what's the fucking problem, then?"

I had been thinking about just this for the past three hours.

Stan was smiling and spoke in a hushed voice. "Doep said we were too close to the base camp to be pulled out. Gungie, this could start a fucking war with FAPLA," he said, with his bush hat pushed high on his head. "The last time South Africa took out FAPLA troops was five years ago, in 1975, in Operation *Savannah*. Those Cubans are itching to have a go at us."

"You think those were Cubans chasing us?"

"Hell, yeah! There are 40 or 50,000 Cuban troops in Angola … where do you think they all are? Right here in southern Angola where the trouble is! Half that FAPLA base is probably Cuban troops. Some of the ones we shot were probably also Cuban."

I pondered this and took a shallow drag of my cigarette that made me cough. I looked back slowly in the direction we had come from. Come to think of it, a couple of the dead FAPLA had looked a bit different, lighter-skinned. I stared into the night.

"That's why they didn't send a Mirage to bomb them. That would really piss Castro off." Stan was standing up now and looked as happy as a pig in shit as he smiled and pointed back into the bush. "I can tell you, that was close … if we had stayed another half-hour, that T-55 would have come right through us and you'd better believe they would have had more than a platoon with them, coming after the South Africans!"

He seemed to relish the thought of us being massacred.

"Yeah, we would have lasted two minutes. How much ammo have you got?" I asked glibly.

"Two mags."

I looked down at my burning forearms and in the moonlight saw a dozen long scratches where the thorns had torn my skin. As I rubbed them I could feel the hard pieces of thorn that had broken off under the skin. Stan was right—South Africa had not had a clash with FAPLA for several years. The Angolan army had always tried to stay out of SWAPO's fight even though Angola let SWAPO set up bases in her territory. Recently, with the escalation of cross-border raids on SWAPO bases, SWAPO had moved their bases deeper into the interior, sometimes right next to FAPLA bases in an attempt to avoid getting fucked up. Trust *Valk* 4 to start a fucking international incident. Go on in and attack the Angolan army and get away with it. I thought how my brother would laugh when I told him about it. Little did I know that he would hear about it the next day on the six o'clock news when it was reported that South African troops had clashed with the Angolan army while carrying out strikes against SWAPO in Angola, killing 16 Angolan troops, and that Angola had complained bitterly and lodged a complaint at the United Nations.

He would only find out months later when I told him that it was my merry bunch of men who had carried out the raid. We would also find out pretty soon that South Africa's policy of avoiding confrontation with the Angolan army was about to change and that soon we would be the spearhead in a massive offensive against FAPLA, deep into Angola.

MORE CONTACT

Misunderstanding—Genesis

We moved a bit farther south and felt safe enough to be resupplied with ammo and food early the next morning. We were also able to stay put in a TB and relax for a couple of days. I stripped and cleaned my rifle that was thick with carbon and dust. We even had the chance to rinse our filthy clothes in a smaller second reservoir with less than a metre of water in it, but enough for our needs. The rains had disappeared. I washed and donned my olive-green FAPLA pullover and scrubbed the thick bloodstain from the SWAPO cap which I pulled onto my head. The pullover still reeked of scented soap from when I had found it in the satchel stashed in the trees at the ambush. Now I saw why during training they had emphasized that we could not use soap on operations, as after weeks in the bush the scent was still strong enough to be picked up from a fair distance. For many years afterwards, whenever I smelled a bar of soap my mind would flash back to FAPLA, the ambush and the dead man's clothes.

At one of our early-evening TBs we came upon a troop of *nagapies*, a kind of small monkey with bulging eyes that comes out at night and once caught is quickly tamed. *Nagapies*, Afrikaans for night apes, or bushbabies, are about the size of a small rabbit, and prized possessions to be smuggled back to South Africa. It was a powerful symbol of a true bush fighter to walk among the juniors with one of these little primates perched loyally on your shoulder. Now I watched as half the platoon, the war forgotten, dropped their rifles and whooped like kids as they ran around some thorn trees where a small troop of *nagapies* had become marooned and were clinging onto the thin branches, staring down and foiling the paratroopers' clumsy attempts to capture them.

The troops formed a circle around the trees and began to shake the branches to try and get them to fall out, but this proved impossible as the bushbabies simply bounced up and down, their long fingers holding on with ease.

Smit, who was a small chap, scaled the trunk of the one thin tree to try and get closer to the branch that four or five of them had moved up to. The little creatures screeched as they leaped with ease to the next branch, where they grabbed on with their strange-looking fingers, glaring at their would-be captors. After five minutes of playing 'musical branches' they took a chance, leaped screeching from the tree, one after the other, and landed almost among the circle of troops beneath them. But, like lightning, they scampered away to the closest clump of trees, kicking up puffs of sand, lost from sight and gone forever.

One, who seemed younger than the others, remained clutching the branch as Smit climbed up. At the last minute, as Smit lunged to grab it, he fell and grasped onto a branch just in time to break his fall, but the awkward manoeuvre left him hanging in the tree, looking like an ape himself. I sat next to my kit brewing a fire bucket of tea, watching with interest and roaring with laughter at the show. In falling, Smit had persuaded the young *nagapie* to make a desperate leap to the ground as his companions had done but with a superb rugby-tackle dive, Lange van Rensburg snagged the creature. Everyone cheered as Lange held up the little bloke triumphantly. After a few minutes the *nagapie* became totally quiet and seemed quite accepting of his new parent. Lange would keep this little fellow for the rest of the bush trip and eventually take him home with him to the Karoo, where Lange would die in a car accident soon after leaving the army.

Even Lieutenant Doep, who had little interest in personal relations and even less in the English-speakers in the platoon, had eased up a bit. He sauntered up to our little group of *soutpiele*.[17] It did not matter that we spoke almost fluent Afrikaans and had been three or more generations in South Africa. He lit up a cigarette, squatted next to us and slowly exhaled a cloud of smoke.

"How're your feet, Korff?" he asked in Afrikaans.

"They're holding out okay, lieutenant ... not bad."

---

[17] Afrikaans insult applied to those of South African/British dual nationality. Literally 'salt dick', it refers to having one foot in either country with your dick hanging in the ocean between

"You'll have to put your boots back on before we get back to the base."

"Ja, I know. I will, lieutenant."

He looked at Doogy who had his LMG propped up against a small tree behind him.

"That LMG of yours has been talking a bit of Afrikaans lately, eh?"

Doogy smiled, gave a quick account of the contact and demonstrated how he'd had to change a broken ammo belt while half on the run. We took the opportunity to question Lieutenant Doep on what had been said to him on the radio about the FAPLA incident. He took a long drag of his cigarette and instinctively blew the smoke forcefully downward so as not to make a cloud. "We went too far north and crossed over the agreed line into FAPLA's immediate area. Angola's agreement with South Africa is that we can't cross this line on operations against SWAPO. We fucked up and were too far north and crossed it ... and we are definitely not allowed to shoot FAPLA troops. There is still going to be shit about this."

"What did they say about it?"

"Angola contacted South Africa and said they were going to wipe out any South African forces in the area north of the line; that's why we had to run for it!"

"We started a fucking international dispute!" John Delaney stood up, did one of his trademark jigs and shook his head in disbelief. "We've started a war! Trust fucking *Valk* 4 to start a war!"

We all smiled stupidly at each other.

"Oh, I can just fucking see it now ... *Valk* 4 will be asked to step forward at parade to be congratulated for finally starting the long-awaited war with Angola and the 50,000 Cuban troops stationed there. We'll get special recommendations and 21 days' leave when Russia and East Germany send in their reinforcements to help against the South African racist aggressors. Then, when America steps in to help us, we'll get even more praise and a chestful of medals for being the match-head that lit the global nuclear war!"

"Did we know about the boundary?" I asked, smiling at John's performance.

"Yes." Doep's brown eyes twinkled for a couple of seconds and he smiled. "Never knew it was so damn close!"

We all chuckled together and finished our cigarettes. Lieutenant Doep field-stripped his cigarette butt and instinctively put the filter in his pocket. Serious again, he looked around at his little group of *soutpiele*—John Fox, John Delaney, Stan, Doogy and me—as he nodded his head stiffly and got down to saying what he had come over to say, somewhat awkwardly.

"You guys have done some good work in the last couple of days; keep it up." He quickly looked at each of us, seriously, making eye contact, then got up, nodded again and left our little group under the tree.

It sounded strange, coming from Lieutenant Doep in the tone that he'd said it, as though it had been difficult for him to say, that he had rehearsed it a couple of times in his head before coming over and spitting it out. He would normally blurt out something like that to the whole platoon when we came back from a run or a chasing, but there wasn't much sincerity on those occasions. This was a different Lieutenant Doep we were beginning to see. Not so lumbering, brash and quick to blurt out orders like a school prefect. It was Doep's first action as well as ours; we were all maturing together ... very quickly.

Yeah! It was about time someone noticed that the *soutpiele* were a sharp bunch and didn't horse around with brown-nosing platoon politics and bullshit, but that we were always there when the shit hit the fan.

We spent a few more uneventful days patrolling the area half-heartedly. Then one morning came the order from Commandant Lindsay for the whole company to head back to South West Africa. The walk would take us a couple of days, as our *valk* had already back-tracked south a fair bit since the FAPLA incident when we had run for half the night. The other platoons were still a day's walk farther north into Angola than us. We would be the leading platoon on the long walk home. We were dirty and fatigued after three weeks in the bush, with bad sleep and rat pack food. We looked like a platoon of SWAPO ourselves, with three weeks' growth and old, crusty, black camo grease that was still applied every couple of days. We were glad to turn south and start the long walk out of fucking Angola.

We walked back, not in the cautious way we had been patrolling the last three weeks, but crashing noisily and confidently through dry brush and across open *chanas* as we headed south in a V formation like marathon bushwalkers … not paying much heed to a quiet withdrawal. No one was going to stand in our way.

Besides, we had met both FAPLA and SWAPO in their own backyards and had licked them both.

"Mess with the best; you'll die like the rest!"

I had my H-frame tied tightly round my chest and high on my back, with my SWAPO satchel over one shoulder, containing my boots and a few water bottles. My rifle strap was looped sloppily over my neck and hung in front of me like a tray on which I rested both arms. Fuck SWAPO and fuck FAPLA. Enough of this bush already. Let's get out of here, have a nice hot shower and a shave. I knew they would definitely give us a big *braai* and piss-up after this operation. Who knows how many kills the company had brought in. Our platoon alone had over 20 in the two contacts we'd had. The company together could probably account for maybe 80 kills. Shit, that's not bad for just legging around Angola looking for trouble, and we didn't even hit a base really. Worth a *braai*, I'm sure. Big pork chops and cold beer. To sleep on an army foam mattress sounded like too much to ask.

I realized I hadn't even whacked off in more than three weeks either. Must be some kind of record.

I was daydreaming of home, of going out with my friends to a nightclub, of dancing and getting rip-roaring drunk, puking and passing out. I was dreaming of Taina's beautiful big breasts and green eyes and little freckles and …

"SWAPO! There! … SWAPO!"

Bang, bang, bang!

Five figures dashed 50-odd metres in front of us, weaving in and out of the thin brush as they ran. The black 101 Battalion tracker walking point had spotted them first and had already opened up on them with his heavy 7.62 G3, shattering the stillness.

I was close to the front of the formation and snapped out of my dreamland in an instant. I pulled my rifle strap off my neck, flipped the switch to 'fire' and started forward, shooting at the running figures as I ran.

John Delaney was at my side, throwing off his bulky kit. I did the same and swore as my SWAPO satchel hooked up in my H-frame but after a few vicious tugs it came loose. I ran a couple of yards, then stopped and fired at a couple more fleeing figures following their comrades. I picked one with a light-coloured shirt and blasted at him as he ran behind some tall grass.

A shout came: "Mortars!"

I had barely hit the ground when a mortar bomb exploded deafeningly 20 metres ahead of me. I was up again, shooting. Because of my forward position in the formation I was in front of the charge with just John Delaney ahead of me and our section leader, Dan Pienaar, abreast of me.

Pop! from behind me.

"Get down, Gungie!" Pienaar shouted.

Boom! ... an explosion again just in front of us. I hit the dirt just in time, landing on my side. Mortar shrapnel whizzed overhead like angry bees.

Boom ... another one close by, not 30 metres away. Both Pienaar and I turned while still on the ground and angrily shouted at Kleingeld who had hastily set up his 60-millimetre pipe behind us and was popping off mortars as fast as he could drop them down the pipe. Then it registered.

"What the fuck are you doing? They're landing in among us! You're too short ... you're too short!" Pienaar shouted at Kleingeld. I made eye contact with the mortar man and he stared at me, momentarily unable to hear what I was saying, but my eyes told the story as I shook my fist at him, pointing to where his last bomb had fallen. By good adjustment or fluke, his next bomb exploded 20 metres behind the last fleeing figure who ran on unscathed until he too disappeared from sight.

More troops had caught up with us now as we ran forward, covering about 30 metres through some scattered scrub and caught sight again of the fleeing band, who were now gaining ground and were about 70 metres in front of us. I came to an abrupt stop and, while standing, let loose a long volley of shots. I thought I saw the lead man falter but he ran on and disappeared again behind trees.

As we came closer I was surprised to see a kraal, a few untidy grass huts nestled behind a cattle barricade made from old dry branches.

"There's a kraal. They ran into the kraal." Delaney pointed out to Lieutenant Doep who was coming up from behind, running crouched with his radio handset loose, slapping him in the face.

"Cease fire ... cease fire!" he yelled, and the call was carried down. He yelled again as one of Kleingeld's mortars just missed the small circle of huts.

"Cease fire ... spread out in a line ... spread out in a line!"

We shook out into an extended line.

"Okay ... forward!"

We advanced slowly towards the kraal. Doogy had caught up and was next to me, holding his LMG low and ready.

"Gungie, where did they go?"

"Into the kraal!"

"How many?"

"I dunno ... five, six!"

I moved cautiously around the side through some dead trees that had been stripped clean of their branches for firewood. A small herd of skinny goats took off, making me spin around and almost pull off a shot. Doogy and I moved slowly forward together. Everybody had stopped shooting as we crept in a semicircle up to 30 metres from the kraal.

"You see anything?"

"No, watch it."

I looked down the sweep line. Lieutenant Doep was signalling us to get down. I dropped to one knee, my rifle trained on the little grass huts just in front of us. They would have no chance in a shootout; we'd cut them down.

"Horn, get ready with that RPG right into that hut if they fire!" Doep barked, running hunched over and catching up with us again. He had been on the radio reporting the contact.

Horn went down on one knee with the rocket-launcher over his shoulder and bent his head to the sights. We knelt low in a semicircle, 20 metres from the kraal now, and waited, our rifles trained on the five huts. Not a soul stirred in the kraal.

"Forward!" Doep waved his hand slowly.

I moved forward, around towards a wide entrance on my side of the kraal.

"Get ready, Doogy."

"I'm ready, *boet*, I'm right here." We inched forward as Doogy and I slowly came to the entrance, stepping inside the perimeter of the branch barricade.

Not a sound was heard from the huts. I duck-walked around the smaller, outer grass huts and came to a low entrance covered with a hanging piece of cloth. I motioned that I was going to check the hut. Doogy nodded at me, standing back and locking his legs into a wide stance with his LMG pointed stiffly at the hut. I noticed as I moved that John Delaney and a handful of troops had gained entrance from the other side and now moved equally as cautiously towards one of the larger huts. John too was duck-walking with his rifle in his shoulder.

I pushed my rifle in front of me, flipped up the cloth that hung in the doorway, then jumped aside and waited for a few seconds. I looked at Doogy with his LMG, who by now had been joined by Kurt and Greef, both with their rifles pointed into the darkness of the hut. Watching their faces for a reading of what they saw, I was just about to spin into the door when I heard a commotion at the big hut and above the din the word 'PBs'.[18]

"Here, over here ... there're PBs over here!"

After quickly searching the small hut, which was empty, we approached the main one where half the platoon was now gathered. Five black civilians were in the hut. One, in a clean white shirt, was lying on his back, rolling back and forth in pain. His comrades, once they saw they weren't going to be shot, started gabbling frantically to one another and to our black tracker who was listening to them with a frown on his forehead. They were all talking at once with wide eyes and frantic arm gestures. After a minute they began to slow down a bit.

"Why did they run away?" Doep almost shouted at the tracker who in turn shouted at the four who were now quiet. They gabbled back, all talking at once again with wild hand gestures, pointing at the kraal and their injured comrade writhing on the floor in front of us.

"They say that they had been drinking beer and were on their way back home to this kraal when they saw us coming and, not knowing who we were, they were scared and ran away."

"Are they SWAPO?" Doep snapped, glaring at them.

"No, they say that they are not SWAPO and that they live at this kraal and these two live in a kraal not far from here."

---

[18] Plaaslike bevolking: local population (Afrikaans)

I bent down to look at the old man lying rocking on the floor, his face screwed up in pain. His tan-coloured pants were saturated in blood from the knee down. I signalled to him to ascertain where he was hurt. He pointed to his knee and then to his grey head, at a tuft of hair scuffed up where a bullet had grazed him, making a small open furrow in his scalp. Then he pointed to his hip. I pulled his shirt aside and also found a nick in the soft flesh just below his hip bone that was hardly bleeding, fortunately only a few millimetres deep.

"Shit, this old guy is fucking lucky," someone commented behind me.

I pulled up his baggy trouser leg as he grimaced and wailed in agony. "Give me the scissors," I said to Kurt, the platoon medic, kneeling next to me. I cut the trouser leg off above the knee to reveal a horrible wound. A bullet had gone right through the middle of his shinbone ten centimetres or so below the knee, shattering the bone completely. The bottom half of his shin had shifted and lay at a grotesque 45-degree angle to the top half. It seemed to be attached only by a few bits of skin, with a huge black bullet hole in the centre. It did not appear that an artery had been hit because the bleeding had slowed and the blood oozed only slowly from the jagged wound.

He groaned in pain as I laid my hand on it. "Where's that Sosagon?" I had quickly taken control of the situation. Not because I knew what I was doing but because no one else seemed to want to do anything. Kurt was standing by and seemed happy to let me do what I could to help the old man, whose face was contorted in pain. Kurt emptied the contents of his medical bag on the floor and handed me the syringe of Sosagon. I quickly popped the seal off and lifted the old man's arm, looking for a vein, while Kurt began to set up a glucose drip. Even though I knew that Sosagon was supposed to be given intra-muscularly, I decided that the situation called for drastic measures, so I was going to slam this old boy into the clouds above because he was going to need it when I tried to move that leg back into place. I found a vein on his skinny arm and slowly drew some blood back into the syringe, mixing it with the liquid painkiller, then shot the full dose into his vein.

"Give me the other one!" I said motioning to the second Sosagon syringe that lay in the medical heap. Kurt looked at me with a strange look but said nothing and handed it to me. I was working quickly as if I knew what I was doing while everyone stood silently around, observing. I took the second syringe and plunged it into a vein in his other arm, mixed blood and pushed the plunger all the way down. I didn't know too much about what I was doing but what I *did* know for sure was that a shot of Sosagon intravenously into 'Papa Joe', the main vein in the arm, knocked you instantly into another world. I also knew that a person could handle two shots, because I had once watched a red-headed, freckle-faced senior on our last bush trip in Ondangwa slam two full syringes of Sosagon one starry night. He'd sat rocking on the sand walls of our Fireforce base, staring up at the night sky until he fell asleep and we had to carry him to his tent. He seemed fine the next day at parade.

Instantly the old man was as high as a kite and even broke into a slow smile. He began pointing this way and that in some explanation that I took to be saying that he lived somewhere else. His speech became slurred and I could see in his eyes that the old boy was heavily stoned as his lids hung halfway over his eyeballs. That was what I had wanted.

I lifted the bottom half of his shin that flopped loosely as I moved it. I picked it up with two hands as gently as I could and shifted it so that it was aligned with the top half. I could clearly see the bottom half of the bone, red with congealed blood. I could feel the two ends of broken bone grind against each other as I pushed them together. I had to repeat the process a couple of times until it all seemed to fit into place, bringing with it a small flood of fresh blood. The old still grimaced and moaned in pain, his eyes tightly shut, but he was able to handle it. I cleaned the sticky blood from around the wound and poured some antiseptic liquid which Kurt handed me into the wound.

"Get sticks for splints!" I called. It it seemed a logical thing to do. Even a boy scout should know this. Make a splint.

Some of the guys quickly returned and handed me an assortment of sticks that I broke up into what I thought to be suitable splints. I placed two field dressings on either side of the wound and then bandaged them tightly into place with a long bandage. Then I put some two-foot sticks on the outside to hold the flopping bone in place and wrapped them tightly too, making a firm splint. The old man, tripping on the morphine proxy, gripped my wrist tightly and babbled on again, looking deeply into my eyes with what seemed like heartfelt gratitude. Even with no medical training, I knew he would probably die if he did not get proper medical attention and even then he would probably lose the leg. I had actually done nothing but put his leg in place and bandage it tightly. I irrationally wondered for a moment whether it had been my bullet.

Lieutenant Doep had just got off the radio, cancelling the gunships and reporting that we had shot a PB. I stood up and looked at him. He nodded at me. We stared at each other.

"What are we going to do with him?" I asked, still in charge as the acting medic.

Doep looked at me blankly. "We should take him with us. It's probably only 40 clicks to the South West African border," he said, knowing it would be impossible to carry the old guy 40 clicks.

"We should get a chopper to carry him back to Oshakati to the hospital. We shot the poor bastard. We can't just leave him here," I insisted.

I quickly learned the reality of war when Lieutenant Doep looked at the old man silently, then at me, and then away from my gaze.

After a minute, I said again, "What are we going to do, lieutenant?"

"Leave him here. We can't take him with us ... we're in Angola. Come on, let's move out!"

He did not even mention the ridiculous idea of having a chopper come all the way, over 40 clicks, to pick up the poor old bastard after we had shot him by mistake. I shook my head and made a disgusted sound and looked down at the old boy who was now happily smiling, still looking up at me.

Kurt had hooked him up on a drip and was showing his friends that they should keep it held high and remove it when it was finished. I left a heap of bandages and ointments and another Sosagon from the other medical bag and told them to give it to him again in his thigh when it started hurting again. I also left a pile of glucose sweets and sour sweets from my rat pack.

We moved out of the kraal and headed south again in a V formation. A deep, dark mood had settled on me. I felt terrible about leaving the old man lying in the hut. I thought back and knew too that I had pulled off a volley of shots at him when I saw him in his white shirt running to the kraal. Why the fuck couldn't Lieutenant Doep just call in and at least request a chopper?

Who knows, they might have even said: "Sure we'll come and pick him up." It would be no skin off anybody's nose to get a bird out here and pick the old boy up and when he'd healed, just drop him at the border and tell him to make his own way back. I knew that when he came round he would half die from the pain and would probably be dead in a few days from infection.

I pushed the thought out of my mind and scanned the bush, my rifle ready at my side. We crashed south uneventfully but the next day at about 10:00, as we were about to cross a big open *chana*, the black tracker walking point stopped and pointed across the *chana* to the other side.

"SWAPO! SWAPO!"

The formation came to a sudden stop and we stared out across the *chana*, shielding our eyes from the bright morning sun. Sure enough, on the other side 300 metres away was a group of figures hanging around and sitting under a large tree which looked to have bicycles leaning against it.

"SWAPO!" he said again, pointing and wagging his black finger.

"Are you sure?" Doep stared across the *chana*.

"Ja, is SWAPO!" he wagged his finger furiously, his bloodshot eyes widening and his tongue darting across his thick lips.

I shielded my eyes from the bright glare coming off the white *chana* and stared across. I could see that they all seemed to be wearing the same colour khaki uniform and that there seemed to be at least a dozen of them. We were a weary bunch of bush soldiers and had little interest in breaking off and sneaking all the way around the big *chana* to try and surprise them in a flanking attack. In any case it looked as if we had been spotted, so we quickly spread out on the side of the *chana,* as if at the shooting range, and *Valk* 4 opened fire from 400 metres. It was deafening. I pretty soon lost sight of the target because of the smoke and then had to stop shooting as a troop in front of me had moved into my line of fire. I did not want to change my position suddenly because there were also troops behind me who were shooting just over my shoulder, so I lowered my rifle and kept still. The lack of one rifle was not going to make a difference from this range.

Fifteen seconds after the shooting started a mortar exploded in a cloud of white smoke 50 metres in front of us ... and then another one a little closer.

"Kleingeld has got off fast with his mortars this time but he's fucking up again … he's way too short. Fuck him!" I thought.

Boom! … another mortar exploded 40 metres in front of us as we all involuntarily got down onto our knees.

"Stupid shithead!" I cursed Kleingeld, but did not look around for him as rifles were once again blasting over my shoulder, deafening me. After a minute the shooting staggered to a stop, as did the mortars.

"Spread out wide … move across!" Doep shouted.

I made a point of looking at Kleingeld who was loading up his mortar pipe and his kit. "You were pretty fucking fast to get those mortars flying off, Change!" I acknowledged. (Kleingeld in English means 'small change'.) "But you were too fucking short again, man … you landed right in front of us," I challenged. I still hadn't forgiven him for almost dropping two of his mortars on me yesterday when we had chased the PBs.

"I didn't get one mortar off. What are you talking about? I was shooting with my rifle. That was their bombs! They were fucking quick to respond," he said in Afrikaans.

I was surprised. Shit! They had been pretty close. Their mortar man must have a damn good eye to have put his first bomb so close at over 400 metres while under fire. I never did ask Kleingeld why he hadn't used the mortar, which would have made perfect sense over that distance.

We walked fast, spread out in an extended line across the huge *chana*. A few bullets buzzed high overhead like bees but soon stopped, as the group of SWAPO made a beeline into the bush, having traded a few shots. With the reckless abandon of having a few successful fire fights under our belts and weeks in the bush, we came to where we had seen them under the trees. They had cleared out but it looked as though they had spent a couple of days in a TB under the trees, because once again we found some bedding, cans of fish and bits of clothing.

We found more propaganda leaflets saying that the *Boere* were white monsters who had no mercy and would not be satisfied until they shot all your cattle and slaughtered your goats and only wanted to terrorize the peaceful people of Angola.

"You see, they found out about the goat. I told you!" Kurt said slowly. "They're not lying!"

big crimson belt buckle with a hammer and sickle on it ıp his booty as we all gathered around to marvel. It was a ıd! Also clear evidence of the Soviet presence in Angola. nd for about half an hour, looking in the trees for more ınd none.

› was on the radio, reporting that we had made contact but ıot seen exactly which way they had run. Their chevron- clearly imprinted in the sand all over and I examined it ıed to have bombshelled almost immediately, splintering ons.

.ıckers," I thought. Their bombshelling technique was a good one, because which spoor should you follow? Would you put a whole platoon on the chase of one or two spoor?

Ho Chi Minh, or whoever, was the father of guerrilla tactics and it was he who had come up with this one and saved many a terrorist's, or freedom fighter's, life, whichever way you wanted to look at it.

Doep was debating following a spoor but we had all sat down for a smoke and had even taken the opportunity to open a quick can of chow. We had no stomach for a chase. He looked at us and read quite clearly how we felt about it.

"Okay, finish up ... let's move out."

That dusk we came to the rendezvous spot in a bushy area. Waiting for us was a platoon of 3 SAI (South African Infantry) who had a few armoured Buffels and had been dug in, waiting for us since the previous day. We were the first D Company platoon to arrive. We flopped down under the trees, laughing and relieved that our four-week patrol in Angola had come to an end. We drank warm Cokes that the infantry had kindly brought and opened long-awaited mail that we scrutinized closely and quickly in the dwindling light.

"The bitch has left me … she says she's found somebody who loves her! She actually did it. I don't fucking believe it!" Stan read through the short letter again. He stood up, looking in disbelief at the piece of paper in his hand and walked around and around in a little circle, rubbing the back of his head with a deep scowl on his face. "The stupid cow ... I don't believe this. She

couldn't wait till she saw me face to face!"

We laughed and hooted at his misfortune.

"What did you do to her, Stan? She must have heard that you were screwing these Owambo women," I laughed heartily, as under the circumstances I found it very funny, because for a year and a half I had been hearing about Stan's up-and-down problems with his girlfriend and I knew all the details. (By pure chance it turned out that it was Taina's neighbour Jimmy who Stan's girlfriend had met. Funny thing was that Stan and his girlfriend lived in Cape Town and Taina and I lived in Jo'burg, 1,400 kilometres apart.)

We were sitting under the tree in the fading light and had put our own letter-reading on hold to console and poke fun at Stan when Kurt came walking slowly into the circle with a couple of white pages clutched in his big ham hands.

"Doreen's pregnant ... from another guy!"

There was a brief silence as we looked at him to see if he was screwing with us—which was usual—when he spoke in that low serious tone but this time he was not as he looked at us quietly with his speckled blue eyes in his big pink face. I cracked up and flopped down on my back, laughing.

Kurt sat down, shoulders hunched, his huge frame bent over as he read the good parts to us. "She's pregnant by this other guy ... I know the guy, too. He works with her sister. I've met him."

I could not stop laughing and had tears in my eyes. Kurt and I were always taking the piss out of each other and bullshitting, and seeing him sitting there, hunched over, talking in his low, barely audible voice was just too much. The tears rolled down my cheeks as I laughed and laughed. I had met his girlfriend. We had AWOLed to her hotel room in downtown Bloemfontein when she had come to visit him and got drunk on wine before going bar-hopping, getting motherless and ending up having five fist fights in one night. I had been arrested and put into a police van while the cops pursued other drunken AWOLees involved in the inter-unit war that was raging outside the disco, but while they were busy some strange dude with hair down to his arse came and unlocked the police van and said in Afrikaans, "*Kom, ma wag vir ons*" (Come, mother's waiting for us) and let me out. It was the strangest thing—and then he disappeared, and so did I. Quickly. I have always thought he might have been some weird angel who had been sent to set me free.

John Delaney and I were two of the few who still had our girlfriends. We bragged about how we knew how to treat them right and poked fun at Stan and Kurt till it was pitch dark when we rolled out our smelly sleeping bags into shallow holes. That night we had the first good night's sleep in four weeks, while the infantry stood watch over us with new South African-made night-vision equipment that had just been issued.

My last thought was of Taina, who in her letter had told me that her father had sent her pet pig to a friend's farm "where he would be more comfortable and would be used to breed". I had raised pigs while at high school and had 22 pink pigs in neat stalls at the back of the plot. I had given her a squealing piglet, the size of a small puppy, for her birthday. Of course the pig grew huge and had the run of their five-acre plot, beating up the dogs for their food and shitting on the front lawn. I hoped that she had believed the breeding part because I knew the next time she would see Pig would be as the sausages her mother cooked for breakfast.

BUSH JUSTICE

In the air tonight—Phil Collins

For us, Operation *Ceiling* had come to an end. 32 Battalion were still busy in Angola with Operation *Carnation*, which had been run hand in hand with our seek-and-destroy operation, *Ceiling*, and would continue for weeks to come; they would still be going strong when the next big ops started, but for us, thankfully, it was over.

The other three D Company platoons all came into the rendezvous by midday the next day and we walked the last 20 or so clicks back across the border in a huge company V formation, swapping war stories with the guys from the other platoons and showing off booty that we had picked up.

Willy Bray told me how he had shat himself when they were mortared during the night and said that SWAPO troops were doing fire and movement into their TB. He felt bad but said that they had no choice but to run, and that they had sat tight through the night in small groups until they regrouped the following morning at their emergency RV on a *chana* many kilometres south. (There was always an emergency rendezvous given before we bedded down so that we could reunite later if the shit hit the fan during the night.)

I told him how we had hit FAPLA—the Angolan army—by mistake, how we'd had to run from the tank or BTR in the middle of the night and how we had hardly any ammo left.

We also heard how *Valk* 1 had had a desperate, almost hand-to-hand contact in some thick shrub that lasted a few minutes, how Swanepoel had been seriously wounded through the groin and how the university lieutenant leading that platoon had been shot in the hand. Both had been casevaced out and more than half a dozen terrs had been killed.

Our part in the operation had been successful—all in all D Company had got over 60 kills and not lost a man. Commandant Lindsay would surely be proud of his boys.

The next morning we stepped over the remnants of a rusty barbed wire fence that was the border and crossed into South West Africa. I was still dressed in my blue sneakers and my assortment of SWAPO and FAPLA clothes and got Doogy to snap a photograph of me standing on the broken-down fence that symbolized the border. I flashed a grin and a peace sign. I took a photo of him as he scowled at me with one foot in Angola and the other in South West Africa. Inside South West Africa I changed out of my terrorist outfit and donned the hated army boots again.

We dropped the V formation and walked the last ten clicks in a loose company group, not at all concerned about running into any SWAPOs who happened to be south of the border.

D Company had proved itself in battle, in a four-week cross-border operation with hardly any support and only in platoon strengths. We were warriors at last. We had faced the enemy in their own country, kicked their ass and had bragging rights to almost 80 kills, if you included the contacts on the previous bush trip. Our senior company, I had heard, had finished up with 130 kills, which I had thought very high, but we were well on our way to beating them. Those 12 months of hard training were now bearing fruit and we were getting all the action we could handle. We did not know that in a few weeks we would be part of the biggest conventional cross-border operation into Angola that South Africa had yet to launch.

We crashed through the bush like happy school kids going home after a football game, joking and shooting the shit.

"Why can't they send some Buffels to pick us up at the border, instead of walking all the way back to base?" John Delaney was walking happily along with a bounce in his step, flitting from group to group, chatting and swapping stories.

"Can't wait to have an ice-cold Coke and a honey sandwich and get these fucking boots off." No one had taken off their boots for three weeks, but I'd had it easier with my sneakers.

"All I want to do is sleep on an army foam mattress and shave. I feel like I'm back on Recce course," John went off on a tirade, telling everyone in earshot how this four weeks in the bush was nothing compared to the seven weeks of hell that he and I had spent on the Recce selection course where we had walked close to 700 kilometres.

"Think *this* is bad? Try seven weeks."

"Well, it couldn't have been that bad if you two almost made it to the end— you both look like hell now."

I looked at Dan Pienaar who had a pair of brand-new SWAPO boots dangling around his neck. "Better than you'll look hanging from a tree by those fucking SWAPO boots."

We soon sighted the white sand walls of Ombalantu base camp and walked through the small gates which were guarded by two serious-looking infantrymen who gawked at us as if a company of SWAPO was walking into camp. We looked at them with the thousand-yard stare we had picked up from weeks of constantly peering through the bush. We walked with the long stride of men who have walked far and fast for a long time. We walked past the little white-brick HQ building and the six-metre-wide baobab tree and flopped our kit down in a heap around the small tin canteen in the centre of the tent square. I felt tired and bone weary from our four weeks in the bush ... but I felt good.

We had seen real action at last.

Most of the guys immediately took off their boots for the first time in four weeks and wiggled their toes into the sand. Cigarettes were lit amidst loud calls for the canteen to open. I had been sitting on my kit for about ten minutes, enjoying my third Camel and grinning at the schoolboy-like activity around me when my ears picked up a hauntingly soulful drumbeat and horn coming from the tin camo-painted canteen some metres away. The solid, moving drumbeat and mournful horn compelled me to find out who and what the heck this song was. I got up and walked to the door of the canteen, still in my filthy, torn uniform, pushed my way through a few 3 SAI troops who quickly gave way, and watched Phil Collins on a music video for the first time, breaking into "I can feel it coming in the air tonight". He crashed into the chorus as he changed tempo halfway through the song. I stood and watched the whole video, mesmerized, and afterwards walked back to my kit with the drumbeat still thumping through my head, thinking it was probably the best song I had ever heard. I still, to this day, think it is one of the best songs ever recorded—the haunting beat still grabs me by the throat whenever I hear it and I am still compelled to turn the volume up high wherever I might be.

3 SAI had occupied the base in our absence. SAI troops with short, regulation haircuts were walking around in twos and threes in squeaky-clean browns and PT shorts. They seemed awed by this company of unshaven paratroopers dressed in bits and pieces of SWAPO uniform and quickly disappeared from view into the tents, gawking from the shadows of the tent flaps.

"These fucking infantry look like they're about to shit themselves," Stan snarled, giving them a hard bush-killer stare as they scurried by, looking straight ahead.

"What are these pussies doing in our base anyway? I'll be fucked if I'm not sleeping on a mattress tonight! Those are our beds they're sleeping on!"

"Take it easy, they're on your side." I sat on my kit savouring the sweet burn of an ice-cold Coke and a chocolate bar that tasted like heaven.

"Fucking morons," Stan was pushing the mad bush fighter thing and motioned with his chin in a 'What the fuck are you looking at?' to a clean-cut infantryman who was hastily walking past. The junior soldier braved a look but quickly turned and looked straight ahead. The company sat around the canteen, laughing.

We had come a long way together since we'd stood under the parade-ground lights at 05:00 twelve long months ago, the survivors of the 700 who had tried to take the PT course to become paratroopers. Now we had been tempered in the heat of battle, the very reason we had all joined this outfit. We had become like one another, knew each other's strengths, weakness and character flaws and now babbled together like a big family, sipping cold drinks and eating chocolate bars, shouting for the bar to be opened. Most had taken off their torn shirts and filthy boots, skinny torsos shining white in the sun in contrast to the crusty Black is Beautiful camo-smeared faces and arms, joyfully wriggling their blistered feet and toes in the hot, fine, white sand.

I looked across at our old tents and saw a group of short-haired, worried faces peering out through the tent flaps.

"Looks like these boys are dug in permanently in our tents—we might not get a foam mattress tonight!" I said, now also appreciating the seriousness of the new sleeping arrangements.

"Yeah, well, we'll see about that."

Corporal Pretorius came strolling out of the HQ and addressed us. "Pack your kit neatly down at the bottom there by the chopper pads. We're not going to be staying here and will be moving out in the morning back to Ondangwa. We'll spend the night outside the walls, next to the pad."

He spoke gingerly, as a new pecking order had been established in the last four weeks of combat and patrolling in Angola and he wasn't at the top of it any more. He had sat on his ass, not wanting to continue, just before the FAPLA contact. Not that I blamed him—I had wanted to turn around too. He smiled awkwardly as he was met with jeers and shouts of anger at the thought of sleeping another night in the dirt while the 3 SAI troops snored in our beds.

To me it wasn't a big deal. I stood up with John Fox and slowly walked across the tent square to the chopper pad and dumped my kit against the outside of the sand wall.

John Delaney, always the first to pick up any news, came and dropped his kit heavily next to mine, spraying a cloud of dust into my face. His eyes were wide. "I hear there's a big op going down ... just heard it from an infantry guard. It's supposed to be a big one. He says they might be going all the way up to Luanda, like in '75. Maybe take the whole of Angola!"

"Bullshit."

"Serious. Ask Lieutenant Doep. And we'll probably be involved."

"You mean we're going to hit FAPLA?"

"FAPLA and SWAPO and the Cubans and anyone else in the way from what it sounds like. I told you we started a fucking war, didn't I?"

I tilted my head back, swallowing the last of my second cold Coke.

"When's it going to happen?"

"I don't know but it sounds like soon. All the infantry guys are talking about it."

I wiped some sweat off my brow and for the first time thought of a shower. Funny, you would have thought a shower would have been the first thing on our minds but after four weeks you get to feel quite at home in filth. I had always wondered how those bums on the street could stand walking around black with grime. Now I knew. After a while you don't even smell yourself or feel the grime.

John stood up and pointed back into Angola. "I know what's going on. FAPLA is getting too buddy-buddy with SWAPO and even training them. That's why we hit FAPLA by mistake … that ambush we did wasn't far from their main base."

We looked at him sceptically.

"Doep told me. Ask any of these infantry cunts—they all know about it." I always doubted John with first-hand news, not because he was untruthful but because I knew he could not resist adding a tale or two.

I looked across the chopper pad trying to decide if I should lift my ass and go and shower, even though I felt quite comfortable sitting filthy in the sun. I saw Kurt coming across the chopper pad, lugging his kit over his back with one hand and with a big cheese, onion and tomato sandwich clutched in the other. His cheeks were bulging and he smiled as he put down his kit.

I caught a whiff of onion and my saliva glands reacted instantly. "Where did you score the sandwich?"

"At the kitchen. The cook."

"Oh, I forgot you're in with the cooks, being an alumnus and all."

"Nah, he'll give you one ... ask him."

He took another huge bite of the sandwich, speaking around the mouthful. "Hey Gungie, the cook says that the sergeant-major here killed those two little cats we had."

"Whaaaat?"

"The cook says he was feeding them, like we asked him to, but one day this sergeant-major stomped on the one cat in the mess while they were eating and broke its neck and the next day picked the ginger one up by the back legs and slammed it against the wall, killing it. He says the cat lay there crying for 20 minutes before it died."

"Who the *fuck* is this cunt?" I said, sitting up, stunned at the news.

"Cook says he's a mean fucker. All the troops are shit scared of him and he runs this camp like he's God, ex-boxer and all."

I stood up and felt a rage flood through me as I looked around towards the kitchen. Kurt, who had stood beside me in a few fist fights, knew that look and smiled slowly.

"Kill our fucking cats ... where's this cook of yours?"

"Easy, Gungie. He's the fucking RSM and sergeant-major of this camp, man. Cool it!"

The cook was chopping a side of beef with a huge knife, stained up to his elbows in watery blood. "Yeah, he stood on the little grey one right here in the mess while we were having supper—didn't even say anything—then left it lying there while the troops ate.

He put down his huge knife and walked up to us, frowning, wiping his bloody hands on his apron. "Then the next day he caught the other one right here and smashed it against that wall and threw it over there and it lay there and cried while it died." He demonstrated how the poor animal had been killed.

"He's a fucking *poes*, this guy. Total cunt, everyone hates him. The cunt runs the camp with an iron fist and these infantry troops are fucking petrified of him. He stomps around here like he's chief of the army or something. He had all us cooks go for PT with full kit because some of the glasses had stains on them, but it's the shit water here that stains them."

I felt murder in my veins. Without a shadow of a doubt, I knew I was going to kill this motherfucker.

"What's his rank?" I asked, not that it mattered.

"He's a staff sergeant, but he's acting sergeant-major of the base."

"Well, he's a fucking dead sergeant-major!" I walked calmly out of the kitchen and stood outside. Kurt and the cook exchanged looks. I caught sight of an infantry troop walking past and called him over. He ran up nervously, almost coming to attention in front of me. I asked him where I could find his sergeant-major.

"He's in the HQ. They're having a debriefing with your officers."

I asked him about the cats and he verified the story the cook had told. He relaxed when he saw where I was coming from.

"He's a real mean bastard," he ventured in Afrikaans.

"Tell your sergeant-fucking-major there is someone in his tent who wants to speak to him," I said evenly.

He hesitated, not relishing the thought of having to face the man but when he realized he could play a part in this prick's demise he smiled slightly and tried without much success to hide a twinkle his eyes. "Okay, okay ... I'll go and try and get him." He shot off towards the HQ building at a brisk walk.

I walked casually into the sergeant-major's tent which had been pointed out to me. It was close to the kitchens and I sat down on a high stool next to a table laden with an assortment of what looked like carburettors and taken-apart radio sets. There was also a metre-long truck screwdriver with a big red hand-grip about 20 centimetres long and a shaft thicker than my thumb. I sat looking out in the opposite direction towards the chopper pad. Through the tent flaps I watched the rest of the company laughing and heading to the showers in twos and threes.

"What are you going to do, Gungie?" Kurt finally asked in his low monotone. We had not spoken since I had sent the infantry troop off to look for the sergeant-major. Kurt sat on the other stool and faced the tent door, with a clear view of the small camp.

"I'm going to teach him a fucking lesson, Kurt. While we are out fighting and getting shot, this asshole is killing our pets. I'll show him what a big man he is, killing two kittens."

I felt cold and calm. It was a dangerous feeling. I had only felt it a few times in my life and had quickly learned to stay away from it at all costs. I would force myself to snap out of it immediately on the few occasions that I felt it rise because I knew it would surely destroy me. It was a feeling of following through with absolute destruction, without the slightest thought of any consequences. It was very dangerous but this time I had opened the door and had let it in. It now coldly and furiously rushed through my veins, overjoyed to have been allowed in for only the second time in my life.

I sat and coolly inspected the many pieces of dismantled equipment on the fold-out table, lifting one up to examine it.

"Here he comes, Gungie! Jesus, he looks like he's about to take off and fly his arms are out so wide."

I didn't bother turning around and continued inspecting the piece of radio equipment in my hand, turning it around and peering at the dozens of little wires and tubes that were now exposed. It took him half a minute to strut across the tent square.

I felt detached from my body and casually watched Kurt's chubby, deadpan face for a signal. As he lifted his eyebrow I put down the radio I was idly inspecting and turned around to face a short, mean-looking acting sergeant-major glaring at us as he entered the tent.

He was stocky and powerfully built. Kurt was not lying; he stood with his arms out like fucking Popeye the sailor man. He looked at both of us but composed himself quickly and glared at me as I stood up. He had the face of a pit bull with the square, jutting jaw of a fighter that he thrust out at me under a thick moustache drooping over his top lip. He had small, beady, dark eyes set deep in his head, with a nose that looked to have been broken a few times and small scars around his eyes that must have come from boxing. He glared at us with his little black eyes and was just about to open his mouth to roar at us when I turned to fully face him.

I got straight to the point. "Are you the guy that killed the cats?" I asked quietly, in English.

He stopped for a second, not sure what he had heard but he quickly got the message and emphatically snapped back in Afrikaans. *"Ja ... en wat daarvan?"*[19] He glared at me defiantly, his black pit bull eyes locked on mine, sparkling in anticipation.

The three weeks in the bush living on dry rat packs had made me skinny and light; at that very moment I actually felt as weak as a kitten. In a microsecond I realized that if I punched this man he would probably laugh at my weakness and then turn on me and fuck me up. He looked very powerful with his legs planted firmly on the ground and his arms puffed out wide, with the broad stripes of a staff sergeant clean and new on his sleeve. He glared at me. Nevertheless, as he finished his sentence, I threw a right-hand punch that came all the way from Angola and as fast as an RPG-7. It hit him square in the mouth. He fell back onto his haunches into the tent flaps. I remember being surprised that he went down so easily. I charged forward, blind with white rage and punched him three or four more times in his unprotected face as he struggled to get up. I was digging in my knuckles as I landed, and

---

[19] Yes ... and what of it?

already I saw a flash of blood from his mouth. Suddenly I was as strong as a leopard and he as weak as a kitten and I wanted to see his blood run and feel his bones break under my boot. He fell forward onto his hands and knees and I slammed my knee as hard as I could into the side of his face, then grabbed hold of his head with my hand and slammed my knee into his face again and again and again. I felt my knee strike home and he collapsed to the ground in a foetal position, covering his face with his hands as he howled a muffled scream of genuine terror.

"You kill my cats, you motherfucker, I'll kill you!" I roared as I stomped hard into his face with the heel of my boot. My senses lost, I looked around and snatched up the heavy metre-long screwdriver that was lying on the table and in an instant of madness held it high above my head like a dagger, preparing to run him through like the knights of old.

"Gungie, no!" Kurt shouted sharply.

I looked at Kurt's shocked face for a split second. In one fluid movement I flipped the big screwdriver around in mid air and snatched the shaft, bringing the heavy handle crashing down on his back and shoulders as hard as I could, three or four times. He screamed, high-pitched like a girl, as he held his arms tightly over his face, still crouched in a foetal position. I tossed the club across the table and grabbed him by the scruff of his neck and, for some reason, dragged him out of the tent like a sack of maize.

"You're the main fucking guy, hey? ... Main fucking guy, killing my cats! Main fucking guy! Stomp on my cats, motherfucker! I'll stomp on *you*!"

I dragged him several metres from of the tent as he shrieked like a banshee about to be bludgeoned to death. By now a crowd had come running and stood silent, watching mutely. I dumped him on the sand like a sack of shit, stood back and kicked him squarely in the face and felt the fingers that he held tightly against his face for protection, crack. A deadly flood of pure hate was rushing through me. I had lost control. I leaped up and with both feet in the air, landed squarely on his neck and shoulders. I wanted to feel him break. I did it again as he tried to cover his neck with his arms, howling, squealing.

"Jump on my cats, hey? ... I'll fucking jump on you ... jump ... on ... you!" I shouted hoarsely, almost falling as I lost my balance on his head.

Suddenly, in a giddy blur, I came to my senses and stood back and glared down at the pathetic figure crumpled in the sand. He was lying in a tight foetal position, sobbing loudly. He had thick, sweet blood all over his face and hands and down his shirt. His staff sergeant's stripes and the castle above them hung torn around his elbow, splattered with blood. Thick snot hung from his jaw that seemed to be at an odd angle. I caught a whiff of shit as he sobbed loudly in the silence that had suddenly fallen.

"Piece of shit ... big man that kills cats! Come on, let's see how big you are now! Come on, let's see! Stand up, fuckwit ... I see you're not so big now, hey?"

I stood over him with my fists clenched like rocks, daring him to move, but he lay quiet, still curled up, sobbing. A pin could be heard dropping in the white sand as I turned around in disgust and walked towards my kit that was lying by the chopper pad.

A sea of shocked, and delighted, infantrymen parted, making way for me as though I was Moses. I strode mumbling that I should have given the motherfucker some more, to really teach him a lesson.

"Piece of shit ..."

The group of about 20 troops stood gobsmacked, not believing what they had just witnessed. A seriously fucking pissed-off paratrooper with a beard, dressed in a torn-up uniform, had pulled their mean-ass company sergeant-major out of his tent by his hair and kicked the living shit out of him. The whiff of shit was still thick in the air to prove it.

All heads turned to watch me as I strode to my kit with deliberate steps. Still not a word was said. I turned my back on the scene and sat down on my kit bag. With very shaky hands I fumbled for my cigarettes, took one out, but was barely able to light it. I sat alone in the mountains of kit. No one dared come near me.

I smoked quickly, threw the butt down half-smoked and lit another one. My hands had started to shake violently and I suddenly felt exhausted. I felt as weak as a skinny kid, like I was about to faint. I took some slow, deep breaths and told myself to calm down and not worry. They couldn't shoot me. I sat alone for four or five minutes, undisturbed, not once looking back at the scene behind me. I gazed over the sand walls of the camp and out

across the open *chana* towards Angola and the thick bush beyond. A picture
of the SWAPO cadre we had ambushed, propping himself up on his elbows,
looking at me and calling for his mother as John the Fox blew his brains out
came into my mind. The dying SWAPO from the ambush showing me a
'fuck you' sign with his fingers on his chest as he died. I then thought of the
poor, white-haired old man we had shot and left to die. His leg was clean and
bandaged. He was smiling up at me with a slow, morphine-induced smile,
clutching weakly at my wrists, looking into my eyes, nodding and thanking
me for saving his life.

"Korff!"

Captain Verwey, our company OC, yelled at the top of his voice as he
walked across the parade ground towards the chopper pad where I sat.

"Do you think you're the God of Owamboland, or what?"

I had never heard Captain Verwey shout before. He was usually a very
quiet and reserved man. This might have been the only time anyone had ever
heard him shout. I quickly got up and went to meet him halfway.

"What in the name of hell do you think you are doing? You can't beat up a
fucking sergeant-major from another unit, man! What's wrong with you? Do
you understand what you have done?"

I had no words and decided it was best to keep quiet.

He was angry and stood looking at me and the gawking troops with
disbelief. He, too, seemed at a loss for words. He had had a deep frown which
slowly grew into the hint of a smile and I thought I caught a flash of humour
in his eyes as he surveyed the scene with all the infantry troops still milling
around, talking among themselves in hushed tones. Even the Parabats who
had now gathered were, for once, quiet.

Troops rapidly gave way as Captain Verwey and I calmly walked back across
the parade ground to the small, whitewashed brick buildings of the HQ.

I stood at ease outside the HQ door with my legs apart and hands behind
my back, staring straight ahead over the sand walls of the small camp and into
the bush. I had gained control of the violent shaking that had overcome me
but still shook my one knee continuously to conceal my tension. I stood like
this for a couple of minutes as infantry troops walked by, gaping. One small
troop walked hurriedly past and, satisfied that the coast was clear, flashed

me a huge grin and a thumbs-up, and then quickly went back to deadpan as a short, fat, red-faced infantry major came barging out the HQ doors like a bull, almost tripping in his haste to get to me.

He rushed at me furiously, stopping only a few centimetres from my face. His round, red, boozy face was contorted with genuine rage. "You're the troop who beats up sergeant-majors, eh? You want to try me? Eh? Eh? Why don't you try me, you *soutpiel*!"

It crossed my mind that, seeing I was already so deep in the shit, perhaps I should just head-butt this stupid fucking idiot on the nose right now and get it over wit, but I decided to ignore him and stared straight ahead. He was about to try and provoke me further when our little Parabat staff sergeant, our acting company sergeant-major, Greyling, came in, elbowed the idiotic infantry major aside and took my arm. He led me away and made a show of holding my arm like I was a captive as we crossed the opposite way across the parade ground to the small camp *kas*, the jail. As we turned our backs and were a dozen paces from the group of rank that had come out the HQ to eyeball me, he looked straight ahead and gave a huge grin.

He did not turn to me but spoke out the side of his mouth. "Korff, what did you fuck up the sergeant-major for, hey? You can't do that, man! Why did you do it? What happened?"

"He killed our two cats while we were away in the bush, staff," I answered seriously, having regained my composure. "I should have given him more," I smiled.

Staff Greyling shook his head and laughed. He couldn't keep a straight face. "Well, you're in the shit now, my mate ... you're going to sleep in the *kas* tonight, here with SWAPO for starters, then a whole world of *kak* is going to come down on you."

He motioned to the skinny black guy in the cell next to me and locked the steel grill.

I never did get to have my shower or change my clothes and I lay down on a thin blanket in my filthy four-week-old bush clothes and listened to the sounds of 1 Para having a celebration welcome-home party late into the night. I had not even got to wash my face.

I spoke to the confused SWAPO suspect in the other cell and told him that

I was a SWAPO sympathizer and that he should tell me where his buddies were so that we could get word to them. I was still trying to do my duty, even in the *kas*. He did not fall for my trick.

The next morning I was let out and told that 1 Para had gone on a rampage, that not one infantry troop had slept on a foam mattress that night. Hell, they had been our mattresses when we'd left four weeks ago!

HIDDEN FROM VIEW

Whipping post—The Allman Brothers Band

The next morning, D Company rode in Buffels in a long convoy back to Ondangwa. It took extra long because we had to weave through the bush next to the white road due to a recent landmine campaign by our friends from across the border. It was standard procedure anyhow, but this time it seemed to take forever. Kruger and Fourie got into a condensed-milk fight, which had started off as a joke but quickly developed into a real fight with the sticky goo sprayed all over the small ten-man Buffel. Fucking idiots.

The knuckles on my right hand were bruised and painful and I was hardly able to close my fist. Even my knee hurt.

"You did good, Gungie. He deserved every bit you gave him."

"Yeah, I saw him at the HQ ... he was fucked ... couldn't even talk. I think you broke his jaw, 'cause he was mumbling through his teeth. Hey, everyone in the whole camp was behind you, I can tell you that. You just had the balls to do something about it. Even Staff Greyling was cracking up when he came to talk to us last night about taking the infantry's mattresses. Show those fucks not to mess with the fucking Bats! You did the paratroopers proud, boy," Stan was chuffed.

I sat quietly, bouncing up and down as the Buffel manoeuvred over the rough terrain. I felt depleted, small and weak. But I felt right. Fuck that! I had revolted against the machine and had done right and I had no regrets. I was the guardian of the helpless, I was the bringer of bush justice to tyrants and bullies. I was the slayer of fucking giants who ruled with might and force and cruelty. I was a soldier, out there doing the real thing, killing the enemy, while the bully killed helpless kittens back at camp.

We arrived in Ondangwa, the Parabat home. The big parachute and swooping eagle painted on the sign at the ops room told us so. This was a paratrooper camp, with no idiot infantry walking around like Popeye. The juniors had come up early and taken over Fireforce duties, occupying all the tents. There was an excited atmosphere in the camp as rank hurried across the tent square with clipboards in their hands. Big German-built Magirus Deutz trucks stood in a long line next to the chopper pad, loaded high with supplies. Choppers buzzed back and forth overhead. The activity carried on non-stop till late into the night, the ops room's yellow lights burning till past midnight. We dumped all our gear against the sand walls at the back and spent the night in the few empty tents.

I had been released and allowed to return with my company, but would go before a court martial in the town of Oshakati, the operational area HQ, 60 clicks from Ondangwa. The rest of D Company was to leave immediately for parts unknown, to start practising for the big operation that was coming off very soon. No one had a clue what exactly was going on but we knew it would probably be against FAPLA,and that this was it. This was the big one. The big game. The rumours were that we might even go in and take over the whole of Angola, including taking on the 40,000-odd Cubans. Others said we were going to occupy southern Angola in a *blitzkrieg* and sandwich SWAPO between the South West African border and our occupying force. But all the rumours had one thing in common—it was going to be the biggest military operation that South Africa had undertaken since World War Two.

"Be sharp, you guys. Keep your heads down. If it moves, shoot it and if it doesn't move, shoot it until it moves," was my piece of stupid advice as I helped Doogy and Kurt load their kit onto the big trucks the next morning.

"When's the court martial?"

"I've no idea. Verwey said I must stay here ... soon I guess."

"Well, looks like you're going to miss out on the big game, bro. Doep says we're going to be right in the middle of it ... I don't know if you're lucky or not."

Lucky or not—the words rang hollow in my brain as I handed up Doogy's heavy LMG to him. I watched the company loading up. We had become like a big family in the last few months. I watched as they excitedly passed up kit, squabbling over the best spots among the kit bags for the long ride to who knew where.

All I knew was that I should be riding out with them, but that now I had to stay behind to be court martialled while I missed the biggest fucking operation in our history! The big operation that I had been waiting for ... trained for and lost all my toenails for ... I was going to miss it!

"Hey Gungie, mail these off for me, please bro." Stan placed a wad of letters in my hand.

Now I was the fucking mail boy.

It caught on quickly. Half a dozen troops came and handed me letters that they wanted me to post off. I watched, clutching a handful of post, as the big trucks rumbled out past the ops room and down the sand road that led out of the vast air force base. I waved and gave a salute. Doogy laughed and flipped me a middle finger.

The next few days passed slowly. I had moved my kit to the farthest corner of the last tent; no one even knew I was there. I sat alone and when I rolled up my sleeping bag and shoved my kit under the bed I was barely noticeable in the sea of naked yellow foam mattresses. I took the opportunity to thoroughly wash every bit of clothing I had, including my war-booty FAPLA outfit. I borrowed a needle and thread from a junior and stitched my favorite ripped brown shirt and pants as best I could, but not being blessed with much knowledge in the craft of needlework, the stitches came out as if Frankenstein had done them. I had to accept that my prized shirt, now faded almost to white, would have to be retired or at least put on light duty till I got home from this bush trip and my mother could work one of her miracles on it.

I kept a low profile and stayed at the back of the camp behind my tent, only coming out to eat with the juniors and then disappearing again. It was a new experience, being alone in the six-man tent and not surrounded by rowdy troops. I savoured the solitude.

I took time to write some long letters to Taina, telling her how I missed her terribly and that she was certainly my true love, and how I would look at our three stars every night in the bush and think of her. I didn't tell her or anyone else about the incident with the sergeant-major, only saying that I had some time to spend doing Fireforce at Ondangwa.

I told her in code that I had been doing what I had joined up to do. At night

I dreamed of Taina lying in bed with me.

I attended the situation report with the juniors in the morning after parade and breakfast. The war was going well; the lieutenant informed us that July had been the bloodiest month of the year so far, with 93 insurgents killed by July 11, and the month ending with 178 insurgents killed in the operational area. I quietly sat and listened, knowing that my name was responsible for a couple of the 178 statistics and that D Company had accounted for more than 50 of the month's impressive tally of SWAPO scalps.

There was a big drop in SWAPO insurgent activity that month, with only a few locals killed in landmine incidents. It was about this time that SWATF's (South West African Territorial Force) General Lloyd reported on the news that the security forces had formed a buffer zone by carrying out a series of raids into southern Angola, east of Oshikango, using specialist airborne troops.

Hey, that was us! Operation *Ceiling* had made an impact on the struggle against terrorism. We had actually made a dent. A couple of days later, a skinny clerk from the juniors' HQ tracked me down in my hidden retreat and told me that I was to go through to Oshakati on the morning Buffel and was to report to the admin offices.

I dressed in my clean browns and polished boots and headed off. After going from one idiot clerk to another I was finally directed into a small office with an empty desk and two chairs. A young red-haired lieutenant came in five minutes later and greeted me softly. He looked nervous when I stood up and chopped him, saluted. He told me to sit down and informed me that he was to be my counsel for the court martial. I was surprised. I never knew that I would be provided with, or even need, a lawyer. I was starting to see the seriousness of the whole thing. He sat down and told me to relate my version of what had happened, without leaving anything out.

I told him how we had cared for and raised the kittens before we left for Angola and how they slept with us on our beds and that when I heard that this prick had killed them, especially the way that he had killed them, I had seen red and kicked his ass. Pretty straightfoward.

"What did you do in Angola?"

"We went up on a seek-and-destroy operation in platoon strength."

"Yes, but how long did you spend on this patrol?" He studied me attentively, making notes on a couple of sheets of foolscap paper. He looked concerned and sincere, but didn't come across as very assertive or sure of himself. I wondered if he had done this before as he seemed more nervous than me. He stared at me, waiting for the response.

"It wasn't a patrol, it was part of an operation—Operation *Ceiling*—and we spent four weeks in Angola tracking down SWAPO."

"What happened up there? Did you guys have any contact? Was there any shooting?"

I held his gaze and looked at him like he too was an idiot. "Yes, we made a lot of contact ... there was lots of shooting ... our company got almost 60 kills and a few of our guys got shot up too."

He stared at me and looked as if he did not believe me, searching my eyes for signs that I was bullshitting, but when I blankly held his stare he bent down and scribbled a long chapter of notes and looked up again, seemingly excited, as if he was onto something.

"Were you involved in any of these contacts ... I mean, personally involved?"

"Yes, I was." I told him about the ambush and how we were led by the SWAPO deserter to his comrades; how we had wiped them all out and how we had to run for it in the night after we had made contact with FAPLA and killed a number of them; and how they chased us with mortars and a BTR or a T-55 tank. I told him about the old man we had shot and how I had bandaged him up and that we had left him there because the lieutenant did not want to call a chopper. He scribbled as I spoke.

"Well, listen, you go back and take it easy ... I'll send for you in a couple of days, and we'll talk again."

"When will the court martial be?" I asked.

"I don't know for sure, but probably in a couple of weeks."

A couple of weeks!

I rode back to Ondangwa and took refuge in my hidden comer. I started to get a routine going and would go for an early-morning run down the long road that ran around the inside of the 13-square-kilometre base. After I returned I would sneak of for a shower and then hit breakfast. I knew the cooks well so that even if I missed chow, which I often did, I could still score a plate of hot scrambled eggs and bacon or sausage. I also stocked up on canned food from the kitchen, so that I had snacks at night.

I wrote almost daily to Taina or my folks and my brother. I also started to do some sketches on a writing pad. I drew the ambush scene the way I remembered it, with the terrs sitting and standing by the fire under a tree and us lying just a few metres away, rifles pointed at them, waiting for the sun to rise. I called it the Breakfast Party. I suntanned in a plastic chair behind the tent and sipped on ice-cold Cokes from the canteen that opened at about 10:00, and for a few days I forgot about the big operation and the court martial.

One morning some Americans and Rhodesians from 44 Brigade, who had their tents just outside our sand walls, pulled in with their Q-Kars. These were Jeeps rigged up with twin MAGs; one even had a 20-millimetre cannon that had been taken off an old fighter jet, mounted with a big steel protective plate in front of it. On the plate was scrawled 'The Voice of America' in thick black Koki pen.

That night I sauntered across as they sat drinking next to a blazing fire. I recognized the lieutenant in command of the small group as being a guy who had been on the Recce selection course with me. He remembered me. I recalled that it was his third attempt at the Recce course. He had not made it. They had just returned from their part in Operation *Carnation* and were already roaring drunk. I was surprised to learn that they had lost one of the Americans a week earlier in a contact. They didn't seem too remorseful about it; in fact they scorned the one troop who had been killed because he'd stood up in the middle of a fire fight to lob a grenade like he'd seen it done in a John Wayne movie and had been cut down instantly.

I spent the night drinking brandy with them and they pissed themselves laughing when I told them the sergeant-major story. They accepted me because of this, slapped me on the back and plied me with straight brandy after the Coke ran out. I spoke to a couple of Yanks with thick airborne tattoos on their forearms who said they had been in Vietnam. I tried to prise some stories from them but they seemed tight-lipped and unwilling to talk in front of their comrades. They just shook their heads as they took long swigs of brandy.

"It was a fuck-up," was about all I could get out of them. (I learned later

227

that one of the unwritten rules when joining a foreign army and its war was not to talk about 'How we did it in Vietnam or Rhodesia', but to forget that you'd been there because nobody is interested in how you did it then. This was another army and another war.)

The one guy was still using his old M16 and said it was the same one he had used in Vietnam and that it was a good rifle. His partner jeered him, saying that it was a piece of shit and said that he had almost got killed in Vietnam when his magazine fell out during a fire fight.

"You've got to push your magazine all the way in until it clicks, shithead," his partner said quietly. He patted the South African-made R4 next to him "This is a rifle ... it's made here in South Africa to shoot kaffirs with," he said in a thick Louisiana accent. He seemed a nice guy, almost out of place. I wondered how he had got involved in a tiny war so far from home.

As the night went on they became raucous and rowdy, with one American falling in the fire and almost catching alight. They laughed and squabbled, and I felt that there could be an argument at any minute, that one of them would pick up his loaded R4 and start shooting around the fire. I decided in my drunken state that I would definitely not like to go into battle with this loose-goose crowd.

They were mostly much older than me, probably in their thirties, but I got on well with a Rhodesian guy around my age, whom they called 'Mad Irish'. He told me that he had lied to join the Rhodesian army at the age of 16 and had been shooting terrs for five years. They mocked him as being totally mad and because he had driven into contact in the Q-Kar with his two .357 revolvers blazing like a cowboy. Mad Irish and I sat by the fire, as drunk as lords, and had long rambling conversations about bullshit, only getting up now and then to puke or piss. We had become quite good mates by the time the night was through and he encouraged me to try and get transferred to his "merry band of losers", which would have been impossible.

I made the mistake of sleeping late the next morning, with a huge hangover, and almost fell out of bed when a voice like a bullhorn bellowed at me, rattling my bruised brain against my skull. I was asked who the fuck I was and what I thought I was doing sleeping at 08:30 in his base?

I stuttered sluggishly that I was from D Company and was waiting for a court martial in Oshakati. This seemed to stir some vague recollection in him and it only made him even more furious.

"Get the fuck out of here, you rotten piece of shit, and start chicken parade around the camp!"

I contemplated trying to kick his ass, which had lately become my standard secret joke when any rank gave me trouble, but decided he would probably shoot me, so I hastily threw on my browns and began to search in between the tents for litter, my brain almost bursting every time I bent down to pick up a cigarette butt.

I had made an enemy and my little holiday was over. The next morning I was on parade with the juniors and put to work in the kitchen afterwards, loading sacks of onions and potatoes. The beady-eyed cunt from the morning before drove me unmercifully and had me doing chicken parade when there wasn't an ounce of litter in the entire camp. For days the juniors sat relaxing around the pool in pants and boots, on standby for Fireforce and sympathetically watching me trudging around the small base looking for butts. Enough was enough. I was no chicken-parade, chickenshit troopie just up from training like this dickhead captain who had come up with the juniors. I had never even seen him before. Probably just got his wings the other day! I quickly figured on a plan to fuck the irritating captain over, and so one morning informed him with a smart salute that I had to go into Oshakati to see my lawyer about the court martial. He mumbled and grudgingly sent me on my way into town with the morning transport.

Hey, I was AWOL, and sat shoulder to shoulder in the Buffel with airborne lieutenants and sergeants I did not know. I wondered if it was compulsory when you got rank to be an asshole. I wondered whether they take classes on how to fuck with troops and make life a misery for them, to make them hate the army, or whether it was just the personal preference of each individual officer. I decided that they probably did give classes on the shit.

In Oshakati, a small civilian town as well as the operational area HQ, I grooved around the base with a mean, purposeful look in my eye. No one bothered me; they probably all thought I had some business being there ... otherwise I would not be there.

I had a peaceful and tasty lunch at the canteen, which was full of noisy medics, MPs and services troops. I even got a look of respect when they glanced at the maroon paratrooper beret which I wore at a rakish angle. I still had most of the R200 left over that John and I had taken from the SWAPO we had shot, so I cruised downtown and put the money to good use. I bought some shorts, a watch and an 'electric' shaver you wound up like a lawn mower with a few good pulls on a cord. It ran for minutes by itself till you had to tug the cord again a couple of times. It gave a great shave.

I walked down to the post office (which was bombed soon after we left the operational area, killing 20 civilians) and called Taina collect. It was unbelievable to hear her voice; she squealed with delight when she picked up the phone and heard who it was. I felt a physical stab of pain in my heart when I put the receiver back in the cradle.

Back at Ondangs the following morning I was informed by the clerk that this time I had to go to Oshakati to see the lawyer for real, so it was back to town the next day.

"Well, it doesn't look too good for you. You hurt this sergeant-major quite badly, you know. He has a broken jaw and a broken collarbone. Tell me ... did you use any weapon or instrument to hit him with?"

"No, not at all," I lied.

I knew that the sergeant-major hadn't seen me use the big screwdriver, because he was huddled up with his hands over his face at the time. He must have thought that I punched like hell. Kurt was the only one who had seen it and I knew that I was safe with him. The red-haired lieutenant looked at me again with disbelief.

"He says you might have hit him with something."

"No, I didn't."

"They are saying that you are some kind of boxer or something. What's all that about?"

"Nothing. I haven't boxed in years. Anyway, I heard he was some kind of amateur champion, so that should even that out."

"Well, that's not the point—you're the one who beat the shit out of him, and he's saying you might have used some kind of weapon. If you did, you're going to be in deep trouble. As it stands, they want to haul you over the coals and I don't think we have much to go on. I'm going to try and push the fact that you were personally involved in a lot of action in Angola and that you were looking forward to seeing your pets. And when you found out they had been killed you weren't thinking straight ... and that you are very sorry for what you have done."

I still felt no remorse for kicking the idiot's ass but nodded my head solemnly in agreement.

There was a pause, the lieutenant assuming we were done.

"What kind of sentence could I get, lieutenant?"

"Well, I've got to tell you that you could spend the rest of your service in DB and, if there was a weapon involved like they say, you could even go to civvy jail when your service is up."

I was shocked. The next seven months in DB, or maybe jail! I had never dreamed that the outcome could be so bad; in fact I hadn't really thought of the consequences at all. I had no idea what to expect, but now the possibility of spending the next seven months in DB shook me to the core. For the first time, I really appreciated the gravity of my situation.

COURT MARTIAL

I heard it through the grapevine—Creedence Clearwater Revival

The court martial was scheduled for the next Tuesday, a week away. I rode back to Ondangwa feeling low and depressed. I had fucked up big time. What a disgrace to spend the rest of my service in DB while my buddies were fighting in the biggest operation at what seemed to be the height of the war. I had let myself down. I had let my guard down and let my emotions get the better of me. I had opened the door and let the demon of chaos in which I could normally control with an iron fist—and now I was to pay the price. Hadn't I learned anything from the numerous temper-related troubles I had been through in the past? I thought of what my parents would say. They would be so disappointed in me for fucking up. My mom and dad were proud that I was in the Parabats doing my bit; now they would have to come and visit me in DB. And all the bullshit training I had been through—now possibly all for nothing. Why did I do it? What's wrong with you, man?

Back at Ondangs I received a parcel from Taina with a bottle of Green Island Jamaican rum in it. I read her letter, got drunk and spent the night talking to the juniors and answering their questions about what it was like to be in a contact. They were all ears.

They had not yet completed their training but had come up early to take over Fireforce duties while the senior companies were on the 'big ops'. I enjoyed the attention and respect and laid on the bush-soldier image a little too thickly, but I felt I had the right. These were our juniors and in the five months on the border D Company had already chalked up 80 kills, so I could lay it on a bit. I told them how we had sneaked up on SWAPO and ambushed them deep in Angola and how we had hit a FAPLA observation base and had been chased by a T-55 tank through the bush, barely escaping with our lives, and causing an international incident. They were impressed and gathered around me, clamouring with eager questions.

"What's it feel like in a contact ... do you shit yourself?"

"It's just like a street fight—keep on punching, don't stop. You've just got to pull your ass tight, go for it and keep shooting, try and keep cool and think. In this kind of close contact half of it is the noise. The side that makes the biggest noise makes the other side crack. Just keep shooting."

I sat coolly on the edge of the bed as if this was how I always acted in a fire fight, smoked one of their cigarettes and looked at the group of eager faces almost worshipping me.

"What about this big operation, senior?"

"Is D Company going to be in it?"

"If they hit FAPLA, won't all those Cubans be with them?"

"It'll be a massive operation!"

"You guys might even be in it if the shit really hits the fan ... you might be up there in Angola shooting FAPLA before you can say lickety-split. They'll just wake you up one night, issue you with grenades, put you on a chopper and half an hour later you're facing a T-55 tank—that's how fast it goes down."

They smiled at each other at the prospect of action so soon. These young juniors I was talking to wouldn't be smiling a year or so later. In fact, their company was to end up seeing the most action of us all—they would lose 12 troops when the Puma helicopter carrying them into Angola on Operation *Meebos* was shot down by anti-aircraft guns hidden among the trees, ploughing into the ground at high speed, killing everyone aboard.

For some reason the tormenting, beady-eyed captain had disappeared from the scene, and so again my days were laid back with long suntanning sessions and cold Cokes. I had been thinking about the whole scene. If I went to DB for the rest of my service, at least I would not get my ass shot off and would be in Bloemfontein. Taina could come and visit me and before I knew it I'd be done and out the army, getting on with my life. This wasn't life, walking around the bush shooting people. Get on with life? Get on with what? I had no idea what I was going to do once I had finished the army. I had given it little thought. My brother was at university getting his marketing degree, but further studies were out for me—I had just skinned by, getting my matric after screwing the English teacher, and that was on my own, studying in the city library. What was I going to do?

I had sometimes thought of signing up and making a career of the army but lately that had turned sour. Fucking up a sergeant-major wouldn't look good on my file and I would definitely stay a private forever. No, to hell with the fucking army. I could belt out some good rock and roll—perhaps I could sing in a rock band, become famous, live the good life and drive around in a Mercedes sports. Music, maybe?

The other thing was sport. If I trained like hell and put everything into boxing I could turn professional and maybe get to the top and make millions, or at least give it a shot. All this thinking just made me more depressed. I decided to go on some long runs. I ran round the big base once in the morning and again in the late afternoon; I went to the little weight gym and worked out hard with the concrete-filled paint cans till I was dripping with sweat and my muscles ached the following day. But I pushed myself to do it over and over again.

One of the pathfinders for D Company arrived and dumped his kit in my empty tent. He had come back because he was scheduled to have knee surgery at Oshakati. I was happy to have the company and some information.

"Ja ... we're all camped up about 80 clicks straight up the main tar road. It's really *kak*; there's maybe a thousand troops there. Every day we're doing the same thing—digging trenches. We spent days digging these long fucking trenches and bunkers, then for the last two weeks we've been assaulting them. There are about 20 Mirages that come in first and do dummy bomb-drops. The infantry's there, medics, panzers with Ratels, everyone. It's a big fucking operation going down. You're fucking lucky you're not doing it."

"What's going on, what's the target?"

"Ag, I don't know ... nobody knows yet but it's obviously a very big base and D Company is the spearhead for one of the attacks. We're going in right up front and we're going to be taking the trenches, with all the rest following up. I think there's going to be a few attacks. We've spent days doing fire and movement into the trenches and then throwing grenades into bunkers to clear them. It's a full-on conventional attack, *broer*. We've got Ratels and

Elands and artillery behind us. You must hear those howitzers, man! Fuck, it's loud … can't believe it! What's going on with you? I heard about the sergeant-major … are you fucking crazy, man?"

"I'll probably get DB till I *klaar* out."

"Shit, china, that's rough … Hey, where can I get some chow here?"

I gave him a few cans from my stash.

★★★★★

I marched into the big gloomy room in double-quick time and came to a sharp halt in the middle of the floor. The walls were dark; my halt seemed to echo off them. In front of me was a long row of tables pushed together, behind which sat seven or eight big knobs with piles of paper in front of them.

I couldn't even tell what rank they were because I had never before seen the kind of stuff they had on their shoulders. They had an ugly assortment of orange and blue and brown berets from different units. I felt a twinge of pride as I stood stiffly at attention with my dark maroon airborne beret at an angle on my head.

"Take that beret off!" a voice boomed sharply at me. The corporal who had marched me in snatched my beret off my head and handed it to me. He seemed as nervous as I was. I stood staring straight ahead of me but in my peripheral vision I could see that this was a group of no-nonsense, mean motherfuckers. They shuffled papers and growled at each other in low snapping tones. I had the distinct feeling that they did not like paratroopers. Finally a thin, bespectacled, mean-looking commandant-general, brigadier-or-something started reading some preamble in rapid-fire Afrikaans that I had no chance of following. I did, however, catch the word 'sergeant-major'.

The thin man finished and sat down, then barked at my counsel who stood up and came forward nervously, shuffling his sheets of paper. He performed just like I was afraid he would. He began speaking in English in a weak little voice that was barely audible in the big room; even I could hardly hear him and he was right next to me. The same voice that commanded my beret to be removed roared at him to speak up. He was clearly shitting himself,

235

overawed by the quantity of scrambled egg on the shoulders of the men he was addressing. He turned it up half a notch, shooting through his delivery of my defence seemingly in one breath. I was done for. I had a sinking feeling in my gut. Was that it? Chicken shit! *I* could have done better than that and I stutter!

The voice boomed again and the 3 SAI sergeant-major whose ass I had kicked marched smartly into the room and came to an impressive halt on the smooth polished floor. I could see that he was a lifer. He sat down on a wooden chair and began to give his testimony of what had happened. He kept his beret on. I was surprised when he opened his mouth and spoke in a small, almost pleading voice, in Afrikaans. All I could pick up was the bit at the end: "And then he kicked me and jumped on me," as he pointed dramatically to his shoulder and neck.

He also said that he had been ordered to get rid of the cats by the camp CO the day before. The brass barked a couple of questions at him, which he answered meekly like a child talking to his father, not at all like the fire-eating, kitten-killing Popeye character I had tried to kick to death a month before.

Perhaps I was wrong and he was a decent sort. Maybe I was the fuck-up. The way he spoke was very humble and human. I glanced at him out of the corner of my eye; he looked small and harmless, and I felt a brief sense of remorse but quickly changed my mind when I remembered the unalterable fact of him stomping the kitten to death. I changed my way of thought. He was probably so humble because someone—me—had finally and properly kicked the shit out of him. This much was true as I later found out from the 3 SAI troops. He was never the same man after his troops had seen the crazed paratrooper giving him the mother and father of all beatings right in front of them.

My counsel seemed to have found some courage from somewhere. He stood up at his wooden desk with his few pages in his hand. "These are young servicemen who have come straight from high school to do their duty. They do it for the security of our country and for their families, as we all do. Those who enter combat units are thrust straight from school into close-combat situations. Consideration has to be given to the fact that the accused is in a fighting unit and had personally been involved in numerous contacts just prior to the incident."

"Yes, that's my man … go for it. You tell 'em!"

My counsel seemed to have found a crack in the proverbial dyke. He persisted bravely, standing somewhat squarely behind his empty desk. He had a determined look on his face as he lifted his notes and made a broad, sweeping gesture with them when he came to the part where I had discovered that the kittens had been killed. It seemed out of character. The panel of slavering pit bulls let him talk for a minute, glaring at him in silence with knuckled foreheads.

"I have a letter of recommendation here from the accused's company commander, Captain Verwey. In it the captain states that Rifleman Korff is a likable, good troop who has always pulled his weight and has never been a troublemaker. He has performed well in the bush and has been at the forefront of recent actions across the border in Angola."

He handed the letter to the corporal, who came forward and then handed it to a short, fat commandant who had been sitting quietly at the end of the long table.

"In these circumstances, away from family and loved ones, the men form strong attachments with pets and suchlike for comfort and possibly feel more for them than they would under normal circumstances."

"Lieutenant, you are repeating yourself. I say to you again, troops are not permitted to have pets of any sort in the operational area, or in their base camps in South Africa!" The voice boomed out in surprisingly good English and cut off the brave red-haired lieutenant in mid-sentence, signalling the close of my defence.

My counsel quickly lost heart and swallowed his words. He sat down and shuffled his papers distractedly.

I stared straight ahead at the brown prefabricated wall behind the panel of pit bulls as they swapped notes and snapped and growled into each other's ears. I felt the same feeling of helplessness I used to have when I was sent down to the school principal's office and stood in front of him. It was a childhood feeling of having been bad and being caught and reprimanded. My brain seemed frozen in this childlike state of catatonic helplessness. I shifted my eyes back and forth along the prefabricated wall in an attempt to rearrange my thoughts and snap out of it. Why did I always end up in these situations? Why was it always me? Why hadn't someone else beaten the shit out of this prick?

I didn't have time to come to a conclusion in my soul-searching. It seemed that they had decided my fate alarmingly quickly. Boom Voice cleared his throat and bellowed on again in rapid Afrikaans for a minute, building to a climax that came quickly. Then he sat down and passed some notes to his colleagues.

The corporal, who'd been standing in the doorway, came forward to a snappy halt next to me, sharply saluted the panel and turned to me. "Right turn! Out the building, double-quick time! Forward ... march! Leftrightleftrightleft ..."

I marched through the doorway like a wind-up toy, unable to step in time to his quick-fire commands. Outside, he dismissed me on the concrete pathway and flashed the shadow of a smile as he shook his head slightly. Although he said nothing, I could tell that he was thinking—"What a bunch of dicks".

The corporal took off and I stood uneasily in the shade of the covered walkway as sundry admin motherfuckers walked past me with piles of paperwork and relaxed attitudes. They seemed to be having a great time, bullshitting and laughing easily. Just like any job in Civvy Street. Five minutes later the red-haired lieutenant came out and gestured to me with his head as we walked briskly to his small office a few buildings down.

"What happened, what did I get?" I had no idea what Boom Voice had been saying on my fate.

"Well, it looks like luck is smiling on you, Korff. You got a one-year sentence, suspended for three years. It's a longer sentence than I expected, but it is suspended. If you put a foot wrong in the next three years you'll go to DB for a year, which will be carried over to civvy jail if your service is up while you are in DB.

I didn't quite get the gist of what he was saying at the time, but all I knew was that I wasn't going to DB. Even though I had prepared myself for the worst, in a way I was not surprised at the verdict as I had never really felt I would go to DB from day one. Somehow the picture of me in DB had never registered in my brain. Maybe God was looking after me after all. Maybe He had used me as his instrument of bush justice. Maybe.

"I think that letter of recommendation from your captain helped a lot. Also that you guys have got this big operation that's going on any time now and they need every man they can get in your unit."

I felt a gush of gratitude towards Captain Verwey. I went to the lieutenant's office and signed some papers. I shook his hand and thanked him.

"Stay out of trouble now, eh—no more beating up sergeant-majors!" He had a smile on his face.

"No, I won't, lieutenant." I came smartly to attention and saluted him. He returned a casual salute and I walked out the door. Outside I felt like jumping up and down and whooping a Red Indian whoop but I walked casually, on air, to the canteen where I could grab some decent chow before I caught the ride back to Ondangwa. I couldn't believe my luck and was unable to wipe the stupid grin off my face as I chowed down. As far as I knew the 'big ops' hadn't started yet, so I might even be able to make it in time to join the action. Now I just had to find out where the hell D Company was.

Back at Ondangwa I jumped off the Buffel, beaming. It was hard to keep the smile off my face. I felt joyously happy. I was a free man ... it was over! My soul soared like an eagle after being released from the dark three-week depression I had slipped into, sitting alone in my tent and waiting for this fucking court martial to be over. I walked among the tents on the way to the canteen and bumped into one of the corporals of the junior E Company, talking to a few of his troops in the doorway.

One of the good things about the Parabats was the respect shown between the senior and junior companies that didn't really exist to the same extent in other units. A senior rifleman could even throw a bit of attitude around a junior corporal and probably get away with it. The only difference between a senior and junior company was the difference of six months between intakes of troops for national service.

I questioned the corporal with new vigour and bearing. "Corporal. Do you know anything about this big op? Has it started?"

He looked at me and, recognizing me as a senior, dropped the aggressive attitude he was inflicting on the group of juniors and answered me respectfully, even though I was just a rifleman and he had two stripes on his arm.

"No, I'm not sure … but I don't think so. But it should be soon, because I know that D and H companies have been up training for it for the last three weeks. They're going to be involved in it."

"Yes I know. I'm in D Company and I need to get back to them as soon as possible."

"Well, you better speak to Captain Swart. He'll be back at 14:00."

"Thank you, corporal."

Captain Swart, the tormentor! I couldn't wait to tell him that my business was done and I'd be moving on. I strolled back to my tent, pulled off my army boots and put on my worn blue sneakers, which had become a habit. I lit a cigarette and lay back against my folded-up sleeping bag as I contemplated my good fortune. A hot ray of sun blazed through an open tent flap and burned my legs. It felt good.

If I could find out exactly where the company was, I could join them immediately. They would probably have to send a Buffel to take me out there. They needed every man for this op … shit, if they're going to hit FAPLA, there's going to be a small war. Captain Verwey said that I was a good troop who pulled his weight. I needed to be with my company!

I felt a new buzz of loyalty to my company and to my OC, Captain Verwey, and a rush of excitement at the chance of making it in time to be part of the mother of all cross-border operations into Angola. I sat back, deep in thought, and lit another cigarette. I had sworn that I would quit after the retching incident, where I was almost shot dead while coughing and puking my lungs out when we'd hit the FAPLA troops. I would have died in mid-puke. What a way to go! I had stopped for a couple of days afterwards but was soon back to puffing a pack a day. I blew a big cloud of smoke and watched it drift lazily to the top of the hot tent.

My 21st birthday was in two days time. This was a good thing, except that for the last two years in a row, the evening before my birthday had been cursed with weird bad luck. On both occasions, almost to the hour, around 23:00, I had been arrested on possession of weed charges and spent both birthdays in jail. I mean, what are the chances of that? It was uncanny and must have had something to do with the alignment of the stars when I was born—not that I believed in that crap, of course, but perhaps there was something to it after all. Anyway, this time it looked as if the spell had been broken and that luck was working for me and not against me. I decided to slip over to the canteen and pick up a couple of ice-cold Cokes and a chocolate bar to celebrate.

On the way I spotted my nemesis, the beady-eyed cunt, Captain Swart. He was in the small mess, walking out towards the kitchen.

"Hey, there's my man!"

I couldn't wait to give him the good news, that I needed to be taken back to rejoin my company. I walked quickly around the back of the mess and planned to catch him as he came out the other side at the kitchen door. He had just driven in from Oshakati in a big supply truck and was roaring at a dozen juniors who were in the process of unloading the truck, but not quickly enough for his satisfaction. I waited on the side for him to finish his assault, then, as he turned to head back to the officers' quarters, I jogged up to him. He spun on his heels and glared at me.

I came to attention in the sand and threw a smart salute. "Captain, I'm finished with the court martial. It's over and I need to get back to my company. They are going on an operation."

He glared at me with nothing short of hatred in his eyes. "What kind of shit, slack-ass fuck-up of a salute is that? Do it over, troop!"

I was taken back by the ferocity of his response but, nevertheless, slammed my foot hard into the sand and swung my arm up to my forehead and chopped it down to my side like a knife and stood stiffly to attention. "My court martial is over, captain. I want to rejoin my company," I repeated, louder.

He looked me up and down like I had dropped from the sky or something and glanced down at my blue sneakers. "Why the fuck haven't you got boots on?"

I had forgotten that I still had my sneakers on. I hadn't planned on meeting him this way. "My feet give me trouble, captain. My lieutenant has given me permission to wear them. He knows about it."

He was quick on the uptake. "Your feet give you trouble but you want to go on an operation into Angola with your company?" He looked me up and down again, like I was a piece of shit, sneering as though I was out of my mind to have even considered such a ridiculous request.

"Well, they're not that bad, captain ... my lieutenant allows me to wear them."

I knew that he had me well and truly pinned in a corner and that something not good was about to happen.

He responded in a second. "Well, I don't give a flying fuck what your lieutenant allows you to do, troop. If your feet are injured, then you will sick-report to the hospital and go on light duty. No, you cannot join your company. Yes, you will sick-report immediately and you will bring me the report so that I can see it! Do you understand?"

He shook his head vigorously to emphasize his point. I saw a glint of satisfaction in his eye as he saw I was unable to hide my disappointment. I stared at him, stunned.

"And you do that right away. I'm waiting for the report! You find me and bring it to me *today*!"

"Yes, captain."

I saluted and turned away, walking back past the mess towards my tent, my mind reeling, shoulders slumped. I sat down on my bed, feeling numb. I stared out at the white sand walls but did not see them. I get through this court martial and now this fucking idiot says I must sick-report and go on light duty! While my company's fighting FAPLA in Angola I must walk around the camp in sandals, picking up cigarette butts!

In a flash, I knew what I was going to do.

There was going to be no way in hell this prick was going to ruin a once-in-a-lifetime opportunity to do what I had joined up to do. I had gone through too much bullshit to get to this point ... days—maybe hours—away from taking part in a massive operation into Angola.

I sat for a while and gathered my thoughts.

"Fuck that, let's go!" I said aloud in the empty tent and stood up. I ripped my folded *balsak* from under my bed and began cramming in clothes, boots and water bottles. I pulled out my big brown H-frame bush-pack and stuffed in my blue sneakers, chest webbing, Fireforce vest and loaded magazines. I peered through the tent flaps to see if anyone was around. There was no one.

I threw my rifle over my shoulder. I was cool and focused once again. I was going to join my company for this operation, even if I had to go AWOL to do it. The captain can go suck on a fucking egg. Cunt!

It was about 14:00 when I slipped, heavily laden, over the sand wall at the back of our tent square with my H-frame on my back, my big *balsak* duffel bag over one shoulder and my rifle over the other. I took the long way, around the air force tents and PF quarters and cut through some workshops, taking the road that led through the huge air force camp to the gates about a click away. I prayed that the dickhead captain would not drive out on the offchance and see me. The chances were slim as he had just returned from a supply run to Oshakati.

Hansen, the pathfinder who had come in for knee surgery, had told me the training grounds were about 80 to a hundred clicks down the main tar road, towards the Etosha Pan game reserve. That was all I knew but it was enough for me. Before I was even out of the main camp, a big water truck rumbled past me. I threw out my thumb. He braked and came to a stop 50 or so metres ahead, throwing up a cloud of dust.

"Yes?"

I ran through the dust cloud with my kit bouncing on my back, reached the door and pulled it open. The driver was a pleasant, overweight chap with a jolly face and a black moustache.

"Where are you going?" he asked in a thick Afrikaans accent.

"I'm not sure where it is, but I'm heading down the main road to where they're training for this operation. I think it's about 80 clicks down that way. Where are you going?"

"That's where I'm headed right now. I'm taking water there ... hop in."

I hauled my heavy kit up to him and he pulled it all into the cab. I knew for sure now that God was definitely looking after my butt. We drove out of the gates of the air force base of Ondangwa and turned left onto the long black tar road that cut through the bush like a mamba.

"What are you doing that you're going down there?" he asked, thrusting an open pack of Camels at me. I gladly took one and pulled my own red lighter out and lit it, enjoying the strong smoke. It had been a while since I'd had a Camel.

"I was in hospital for some check-ups, but I'm medically okay and now I have to get back to my company," I lied.

He puffed on his Camel, pleased to have the company. "You a paratrooper, eh?" he said, glancing at my maroon beret. "I saw your guys training at the grounds. Looks like it's going to be a big operation. I heard they're going to hit all the FAPLA bases and the Cubans at the same time and sort them out once and for all. About time."

"Yeah, it's about time, alright," I agreed, puffing on the smoke. Shit, I hadn't heard about the Cubans bit. That was news to me.

"Are you guys going to jump in? Don't you get scared jumping out a plane?"

"Naw, you get used to it … it's like falling out of a tree … you just let go."

"You'd never catch me jumping from a plane. I've been up here six months straight. I usually drive a honeysucker but I've been taking water up to the training grounds for the last three weeks. It's pretty shit out there, all fine red sand, you'll see. All the guys are sleeping in holes and they've been at it for three weeks now. It must be a big operation if you have to train for three weeks!"

"Yeah, must be," I puffed on the Camel.

He changed down and the heavy truck shuddered so hard I thought it would fall apart, the gear knob rattling like a Ginger Baker drum solo.

"Does this truck always ride this smoothly?"

"Ja, it's a piece of junk. This is its third engine."

We settled down for the ride and I stared out the window at the passing bush and contemplated my situation. Since I had made up my mind to leave I had felt as happy and excited as a runaway kid, but now a flutter of worry lay in my gut.

I had just been court martialed that morning, not even three hours ago, and told not to put a foot wrong for the rest of my service and beyond or I would go to DB for a year. Yet here I was, not three hours later, defying the camp CO's orders and going AWOL out of camp. And I wondered why I was always in the shit?

I studied the thick thorn trees next to the road and automatically started scanning the bush. Our senior company had killed six terrs walking on this same road just eight months ago. It had happened the first hour we had arrived at Ondangwa as juniors and we had been impressed no end.

I pulled my rifle closer to my leg and slipped off into a fantasy of us running into a group of terrs walking casually next to the road. I knew exactly what to do—shout at the truck driver to drive his truck at them as far as he could as they scattered into the bush, and then to give cover with his R1. As they scattered I would jump from the truck and calmly pour fire into them as they ran. They would be green troops on their first infiltration, and panicking. I would take two or three of them out before they could react and run away. Having no radio contact, we would load the dead terrs onto the side of the water truck and carry on with our journey to the training grounds, rolling to a stop in front of the boys of D Company. As they'd gather around the truck, dripping with SWAPO, I'd hop out of the cab and casually tell them I'd run into some trouble on the way.

I laughed at myself, closed my eyes and tried to catch a snooze but it was impossible in the rock-and-roll water truck.

"It's not to much further ... I can't take you into your guys. I'm going on a bit further, but I'll show you where to go."

A while later he brought the heavy truck to a stop and pointed through the cloud of red dust. "Just go straight through the bush about two clicks in. You'll come on them."

I followed his finger and saw no road or path, nothing but virgin bush. "Where? Through there?"

He laughed, seeing my doubt. "Yes, this is a shortcut, otherwise you'll have to go all the way around."

"Okay ..."

"Go straight, I'm telling you. You're going to come right onto your guys."

I heaved out my kit and thanked him. He waved a beefy hand as he pulled the heavy truck back onto the road, billowing black smoke. I watched him go and stood enjoying the sudden silence and solitude of standing alone next to the hot tar road in the quiet bush. When the truck was a speck in the distance I hauled up my kit and cheerfully broke into the bush in the direction he had pointed.

Immediately my boots sank into the fine red dust, scuffing up small puffs as I plodded along, pushing branches out of my way. He wasn't kidding about the fucking red sand! I struggled through the bush with my load and was soon breathing hard and swearing as the awkward *balsak* kept slipping off my shoulder. A beautiful-looking bird with a half-metre-long black tail sat on a thorny dead branch and shrilled at me as I walked past. The truck driver must be mad—there is no one out here! The bush was still, except for the bird that now followed me in a slow manic flight, with its long tail seemingly too heavy for his body. It found a tree in front of me and shrilled incessantly; it seemed to be cursing me for disturbing it. I put my head down and pushed on for a few hundred metres and, as I came out of a thicket and was just about to start cursing the driver, I saw a couple of water bowsers some distance ahead. They were hardly visible and blended into the bush with their matt-brown colouring, but a couple of shirtless troops bent over and washing huge pots caught my eye. I walked towards the trucks.

"Hey, you guys know where the Bats are staying out here?"

One troop pointed casually straight ahead and went back to his chores. I plodded on breathlessly through another thicket, and then literally walked into D Company. I didn't recognize them for a second because they all looked like hell. They were sitting around in small groups, fiddling with kit and rifles. They were long-haired, unshaven and grimy with red dust. I walked into the midst of them, beaming from ear to ear.

"Hey, hey … look who's here!"

"Oh no, look what's come out of the bush ... better warn the sergeant-major!"

"Hey Korff, what happened to you?"

I walked through the small groups of guys, grinning like a Cheshire cat and answering their questions with witty chirps. I saw *Valk* 4 over by some tents and trudged over to them, dumping my kit down against a thorn tree.

"Hey, Gungie!" John Delaney looked up. He was sitting cross-legged in the sand, filling his magazines from a pile of shiny new 5.56 cartridges piled in his bush hat, and laying them out on an army towel. He looked sullen.

Stan came zipping out of a tent, looking equally as dirty and worn, but with a big smile. "Hey, *braa,* what's it? Tell me the news!"

I smiled and lit up the extra Camel that the truck driver had given me. "Aww, I got a suspended sentence. No big deal ... it was worth it. What's going on here?" I glanced at the sullen faces around me who barely gave me a cursory nod. The platoon carried on with its seemingly urgent rifle-cleaning and packing the big H-frame backpacks, unexcited about my homecoming.

Stan seemed to be the only one smiling. "We're going on a big op, Gungie. We've been fucking training here in this dump for three weeks. We're going to hit FAPLA's main base, boy. It's fucking huge—there must be a thousand troops involved as back-up and stopper groups. Artillery, Mirages, Ratels ... the works, and guess what? They're all behind us. We're going in front and will be doing fire and movement into their trenches."

"Trenches?"

"Yeah. Trenches and bunkers. We've been practising taking them out every day. And we're crossing the border tonight, my man. You just made it. Did you know that we were leaving?"

"Naw ... I fucking AWOLed Ondangwa and hitched up here, *broer.*"

I had made it just hours before the op. What luck!

"Hey, you better go tell Sergeant-Major Sakkie you're here."

I looked at the pile of M27 grenades lying on a tarpaulin under a tree.

"Sakkie is here?"

"Yeah, they sent him up for the op."

It must be something special if they had sent Sakkie up. Sergeant-Major Sakkie was the RSM back in Bloemfontein. He was the symbol of 1 Parachute Battalion. It took me a year to realize he was only a fraction taller than me as he projected a physical aura so overwhelming that, to me and everyone else, without exception, he looked like a monster. He was a model soldier ... with muscles on his jawbone. When he spoke casually it was almost as loud as a normal man's shout; he could easily hold a conversation with someone 100 metres away. When he shouted, which he loved doing, it was something to behold and you came away thinking you had experienced some kind of awesome natural phenomenon. He was the pride of the battalion at inter-unit parades too, when he brought the whole Parachute Battalion to attention four times louder that any other unit's sergeant-major in flawless and perfect time. I always thought he would be killer as a rock and roll singer and had missed his calling.

I looked around quickly over my shoulder.

"He's over there at the tents. You better go."

I walked over to the tents and came up to Sakkie who was roaring at some services troops to pull down a group of tents. He looked to be having a good time cheerfully yelling at the sweating soldiers. I figured he was happy to be up in the bush, away from 1 Parachute Battalion. He barely looked at me as I came to a relaxed bush attention.

"Sergeant-Major, I've just come in from Ondangwa. I've missed all the training. I just got here now."

I respected him. Even though he could rearrange your hairstyle with his enormous voice, he wasn't like a lot of the rest of the rank who seemed to have a personal prejudice against the troops. Although he could be a mean bastard (the story went that he once killed a troop doing CD—corrective drill), he was naturally good-natured.

He seemed in a good mood. "Korff ... you the one that fucked up the infantry sergeant-major? What happened to you, shit-for-brains?" he asked matter-of-factly. Word had spread far and wide.

"I got a suspended sentence, sergeant-major."

"You're lucky. They should have locked you up," he said with dry humour.

"Yes, sir ..."

"You can't go around re-orientating infantry sergeant-majors. What do you think they'll think of paratroopers now? They'll think we're a bunch of hooligans!"

He turned to *Valk* 4, some 50 metres away, and shouted at them. "You men, show this man where he can pull new ammunition, grenades, field dressings and rat packs. Show him what we've been training for here. Go through trench deployment and bunker clearing and how to work with the panzers."

I paused and caught him as he started walking away.

"Sergeant-Major, there might be a bit of trouble ... er, the captain at Ondangwa didn't want to let me join my company ... but I came anyway."

He stopped for a second, eyebrows knitted, trying to figure out what it was exactly that I was trying to say. Then he realized that I was telling him I had effectively gone AWOL to join my company for this operation. The penny dropped. I thought I saw the hint of a twinkle in his eye as he raised his chin defiantly, seeming to take the matter as a personal challenge.

"Didn't you just get court martialed …?" he asked loudly and clearly.

I said nothing, and looked at him earnestly.

"No, no, no," he was shaking his head, his mind firmly made up. "There'll be no trouble from Captain Swart. There are bigger things going on here. Go with them, now," he pointed an arm towards Stan who was standing nearby.

"Yes, sergeant-major."

Yes!

I was back home and had just got a reprieve from the man himself. I'd like to see that dickhead captain try and fuck with Sakkie.

OPERATION PROTEA
August 1981

Jinx Blues—Robert Pete Williams

The commander of South African forces in this disputed territory said today that their assaults into southern Angola this month had shattered the command structure of two of the three regional headquarters of the insurgent South West Africa People's Organization and forced the insurgents to regroup 30 to 35 miles from the border. Maj. Gen. Charles Lloyd denied reports from the Angolan capital of Luanda that his troops had occupied seven small towns in the region. New York Times, 1 August 1981

Angola said today that two South African armored columns had crossed into southern Angola from South West Africa and were mounting attacks as much as 60 miles inside the country. The Angolan Government announced a general mobilization of its armed forces. The actions, reported by the Angolan press agency Angop, were neither confirmed nor denied by the South African Government, but a military analyst in Johannesburg said South African forces were involved in a major drive against black guerrillas.
New York Times, 26 August 1981

Stan took the job of cramming three weeks of training into a half-hour crash course very seriously. I sat and cleared my magazines of all the old rounds and took a bush hat full of shiny new bullets from an open crate nearby. I went to collect M27 grenades. I took three.

"Take more," Stan instructed. I finally took seven and stuffed them into a special grenade pouch I had never seen before, which I attached to my web belt. I picked up three or four thick field dressings, while Stan helped me carry a week's supply of rat packs back to the tent.

I had picked up on the sombre mood that hung around the dirty collection of paratrooper tents. I had never seen D Company like this before. Everyone sat gloomily, frowning deeply as they arranged their kit and cleaned weapons that lay stripped on towels and sleeping bags. It certainly did not look as if they had been having a good time recently.

I felt my jubilant mood disappear as I gazed around the area for the first time and saw that it was, in fact, a huge hidden tent city in the bush. Tents were tucked away behind trees as far as I could see. The red sand lay everywhere, like well-trodden heaps of red flour. The tents and trees and vehicles were all covered with a layer of fine red dust that was kicked up with every step.

I could make out a long row of about 20 Ratels with 90-millimetre cannons, parked in the shade. On the other side I saw half a dozen field ambulances. I had the feeling that everyone knew something that I did not. A Mirage fighter came roaring low overhead with an ear-shattering noise and I ducked instinctively. I had never heard anything that loud before.

"Wait till they come *really* low. There's about 20 of them we've been working with … you should see them coming straight down, firing rockets. Looks unreal."

"What base are we going to hit?"

"Ongiva. It's a town and a big FAPLA base about 40 clicks into Angola. It has ten square kilometres of trenches and bunkers. Some trenches are almost three metres deep, with cement World War Two-type pillboxes. They've got a battalion of tanks and a thousand troops in the base and we're going to be up front!"

"Whaaaat?"

"Yeah … the Mirages are going to come in and bomb them with thousand-pound bombs—big fuckers—probably for half an hour, then we go in. We're going to do fire and movement into their trenches. That's what we've been doing here for the last three weeks. They also have anti-aircraft guns all over the base, dug into the ground, which they'll probably put onto us when the Mirages have gone, like they did in Operation *Smokeshell*."

"Why are we hitting FAPLA? I thought they were protected game in this war. Shit, we almost caused an international incident when we shot a bunch of them by mistake a couple of weeks ago!"

"Not any more, boy ... fair game now. Something about allowing SWAPO bases to be built too close to their own, for security. Who cares, anyway ... they're all in this together. They've all got fucking AKs."

Stan's words made me queasy inside. I had spoken to an infantry troop who had been on Operation *Smokeshell* when it went wrong. He had told me how they'd been advancing slowly towards one of the many small bases through some trees, and his section was obliterated in an instant by a fucking anti-aircraft gun that was dug in and shooting at ground level. He shook as he remembered his partner being cut in half and his section leader's head being blown clean off. He was hit by shrapnel but crawled away and finally flagged down a big Ratel troop-carrier that pulled him in. The same guns then took out the Ratel, killing a few troops, and he was hit again, shrapnel gouging out his eye and taking a big chunk out of his head. He said the guns had been so tremendously loud that your brain couldn't think. He said he dropped everything and ran. I remembered how he was covered with goose bumps and the way his hands shook when he spoke about it.

Stan took great glee telling me in some detail about our impending doom and had a constant smirk on his face as he smoked and watched me fill my magazines. "This is it, Gungie, the real thing. A full-on conventional attack and you just fucking made it too, my bud. We're leaving tomorrow at 03:00."

I sat absorbing the unreal information he was feeding me and definitely felt my carefree mood going AWOL. Soon I too had a deep frown on my brow like everybody else.

Our section leader, Dan Pienaar, came into the tent chewing on a rat-pack chocolate bar, with his usual sleepy look and droopy eyelids. "You all got to go and give blood down at the medics, and hurry—we have to be finished in an hour. Also, mark your shirt and helmet with your blood group.

"Who's the blood for?"

"It's for you, who else?"

"Oh."

This was depressing. We went off and stood in line to give a pint of blood for ourselves and I came away feeling light-headed. We went back to the tent and I found John Delaney and Kurt sitting next to their almost-packed kit. Even the irrepressible John Delaney was down in the dumps.

"Big op, Gungie. There's a thousand troops in the base. Cubans and East Germans too. They're dug in with …"

"I know, I know. Fucking anti-aircraft guns and all … I know."

"Yeah, and tanks. Did Stan show you how to go into the trenches?"

"Ja, kind of. The first man in shoots down the trench and when it's clear the others roll in, like in the movies."

"Right, and when you see a bunker, call for an RPG-7. If you're closest to it and you can, you lob a grenade into it and roll away. That's all we've been doing here, over and over again—it's been like fucking hell. You're lucky you missed it. What happened with you, anyway?"

"I got a suspended sentence." All my good news seemed irrelevant now.

Dusk was settling; the bush was alive with troops loading up gear and locking up kit that was to be left in the tents until, if ever, we returned from the operation. Generators kicked into life and hummed, lighting naked bulbs that hung in the trees and giving the oppressive scene a surreal, gaudy, resort-like atmosphere. We lined up for a hot meal. Cooks slopped a stew onto sticky rice, which we ate in our tents. It all had the atmosphere of the last supper.

"Orders at 18:00. Everybody has to be there."

At 18:00 each platoon duly gathered around its respective lieutenant. I was in the front row, sitting on my ass in the dust. Lieutenant Doep slowly drew a map of long trenches in the red sand. When he finished he stayed on his haunches and looked at us. He spoke solemnly and I could see how he had matured in the short time since I had done the jump course with him, not knowing at the time that he was going to be my lieutenant.

"Men, as you probably know, we are going to be doing a number of attacks. The first one for us is the FAPLA base next to the town of Ongiva. It is a biggish town with a civilian population and military personal living in the town. Don't get any ideas; the infantry and 101 are going to be taking the town … let them take the easy one. We are going to come around from the

253

north and attack the FAPLA base, which is next to and just east of the town."
He pointed with a pen. "This is a big base and at this time it is fully occupied.
On this side is an airport which we have to secure." He drew some more
lines in the dust. "Here are the first trenches of the base, which begin at the
side of the airport. *Valk* 4 is going to take these trenches here." He indicated
with the pen to the network of trenches in the sand.

"We're going to drive in with Buffels in a spread-out line across a big *chana*
here at 06:00. The air force will be strafing the base with thousand-pound
bombs at 06:00 sharp and will keep on until 06:30. At this time we will have
advanced across this *chana* and will disembark from the Buffels in front of
this tar road. Twenty yards past the road are these banana-shaped trenches
here," he pointed with his pen.

"There are bunkers on either side. RPG men—take them out as soon as
you can. The Ratels will also be in our line at this time and they will also
go for these bunkers straight away. Once we get into these banana trenches
[from above they were shaped like two bananas next to each other with the
ends meeting], we are to advance to the next set of trenches here, do the same
thing ... and so on."

Doep looked around at his troops.

"This is a major FAPLA base and, as you know, it consists of ten square
kilometres of a network of trenches and big bunkers throughout. There are
also many smaller ones hidden throughout the area. Be sharp. Do it like you
are supposed to. The way that we have been training here."

"What training? I just got here two hours ago!" I mumbled to myself.

"Any questions?"

I was the first one to put my hand up and almost fell into the sandy mock-
up as I got to my haunches. Doep showed no surprise at seeing me there.
"Where are these AA guns?"

"They're all around the base but the closest to us are here to the side and
we don't know yet if they're visible from where we will disembark. But be
prepared—they might be active if the Mirages don't take them all out."

If the Mirages don't take them all out! I thought of Operation *Smokeshell*
and the senior I had spoken to—his section had been obliterated in an instant
by the anti-aircraft guns' three barrels lowered to ground level.

Lieutenant Doep stood up, looked around and answered a few more concerned questions. Captain Verwey had come across and stood next to Lieutenant Doep with his hands thrust deep into his pockets, as was his trademark. With his stoop he looked like a tall stork.

He casually addressed us: "Remember to keep your fire and movement short. No more than three paces, then down. It's all open ground and they'll take you out if you stay up any longer than that. Only shoot if you see a target. Aim for the belt buckle. If you see Boy go down, put another round in his head as you go past—we don't want him standing up behind you. We've got a lot of back-up and everything we need if we get into a tight spot, so take your time and double-check before every move. Be sharp men and let's show them what the paratroopers can do."

Captain Verwey nodded at us, stood back and moved to the next platoon to convey his message.

Lieutenant Doep continued: "After we have taken Ongiva, the whole fighting group will move farther into Angola to another big FAPLA base at Xangongo, about 100 clicks to the west of Ongiva, and we'll do it all over again."

We listened in silence. When he'd finished, he added something that made us all fully aware of the scope of the attack. His blond hair was long now from seven weeks in the bush, as was everyone else's—except mine. It hung in curls well over his collar. His brown eyes screwed up, his thin lips were a slit in his face under the shadows thrown by the naked light bulbs hanging in the trees.

"Men, this is a big operation and we're expecting tough resistance. Some of us might not be coming back from this one." He glanced around at the platoon and said meaningfully, "Those of you who believe in Almighty God better have a prayer tonight; those who don't might want to think deeply about it. Get to sleep early and get your stuff on the Buffels; we're leaving at 03:00 sharp."

I knew then that I was going to die. The run of good fortune I thought I'd had was just a twist of fate to get me into the front lines, attacking a base manned by 1,000 men on the day of my 21st birthday. My bad-luck birthday spell had not been broken ... I would probably be one of the ones not coming back and would die in a trench on my 21st birthday or be cut in half by a 23-millimetre anti-aircraft gun.

Stan and I slipped off on our old after-dark recce and returned with two cases of Castle lager. Captain Verwey walked right past us and bust us red-handed with our arms full of cans of beer but said nothing and walked on as if he'd seen nothing. We sat down around the fire that was full of old ash from three weeks' nightly burning and began some serious beer-drinking. I had a genuine feeling of doom and spoke about it quietly around the fire.

"Think about it. On my last two birthdays I was busted, almost to the exact same hour, and spent the night in boop—and now this year, on my 21st, we're attacking fucking Ongiva!"

"Well Gungie, could be that third time is lucky. Ever thought of that?"

"That's what I thought when I got off going to DB and then managed to get back here to you guys hours before you left. But now I don't know. It's just too fucking weird. Think about it; what are the odds of all these things happening on the same date?" I was not a superstitious person in the least, but this all seemed too much.

"What do you think's going to happen?"

"I think I might get killed, that's what might happen!"

"Bullshit! Any of us might get killed."

"Yeah, I know, but I feel jinxed ... seriously." I sat on an empty grenade case and drained my first beer in three big pulls. It was warm but tasted wonderful. I crunched the can and reached for a second. There were six or seven small fires here and there under the trees. The gloom was slowly lifting with some help from the warm beer. There were bursts of laughter that seemed too loud and forced. After the third beer my feelings of doom had subsided and after the fifth I was mimicking the 3 SAI sergeant-major at the court martial, saying in a whiny voice: "He stomped on me and jumped on me and then dragged me out the tent." Everyone laughed.

"Hey, John, if you catch it at Ongiva, can I have your watch?"

"Yes, you can. Seriously ... you can have it, but if you get nailed I want that bush knife."

"Yes, you can have it, brother." We all laughed too loudly.

"No, if you get killed, Johnny, I want Jennifer. You know and I know she fancies me. I want your word that I can move in on her and tell her it's what you would have wanted. She'll go for that." I had John Delaney cracking up.

"Sure, but I want that babe of yours if your birthday curse comes true." I had once shown John a sassy picture of Taina standing with her hands on her hips and her top off and he had been in love ever since.

"Sure, but I don't think you'll get it up because my ghost will be squeezing your nuts too hard."

"Well, my man, if you get hit by a 23-millimetre AA shell, even your ghost will be in pieces, so I'm not too worried about that!"

We all cracked up.

I was doing two things: celebrating being back with the boys and trying to make like all the shit I had heard in the last couple hours wasn't true. But right now we were warriors and like warriors of old we were getting well plastered before battle. Stan was well and truly drunk and walking around the fire doing his usual pantomime thing, wagging his finger at everyone like a teacher: "No, no, no. You must listen now; you don't understand ..." and then breaking into a Pink Floyd song: "*Forward they cried, from the rear, and the front ranks diiiiieeed ...*"

Even John Glover was standing and doing a jig in the firelight and joining Stan in song, which was very unusual for him. I sat smiling, just enjoying being back.

Pennefather came over from the other platoon's campfire, holding a fire bucket. He sat down at our fire and swirled the bucket around, mixing its contents. "Take a swig of this, it'll fuck you right up."

"What is it?"

"Liquid Valium. From ampoules mixed with sugar water. Tastes like hell, but hey ..." He handed it around. I took the fire bucket and looked at the wet shadow at the bottom.

"Drink it fast. You can't sip it or you'll puke. Guaranteed."

"Have you had some?"

"Yeah, man ... it's fucking awful. We got it from some of the medics. Riley knows them. We got some Sosagon too."

What the hell; tomorrow we die. I tilted my head back and downed the evil-tasting concoction in one swallow. I had to fight to keep it down.

Later that night I sat and watched the low flames of our fire flicker around the pockets of glowing embers. They licked around the log and erupted in a small explosion of green as they found some sap and then leaped with new vigour to attack the still-green bark. The green bark fought back, determined not to burn like the rest of its body which glowed in broken embers, but each time it bled a drop of its blood the green explosions erupted again and brought on a new attack of flame. I thought the green bark was doomed and would not withstand the attack. I looked deep into the cherry-red embers and saw a thousand shapes spring to life. I turned and rolled onto my side and looked into the darkness. Before my eyes I saw a beautiful old ranchhouse in vivid yellow and red with long ploughed fields of chocolate-brown soil. A fence of blackwood stretched as long as a railway line, huge trees flickered in a hundred shades of green, red and yellow. It was an indescribably beautiful, peaceful scene and I didn't want to leave it. The trees changed to purple but the fence stayed black. My eyes were wide open; I was seeing the scene as if I was hovering above it and could reach out and touch it. I realized what I was seeing in front of my eyes was my home, the farm ...

I tried weakly to get up but could not and laid my head down with my eyes still open. I was as high as a kite on a thousand-metre string and for the first time in my life was having a real hallucination. I became aware of Lieutenant Doep standing close to me and talking to me but I don't know if I answered him. He might have been an hallucination too.

★★★★★

"If you want to piss you'd better go now; there wont be time later!"

Half the company jumped down from the Buffels and steam rose in the air from several dozen piss spots in the chilly dawn. I was nervously forcing out the last drops against a thin tree (I remember that tree like I saw it yesterday) when an ear-shattering explosion like I had never heard in my life split the silence of the dawn half a click away.

"Hey, hey, hey!" I whooped as I shook my reluctant lizard.

"Come on, lets go ... c'mon now!" Doep was beckoning. We ran back and jumped into the Buffels as another huge explosion crashed a click away from us, sending a plume of grey smoke 30 storeys into the air. Small flocks of birds flew over our heads like bats out of hell. It was on!

"Start moving across the *chana*! No, slowly ... slow down!"

Our long line of 20 Buffels slowly emerged from the trees where we had been waiting in the dark for the last couple of hours. We were directly across from the airport runway and half a kilometre from the trenches of Ongiva. A lonesome machine gun opened up in the dawn far away to our right and was answered by sporadic and distinctive AK-47 fire. The fist shots had been fired.

"Slow down, you moron! Stay abreast with the others ... fuck it, man, listen to me! Wait for them!" Doep swore in Afrikaans at the driver of our Buffel who seemed determined to be first to reach the trenches and offload us so he could be first back.

We had been told to start the advance when the air force began bombing but, true to form, someone had fucked up again because in the half-hour that the air force strafed the base we could have crossed the *chana* four times. So we'd all stopped—20 Buffels spread out in the middle of the huge open *chana*, waiting, observing the show. It was like watching a movie.

Mirages came darting straight down from the heavens, only visible as tiny shiny specks, then becoming small silver arrows in a vertical dive, then pulling massive Gs as they let go their thousand-pound bombs and pulling horizontal, leaving a high column of smoke and a boom ten times louder than any thunder I had ever heard.

"Hey, they're shooting back ... check it out!"

"Fucking hell ... look at that!"

A new sound had taken over now. It was the loud *burp* of the FAPLA anti-aircraft guns that had begun to open up. The early morning blue-and-pink sky filled with small white puffs of smoke.

"Look, they're almost on the Mirage. I think they got him."

A Mirage dropped like a pinhead from the sky, followed all the way down by puffs of white smoke that seemed right on his tail.

"These kaffirs can shoot ... look at that. Aw, fuck."

I was coldly impressed. We had been led to believe that when the big bombs started falling the Angolan army would try and find a quick way out, but not so. The gunners were staying right there and keeping their heads with thousand-pound bombs falling among them and they were almost shooting down the Mirages. (A handful of Mirages were in fact hit by shrapnel.) We watched the show, fascinated. Every time a little pinhead dropped out the sky at incredible speed we pointed it out to each other, and every time there was a cluster of flak puffs just behind it. We cheered as the bombs exploded, sometimes two at a time.

Bullets had begun to buzz overhead like angry bees and we put our heads down behind the protection of the Buffels. I risked poking my head up and snapped a picture as a thousand-pound bomb erupted into a huge plume close to the tree line on the other side of the *chana*.

Kurt was grinning at me with his head bent low. I grinned back.

TRENCHES AND BUNKERS

Fortunate son—Creedence Clearwater Revival

South Africa said today that it had destroyed Angolan radar installations and killed at least 240 Angolan government troops in its assaults this week in southern Angola. Anti-aircraft installations protecting the radar units were also knocked out, according to South African officers in the area.
New York Times, 30 August 1981

Boom ... boom ... the hollow-sounding explosions of big 82-millimetre mortars.

Shells started to drop among our Buffels. The movie was over; now we were getting involved.

"Drive! Drive!" Doep roared, as we slowly started moving forward.

Boom.

Sand covered us from a mortar exploding 40 metres away. Doep shouted to us that one of the Buffels had been hit by a mortar and couldn't continue. I don't know why but he shouted it a couple of times to us. (We found out later that the mortar exploded right next to the vehicle.) I was bending down low and had forgotten about the bombing.

I was saying a quick prayer but could think of no words but "Please, Lord—look after me." I crouched low and tightened my bootlaces for at least the third time that morning and checked the magazine in my rifle for the tenth time. I smiled at Doogy who was fiddling with his LMG. He had solemn look and nodded back at me. We rolled slowly forward. I was no longer the cold killing machine I had been on the ambush, or when we'd hit FAPLA on Operation *Ceiling.* I had the jitters.

Perhaps the feeling of impending doom was the legacy of my birthday curse, or perhaps it was because I had gone through no training for this op and had just walked in cold after three weeks of lazy *bal bak*, goofing off, at Ondangwa. The bombing had stopped. How a half-hour seems to fly when you're having fun! A couple of anti-aircraft guns were still firing in long *burps*—the Mirages had obviously not taken out the guns, the main objective of the bombing.

I knew it would be like this. There was some commotion and bullets pinged musically on our Buffel. We were taking some fire from close by. I could not see where from and nor did I really want to look, but Doep had his head half over the side of the Buffel and was pointing to some small huts about 100 metres away.

"Green! Green! Fire with the LMG into those huts!"

It took Doogy a good few seconds to get his shit together but finally he stood up and, even though bullets were buzzing around us, he let rip with a long burst from his MAG. He fired into the huts and down the small tar road that was the landmark both for the beginning of the base and for us to disembark at the banana-shaped trenches. I didn't see anybody fall or run but Doogy still let out a yell of triumph as he quickly ducked down inside again.

We had fired our first shots.

"Get ready to deploy!" Doep shouted as loud as he could. Bullets cracked over our heads in earnest, twanging on the side of the Buffel. I tried to empty my mind of all thoughts and become as single-minded as I had been in the other contacts but I wasn't having much success.

"Get ready to deploy … get ready!" Lieutenant Doep was shouting very loudly, almost hysterically.

"You must be fucking mad! What do you mean, deploy? Can't you see we're taking fire, you stupid fucking idiot?" my mind screamed. I grasped my R4 in a death grip, my knuckles standing out starkly white. I shifted my body and readied my feet to kick open the steel side panels of the Buffel.

Bullets cracked close over our heads, sounding like the target pits on the shooting range back in Bloemfontein. Now I thought I had some idea how those poor bastards must have felt landing on D-Day. Doep had the radio receiver to his ear, glaring fiercely as he tried to listen into the receiver.

"Deploy! Deploy! Deploy now!" he screamed in Afrikaans but no one moved. "Deploy! Deploy!" but still no one moved; we crouched low in the Buffel with our heads down.

"You fucking stupid person," I thought. "Why do you want to go out there? Can't you see we'll all get killed?" I wanted to scream at him.

The troops at the side of the vehicle fumbled at the heavy pins to release the panel, as we all kicked it over with a loud clang. I leaped out and tumbled to the ground. I immediately got up, ran a couple of metres and hit the dirt. Everybody was hugging the dirt.

"Fire and movement ... go!" my mind shouted at me. I looked at Stan on my right and he nodded furiously. He leaped up and ran a couple of metres and dropped. I looked around and did the same. The tar road was 20 metres in front of us but we were in an open *chana* as flat as a bowling green with not a stick for cover. Bullets cracked and kicked up dirt around us in big squirts. Stan moved again but quickly dived for the deck. I, too, leaped up in sequence but dived for the sand almost at once. I leopard-crawled some metres to a shallow depression in the sand, quickly looked up and saw no targets in the bush line 50 to 70 metres away, but the sudden loud crack of a bullet very nearby made me shove my cheek into the sand.

"We're taking too much fire, stupid motherfuckers ... we can't move," I swore at no one in particular. I looked at Stan who also had his head flat against the sand with his ear on the ground. I dared not get up. I dared not move a centimetre. Without moving my head I could see that the whole advance had stopped and was lying prone in a scraggly line. Some had not moved from where they had landed next to the Buffel, which was now very quickly backing away. We were pinned down; we could not move. We could not even look up, never mind shoot back. Sand kicked up around us in terrifying sprays.

I lay still and involuntarily tried to wriggle my body deeper into the soft sand. I could hear myself breathe. It was not even 07:00 and already the sweat was pouring into my eyes, stinging them. I was afraid to even move my hand to try and wipe them. I closed my eyes and lay still.

"Any time now I'm dead ... any time now." I expected a bullet to blow the top of my head off. I would not even feel it. My brains would lie there steaming in the morning chill, just like the SWAPO's at the ambush had done. These might be the final seconds of my life right now, right now as I lay thinking about it. Stupidly it crossed my mind that it would be sad and wasteful if I were to be killed here today.

"Fourie is down! Medics! Fourie's hit!" the shout came down the line. I shouted the message on without turning my head. I could do nothing so I just lay still with my cheek in the sand. It was strangely relaxing; my mind was working in slow motion and I felt almost that I wasn't really there at all but I was an outsider looking on. I took the chance to breathe deeply and get a grip.

For some reason I became fascinated with my rifle, centimetres from my face, as its image burned into my brain. I looked at the four notches scratched into the chipped green paint above the hand grip. Each symbolized a man killed with this rifle. Two were already scratched into the rifle when it had been issued to me. Suddenly I almost forgot where I was and felt an acceptance, a relaxing, cozy detachment from the present, as if I was lying in the sun in my backyard while bullets cracked head-high.

I inspected the granules of white sand that covered my sweaty forearm and noted how my arm hairs pushed out through the sand and glistened with sweat. I suddenly noticed a tiny, almost transparent green bug struggling across the wet sand granules on my forearm. He wasn't much bigger than a grain of sand himself. His little antennae waved frantically and his green legs worked as he climbed over each grain one at a time. "Where the hell does this little bug think he's going? Doesn't he know what's going on here?" I watched him with amazement. I had never seen a bug so small. He struggled on, slipping and falling back, but carried on, determined to get where he was going. "What's his fucking objective? What's this little thing's purpose? For what possible reason on earth does a bug this small exist?" I questioned. Idiotically I noted too that if I had not been lying in this position, unable to move and with my face so close to my arm, I would never in my life have seen this wonderful, stupid, determined little bug.

"Kruger is hit ... Kruger's hit!" the call came down the line. Numbly I shouted the message on. It was sinking in now. It was a fuck-up! We were pinned down in the open and we were all going to get shot to hell. Two guys are down and we haven't moved ten fucking metres. And we only have another 13 kilometres of base to get through! We had been pinned down now for about ten or 15 minutes and nobody seemed to know what to do.

"Why don't the fucking Ratels come forward? What are they here for?"

"Keep your heads down ... the Mirages are coming in for a run!"

I didn't bother relaying the message. Everyone had heard it. I turned my face up to see if I could see the Mirage dropping out of the sky but saw nothing. Thirty seconds later I caught the flash of a plane darting in low above treetop level and a couple of huge explosions followed almost at once, 300 metres in front of us.

They were not as big as the thousand-pounders but big enough to shake the ground under me. A cheer went up and the shooting stopped. After 30 seconds I reckoned it was safe to get up on my haunches. The bomb smoke drifted lazily over the trees just ahead.

"*Vorentoe*! Forward!"

At the far end of the line one Buffel with a bit of cover had advanced about forty metres ahead of us, having taken advantage in the lull in the firing. Paratroops were even futher forward, running bent over and not even doing fire and movement. They were about 50 metres ahead of our side of the line. Suddenly, when I looked again, they had all turned and were sprinting back at full speed, breaking into different directions.

"What the fuck's going on to make them run like that?"

Soon the shout came down the line. "Tanks! There's a fucking tank coming!"

I stayed put and could now plainly hear the clank and squeak of something approaching on the far side from the trees.

"Tanks, tanks ... we got tanks coming out right on us!" Lieutenant Doep was close to me to my left and shouting as loud as he could into the receiver.

I sat watching with a numbness in my gut. The whole line had started to scatter wildly in all directions.

John Delaney was shouting as he ran doubled over towards me. "Tank, right here ... right here!"

I sat and watched, unable to pull away from the movie scene unfolding before my eyes. Sure enough, an old T-34 emerged from the tree line about

100 metres to our right and stopped, only partially exposed in the trees. I could see its long barrel sticking out confidently and could now hear its big motor roaring at high revs. Perhaps he was stuck in first gear or something. I turned and ran crouched a little farther to my left, away from the tank, then stopped and turned. There was nowhere to run to. We were on a bowling green of fucking sand! I flung myself flat on the sand.

Stan almost fell over me as he too ran doubled over past me. Minutes passed that seemed like hours, before I heard an engine gunning behind me. I turned to see one of our small, odd-looking Eland armoured 'Noddy' cars with its long 90-millimetre gun barrelling towards us at almost top speed from across the *chana*. He became airborne as he bounced over bumps and turned nimbly, kicking up a cloud of dust as he came directly through our scattered line and then turned again, this time towards the tank. The little armoured car came to a quick stop right in the middle of the open ground about 80 metres from the tank, waited a couple of seconds and then fired one shot from his 90-millimetre with a loud bang.

The shot was right on target. When the smoke drifted away the T-34's turret was lying off to one side and the open body was burning, belching dense black smoke. I couldn't believe it. My admiration went out to the panzer men in the Eland. The panzers had been our neighbours in Bloemfontein, the traditional arch-enemies of the paratroopers during training. We used to jump over the fence at night to kick their arses but I knew that from here on they would have my full respect. I quickly pulled out my camera and snapped a shot of the burning tank billowing black smoke.

"Forward!"

We weren't out of the woods yet. Fourie had been shot in the leg and was hobbling away with a medic on either side of him. His trouser leg had already been cut off, with bright blood seeping from a hastily applied field dressing. Kruger had a hand wound and was walking doubled up behind the medics, clutching his hand with the other. We were still taking light fire but advanced with fire and movement over the tar road to the banana-shaped trenches, finding them to be old, broken down and abandoned.

The big Ratels had only now moved up among us after the tank scare. About time too. They slowly rolled forward with their huge wheels as we started forward with buddy-buddy fire and movement next to them. We went over the crumbled trenches and into some scattered trees, still with no visible targets. Stan, who was my partner on this operation, bolted four or five metres in front of me and dived into the dirt. I looked around and jumped up, flipping my rifle to 'fire' as I did so. I had taken two quick steps when the unmistakable *whoosh* of an RPG-7 anti-tank rocket went over my head, probably aimed at the big armoured Ratel that had come in directly next to me on my right. I collapsed instantly like a man shot through the head and fell hard to the ground with a loud grunt. It was not a controlled fall; my rifle ploughed into the sand with the fire-selector open and sand poured through the open slot into the working parts. The rocket had missed the Ratel, for no explosion came. I lay on my side and worked the bolt, ejecting a couple of rounds, hearing the sand grinding inside the rifle.

"Fuck it!" I looked towards Stan, who had found cover in a shallow depression and was beckoning me to come over. I leopard-crawled the 15 metres like a snake, just like in the training manual, and fell into the little hole. Thank heavens for basic training.

"I got sand in my rifle!"

"You better clean it! Do it now!"

I flipped onto my back and stripped the R4 in triple-quick time, working like a sea otter and putting the working parts on my chest like seashells as I pulled my bandana from around my neck. I worked fast and smoothly. In training I had always struggled with weapon stripping and assembling, never mind speed-stripping. Now my fingers worked like steel pins, easily forcing the parts together and snapping them in. Amazing how quickly and easily one can strip and clean a weapon and reassemble it under fire. Every part went back into place at the first atempt, with not the slightest hitch.

"Fuck ... RPG almost took my head off. Did you see that?"

"Ja, it came from those trees there."

I crawled to the top of the depression, wiped my eyes with my bandana and adjusted the heavy jump helmet that kept falling over my eyes. We were about 50 metres into the base and were now among scattered trees. I was already drenched with sweat. I saw a sand wall up ahead with thick trees behind it.

"Where? Over there?"

"Next to that wall."

I put my rifle over, aimed at the top of the wall and squeezed off four or five shots. Stan followed suit. They were the first shots I had fired. I still hadn't seen a target but it felt good. I was just looking up to search the trees again when a huge *burp* filled our world as the anti-aircraft guns opened up ahead of us again.

"Jesus!" I dropped down.

"Hey Gungie, look!" Stan lay on his back and pointed to the sky where a small Bosbok (Bushbuck) spotter plane was in big trouble. The spotter plane had thought, as we all did, that the AA gunners had all deserted their guns after the thousand-pound bombs were dropped on them but there was one stubborn gunner who had stayed at his post and seemed determined to fight till the end. The small single-engined aircraft was so high he was just a speck in the blue sky but not too high for the sharp-eyed FAPLA gunner.

The Bosbok seemed unaware that he was being shot at and was putt-putting along slowly, but he must suddenly have realized that he was in the jaws of death. The spotter plane weaved and dived as white puffs of flak exploded around him. At one stage he was totally engulfed in a cluster of about 20 puffs but he emerged from them diving at a 45-degree angle and high-tailed it out of there like a bat out of hell. I've never seen a small plane move like that before. He made it out, full of holes, only because the anti-aircraft guns had stopped shooting for some reason.

"Jeez, I never knew a Bosbok could move that fast!" I was grinning and Stan was laughing.

"That's one lucky damn spotter. Did you see him change down to first gear very quickly?"

"Ja, he turned into a Mirage pretty quick."

Our chuckling was short lived. The brave FAPLA anti-aircraft gunner was back in the game. He had trained his barrels on us at ground level and sent a salvo of shots over our heads with a sound like doomsday that took the breath out of me. I had been on one knee after the spotter had high-tailed it out and was scanning the bush in front of me but dropped into the sand like a sack. It was the loudest and most frightening sound I had ever heard—ten or 20 anti-aircraft projectiles split the air just metres above our heads in less than a second! The gun, we discovered later, had four barrels.

The anti-aircraft gun was five times as loud now that we were on the receiving end of it. I saw a huge limb crash down from a tree behind us; leaves rained down like a thousand drifting snowflakes. We hugged the little cover that we had.

"Fuck!" My brain was still trying to process and catalogue the sound but it couldn't. It had never heard a sound anything like that before. We had also begun to take some heavy small-arms fire as rounds cracked close overhead. The anti-aircraft gun was not very constant, but every few minutes he would cut loose again and more limbs would come crashing down.

"They're not dug in. They can't shoot lower than seven or eight feet ... they're set too high!"

Stan and I stayed in the shallow hole and hardly said a word, our full concentration on what was going on around us. The whole company was hugging cover again and no one moved. The anti-aircraft gun would *burp* every so often, sending foliage flying, but we soon learned that his guns indeed were not dug in and so his rounds could only fly two or three metres over our heads. They could scare the shit out of us but couldn't seem to hit us.

We appeared to be pinned down again but at least now we had cover. We had hardly fired any shots at all. So far FAPLA was the one dishing it out as we had done little more than dive for cover all the time. I still had not seen a FAPLA soldier. All the fire was coming from a spread-out area behind sand walls, inside deep trenches and tree lines and we were doing a good job at keeping our heads down. It was hard to gauge time accurately; looking back this had all happened in 45 minutes or perhaps an hour.

I lay on my back and took the opportunity to get my breath. The anti-aircraft gunner finally seemed to have quit his post—at any rate, we hadn't heard from him for a while—but now a machine gun was rattling sporadic ally from a hidden position ahead. I wiped the stinging sweat from my eyes with my soaked bandana.

I was surprised what a slow process it was. Not having trained for this full-on conventional attack, I thought we would hit it in a *blitzkrieg*, charging forward and shooting like in the movies, but apparently not. We had been at it for well over an hour and were moving merely yards at a time, if that.

"Where is the spare headset?" I heard Sergeant-Major Sakkie's voice roaring during a lull in the firing. I lay still, not much bothered, but then in a flash I remembered that I had been appointed to carry the spare radio receiver and had stuffed it in the side pocket of my pants.

"Aw, shit!" I popped my head up and saw that Sakkie was about 30 metres to my left, a little closer to the sand wall where all the bullshit was going on. Sakkie boomed again as if he was on the fucking parade ground.

"Stan, cover me. I've got the receiver."

"What?"

"I've got the fucking spare radio receiver."

"Well, you'd better go!"

"I know! Cover me!"

I shouted as loud as I could that I had it and that I was on my way. Stan seemed reluctant to lift his head too high but he nodded and pulled his R4 up to his shoulder. I readied my legs under me, took a deep breath, jumped up and ran across the 30 or 40 metres in one mad dash, jumping feet first into a two-metre-deep hole that seemed like an old bomb crater or a broken-down bunker. I heard Stan's covering shots behind me.

I was a few yards from Sakkie and a couple of troops who were huddled behind some trees. I tossed the headset over to them.

"Good man!" Sakkie shouted. He seemed to be enjoying himself. I slid back into the crater.

There was also a medic lying in the hole; we smiled at each other. "Can you believe it?" he said, shaking his head.

"Fucking hell," was all I could say and I also shook my head. Safe in the two-metre crater I lay on my back, pulled a crumpled box of Marlboro from my top pocket and offered him one. He took it and I lit it for him with my red lighter. We puffed in silence.

Sakkie's famous parade-ground bellow came again, like a bullhorn on the front line of battle. "*Waar is die LMG? … bring daardie donnerse LMG vorentoe*," he roared across to *Valk* 4 who were spread out over 70 metres of pretty-much flat ground. Each para lay flat in the tiny bit of cover he had managed to find.

"Here! The fucking LMG's here, sergeant-major," Doogy's faint voice drifted through the din.

With the medic next to me I had to keep up the paratrooper image, so I moved up the hole and lay on my shoulder with my head just sticking over the edge, still smoking my Marlboro and monitoring the scene while the medic lay at the bottom of the hole. I clutched my rifle, ready. The FAPLA machine gun fire was sporadic, but constant with its long 20- and 30-round bursts.

I watched Doogy, with his MAG, doing the same gauntlet run that I had just done but further, as he had to come from the far right of the line. He ran doubled over, carrying the heavy LMG, with his number two behind him.

Sakkie was now standing up as though he was on a fucking parade ground with another troop crouching next to him behind the tree. He seemed to have pinpointed where the FAPLA machine-gun fire was coming from. Doogy came sliding up to him. Sakkie put one arm on Doogy's shoulder, and with the other pointed towards a high sand wall 100 metres ahead, beyond the trench 30 metres in front of us and shook his hand vigorously.

Doogy wrapped the LMG's strap over his shoulder, took a wide stance and opened up with long bursts. The sand wall exploded in a cloud of dust and leaves flew. He kept on shooting, his number two feeding in the belt. He changed belts and fired again, almost disappearing in his own gunsmoke. The FAPLA machine gun fell silent.

We kept our positions for a while as no one really knew what to do. I saw a round brown helmet bobbing up ahead to my right, at the sand wall of the trench ahead. It was some of our guys. *Valk* 3 had entered the trench from the right flank and were now in it, moving down towards us, going from bunker to bunker. Shots rang out but no return fire. A few shouts went up.

"C'mon, lets go!" I jumped out of my safe, two-metre-deep crater, leaving the medic still sitting in the bottom. For the first time we were able to get up without the crack of bullets flying past our heads. I ran crouched the remaining 30 metres to the trench ahead, and jumped in. It was a model trench with a level floor, straight walls and wooden steps with little nooks cut into the walls. It was well maintained and clean, except for the piles of spent AK-47 cartridges that lay everywhere and clothing and equipment that had been hastily abandoned. A grenade thumped and a cloud of dust erupted from a bunker at the end of the trench.

Lieutenant Doep was now back on the scene, shouting the odds. He waved one arm excitedly as he leaned against the wall of the trench and fiddled with the radio receiver on his shoulder. It was the first time we had been together as a platoon since we'd disembarked the Buffels almost an hour and a half ago. A few guys lit up cigarettes. In the mad scramble of taking heavy fire as we disembarked the Buffel, with almost no cover and what with the Canberra jet coming in low and dropping a bomb close in front of us and the fucking anti-aircraft fire, it had been pretty well every man for himself, with no real leadership except for Sergeant-Major Sakkie calling for the LMG. But now Doep was back in charge.

"Don't pick anything up, don't touch anything! Be careful of booby traps and don't go into the bunkers!" Doep shouted.

He bent his head and started talking into the receiver in rapid Afrikaans. "Tango Lima… Tango Lima, Victor Four. We're in the third row of trenches. Under control and clear at this time."

I saw Kurt and I lifted my eyebrows at him but could not smile. His shirt was black with sweat and he looked at me blankly, his usually pink face flushed bright red as he stood quietly catching his breath and gripping his rifle tightly with both hands. He did not look as though he was enjoying himself, probably thinking that it would be a lot nicer to be back in a kitchen right now, standing over a pot and stirring potatoes as they boiled.

Stan was next to me and looked grim with his helmet pulled low over his eyes. He resembled a German stormtrooper, his desired look, as he took long, quick pulls on a cigarette. His face was also red with exertion. Mortars still boomed a few clicks to the east in the civilian town of Ongiva as black smoke curled in a thick column 300 or 400 metres into the sky. It looked like we weren't the only ones having fun. The infantry had thought that taking the town would be easy. I peered into a neat-looking bunker that had a wooden door hanging on a hinge, now flung open, and saw what looked to be crates of ammo and supplies stacked inside.

There were dozens of shiny new AK-47 rounds lying on the dusty floor that must have been dropped in a hasty ammunition hand-out. There was no sign of FAPLA or of any bodies. I took a deep slug from my water bottle. The water was hot but slid down my throat like chilled Champagne.

"Okay, form up. We're going over here and forward. Boy's moved to the next trench line. Keep your eyes open and watch for bunkers. Okay, form up ... let's go!" Doep shouted, too loudly.

He seemed more under control now; he was still loud but not shouting orders at the very top of his voice as he had done in the Buffel.

We were now in the thicket of trees which until now had been pretty much all we could see. Now, as I peered over the top of the trench for the first time, I could see the vast FAPLA base spread out in front of us. It was a huge expanse of sand mounds and scattered, single-storey brick buildings built on acres of ground that was a combination of open *chanas* and trees. The small buildings seemed to be mostly under trees; some had camouflage-netting spread over them. There were telephone poles and well-used sand roads running between the trees and buildings that lay up ahead and close by a few dark-green Soviet GAZ-66 trucks were dug into ramps in the ground, just visible. The ramps were hidden from the air by a roof topped with branches and netting.

The terrain was a spiderweb of small, well-trodden footpaths leading in every direction. Immediately in front of us was an open *chana* about 100 metres wide, with a few lonely clumps of trees scattered in the middle. Around these trees were small mounds of sand that seemed to be bunkers. I noticed that I was stuck in a sort of tunnel vision, unable to take in much with my peripheral vision. Like an animal, I could only focus on a small area almost dead ahead with unnatural clarity, but had to move my head like a crow to take in what was around me.

"Let's go!"

The guys closest to the wooden steps gingerly clambered out and when they drew no fire the rest of us jumped up out of the trench and lay flat, looking around.

"Fire and movement, c'mon. Across this *chana* straight ahead!" Doep was clearly back in charge.

I ran forward and dived into the ground. *Ooooff!* Up again, three paces, then down. Up again, three paces, then down. Sweat poured off my body. I could hear myself breathing heavily, grunting as I landed in the sand. Shit! I hadn't spent three weeks training for this like everyone else had. I must be the only troop in the whole operation with three weeks' training stuffed into a half-hour crash course, and I felt like it. Every time I hit the ground my heavy jump helmet banged down under my eyes, blinding me and I had to shove it up again. Then it was my turn to get up and run three paces and dive down again. I decided that, seeing we were not taking fire right now, I would rather go onto my knees first then drop down, and also run a little further than three paces because I wasn't getting anywhere very fucking quickly. Also, I wanted to reduce the number of times I had to plough into the dirt. I did it a few times; it felt a lot better. I ran about eight paces, then slowly sagged to my knees and lay down, rather than diving.

"Korff! They're going to take you out! Keep it short. Just three paces at a time!" Doep shouted. He was three men down from me, on my left.

I felt embarrassed to be singled out and reprimanded. Minutes later, the chance came to castigate myself for my stupidity. Twenty metres straight in front of me, under a tree, was a small mound of sand with a square wood-frame opening on top.

Doep turned his head towards me as he lay in the sand. "Korff ... Green ... clear that bunker!" he yelled furiously, his face flushed red against his long blond hair.

21 AT LAST

Hellhound on my trail—Robert Johnson

I looked at Kevin Green on my right. He looked back at me deadpan. I rolled onto my side and fumbled in my little pouch for a smooth M27 grenade. I nodded at Kevin and, with the whole platoon keeping cover, we both leaped up and ran across the short space to the bunker and dived down close to it. Although I had never thrown a live grenade before (I must have missed that class during basic training for some reason), I felt no hesitation about doing so. I pulled hard on the pin and held the lever down. Kevin lay on his stomach a few yards from me with his rifle trained on the bunker. I rolled over as I had seen it being done in the movies, lobbed the grenade into the dark hole and rolled away again, stopping only a metre from the bunker with my arms over my head.

Whomp!

The ground beneath me shook and a cloud of white dust and smoke billowed up from the small hole about a metre off. The bunker seemed to be empty. If it wasn't, they died quietly. We reached a small trench and a long mound of dirt. Shots cracked over our heads.

Fifty yards ahead was a group of FAPLA troops who seemed to have been caught in mid-crossing to another trench. They ran with long strides to make the best of what little cover they had. Fucking targets at last! Their gunsmoke marked them clearly as their comrades already in cover blasted away at us. We got behind the cover of the long mound of sand and fired furiously. I was on one knee with just my upper body exposed above the wall of sand. I could see a couple of woolly black heads bobbing as the group of five or six who had been caught in the open now ran, bent over and at the speed of sound, diving for their lives into the thin trees, where a few brave

275

comrades already lay in the scanty cover. These gentlemen kept up a furious rate of fire in single shots and not automatic, which was the norm. At least when they fired on automatic fire they usually shot high but not this time. Bullets cracked around us. Fighting the instinct to duck down, I stayed up and aimed at the rapidly disappearing bobbing heads. I knew I was shooting too fast and moving my barrel from side to side without staying on one target but I was stuck in a mode and unable to slow down as I pulled the trigger as fast as I could.

They were pretty good shots—a shot cracked past my ear like a ringmaster's whip, the closest I had ever experienced. This time I did duck down. I took the opportunity to try and wipe the sweat from my eyes against my sleeve but this only made it worse. I'm convinced that the sweat in a fire fight is different from normal sweat. I had noticed this before, when we hit the FAPLA troops by mistake a month ago after the SWAPO 'breakfast party' ambush. This variety of sweat seems a lot thicker, saltier and slimier; it floods out of your pores in rivers, almost covering your skin with a goo that is hard to wipe off. Years later, when I boxed, I used to sweat like hell but it would run like water. I looked up again and started shooting but now could hardly keep my eyes open because the sweat was in my eyes, making it almost impossible to keep them open.

"Here I go again—can't see what I'm shooting at!"

I fired almost blindly. When the shooting finally abated I sat down, took my bandana from around my neck and wiped my eyes. I struggled for more than a minute to clear my stinging eyes. What was this stuff? Adrenaline or something? I could see at least three bodies lying sprawled under the trees.

"*Valk* 2 needs help! Turn around and go back!"

A desperate fire fight had broken out behind us to the left, the gunshots sounding like a string of fireworks that had been tied together and lit. I couldn't imagine anyone coming out alive from a fight so furious. We turned and headed back the way we had come—back over the small *chana*, past the bunker I had cleared—and turned towards the fire fight where gunsmoke and dust hung over the thicket like fog.

"There! There!"

In front of us was a group of four or five black troops in camouflage who were fleeing in long strides but still stopping to take quick shots behind them. From our angle, we were partially hidden by some bush. In their preoccupation with making a good getaway after holding down *Valk* 2 from a superior position, they didn't see us.

We had no time to get into position; we just stood there and blasted at them. They didn't know what hit them. Two dropped spinning to the ground as their luckier comrades disappeared into the trees like greased lightning. The shooting died down and we met up with *Valk* 2 who were grinning with shock as if they had just come off a roller-coaster ride and had been lucky to make it off. None of them, as far as I remember, was seriously wounded. We inspected the little barricade where the FAPLA troops had made their stand and found two-metre-deep trenches with walkways to stand on if you wanted to look over the top, cement plaster on the walls and bunkers as big as bedrooms dug into the side walls. There were desks, shelves and beds in the bunker. It looked like some kind of guardroom. One Angolan soldier lay still, half-hidden under a tree. He looked dead. A single shot rang out. Now he was definitely dead. A little farther on, next to the big bunker, we found a parked T-55 Soviet tank. Dug into a pit with a ramp, it was invisible from 15 metres away. Made of crude, rough metal and painted green, it looked just like the ones I had seen in photographs of the Eastern Front in the Second World War.

The shooting had died down, except for the odd shot that buzzed over our heads from afar. We moved forward slowly and occupied a trench, and then sat tight for a while, snooping around and waiting for I-don't-know-what before we moved onto the next section. Every now and then shots rang out, signifying that an Angolan soldier had been found hiding in a bunker and had just joined the ranks of the deceased. We had probably been into Operation *Protea* for about three hours now. It seemed that the worst was over, with only sporadic shooting coming from ahead. We moved forward over some trenches and came upon a small complex of brick buildings. We entered the building.

"Hey, look! Here's Kruger's bush hat! Look, here's his name on the inside!" Badenhorst held up an SADF bush hat he had just found in a desk drawer. He had a huge grin on his face. I was kicking through some clothing lying on the small office floor. I stopped and moved over to have a look.

"Check right here ... Kruger ... there's his name!"

I looked at the brown South African bush hat and, sure enough, there was Kruger's name in faded black pen, visible next to the bright orange DayGlo sticker on the inside of the hat. Soon a group stood around inspecting the bush hat. "Jeez, how about that. It *is* Kruger's bush hat! He lost it when we hit those FAPLA in *Ceiling*. They must have found it and brought it here to the HQ."

I grinned. Kruger's bush hat had travelled far. The area where we had made contact with FAPLA by mistake and had to run for it in Operation *Ceiling* was hundreds of kilometres away. They must have brought it all the way to the HQ here at Ongiva to use as evidence for the their inevitable complaint to the United Nations Security Council that the 'white racists' had attacked them. I chuckled. What were the odds of pulling open a desk drawer and finding the bush hat you had lost almost two months earlier in another operation. Kruger had been pulled back to the medics after being shot in the hand earlier but was going to be pleased to get his hat back .

And an HQ indeed this was! Recklessly we opened cabinets and drawers and found piles of packaged documents and dozens of maps with areas circled in red pen.

"Look at this! These are fucking SWAPO locations! Damn, look at this!"

I turned and looked at the pile of maps that Paul Greef was holding. I could see S.W. written in red pen next to at least a dozen circled areas.

"Show Doep."

Doep pushed his helmet back and shuffled through the pile of maps. His eyes shone as we pointed out the marked spots on the maps as troops brought more maps they had found in some of the other cabinets. We had happened upon one of the main FAPLA intelligence offices in southern Angola.

Doep pressed the receiver attached to his epaulette and it crackled into life. "Tango Lima, Tango Lima, this is Victor Four ... do you read, over?"

"Go ahead, Victor Four ... over."

"Tango Lima, we have found what looks like the operations building and have a pile of maps with marked SWAPO locations. We need someone to come and pick them up. Over."

"Affirmative, Victor Four. Intelligence will be on the way. Stand by and be ready with smoke."

The base was so spread out that we had to pop a smoke for them to find us. We hung around the buildings and the guys rummaged through every office desk and cabinet. Some grabbed booty and souvenirs and stuffed them into their webbing. I did not. I decided this was too serious a time to be scrambling for souvenirs. I couldn't think of a worse way to meet your end than to get blown up by a booby trap while scrabbling for booty. (I saw a lieutenant blown to bits by a booby trap in a bunker in a later trip, on Operation *Daisy*.)

I squatted outside the small group of buildings, smoked a cigarette and scanned the area while they squabbled over prized Eastern Bloc webbing and equipment. A good few kilometres of the base still lay ahead of us but it looked pretty quiet from here. Probably all still hiding in the trenches. Behind some small prefab buildings, behind the ops rooms under some trees we found a large sand model of about four metres square. I couldn't make head or tail of it but Doep informed us that we had to stay put by the model until the intelligence outfit came over. After half an hour someone popped a green smoke and they arrived with big suitcases and a few infantry troops as escorts. Not far from the sand model under some trees, lay an old stripped-down hulk of a plane that was missing wings, tail, undercarriage and engine and nose. It looked so small that I didn't even pay attention to it. I thought it must be spare parts or an old civilian plane but later learned it was what was left of a South African Impala Mk II that had been shot down during Operation *Sceptic* a year before. Our Platoon, *Valk* 4, had stumbled onto one of the Angolan army's main intelligence centres. Later, South Africa launched another equally-large mechanized operation because of intelligence gleaned during Operation *Protea*. I firmly believe that it was this intelligence that the led to next big operation into Angola, Operation *Daisy*.

We spread out and moved on. A black youth leaped out of a bunker six or seven metres in front of us and took off like a jackrabbit. He was extraordinarily tall and muscular ... and unarmed. He had stripped off his shirt and had only his camouflage pants and boots on. His skin was smooth and black as tar. His back muscles flexed and bulged as he ran for his life across the small piece of open ground, heading for a thicket 50 metres away. Five or six of us took a second or two to react, then opened fire at the fleeing man. I bent my head to my sights and aimed between his shoulder blades. My rifle kicked into my shoulder as I fired five or six shots. Dust kicked up all around him as he gained speed, zigzagging and running like the hounds of hell were after him.

He was already maybe 50 metres from us, with his arms pumping in a steady rhythm like an olympic athlete in the race of his life. I quickly changed my footing, held my arm steady and took better aim this time, a little higher, and pulled off another salvo of shots. Through the smoke I saw that he seemed almost charmed. Although the ground around him was alive with spurts of dust from the bullets of the six men who were shooting at him, he ran on untouched. I paused. Inexplicably I took my finger off the trigger and stopped shooting but kept my rifle up so the others could not see I had stopped shooting.

"Go for it, mate, you're going to make it … Go! Go!"

I lifted my head and watched through the smoke.

"Go, you're almost there," my mind willed quietly. Just before the tree line he stumbled and seemed to trip over his feet. His long arms went down to break his fall and he rolled in the sand and lay still.

"Fucking hell … that kaffir can run. He almost got all the way across the *chana* … see that ... with all of us shooting!"

"Shit, doesn't say too much for our shooting. See how he went down? Looked like he was going to make it," Fourie hooted.

I said nothing and felt a sadness. We moved past the dead unarmed youth who lay in the sand with his eyes open. Someone put a shot through his head, just to make sure.

By about two in the afternoon most of the shooting had stopped. We had been at it since 06:00. The 1,000-man army we had expected wasn't there but FAPLA had left a few hundred diehards to face us and now it seemed that they too had retreated through the maze of trenches.

The worst was over. By now we had all got the hang of this thing and were moving methodically, like veterans, though the cavernous trenches, giving hand signals, moving rapidly in small groups. We were about halfway

Paras drive past a knocked-out FAPLA tank.

Mountains of FAPLA war matériel, captured during Operation *Protea*, is stacked behind the South African APCs.

Mechanized Fighting Group 20, back in South West Africa after three weeks in Angola on Operation *Protea*, the biggest South African military operation since the Second World War.

From an Afrikaans newspaper cutting: SADF troops inspecting a captured FAPLA anti-aircraft artillery piece.

Digging in for the night in Angola during Operation *Ceiling*.

A SWAPO turncoat being dropped off with the paras in Angola. The following day he led the paras to SWAPO's 'Navy HQ', where the paras sprung a dawn ambush and killed all 17 SWAPO guerrillas in situ.

John Delaney and Granger Korff about to emplane at Ongiva after several weeks of continuous fighting around the airstrip (in the background).

Valk 4 flying in fast to a contact during Op *Daisy*, Angola, November 1981.

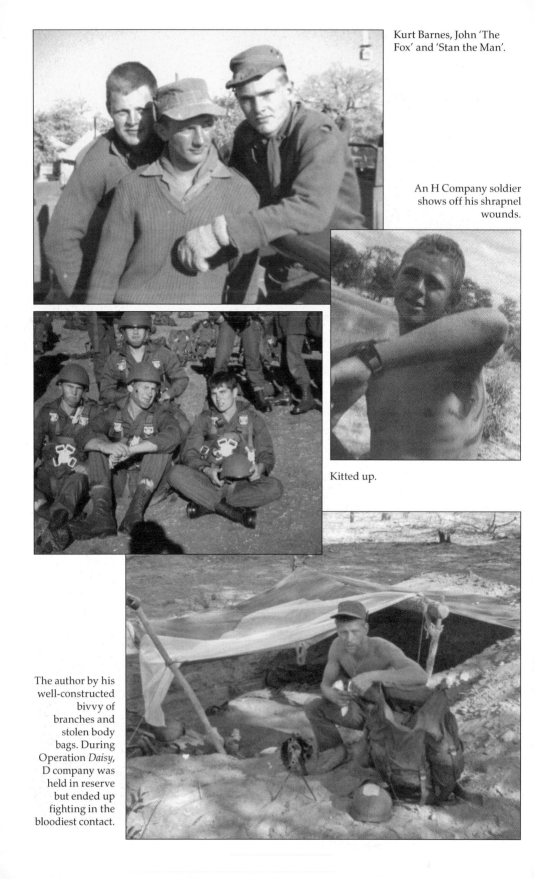

Kurt Barnes, John 'The Fox' and 'Stan the Man'.

An H Company soldier shows off his shrapnel wounds.

Kitted up.

The author by his well-constructed bivvy of branches and stolen body bags. During Operation *Daisy*, D company was held in reserve but ended up fighting in the bloodiest contact.

Kruger (*seated left*), 'The Fox', Stan, Korff and mortar man Kleingeld taking a break in Angola.

The author sitting on a SAAF Impala jet that had made a successful emergency landing in an open *chana* close to Ondangwa air force base. The paras stood guard until the plane was retrieved.

Stan and who-knows-whose finger—probably Gungie's.

H Company troops search the corpse of a SWAPO cadre. The paras had walked into an ambush but turned it around when they charged their assailants.

Final *klaar* out parade.

Korff with a deep cut. He fought on to lose on a points' decision.

Granger Korff knocking an opponent out of the ring, raising his arm in victory. Note his opponent's feet sticking up in the front row—coincidently where the judges are seated.

through the huge base. The midday sun baked down on us as we cleared each bunker with fire or grenades. We had got the order to stop using M27s and to use our 'Willy Pete' white phosphorus grenades instead, as some FAPLA troops had been hiding in bunkers covered with mattresses and survived the M27 blasts. Later I heard the story of how one plucky FAPLA sergeant had climbed out of a bunker after a grenade had been tossed in and, armed only with a piece of wood, had laid into a South African lieutenant. He had been clubbed down and taken prisoner.

We had just come through a long field of trenches. We turned our sweep line at a 90-degree angle to our right from the way we had come and were preparing to sweep through a long open field in front of us that was knee-high with patches of dead grass.

"Okay, go down and take a smoke break," Lieutenant Doep barked.

He was two men to my left. It was our first official break in eight hours. Feeling pretty safe and in control, most of us took off our heavy jump helmets and sat on our haunches, still holding the formation of our sweep line. It was the first time in eight hours I had taken my helmet off and it felt great to feel the hot air on my head. My hair was drenched with sweat and I had a sharp headache down the middle of my head from the weight of the helmet. I lit a cigarette and inhaled deeply.

Once again I took the bandana from around my neck and wiped my eyes. "They should make a headband standard army issue—a person could get killed with sweat in his eyes," I thought. I made a mental note to mention it to someone later on.

"Hey, Gungie! What do you think about your birthday curse now? Looks like you're going to be okay, eh?"

I had completely forgotten that today was my 21st birthday. Everyone in the *valk* knew of my uneasy feeling about this op. A chorus of laughs went up around me. Even Lieutenant Doep turned to me with a big grin on his thin, shark-like lips and said in Afrikaans, exhaling a cloud of smoke: "Well Korff, are you going to make it?"

"Looks like it, lieutenant," I answered sheepishly and laughed too.

We sat on our helmets for five minutes, chatting and laughing down the line. Fourie was still going on about the FAPLA troop who almost got away.

"I've never seen a man run that fast! I know what they mean now when they say it's hard to hit a moving target. That guy looked as if he was always just in front of the bullets."

I thought about why I had stopped shooting. I had no real answer. "Stupid! If he had got away and picked up an AK, do you think he would have stopped shooting if he had you in his sights?" I asked myself. The small voice inside me answered clearly: "He was unarmed and running for his life, that's why you stopped." The other side of me said: "So what? He would have shot you." I was glad no one had seen me stop shooting. I laughed and agreed that I never knew how hard it was to hit a man running.

Lieutenant Doep was the only one standing. He walked in small circles, talking loudly into the handset pushed to his ear. I was looking his way, just finishing my second cigarette when a loud shot cracked out from the dry grass ten metres in front of us. Doep flipped violently backwards, his feet kicking forward from under him with the receiver flying into the air. He fell flat on his back. I snatched up my rifle. A single puff of grey smoke rose from the grass, just metres in front of us. The six of us closest rose as one man and, with helmets off, charged the suicide sniper's position, shooting as we ran. The FAPLA troop did not even have time to turn over. He died on his belly, still in his shooting position, in a hail of South African bullets. We stood over the FAPLA soldier for a moment. A second later I turned to see that Lieutenant Doep was not dead. He was now flying towards us, almost in mid-air, with his long wet blond hair flowing behind him and his face flushed red, locked in a murderous mask. His eyes bulged with rage as he landed and fired four or five shots into the already-dead soldier, almost decapitating him. Lieutenant Doep was visibly shaken. He put his rifle down, his eyes still bulging. He felt his head with his fingers. The skin was not broken but he said he'd felt the bullet pass through his hair. He checked himself, not believing he was unscathed, but after a minute when he found himself intact he broke out in a huge boyish grin.

Lieutenant Doep was the luckiest man on earth. The FAPLA soldier had lain quiet, not ten metres in front of us for more than five minutes. He had probably lain down in the grass when he saw us coming. He knew that he had no chance of escape in the open field, that he had one shot before he died. He had probably held each of us in his sights at some point during that five minutes as he chose a target to take with him and had correctly identified Lieutenant Doep as our leader. He had five minutes or more to take his shot but he had missed and had died like he knew he was going to. With the violent way Doep was thrown back, the brave FAPLA soldier must have died thinking he had taken a Boer officer with him. In a way, I thought he was a brave man. He could have stood up and surrendered and taken a chance that no one would have potted him.

The whole operation was a slow-moving process of trench-to-trench and wait. By nightfall we still had many kilometres of trenches ahead of us.

"Hey, listen up. We're going to dig in and spend the night right here in the base. Dig in properly and set up double-watch. No flame. Only cold food," Lieutenant Doep instructed.

We dug shallow shellscrapes in the middle of the FAPLA military base to spend the night. There was no doubt that the maze of trenches ahead of us was still occupied as shots had buzzed past us all day and, as we knelt digging in for the night, the odd shot still rang out.

I rolled out my thin inner and lay on my back, fully dressed, with my rifle next to me. The whole scene took on an surreal feeling as everything around us was plunged into darkness. I lay and listened to a night that was still alive with the sounds of shooting, but it seemed kilometres away at the other end of the base. There was the roaring, far behind us, of some of the Ratels moving their position for the night. There had been a few bunkers of ammunition that had burned for hours throughout the afternoon, cooking off thousands of AK-47 rounds that popped and crackled and sounded like a never-ending fire fight, but they too had now burned out. I drew slowly and carefully on one of my last cigarettes and looked up at the dark night sky. There would be no moon tonight. It was pitch black and here we were, sleeping in the middle of a FAPLA base.

What a day!

I thought of how the RPG-7 rocket had missed me by centimetres, of what an almighty mess it would have been if it had hit me. Fuck it. I realized as an afterthought that it was my birthday and that I was 21 today. What a way to turn twenty-one. Other guys have parties, give speeches and get wrecked. I thought of my brother's 21st, when every *joller* in town had been there and of the speech my dad gave as he handed my brother an oversized brass key that my dad had received on his own 21st birthday. But of course, not me. Instead, I get to dodge fucking rockets and anti-aircraft fire and face fucking T-34 tanks. I thought of my family who would be thinking of me today and wondered if they had any idea how I was spending my big day. Well, as the story goes, it's the day you become a man. If that's the case, then I guess it's somehow fitting that I spent the day dodging bullets. What better way to see in manhood?

The artillery began a 15-minute barrage from several kilometres behind us. I had never heard the howitzers before and lay amazed, listening as the rounds whistled high overhead in the darkness and then crashed like rolling thunder many kilometres away, somewhere in the dark bush. This became a nightly routine with the artillery. The day's activities had made me feel small and humble. I closed my eyes and tried to doze but the adrenaline still coursed through me like fire and I lay listening in the darkness like an animal. At about 21:00 I snapped out of a surprisingly restful state of being as we heard voices chatting casually to each other in what sounded like Portuguese. They were coming from the big trench that was about three metres from where I lay. Between the trench and me were John Delaney and John 'The Fox' Glover who was closest to the trench. I pulled my rifle soundlessly onto my chest and lay, hardly breathing, so I could hear better as they came closer. They appeared unafraid or unaware, talking loudly and seeming to be arguing in short sentences. I waited, my finger on the trigger. I knew everyone else was lying waiting in exactly the same manner.

What were we going to do? If we all jumped up shooting we would probably shoot each other in the pitch darkness. I knew that if anybody was going to do something, it would be have to be us on the end closest to the trench. The voices were quiet now but I could hear them shuffling in the trench, probably not six metres from me.

"Come here!" John Delaney shouted and broke the silence like a POMZ.

"Huh?" came a surprised grunt from the trench.

John's grenade exploded metres from us but must have missed the trench, as seconds later bursts of green tracers flew over us almost at ground level, zipping a metre over my chest and off into the night. Silence. Another green burst. I lay on my back and watched the tracers flying in front of my eyes with dumb interest and thought, "Well, they're definitely not our boys."

I could hear scuffling as they ran down the trench into the darkness, making good their getaway. Damn! Good thing Doep had made us dig in because if we hadn't, we could have been nailed. No one said a word or made a sound to jeopardize our position. I lay breathing, snatching shallow gasps, still holding my rifle on my chest. What a wonderful day I was having ... and it looked like the party wasn't over yet. I tried to doze again.

At about 03:00 our Fighting Group 20 and anybody within a couple of kilometres was brought to their feet by the thunderous sound of a thousand vehicles starting up at the same time. It sounded like the start of a huge midnight Grand Prix for trucks. It came from directly ahead of us. Acting on reflex, I was on my knees in a flash, peering into the darkness. John was also up from his hole next to mine.

"What the hell is that?" I hissed.

"I don't know!"

"It's fucking vehicles ... lots of them!"

That's it, I thought instantly. They've regrouped and they're making a massive counter-attack. Clever motherfuckers to wait until the small fucking hours of the morning. Who would have thought there were so many of them so close to us ... and to think I was lying here dozing with 1,000 fucking FAPLA sitting in BTRs half a click in front of us! My blood ran cold. Everyone was up, huddled together, on our knees, peering into the blackness and chatting nervously.

"It's that battalion of tanks they said was here. Now we're in the shit!"

"Where's the fucking Ratels? Aren't they supposed to be with us?" I looked around behind me and could just make out the shape of the small Eland armoured car that was parked 30 metres behind us. I had seen him park there when we'd dug in earlier and knew that he didn't have a 90-millimetre cannon, only a 20-millimetre which was not much joy against a BTR or a tank.

The thunderous sound filled the night for long, never-ending minutes. It sounded as if every driver of the thousand vehicles (we discovered much later it was actually about 50 vehicles) had his foot flat on the gas. If they were trying to scare us, they were doing a good job.

"Okay … *now* the fight only starts. They've been holding back all this time, the fucking bastards," I said quietly.

Greeff was next to me, shaking his head. "Fuck it, man, why do they do this to us? They knew there's a battalion of tanks in this base but they send us in with a few lousy fucking Ratels and they're not even here!" He grumbled like a petulant child.

"I dunno," I answered quietly and shook my head too. I also wondered why the big armoured Ratels had retreated for the night, leaving us with scant protection. I was in a bit of a mind-spin myself. It sounded like hell itself was about to come crashing towards us.

"Kit up! Kit up!" Lieutenant Doep shouted, not bothering to be quiet.

I shot to my hole, rolled up my sleeping-bag inner in double-quick time and hauled my kit onto my back. I was just in the process of fastening my chest strap when I heard an engine come gunning towards us through the darkness. I stopped, just in time to see a big black form barrelling onto us out of the night. I barely had time to jump aside and run a few paces as the Soviet-built GAZ-66 supply truck came hurtling past me in mid-air with his engine screaming at a crazy pitch. He was airborne as he bounced at least a metre off the ground in the darkness. I was so close that in one brief second I could just make out a figure, his head hitting the roof of the cab and his arms stiffly braced on the wheel, trying to control the truck as he drove for dear life. We all scattered helter skelter.

"Shoot! Shoot!"

"Hold your fire, don't shoot!"

No one shot.

The GAZ-66 truck had passed right in among us. We watched as the dark shape bounced like a huge shadowy rock, rolling down the hill past the Eland armoured car. Seconds later the Eland's machine gun lit up the night in a reassuring 30-second burst of fire. The driver must have got away. I never did get to see the truck in daylight the next day.

"They're moving … here they come! Get ready, *manne!*"

THE END OF
OPERATION PROTEA

If 6 was a 9—Jimi Hendrix

The big armada of vehicles had started to move and we knelt in the dark. I held my rifle tightly and pulled out three grenades from the pouch and stuffed them into my pants pockets.

"Spread out, spread out!" Doep yelled. Instinctively we had grouped together in the dark.

"Horn, get that RPG ready! Green, set up your LMG with your second!"

Doep's radio crackled to life. "Tango Lima, Tango Lima, Victor Four … do you read me?"

"Yes, I read you, Victor Four …"

"We have a big movement of vehicles approaching; sounds like hundreds of them, over."

"Yes, we hear them too, Victor Four. Sit tight for now." The voice sounded cool and calm on the other end. It was alright for him; he was away at the back somewhere, surrounded by Ratels.

Sit tight for now!

The noise of the vehicles filled the night. I got down on one knee and pulled out the two magazines taped together and snapped in a fresh, full one. I was not sure how many rounds I had left in them and I had no desire to hear the click of a empty mag in the heat of combat again. I had learned that lesson. I pulled back the bolt and put a round in the chamber. I stayed down on one knee and cocked my head to listen. After a minute it sounded like the revving engines were getting fainter. I held my breath to hear better. They were definitely not coming forward!

"They're going away!" No one said a word as we all listened quietly.

"Yeah, they're moving away. They not attacking! They're making a run for it in the dark!"

I felt neither relief nor joy. I had prepared myself for an almighty shootout—and death—and was numb, detached and empty inside. We listened as the thousand-sounding engines faded into the night, making good their escape. I stayed on one knee with my head cocked and listening, holding my rifle in a death grip. No, we would not die tonight.

Neither they nor we knew that they were on their way to a rendezvous with the 'Terrible Ones' of 32 Battalion who were lying in wait miles away as stopper group on the very road they were travelling. An air strike was also called on them when they put up a fight and some of the convoy tried to flank 32 Battalion. It was like shooting fish in a barrel. Most would be killed, including several Soviet personnel as well as the wife of a Russian warrant officer, who, we later read in the newspapers, put up a fight lying next to her husband and firing with a pistol. Her three children were never found even though the SADF, at the surviving Russians' request, sent out a large search party to look for them the following day. At least that's what the newspaper that my mother kept for me said, when I read it weeks later.

It had been a very long night in the middle of a still-occupied enemy base. No one had got any sleep. The chilly dawn brought a long-awaited first light that bathed the bunkers and trenches of Ongiva in a soft grey. We had been up for hours but at first light we jumped into the big trench next to us and saw the spoor of our midnight visitors who had sprayed us with tracers. John's grenade had missed the trench; we saw the burned white sand a metre and a half from the edge. It had been close.

We walked carefully down the trench and came to a fork and a section where it petered out and we could see open ground. One hundred metres away, the nose of an unoccupied Soviet GAZ-66 truck that seemed to have taken the wrong turn in the great escape poked out from behind a mound.

"Lieutenant, should I take out the truck?" Horn was eager to use his RPG-7 rocket-launcher.

Doep paused. "Ja ... take it out."

Horn grinned, pulled the safety clip from his rocket and knelt down.

"You'll never hit that, Horn. Why don't you go closer?"

"Watch, stand away behind me."

Horn was a farm boy of few words. We watched in silence as he bent his head behind the long sights and closed one eye.

Bang. The launcher lurched in his hands with a huge report. The rocket flew with a *whoosh* in a rickety line but held its course and, sure enough, caught the truck just above the front tyre and exploded in white smoke. I recognized the *whoosh* of the rocket flying through the air as the same sound that flew just past my head the day before.

"Shit Horn, not bloody bad … those vehicles were lucky not to come our way last night."

Horn grinned as the whole platoon ooohed and aaahed.

The fight seemed to be over and the rest of the day was spent in much the same way as the previous afternoon—moving from bunker to trench, but now there was no firing at all except from our own troops as they fired deep into bunkers, moving around at will. New ammunition caches started cooking off again, sounding like fireworks.

We found one of the ZU-23-2 anti-aircraft guns that had been shooting so well at our Mirages the day before and had scared the shit out of us. The two barrels still pointed skyward. The area around it was littered with big empty shells.

I was amazed to see a thousand-pound bomb crater that was the size of a small house and three metres deep, with burned white sand clods the size of TV sets scattered for 30 metres around it. The bombs had not come too close to the AA gun positions and we didn't find any bodies at the guns. I heard the infantry found a gunner who had died at his gun while shooting at ground level; a Ratel took him and his position out with 20-millimetre fire. We also came upon the kitchen stores, which was a row of brick rooms filled to the roof with cans of pilchards and ham. In one room there was a mountain of canned chocolate milk. We found cartons of cigarettes, beer, porn magazines from Europe and even a handful of marijuana which we tried to smoke but after a couple of hits tossed the shit away.

We found and captured a skinny man with desperate, burning eyes who was lying flat in an open field next to the buildings. He was dressed in civvies and said that he was trying to get home but when we searched him we found a camouflage epaulette with two black stars in his pants pocket. We trussed him up with parachute cord and put him up on a Ratel where he sat looking quite relieved. At midday we made a loose laager with the Ratels and Elands and sat down under some trees to feast on fish and chocolate milk. There were at least three of our platoons and thirty other personel walking around laughing and chatting in the lightness of the moment. Half an hour later we all jumped as gunfire erupted in the middle of the laager. I looked up to see John Glover standing, legs wide apart, shooting into a deep narrow hole about the size an antbear hole. After seven or eight shots he emerged from the wreaths of gunsmoke and spoke loudly to the hundred surprised faces looking at him.

"There's a terr right here in the fucking hole! I'm sitting brewing some tea and I hear this rustling in the hole. I look down and see a pair of fucking eyes looking up at me. He must have been sitting in there for two days!"

I didn't even go over to look. I sat with my back against the tree, enjoyed my pilchards and washed them down with warm chocolate milk. I had another five cans in my kit.

Soon the whole area was teeming with Engineers and all sorts of other troops, loading up mountains of ammunition crates, equipment, generators, tools and office equipment. Abandoned FAPLA T-55 tanks roared into life, billowing black smoke as SADF drivers drove them out of their underground ramps and parked them in the open. Dozens of anti-aircraft guns were being towed away or loaded onto rows of captured Soviet-built GAZ-66 and Ural-375 trucks. The SADF booty from the operation was enormous. I later saw photographs in a magazine of the equipment and vehicles captured—just the crates of ammunition alone would fill a football field, never mind the more than 200 trucks, 16 tanks and more than 50 artillery and anti-aircraft pieces.

It had taken two days to overcome the big FAPLA base at Ongiva but we had done it. Apparently the operation was a huge success.

The armoured Buffels that had brought us to Ongiva had been brought forward. As we walked warily in a long broken line through a thicket of trees towards them, I carried my kit over my shoulder with one hand and my rifle at the trail in the other. Botha, who was a few metres in front of us, suddenly stopped and started firing into the bush next to him. I dropped my kit and John and I ran forward. A FAPLA soldier, already mortally wounded by Mark's fire, lay huddled under a thick bush. I aimed and put two shots into him. He jerked but was still moving. Botha and I shot again. Half his head was gone but he still writhed and kicked and his chest heaved as he took big gulps of air. I felt very distressed by it all as we all dumbly watched him thrashing. All I wanted was to put the poor bugger out of his misery but he would not die. John the Fox hopped over the little ditch, leaned over into the bush and held his rifle in one hand like a pistol, placing the muzzle point-blank on the poor soldier's heart and pulled the trigger. It seemed to do the job as finally he lay still. It was very messy. I walked away trying to push it out of my mind. Why couldn't we have taken the poor man prisoner? I didn't see an AK lying anywhere near him. As we were walking away Botha, who was a part-time company clerk and a slight, anaemic-looking fellow with yellow-blond hair and glasses, boasted that he had got 14 kills in the last couple of days. One of the other troops in his platoon backed up his claim when we told him he was talking shit. Botha, the company clerk, with 14 kills?

That night we slept in a big laager of Ratels and listened to the howitzers shelling who-knows-what many miles away. The only excitement came when a machine gun from a Ratel opened up just above my head at a sound in the bush around us. I had heard it too. It must have been a donkey or something. I dozed off into the first sleep in days, safely under the wheels of a big armoured Ratel.

The following day we drove through the ghost town of Ongiva. It was a surprisingly built-up little town, with a town centre that consisted of a couple of main roads with street lights and several three-storey, modern-looking buildings. The orange tile roofs of several of the buildings were caved in from mortar hits and thick black smoke from a building that had been smouldering for two days still rose in a pall on the outskirts of town. About a kilometre from the town centre were the suburbs—long rows of a few hundred deserted, small brick houses, their contents spilled out into the streets. Paper, furniture, money and everything imaginable littered the roadways and sidewalks, and before long we all had thick wads of useless

Angolan money. It looked as if the infantry had done a thorough job of going through the town with nothing left unturned. There were still large groups of infantry or intelligence troops going through the buildings with fine-tooth combs and examining every document.

During the day some civilians emerged from somewhere and gawked at us warily. The kids were not as suspicious and laughed as we threw them sweets from our rat packs. I finally gave my wad of money to a skinny woman in tattered clothes with three kids running around her. It was useless to me. I couldn't see myself ever coming back to Angola on a shopping spree. I even saw an old white man who sat on a chair and quietly watched us. He was probably a Portuguese leftover from the colonial days, one of the few who did not leave with the others when the communist-backed MPLA took power.

We spent the day moving around and riding shotgun while an army of troops drove out, loading up everything of value from the big base and the town. We swept the surrounding bush on a few false alarms, until it was finally announced that we were moving onto Xangongo.

Xangongo was another FAPLA base almost as big as Ongiva, about 80 clicks away to the east. Xangongo had been hit by our sister H Company, infantry and another mechanized fighting group a few days before we hit Ongiva, but a battalion of FAPLA tanks had apparently reoccupied the base and had sent a message that they were waiting for us. Or that was the story that was being passed on through the troops.

The entire kilometres-long Mechanized Fighting Group 20 took off slowly along the tar road to Xangongo. On the way out of Ongiva I saw a black civilian I remembered having seen sitting under a tree with his bicycle when we had started the attack three days before. I recognized him by his bright red pants, I was amazed that he hadn't moved from under that tree in three days. He sat casually and smiled and waved as we passed him in the Buffels. I think he was glad to see us go. Presently I saw an old donkey, also a casualty of war, and quite a sight crossing a big *chana* all alone, dragging his shattered back leg behind him away from Ongiva.

It was a painfully slow journey, because long sections of the road were lined with trenches and bunkers containing more ammunition and supplies. Some trenches were old and collapsed, while others looked well kept. We stopped while each one was searched and the contents loaded up. Some suspicious bunkers were blown up which erupted in huge explosions that set off thousands of rounds popping in the inferno. We crawled along at a snail's pace, spending the night in a big armoured laager. The following morning we finally crossed a small bridge and came to Xangongo, halting in sight of the base. It was deserted. There were no tanks to meet us. We spent a couple of days moving around Xangongo which looked similar to Ongiva with a maze of trenches and thick World War Two-like cement pillboxes with machine guns at intervals along the trenches. Some of the trenches had cement-plastered walls.

After about two weeks of chasing phantoms in the bush and with Eastern-Bloc canned fish and chocolate milk coming out of our ears, Operation *Protea* finally came to a end. We headed south, out of Angola, on a tar road in a slow 16-kilometre-long column of Buffels, Ratels, bellowing T-55 tanks and an almost endless column of hundreds of captured Soviet trucks.

The operation had been a great success. On the radio (every troop now had a transistor radio because there had been one or two in just about each bunker or trench that we entered) we heard a slow-talking, reassuring newscaster's voice assuring everyone in South Africa that all the SADF troops had been safely pulled back out of Angola days ago (we were still some distance inside Angola at the time). The radio said that 1,000 FAPLA and SWAPO troops had been killed in the operation. Among them, apparently, was the SWAPO deputy commander-in-chief and the deputy for political affairs. The SWAPO artillery commander had also been captured.

The SADF had lost only ten men, most of them when a Ratel troop-carrier fully occupied with infantry was taken out by anti-aircraft guns shooting at ground level, just as in Operation *Smokeshell*.

The long slow convoy drove back to the staging area in the Etosha game reserve where we had trained for the op. We spent two depressing days sitting around in the red sand and getting drunk at night, celebrating our success. Everybody seemed to be sick of this bush crap. D Company (with the exception of me who had spent three weeks sleeping in a bed waiting for my court martial) had been roughing it in the bush and sleeping in holes in the ground since the start of Operation *Ceiling* more than two months ago.

"I can't wait to walk into a Black Angus steakhouse, sit down and order a juicy steak with pepper sauce. Then two slices of cheesecake and an ice-cold beer. Stroll down to the beach and check out the dolls. Lie on the beach and sniff that good old Cape Town salt water." Even hard-nose Stander was getting homesick.

"Cheesecake and beer? Makes sense ... you'll probably be in your browns ... you know it's pretty hard to walk on the beach with jumper boots. Also, it's not allowed, you know ... the MPs tend to frown on it."

"Fuck the MPs ... if I want to walk in my browns on the beach, I will. I don't give a shit about the MPs. If I want to eat cheesecake and drink beer, I will. We've just come from the front line of one of the biggest operations the SADF has ever done. Fuck the MPs. There were over a thousand kills in this operation. No other operation has come close ... and we were front line!"

We were sitting around the same ashy fire-pit where I had got wasted and passed out the night before the op and hallucinated. I sipped my warm beer.

"That's bullshit. Where do you get a thousand kills?"

"That's what it is ... there were a thousand kills in the whole operation ... that includes Xangongo and the small bases that were hit around the area too."

"Well, I still say it's bullshit. I didn't see a thousand dead bodies lying around ... did you?"

"It was the whole fucking area, man! You know how many of our troops were in on this op? Probably well over three thousand, what with all the stopper groups."

"Well, then, they must have had all the kills because I was there on the front line attacking the biggest base of the operation and I didn't see anywhere near a thousand kills."

Stan and I were at it again. He told me I didn't know what I was talking about and I told him that my eyes didn't lie and that I hadn't seen many rotting corpses at Xangongo either. He shook his head in disgust.

"Hey, cool it, you two. Let's go back to where you were sniffing the salty sea air, but I'm telling you I'd rather be sniffing some good salty Cape Town babes."

We all cracked up as the conversation changed to girls.

A chaplain stood on a Ratel, read from the Bible and gave a long prayer of thanks to God for watching over us. I couldn't hear a word he said. A thousand troops from different units assembled in the fine red sand and were given sky-blue T-shirts with 'Operation Protea' on them in tiny letters to show that the wearer had been there. Mine was too small and I was never able to wear it. We were told what a good job we had all done and what a setback for SWAPO this operation had been. A brigadier or a general, who had a bigger voice that the chaplain, told us we had set back SWAPO's activities in southern Angola for many years to come and that South African presence would be maintained in Ongiva and Xangongo, forcing SWAPO to pull its bases and training camps much farther back into Angola. We had taught the Angolan army a huge lesson about aiding and abetting SWAPO and allowing them to set up bases under their protective wing. FAPLA forces had also been driven back and South Africa would henceforth basically control southern Angola. We were then all dismissed from Fighting Group 20 to return to our different units.

The Parabats drove back down the long tar road to good old Ondangwa in a long, weary column, arriving late that night. There was no chow for us and we had to sleep on the dirt around the swimming pool as the juniors still occupied the tents. Still, it was home. We laughed and joked as we jockeyed for places to sleep on the soft, well-churned-up sand. It was good to be back again, in one piece.

We were just getting comfortable when Lieutenant Doep appeared through the darkness and told us what we really didn't want to hear. "Hey, listen up, D Company. Don't unpack your kit and don't hand in your ammunition. We're going back to Ongiva first thing in the morning. There's a garrison of 200 FAPLA who've reoccupied the town and we have to go and sort them out. Good night."

I thought my ears were playing tricks on me after the long drive in the noisy Buffel, but John the Fox confirmed the information.

"I'll bet we're the only ones going back ... wait and see. I'm telling you!"

I had recently come to understand more clearly how the South African army worked. The Afrikaner did not overreact as some other nations would. I had seen this on TV when they would send eight policemen with dogs and shotguns to handle hundreds of rioting blacks. They would think nothing of sending 40 men to take on 300 enemy (as they did in Operation *Super* in March 1982 when 45 troops from 32 Battalion attacked a base and killed 201 SWAPO terrorists). They definitely did not believe in the old rule about outnumbering the enemy three to one.

That night I had the first episode of a nightmare that would recur for many years: Our platoon was walking on patrol, deep in Angola. We walked through a dark, petrified forest-like area that seemed to have been burned and then we found ourselves walking into the middle of a small town with rows of small brightly painted houses like those in Ongiva. The dirt streets had big potholes and rubbish lay strewn everywhere. The little town was alive with activity; the black Angolans stood calmly on their *stoeps* chatting with each other and jeered at us, unafraid. Kids ran around us, laughing as we walked through in formation. Something was obviously wrong; we should not have been there but we kept formation and walked through the uneven, littered streets. Then a local came up to us, grinning, and casually told us in some language we could more or less understand that we had better watch out because someone had gone to call the government troops and they would be here any minute to kill us.

But we kept on with our patrol.

Early the next morning D Company—and D Company alone—took off back into Angola, above the old potted tar road that crossed the border and linked the two countries, as well as leading straight into Ongiva. It was the old road that had been used in the days of the Portuguese to cross to and fro over the border to South West Africa. The tar was cracked and the edges of the road had long since crumbled away. We passed the last dribs and drabs of South African troops driving back to South West Africa in Soviet GAZ-66 trucks, loaded high with Eastern-Bloc ammo and towing AA guns or civilian cars. We were the only idiots going the wrong way. Our three-month bush trip was soon to be over; we were scheduled to return to South Africa in a couple of days (most outfits did a six-month stint but one of the perks of the paras was that we only did three, the logic being that we would see more action than the rest), so no one particularly felt like heading in the direction we were.

"This is crap. We should be suntanning and getting ready to go home.

Send someone else back! Send the juniors in ... they need the experience. We've spent almost the whole bush trip in the fucking bush. I cant remember what a bed feels like," Roberts sulked.

"That's why they call it a bush trip, dumbo."

We soon came to the town of Ongiva but this time there were no bombs and anti-aircraft fire. It stood like a ghost town. We came in from a different direction this time and didn't see a soul. Even the few locals who had come out of hiding after the op seemed to have disappeared .

We stopped on the outskirts of town and got out of the Buffels. The company spread out in a long sweep line and slowly advanced into the town, with the Buffels following behind. It was a very different feeling to what it had been before, when we'd had hundreds of troops, artillery, fighter planes and armour behind us. This time it was one company of paratroopers, with a Buffel-mounted 82-millimetre mortar.

Fuck the army!

Not a word was said as we got into town and walked cautiously through the deserted streets like a gang of bad guys in a spaghetti western as all the townsfolk hid away. Only this time there were no townsfolk. We walked down the main road and through the old town square that was still cordoned off with rusted chains draped from cement bollards left over from the times when there was grass and flowers in the little square. We walked cautiously through the rows of pink and blue houses and finally to the other side of town where the trenches of the military base began. This was a few kilometres from the airfield where we had fought a week earlier. The trenches and bunkers were deserted. We did not run into a garrison of 200 FAPLA or even two dozen FAPLA. All we found was an eerie ghost town and a FAPLA army base. Ongiva was certainly aptly called the 'Town of Death'

We dug in on the outskirts of town, close to the main tar road (the same road FAPLA had used to make their midnight escape with their ill-fated convoy of vehicles) and soon found that we were not alone. In the distance we could hear the occasional sounds of vehicles or gunshots.

One morning a shout went up as a white Jeep came racing along the tar road 300 metres away. Kleingeld dived for his mortar tube and popped off some 60-millimetre mortar bombs that landed pretty close to the speeding vehicle, but which didn't stop it. The Jeep made the gauntlet but returned half an hour later with a white flag flying out of the window on a long stick.

"Get in position! Spread out! Spread out!" Doep shouted excitedly as the Jeep drove slowly over the *chana* towards us with his white flag flapping. I dived into my little hole and trained my rifle on the approaching vehicle. It pulled up to our position and, to our surprise, a short Portuguese priest, complete with dog-collar and all the rest of it, hopped out of the driver's seat and immediately began berating Lieutenant Doep, wagging his finger in Doep's face and rattling away in broken English. I couldn't hear everything that he was saying but he was unafraid and shook his fist in rage, pointing to us lying in the dirt. He pointed to the town behind him and shook his arms in the air as he stamped his foot in the sand. Doep listened sheepishly and was also waving his hands trying to calm the padre but to no avail. With a last wag of his finger he turned without looking back, jumped into the Jeep and drove off over the *chana*, his white flag still flying.

Doep was smiling as he sat down, leaning his rifle against a tree. "He said that the United Nations is going to fix us, that we will have to answer to them and to God for what we have done by attacking the innocent people of Angola."

"Hey Kleingeld ... *gooi morters*, fire mortars; it's your second chance," one of the troops joked as we watched the padre's white Jeep disappear.

At night I did not sleep well. My old fear of being shot sleeping in my foxhole was alive and well, and justified. I couldn't understand the army at all. It takes a whole fucking mechanized fighting group eight kilometres long and with 20 fighter planes to take the base and then they send in one company of paratroopers to try and prevent it from being reoccupied. They either thought very highly of our fighting abilities or they were stupid. I opted for the latter. The troops were grumbling. The due date for our return to South Africa had come and gone days ago. Everyone was up to their necks with Angola and the bush. We spent the days sitting in our foxholes eating rat packs and talking about Civvy Street. Doep said we might spend another month on the border because of the shit that had gone down. It was bad news.

We weren't doing any *kak soek* patrols, just monitoring the tar road and watching the area with binoculars. The only real excitement and scare came when, just before dusk one night, Doep shouted that a recce group farther up the tar road had said that a convoy of BTR armoured troop-carriers and a couple of old T-55 tanks were on their way up the road to our position. We flew out, hanging onto the sides of the Buffel and set up a hasty ambush by the side of the tar road. All we had was a couple of RPG-7s and a 60-millimetre mortar. I lay with my puny 5.56 rifle tucked into my shoulder and thought how the 14.5-millimetre guns on the BTRs would turn our little ambush into mincemeat. Then the tanks would ride over us just to finish the job and we'd all die just because they couldn't spare a couple of armoured vehicles to accompany us. Darkness thankfully enveloped us and no tanks arrived but we did hear vehicles far away in the distance. At about 21:00 we broke the ambush.

At dawn one morning, after eight or nine days of sitting at our little observation post, Lieutenant Doep came with very good news indeed. There was a Flossy (Hercules C-130) sitting on the runway in South West Africa at the paratrooper base at Ondangwa right now as he spoke and it was waiting for us. Replacements were on their way in choppers that would take us from Angola to Ondangwa. Then straight onto the C-130 and home to South Africa. Within two hours we would board the Flossy, fly 1,600 kilometres and be back in Bloemfontein, South Africa ... today.

It was fantastic news. We chatted and laughed like school kids as we kitted up and walked the few clicks to the deserted airfield we had attacked two weeks ago, to lay an area defence for the choppers. True enough, 40 minutes later, eight big Pumas came hammering in low over the trees and landed on the deserted FAPLA airstrip, unloading a company of wide-eyed black South West African troops from 101 Battalion to replace us.

D Company had the distinction of being the first of many thousands of troops to monitor and occupy the Angolan town of Ongiva, as from then on the South Africans pretty much controlled of the whole of southern Angola and Ongiva for the next eight years. I walked with John Delaney down the runway to the choppers. Kurt snapped a photo of us just before we jumped in. I scratched my two weeks' beard and watched the ghost town of Ongiva with its rows of bombed-out houses and its miles of trenches and bunkers disappear below the horizon. We flew at treetop level which was standard procedure in the operational area. I lay on my kit, relaxed and enjoyed the long chopper ride back as I watched Angola flash beneath me like a wide green sea. At least we did not have to drive the long bumpy journey out of Angola.

As we disembarked at Ondangwa we saw the C-130 sitting fat and squat on the tarmac and we chatted and laughed with the realization that we were truly flying out that day. There was our plane, right in front of our eyes. I was ready just to walk straight from the chopper to the Flossy but we headed instead to the paratrooper tents close to the chopper pads, where we found that all our kit we had left at the training area almost a month ago had been piled into one tent (the one I had stayed in on my three-week court-martial vacation). There was a quick hot meal of army slop in the tin-roofed kitchen and even time to catch a shave and shower to wash off the now-hardened Angolan grime before we shouldered our heavy *balsaks* and tramped across the hot tarmac to the big camo C-130 that sat eager to return to South Africa. I slept cold and cramped in the netting seats, not having had the time or the forethought to dig out a bush jacket for the long, high-altitude flight home. But it didn't matter.

Landing at Bloemfontein we were told to our surprise that there was a big welcome-home parade going on in downtown Bloemfontein for us and the other units that had participated in Operation *Protea*. We were immediately loaded into big Samil trucks and taken from the airport straight into downtown Bloemfontein where, to our amazement, there was a full-scale military parade outside the city hall on the main drag. All the streets had been closed off for kilometres around with thousands of civilians and families cramming the pavements as we drove in. Battalion after battalion of infantry, paratrooper, services and panzer troops lined the road, neatly in closed-order formation with patriotic orange, white and blue banners hanging from lamp post to lamp post over the wide main street.

"What the hell's going on here? Is somebody dead?"

"Yeah, there are a thousand FAPLA and SWAPO dead. This is for us. We're the fucking heroes!"

When our small convoy of trucks drove up the wrong street, people at the roadside thought that the parade had begun and waved and smiled. We waved back sheepishly. Finally the drivers were directed to the right spot at a parking lot near the centre of town and we hopped off and dubiously eyed the scene in front of us. A few hundred panzer troops who had taken part in the operation were lined up in the parking lot as well. They had some Eland armoured cars with them that they lounged against. It looked as if they had been waiting for a while.

It was unbelievable that the army could have put together such a well-timed manoeuvre. Whoever had planned on having the Parabats present at this parade had done so with precision planning, flying us from deep in Indian country in Angola, then immediately onto a C-130 at Ondangwa to South Africa. Three countries in one day. Perhaps it was just luck, perhaps they would have continued with the parade without us, as they did with our sister H Company which was nowhere to be seen.

We looked a ragged bunch, still dressed in our torn bush browns, faded to light khaki with pockets ripped off. My clean shirt that I had hastily pulled from my *balsak* in Ondangwa was stiff with white sweat rings and black with dirt on the collar and sleeves. Our boots were scuffed white from more than two months of kicking sand in back-to-back operations. I still had my two quick-change magazines taped together with dirty white medical tape in my rifle. Our hair hung two or three inches over our collars. We looked like veteran bush fighters with our maroon berets on our heads. We were the heroes, welcomed home and cheered. Warriors at last, who had defended the country and fought for the security of all. We formed up into a company in the parking lot and, with a military band leading the way, began marching down the main road.

Civilians packed the pavements and kids waved from their fathers' shoulders. After months in the bush my eyes were like a hawk and I quickly picked out the beautiful, and not-so-beautiful, girls in the crowd that lined the road waving. In truth, they all looked beautiful, all of them waving their hands and smiling. Lipstick and pretty dresses and soft brushed hair. I stared at them out of the corner of my eye as we marched down the thronged main street with the casual cocky attitude of proud combat paratroopers.

I saw the fresh-faced paratrooper recruits in clean new uniforms staring at us as we marched by and knew how they felt. I had stared in the same way when I first saw a combat-seasoned Parabat company returning from the border and being congratulated on their successes. We came to a halt outside the city hall. Sergeant-Major Sakkie's legendary voice drowned the 20-piece band as we formed up in open formation. Finally the band stopped and we listened as speaker after speaker congratulated and thanked all of us involved for our part in the biggest and most successful military operation since the Second World War.

A prayer was offered for the infantry troops who had paid the ultimate price and finally the mayor of Bloemfontein, a big man with a belly that started from his chest, gave an impressively patriotic speech and then came huffing down from his podium to walk down our open-order ranks and shake hands with every troop as he thanked us. As he got to me a TV crew hurried forward, busy filming. I put out my hand as he grasped and almost crushed it.

"Congratulations on the victory. We all thank you very much."

I remember looking at the thick, studded mayoral gold chain that hung around his neck and then into his small earnest brown eyes beaming at me as I nodded my head.

Afterwards we were dismissed and told to come into the hall for food. Long tables had been laid out and women with sweet voices handed us paper plates and we loaded up with cold meats and delicious desserts. All of a sudden we were like kids at a church picnic—we laughed and giggled as we stood in line for second helpings and answered, around stuffed cheeks, the women's queries on how we liked the food. Outside we had a chance to mingle with the civilians for a while. We stood on the city hall steps and smoked as we eyed the girls and they eyed us back. With our long hair, dark brown suntans, torn uniforms and worn rifles slung over our shoulders we looked the part and kept the civvies staring. We *were* the real thing; just flown out of Angola and into the city hall in Bloemfontein. Seven hours ago we had been sitting in Ongiva watching for FAPLA—now we were chewing cold meat and devilled eggs and eyeing pretty Afrikaans girls in fresh make-up.

The next morning, after another smaller parade and further congratulations from a jubilant Commandant Archie Moore, we were sent off on an unbelievable but true 21-day pass. My mother and Taina were waiting at the gates. After almost breaking my ribs (she was strong as well as beautiful) Taina held me at arms' length and examined me, her big green eyes taking in every detail with concern before informing me that I had changed and somehow looked different. She said I looked like a man now. Well, thank you very much. I never knew she had looked on me as a boy before. But she was right. I could feel it too—a part of me did not feel the same.

When we pulled into the driveway on the farm it was snowing. It had not snowed in Johannesburg for 20-odd years but now everything was covered in a blanket of white snow. The 'welcome home' banner that hung over the garage looked in danger of collapsing under the weight of the thick layer of snow on top of it.

It was great to be home again. Fuck Angola, fuck the army and fuck SWAPO and FAPLA. I was still gung-ho but had seen that it was not a game any more and that people got killed. People got shot to pieces. Old men died and no one cared. Young men who had joined with the same eagerness for adventure as me got ambushed while cooking breakfast and had their brains shot out and eaten by pigs and were notched on someone's rifle as one more kill. I had no doubt that they would have killed me had I been sitting cooking canned steak and onions but in the back of my mind there was a vague notion that even though I was sure I was doing the right thing, somehow it was still all bullshit.

Fuck everybody.

GLORIOUS 21-DAY PASS

Walking on the moon—The Police

That night I saw myself on TV on the six o'clock news, shaking hands with the mayor of Bloemfontein. I was surprised how skinny and forlorn and serious I looked as the mayor vigorously pumped my hand up and down. My moustache looked huge and almost ginger on my face. They showed my handshake as one of the main features after the march-pasts and speeches. Taina squealed with delight and my dad smiled. The report went on to say that Operation *Protea* was the biggest and most successful external operation to date; aimed primarily at knocking out SWAPO headquarters at Xangongo, and secondly at destroying the enormous quantities of heavy weapons and conventional equipment that had been stockpiled by the Angolans at Ongiva, a stone's throw from our border. I was learning more from the television news bulletin about why we had been there and what we had done than I had known when I was in a trench in Ongiva.

I told my brother and father how we had hit the FAPLA troops by mistake in Operation *Ceiling*—before FAPLA became fair game in Operation *Protea* a month later. My brother told me he had seen on the news that South African troops had attacked FAPLA and that Angola had complained bitterly to the United Nations about the aggressive racist regime. He shook his head when I told him that it was my platoon alone involved in the unfortunate mistake. I told him how we shot the hell out of them and how I had almost had my head blown off, puking, while a terr was setting up to blast me from five metres away. I told him how we had run through the night when the BTR had come after us and how we had later shot the old man by mistake and callously left him lying there. And how we had carried out the perfect ambush early in the morning, killing all present and about the steaming heads and the snuffling

305

pigs; the hard-looking terr showing me a 'fuck you' sign on his chest as he died; the 16-year-old SWAPOs we had cornered in the thicket of dense bush and shot to pieces and the 1,000-pound bombs that sounded like thunder and the chaos of being pinned down with anti-aircraft fire ripping over our heads and dashing from trench to trench. I spared my dad some of the details but my brother wanted to know them all.

I cracked up with laughter when my mother (who was also a corporal in the reserve force) told me how she had single-handedly protested the fact that lately there had been so many young troops dying while serving time in DB. There had been a spate of deaths reported in the newspapers. She had been on parade with her unit in Johannesburg; the parade was dismissed and the two companies turned to march off the parade ground but my mother had stood her ground and refused to move. Troops walked around her, cussing in her ear to "Get out the way, you silly bitch!" Pretty soon my mother was standing, at ease, alone on the parade ground. The RSM had a fit and told her to fuck off his parade ground immediately and what was her fucking problem. She told him that she was a mother with sons on the border and that she was protesting the deaths of young soldiers in DB. He threatened and cursed and shouted in her face that if she did not remove herself from his parade ground at once she would be charged and put in DB herself. But no threat could budge my mother. She stood alone on the empty parade ground for half an hour while various officers tried in vain to get her to leave, all getting the same response. Finally, to her relief, an army chaplain came to her and asked if she wanted a cup of tea and to talk about it. To which she replied "Yes, please" and walked off with the chaplain. She had made her point. My mother—the original rebel. Now I knew where my streak came from.

We went to the famous Kyalami race track for the Formula One Grand Prix in Darryl's brand-new AlfaSud sports car which he had just bought. His first new car. He clucked and pecked like a old mother hen over his new piece of tin. I laughed when he fussily said that I shouldn't lean against it. Knowing me as being heavy handed, he instructed me carefully on the correct way to slowly close the door and, though we were both dying for a cigarette, he said we couldn't smoke in the car. The new sound system with graphic equalizer blasted out the Police's 'Walking on the moon' that drowned the horn blasts of the racing enthusiasts behind us as Darryl crawled at a snail's pace over the speed bumps leading into Kyalami.

As Mario Andretti and his mates roared past us in their Formula One rockets, we sat in the front seats of the AlfaSud and did some serious damage to a bottle of good South African brandy. Shouting above the roar of the engines, I told Darryl about the last three months in the bush. Thick with brandy and emotion, I emphasized the point by slamming my right fist into the windscreen of Darryl's brand-new Alfa. The emotion of the moment was bigger than the shattered windscreen in front of us that splintered instantly from corner to corner into a spiderweb of shiny cracks as I carried on with the story, without pausing, still punctuating it with occasional punches. Darryl showed the true colours of our long friendship as he sat silent for half a minute and let me finish my story before we both took in the damage to the brand-new car's windscreen, my bleeding knuckle and then roared with laughter. By chance I met Badenhorst who was in my platoon. He was also wandering among the crowds with a friend, drunk out of his mind mumbling about shooting SWAPO. I poured him a stiff three-finger brandy. Soon afterwards he and I both passed out on the ground. I was drunker than I could ever remember being in my life.

Stan hitchhiked from Cape Town up to Johannesburg and spent a couple of days with me. Lance, my old friend from high school, was also on leave from the border; the old gang was together again. Lance had made it to second lieutenant with a Bushman tracker unit and had been close to the area where we had pushed vehicle patrol. I had often asked after him but had not bumped into him on the border. We swapped war stories.

He was bummed that he had just missed the two ops. "We were securing the area for you guys so that you could get into Angola without a contact. If it hadn't been for us the whole operation would have been compromised!"

"We had a 16-click mechanized convoy with us going in ... I don't think we would have had a problem."

We argued inter-unit politics and pride and drank. Stan got on well with my old gang and we partied at all the old haunts. We swaggered into the discotheque in Boksburg and danced to Bananarama's 'Cruel Summer' then smoked doobies at the dam.

At a roadhouse that served late-night chow, a notorious Lebanese gang pulled in en masse. They were punks with long reputations of ganging up and kicking the crap out of anyone they decided needed an ass-whipping. They had also been involved in a few stabbings and shootings. One of the well-known Lebanese brothers sauntered by and muttered something to Stan who was glaring at him like a Nazi stormtrooper. The little prick sneered and made a hand gesture. Before Stan or anyone could react I had smashed my plate of burger and fries into his face and followed up with a punch that did not catch him flush. He whirled to run with his face full of ketchup, blood and gravy and I gave chase but ran into two of his delightful 'cousins'. It turned into a free-for-all with everyone involved. I ended up doing pretty well, with two punks in a head-lock under each arm like in a Bud Spencer movie. I was starting to jump up and down, shaking them around. Out of the corner of my eye I saw Stan reel back as he got caught by a good punch. Derek Worthy floored a skinny Lebanese with a long right-hand. I was just starting to have fun when some off-duty cop sneaked up and sprayed a canister of tear gas into my face from 30 centimetres away. I dropped like I had been shot as did the two Lebs I was holding, who also got the benefit of the blast, and, in agony, unable to breathe, the three of us crawled blindly on our hands and knees with our eyes burning like fire. I ended up leaning against the prick cop who had blasted me.

Finally Taina and I took off together and spent a week in Cape Town. We drove down through the flat, hot Karoo semi-desert and swam naked in one of the wind-whipped, remarkably ice-cold reservoirs that lined the side of the desert road. In Cape Town we went on long drives through the old wine routes. We went for long walks, disappearing off the paths to make love in fields of tall grass and wild flowers.

★★★★★

"Look at it from their side. All they're doing is fighting for the right to govern themselves in South West Africa. Wouldn't you be doing that if you were born black, Granger?"

I felt frustrated and out of place among the idiot university crowd. They all seemed like dipshits with their long hair and bullshit. Stupid motherfuckers. What did these jerk-offs know about a T-55 coming out and chasing you, or running the whole night without ammunition, or clearing bunkers while anti-aircraft fire made you almost shit in your pants, praying that the next one wouldn't turn you into a heap of guts and bone?

One morning I was woken by a loud knock on the front door of the flat where Taina and I were staying. Sleepily I got up and opened it to find Stan standing in full step-out uniform, maroon beret and *balsak* at his side.

"What the fuck's going on with you?" I inquired, still half-asleep and with a dreadful, throbbing hangover.

"We've all been called up. We have to go back to 1 Para ... there's big shit going on. They called my dad's house."

I stared at Stan through misty vision, not able to believe my ears, or the sight of Stan standing in uniform in front of me, telling me to get dressed immediately and get back to 1 Parachute Battalion.

"What? Bullshit. You're kidding?"

"No, I'm not kidding. They called my dad's house, man!"

"Bullshit. I don't believe you."

"I'm telling you, Gungie, I'm not kidding! I'm leaving right now and hitchhiking to Bloem! Come with me."

"Well, fuck that. I didn't get the message, did I? Nobody knows that I'm down in Cape Town. I'm not going ... you never saw me. Got it?"

Stan lectured me for five minutes, telling me I was not a good soldier and that I would be in big shit and was letting the company down.

I was not interested. As I saw it, nobody even knew where I was except for Stan. I would just say that I never knew. I turned around and went back to bed with Taina.

Stan went off in a huff and hitchhiked the whole 1,000-kilometre, two-day journey to 1 Parachute Battalion in Bloemfontein only to be told on arriving that it was a false alarm. He turned around and hitchhiked back. Apparently only a handful of D Company had responded to the emergency call-back from our precious 21-day pass. Stan was pissed.

★★★★★

"I'm afraid that's the way it seems to be going, son. There's talk that they might one day release Mandela and that the ANC could become a legal political party. I doubt that it'll happen but either way I think there are going to be some big changes here. It can't go on like this. These world sanctions are killing the country. The Americans won't sell us a thing. Everything's so expensive. Bombs going off somewhere almost daily. I'm afraid the day might come that life as we know it will change."

"Fuck the Americans," I thought. "They're a bunch of do-gooders—a naïve, McDonalds-guzzling, fat-ass nation that thinks whatever they do, the world should do the same. Fuck the British ... and the whole world too."

I held no hatred for black South Africans nor did most of the people I knew. We would go out of our way to help them. I had known since I was a kid, without being told, that apartheid was wrong and would end one day, that black people should get a better shake. But the ANC becoming a political party, with Mandela coming out to lead them after 22 years in jail? What horseshit was that? It sounded like a bad Hollywood screenplay. The ANC wass backed by the same commies I was shooting on the border. I smiled and shook my head and tried to let it go. I wasn't going to let politics ruin my 21-day pass. When I thought about it I actually didn't really give a shit because it would never happen. That would be the day, that South Africa would give in to world pressure and communism.

"Well, you've only got three months left in the army, son. Have you thought what you're going to do when you get out?"

"No, I haven't, pa ..."

"You should think about what your friend Ricky Jones is doing ... plumbing. It's a good trade ... you'll always find work, wherever you go."

"Plumbing ... you've got to be kidding. The hell I'll walk around in dirty clothes, swinging a monkey-wrench and fixing fucking pipes," I thought to myself.

"Yeah, I'll think about it," I said to my father.

OPERATION DAISY
October/November 1981

The song remains the same—Led Zeppelin

We were back up in the operational area on our third and final bush trip. Nothing had changed much at Ondangwa in our short absence. We sat packed and sweating in the hot, tin-roofed canteen next to the small pool and had a welcome-back briefing on what was happening in the area.

Over 2,000 insurgents had been killed since the beginning of the year, with 1,295 being confirmed. This was not including the external operations, where they claimed 300 had been killed by bombings alone and 1,000 in Operation *Protea*. The SADF had lost 49 troops which they claimed was less than the previous year. The local black population had suffered heavily, with 91 civilians murdered by the insurgents and another 62 who had died in landmine explosions. A further 103 had been abducted into Angola to forcibly join SWAPO. We were told that Operation *Protea* had dealt a devastating and humiliating blow to FAPLA and that cross-border insurgent raids into South West Africa were down in the last month, as SWAPO and FAPLA were still reeling from the enormous loss of men and equipment. We had shown FAPLA it was not wise to interfere with us while we were dealing with SWAPO. The good news of the briefing was that D Company was going to be on Fireforce again, which meant at least one platoon at a time would be on reaction force, lounging around the pool waiting for the siren to wail.

With no immediate action planned for us I started working out in the little gym and going on runs. I set up a punch-bag filled with towels and sand next to the laundry room and started to work the bag.

"I think I'm going to box when I get back to Civvy Street. Turn pro and get a title."

Stan laughed. "Turn pro and get fucked up is what you mean! You can't just decide to turn pro, china. You've got to come up through the ranks from a kid—fight your way up, get provincial colours, national colours. Its takes a mindset like one of these idiots—like that Ackerman. He's been boxing since he was five years old. He's like a machine."

"Bullshit. I'll take Ackerman out. He's no machine. I'll whip that boy before he can say 'Stand in the door'."

"Oh yeah?"

"Hell, yeah!"

I held Stan's sneer.

Stan still had a thing about Ackerman, whose brief reign of power had fizzled over the last months of combat, of which he had missed a lot. Yet he still waddled around the company like a short, squat tank with eyes like a snake and a fist always ready to knock someone out. Just a few weeks ago in a disco in Bloemfontein we heard that he had knocked a civvy cold with one sucker-punch in the middle of the dance floor. Ackerman had always been wary of me because he couldn't figure me out. I was not a loudmouth and didn't swagger my stuff, like a good macho Afrikaner boy would. He and I had sparred with each other on PT course where I had caught him with a few educated punches. The incident of beating the acting company sergeant-major shitless at Ombalantu had caught even his reptilian attention. (He had not been around at the time it happened and had missed all the operations because he had been called back to South Africa to box for 1 Parachute Battalion in inter-unit tournaments but he had heard about it—as had almost every troop in the battalion.) He had always had a dislike for Stan, eyeing him coldly, waiting for an opportunity to arise. Stan knew it too and I think he had bad dreams about bumping into Ackerman late one night when no one was around.

I slammed the bag with a left-right-left hook combination, then sat down panting. "I think I can do it. I think I can be South African champ. Just got to get back into shape."

Stan laughed.

312

After a few weeks doing short patrols and happily hanging around the pool on Fireforce, there came word of a night operation on a SWAPO base in Angola. It was apparently going to be the first night attack that South Africa had ever done in the Angolan conflict. It was to be a combined operation with 44 Brigade, which was disbanded a year or so later to be built into a para unit. At that time it was the small but notorious unit with all the crazy ex-Vietnam Yanks with parachute tattoos on their arms and ex-Rhodesians who had joined the SADF.

We drove out in trucks to meet them at a secluded spot to practise for the op. It was 100 or so kilometres back into the Etosha National Park, close to where we had trained for Operation *Protea*.

44 Brigade had three or four Q-Kars with them—army Jeeps with twin MAGs mounted on them. We spent cold and miserable nights doing fire and movement with live ammunition, once again going through the motions of clearing out trenches and bunkers with RPGs and grenades. The night lit up with red tracers bouncing off the ground as we dived into the dirt and opened fire.

"Bunker at 2 o'clock ... RPG take it out! Forward! Keep the line straight ... don't bunch up!"

For three nights we practised till well after midnight. Then we would try fix a hot meal in the dark and catch some sleep, still full of sand from diving into the dirt. To help matters a bitter cold and windy spell had sprung up since our return to the border.

The target base was manned by 300 SWAPO terrs, very deep in Angola. Once again the leaders had in their wisdom decided to send just over 100 of us to do the job. Everyone seemed relieved when the day before we were supposed to go in, a cold windy morning, we were brought together and told that the president himself had called off the operation the night before, deeming it too dangerous. (I found out later that apparently every cross-border operation had to be approved by then President P. W. Botha.)

We returned to Ondangwa happy to resume Fireforce and our suntanning duty, but after a week of chilling out, a jubilant and smiling Commandant Lindsay hurriedly called us together next to the pool and announced that another very big operation was in the offing. The man loved war with a passion. He once again paced with enthusiasm in front of the company in his short pants, flashing his teeth. He told us that this was going to be as big as Operation *Protea*, but that this time we would be going even deeper into Angola to look for Boy who had retreated from the bases close to our border, but was still running the training camps hundreds of kilometres inside Angola— business as usual. Lindsay told us that all this new information had come to light from the enormous quantity of maps and intelligence we had gathered in Operation *Protea*. (I realized later that all this new info, without a doubt, had come from the mountain of maps and documents that *Valk* 4 had discovered in the FAPLA ops room at Ongiva, where we had found Kruger's bush hat in the desk drawer.)

It was going to be a full mechanized fighting group, just like Operation *Protea*, where the convoys of each group were perhaps eight or ten clicks long. The target was a cluster of SWAPO training bases hundreds of kilometres into Angola. This was going to be the deepest operation into Angola since *Savannah* in 1975. This time our sister H Company, with infantry, who were already in training at Etosha, was going to spearhead the attack on the bases at Bambi and Cheraquera farther north, while we would be on standby as reaction force at a FAPLA airstrip called Ionde, 120 kilometres into Angola. Ionde was still to be captured. Three C-130s would be dropping a few companies of paratrooper 'campers' (paratroopers who had completed their national service but who were doing their compulsory annual three-week to three-month camp that was required of every army-going South African for 15 years after their initial spell of national service) who would be stopper groups waiting behind the target areas.

The long mechanized attack convoy took off pre-dawn one morning and we snaked our way slowly through the bush. The dawn light was still blue-pink. We had just crossed the border into Angola when we hit our first landmine. There was a muffled explosion up ahead and the column ground to a halt. The news filtered down from vehicle to vehicle that the lead Ratel had hit a landmine. We waited an hour, huddled shoulder to shoulder and shivering in the cold before we started moving again.

No one felt like doing this operation. We only had about seven weeks left in the army. Operation *Protea* had been a massive operation and enough excitement for anybody for a while, and that had only been some seven or eight weeks ago. The long 21-day pass had also softened us up and the talk was more about tits, ass and Civvy Street than about shooting Boy. We lacked the resigned gloom and morbid focus that had been present just before Op *Protea*. I guess being downgraded to standby Fireforce was also part-reason for the lack of commitment.

Late that afternoon the convoy stopped. We were probably some 50 or 60 kilometres into Angola. We heard shots popping from far up front. After half an hour we heard that three big knobs had been killed when they saw some black troops in the bush and, thinking them to be UNITA (Dr Jonas Savimbi's boys, also fighting for democracy in Angola and therefore supported by South Africa), jumped off to speak to them and the rag-tag group gunned them down. It had been a group of SWAPO who then quickly disappeared into the bush. We never did get the details of what really happened.

"It's a bit off a cock-up, ain't it?" John Glover scoffed.

"Haven't even got to the target yet and we've already lost three brass and hit a landmine. Sounds to me that someone knows we're coming."

"Ja. I thought they said SWAPO wasn't even this close to the border after we fucked them up."

It seemed to take forever, crawling stop-start through the bush but the next day we finally came upon the small FAPLA airstrip. All it consisted of was a handful of small brick buildings with a potholed runway situated between two big *chanas*. It was deserted. We drove in without a shot being fired. We were told to dig in for a couple of weeks among the scattered trees, 50 metres from the airstrip, where we would be on standby if the shit hit the fan with H Company. The main column of Ratels, water trucks and Buffels carried on northward to the targets at Bambi and Cheraquera 50 or 60 clicks away. In a relaxed picnic atmosphere we dug in under the trees. I built a bivvy from branches and managed to get my hands on some clear plastic body bags which I cut up and stretched over the frame to build a fine, sloped roof. There had been a slow on-off drizzle, brought in by the coming winter winds. I was pretty proud of my architecture and checked it against the others to compare. Mine was structurally sound and had no leaks. At least I would be dry.

Early the next morning before dawn I woke to the sound of heavy droning engines in the sky above and looked up to see the big shadows of three C-130s flying directly overhead in the moonlight and heading north. I could just make them out. It was our Parabat stopper groups who were being dropped behind the targets.

By midday we were all told to hand in our water bottles for the stopper group who for some reason or other had no water. Later it became widely known that there had been a major fuck-up in the drop zones and that the poor paratrooper campers had stood in the door with full kit, ready and hooked up for 45 minutes, while the C-130s flew up and down looking for the DZ. (As any paratrooper knows, once you have stood up and hooked up with full kit, there is no sitting down again.) Everyone was puking in the plane and, to add to it, when they finally did the bush jump, for some reason they were critically short of water.

We sat under our trees kicking back and smoking. An old DC-3 Dakota was parked on the runway. The wounded had begun to arrive. We watched from under the trees as they loaded a couple of badly wounded black soldiers onto the DC-3 to be flown back to South Africa.

"This operation is fucking jinxed. They hit the main SWAPO base and only got 20 kills and a few of ours wounded."

"Uh huh."

I sat next to my bivvy and smoked as we watched from a distance. By the fourth day it was beginning to get boring.

"Hey … you guys, kit up! *Valk* 4, c'mon, lets go!" The call came for us to move. We piled into the Puma choppers and shot off at high speed, just skimming the treetops. H Company was apparently in trouble and we were going to help them out. When we arrived at the front with the fighting group we hung around some armoured cars and Ratels for an hour, before we were told that we were not needed and that it was a false alarm. We got in the Pumas and flew back to Ionde.

We were deeper in Angola than we had ever been and the bush was very different to what we were used to. Gone were the desert features and scrubby, scattered trees of Owamboland. They had been replaced by sizable tropical koppies and small rocky mountains. The trees were thick, high and green.

Beneath us a huge herd of 300 wildebeest scattered and galloped wildly, tossing their heads as our Pumas hammered low over them. I nudged John Delaney sitting next to me and pointed it out to him. It was a sight to see. I thought they looked happy that the noisy choppers had provided a break in the boredom of grazing in paradise. Some of them kicked up their back legs and pranced as they ran.

Back at Ionde we couldn't believe it when Commandant Lindsay, who was a running buff, made us run up and down the airstrip early one morning.

"He's fucking crazy, running in the middle of fucking Angola on an operation. He's carrying this paratrooper thing too far. Just because he's addicted to running, we have to follow?" Stan was pissed.

"Keeps you in shape, man. What you talking about? You want to be a top-notch paratrooper?"

"Don't need to run to be a top-notch soldier. You think the German Wehrmacht had time to run on the Eastern Front?"

"No, but they did plenty of running at the end."

"That's bullshit ... but anyway, do you think then that the Russians had time to run in the middle of the winter?"

He had a good point.

We sat around smoking, arguing and debating over stupid things. I told Kevin McKee, who had boxed professionally as a club fighter before the army, that I wanted to maybe box seriously when I got out.

"It s a hard game, my *broer*. But you can do it if you get into it. You've got to stay focused. It's like going on a operation—if you let your mind wander for a second you get nailed. It just takes one good punch to change the fight and turn it all around. You think that you're doing all *lekker* and then, *boom*! You seeing fucking stars and the crowd's shouting for your blood. It also takes a while to learn to be relaxed in the ring. You got to be relaxed, my *broer*. Your mind should be almost as relaxed in the ring as we are talking to each other now. But if you got a good punch, Gungie, it will help a lot and save you in tight spots."

I pondered on it. I did have a punch. I could punch with both hands. I also had a cold, dead, unfamiliar anger that had recently come to light. The drizzle had set in and I spent more time lying in my hooch under the body bags. My mind was on Civvy Street which was only six weeks away but seemed like six months. I thought what it would feel like to get back into the real world. Or was this the real world? Which one was reality? This seemed pretty fucking real right here. I wondered if I would be able to hang with all the bullshit things that we used to do and talk about. I thought about the band and wondered if I would be able to get back into music again and sing. Get into a good rock band and hammer out some good hard rock and maybe make an album and play at some top Jo'burg clubs. But it felt as if I had no more music in me, that it had all been hammered out. All the dreams of doing things and flying high. I realized that most of my dreams had disappeared. I toyed with the idea of signing up short-term, even going back and trying for the Recces again. I would probably make the tough selection course now that I knew what to expect. (I spoke to an American SEAL in later years. He said they didn't even do the long, gruelling selection that we did, although they had a few weeks of non-stop hell that they called 'Buds'. Even my platoon buddies didn't believe the shit we had gone through on Recce selection and how far we had walked with next to no food.)

I moped around moodily in my bivvy as the drizzle dripped off the body bags. The clouds had set in. The stink of shit was starting to permeate the area as we had been dug in for eight days now and the little tufts of white toilet paper half buried in the sand were getting closer. The word from the fighting group was that there were many small bases but they were having miss after miss—each time SWAPO slipped out just in time.

It was on one of these gloomy, drizzly days that we flew out, speeding over the treetops for the umpteenth time. We landed in a SWAPO base that had been hit by H Company and looked to have been cleared out. It always looked the same: the trenches cut the earth in between the bush in zigzag patterns and mounds of earth signified the many bunkers that were camouflaged with grass and branches. There had been some fighting but the talk was that they had got only about 15 kills in the whole base which, by the looks of it, seemed to be quite large. We stood under a tree feeling like outsiders and watched. It looked as though it was going to be another lemon but we were thankful for the break in the boredom of sitting as Fireforce at Ionde. We sat and watched the scene. A Buffel had pulled up close by and H

Company paratroopers were loading a small mountain of captured SWAPO ammunition. Cases of RPG-7 rockets, landmines, AK ammunition boxes and food. The loaders laughed and worked with confident ease, handing the heavy boxes up into the Buffel. I watched them and smoked.

Derek Wood (aka Woody) was huddled over on top of the Buffel moving a heavy box when an explosion erupted inside the Buffel in a flash of white smoke and flame. He arched from the top of the high Buffel like a Mexican rock diver and landed flat on his back about ten metres away. A stunned silence followed as everyone stood and looked at Woody who was writhing on the ground in pain. Some H Company troops rushed to his aid. A fire had broken out in the Buffel next to him as the flames quickly licked up and reached the kit bags that were strapped to the roll bar. The Buffel, loaded with ammunition, RPGs and landmines burned for a minute, with no one really seeming to comprehend the danger. After a while we all began to edge away from the area and the burning vehicle, whose rear was almost fully engulfed in flame. Suddenly a skinny major leaped in and started the Buffel up. He drove the burning Buffel into an open *chana* 100 metres away, calmly jumped out and trotted back. His quick action might or might not have saved some lives but he had unwittingly parked the now blazing and popping vehicle closer to the choppers. It was amusing watching the usually cool and drag-ass helicopter pilots sprinting across the *chana* to get to their choppers which they quickly lifted off out of the brown smoke.

We watched as hundreds of rounds now started popping off and explosions boomed in the blazing Buffel, realizing what a sharp move the major had pulled. I heard later that he was awarded the Honoris Crux, the top South African award for conspicuous bravery, for his action. Hey, if I had been on my toes and not thinking like a *dom troopie*, I could have got the Crux. I was right there.

It wasn't half an hour later and we'd lost interest in the almost burned-out Buffel, when another loud explosion erupted 50 metres away. I turned to see a cloud of smoke and dust billow into the air. No one knew what had happened but we soon got word that a lieutenant had killed himself when he triggered a booby trap in one of the many bunkers in the SWAPO base.

Everyone was ordered not to touch anything and all loading was brought to a halt. We sat and watched as they carried the lieutenant's body away on a stretcher in a clear body bag, like the one on the roof of my bivvy.

"What a fuck-up."

"Yes."

"Can you believe all the shit that has happened in front of our eyes ... just in the last half hour?"

"I know ... it's been a fuck-up from the start."

"Man, I'm glad we are Fireforce for this op. These guys have been chasing ghosts for weeks and all they're doing is fucking themselves up."

"Ja ... Shit ... see that lootie get blown up, hey?"

After another hour of waiting we were told to head back to the choppers, that we would be going back to Ionde. Next to the choppers was a water truck with several dozen taps sticking out of the side. Mindful of the lack of water at Ionde, I took the opportunity for a quick wash. I put down my kit and stuck my head under one and opened it. The water was ice-cold and ran down my body, wetting my whole shirt. I gasped with surprise at the coldness.

"*Valk* 4 and *Valk* 3, are you the guys on Fireforce?" a chubby truck driver shouted, looking unsure as he came trotting breathlessly up to us.

"Yeah, we're Fireforce ..."

"You've got to get to the choppers right now. They need you."

Moments later, Lieutenant Doep came running from the group of parked Pumas and Ratels. He was breathless, pulling on his chest webbing.

"*Valk* 3 and 4, get kitted up, get your stuff and move to the choppers now. Quick!" His brown eyes darted from man to man urgently.

"Commandant Lindsay has located a group of terrs from the spotter plane."

We all sprang to life as we heaved on webbing and tugged on jump helmets. I was one of the first to jog after Lieutenant Doep, my helmet bouncing up and down heavily on my head. There was excited activity at the choppers as the two Pumas' turbines whined loudly and the big blades started to whip round and round till they were a blur. Some captain was waving his finger across a folded map. Lieutenant Doep stood looking on with the tight chinstrap of his jump helmet making his cheeks bulge out like a chipmunk. He nodded his head up and down in agreement while the captain spoke, then snatched the map as the captain made a bee-line out of the building dust storm. Doep stuffed the map down the front of his shirt, turned and beckoned us to the choppers. I piled in first and had to move to the back of the chopper as *Valk* 4 piled in behind me. My wet shirt was clingy and cold now. It stuck to my skin and I regretted doing the wash thing.

This was going to be no lemon. I could tell already.

ENOUGH IS ENOUGH

Dreamer—Supertramp

The Pumas lifted out of the trees like dragonflies off a pond. We quickly straightened out and headed in goodness-knows-what direction; I hadn't a clue. I looked out of the small window and watched the treetops flash by below us, almost within arms' reach. Commandant Lindsay, flying in a spotter plane over the area, had pinpointed a group of 40 or 50 terrs who had escaped the earlier failed attack on the SWAPO base and who were now fleeing through some hilly terrain and making good their escape.

Luckily we had been on the spot and ready to go. Another ten minutes and we might have been on our way back to Ionde. I felt a tinge of apprehension flutter through me. I tried to dredge up the feeling of cold, numb, uncaring resignation that I had come to rely on, but it had become increasingly difficult to conjure up this strange, dead, necessary feeling on this last bush trip.

As had become my habit, I clenched the silver crucifix that hung round my neck in my teeth and bit down on it. It was silver and soft, already well-dented with the tooth marks of many such moments. I said a quick prayer, asking the Lord for safety. Why should He listen to me? I bet that the terrs were praying right now too, as they heard the choppers coming in on them. Who would the good Lord favour? Us or them?

We flew for what seemed no more than two minutes when the Pumas came down on a grassy patch of veld. We jumped from the chopper and ran crouched over through some tall grass flattened by the prop-wash and went down in a defensive circle. The first thing I heard was the loud noise of 20-millimetre cannons from what sounded like two Alouette gunships not more than 100 metres away, but I couldn't see them. After the Pumas had lifted off and their hammering blades had faded into the distance, the loud silence of the bush took me by surprise again. Just the 20-millimetre fire boomed away. It sounded as though it was pretty earnest and not just speculative fire, which they sometimes used to flush terrs out of the bush. After a minute in the grass we stood up.

"Form up, spread out ... let's move," Doep pointed in a direction that flanked the sounds of the fire fight.

After two years of training and living together and now as veterans of numerous actions, we formed automatically into our familiar sweep line and slowly picked our way through the scattered bush. First in and last out of the Puma, I was the last man on the right flank of the sweep line, again. To our left was a steep hill with large rocks, probably about three storeys high. The fire fight seemed to be on top of this hill, not much more than 100 metres in front of us.

My helmet kept slipping down over my eyes. I pushed it up. I hated the fucking thing. Why couldn't we just wear our bush caps? I scanned the bush in front of me. It seemed peaceful except for the Alouette gunships and the hammering of their cannons. I searched through the bush around me. The line moved slowly and straight, wth the last man on the far left of the line walking on the slope of the unusual rocky hillside as we walked parallel to the hill.

Kevin McKee, the small ex-pro boxer with the thick scar that ran from eyebrow to chin (he had run slap-bang into an ambulance during PT course, cutting his face terribly, crying in pain and wailing that now he was going to be even uglier), was to my left, glaring into the bush with his small, beady brown eyes and holding his rifle high to his chest. Kevin Green moved cautiously next to him. Suddenly, up ahead of me, as plain as day, coming out from behind some bush and going into a small clearing, I saw a camouflage-clad figure walking casually and carrying a rifle over his shoulder like a hobo carrying a stick. For a second I felt no concern because he was walking so nonchalantly. I thought for sure he must be one of our guys who was in camo for some reason. Either that, or he was Koevoet (the South African Police's Koevoet also wore camo on the border).

"What the fuck is Koevoet doing here?" I thought.

All these thoughts were in slow motion but in split second I realized this

323

was a terr, calmly walking not 20 metres in front of me. I was the only one who had seen him. I stopped and lifted my rifle to my shoulder. I aimed at his midriff, then for some strange reason I called out to him, maybe thinking of trying to take him prisoner because he looked so lost and ill at ease.

"Hey!" It came out too softly.

He did not hear me. Kevin McKee had also seen him now and he shouted loudly. The terr spun around, his eyes large and white as he looked at us.

Kevin waved his arm. "Hey Illa!"

The terr took a second to register who we were and that he was dead. He and I locked eyes for a split second before I shot him and he began falling to the ground. I fired two shots and knew I had hit him. I ran forward ahead of the sweep line. Branches whipped into my face as I ran forward with my rifle still tucked into my shoulder. Together Kevin and I came onto the terr lying behind the bush. He was rolled up into a ball with his AK lying in the sand next to him. Kevin took aim and blew the top of his head off with two well-placed shots. The rest of the sweep line caught up and although all heads craned to see what was going on, they kept their positions. Lieutenant Doep was close by and came over quickly. He inspected the dead terr and looked at Kevin and me.

"Korff saw him, lieutenant."

Doep glanced at me, nodded and said in Afrikaans "*Mooi*, Korff, well done."

"I almost thought he was a Koevoet, lieutenant."

Doep grunted.

We quickly searched the dead terr but found nothing. I reached into my pants-leg pocket, pulled out a small camera and took a picture. The early afternoon light was just right. It was a perfect Kodak moment. I was to take a photograph that haunted me for years until I burned it many years later.

"Left wheel, left wheel!" Doep shouted.

We turned the sweep line around and unavoidably grouped together as we scaled the steep koppie to get to the top, where the gunships had the terrs pinned down. As we topped the rocky hill we could, for the first time, see the two gunships that were flying in tight circles 30 metres in front of us and hammering down into the thick trees.

It was a nightmare scene. We could see figures running and crouching behind trees in the haze of dust and smoke as the gunships circled above them at an angle that looked as though the gunners would fall out but did not. Their long 20-millimetre cannons flashed and the explosive heads blew up waves of white sand. The smoke and dust was as thick as fog.

"Straight ahead! There, straight ahead!"

I dropped to one knee and aimed into the fog at the ghostly figures. I shot as fast as I could. My barrel moved from one spectre to the next, unable to stay on one target for long. I whipped over my quick-change magazine and kept on firing. I had fired 60 rounds. Our own gunsmoke enveloped us, burning my throat and eyes. Now I could see no targets. I pulled another magazine from my chest webbing and dropped my two empty mags into the sand. I fired the third magazine out into the haze.

"Cease fire... cease fire ... cease fire!"

Slowly the mad shooting stopped. The gunships had ceased fire and hovered in tight circles over the dust and smoke-filled killing zone, their rotor blades chopping loudly, *whap, whap, whap*, as they turned.

"Forward ... spread out ... spread out! Forward!" Lieutenant Doep turned and looked down the line, shouting at the top of his voice.

I sprang up and began to walk forward with my rifle socked tight in my shoulder. I stared intently into the smoke and dust haze now 25 metres in front of us. I saw no movement. I stepped over a log and almost stumbled to my knees as my boot hooked something. My eyes did not even waiver as I stumbled, viciously pulling my foot free. I walked fast, as usual, believing in the *blitzkrieg* policy that says moving fast into a situation gives you an edge. It was a tactic I always used in street brawls. To cut through the bullshit and get in before the other guy could get his mind working.

John Delaney was off to my right as we walked into the fog. I looked around at the carnage and in a second I realized there was not much danger here. The ground around me had been torn up and was burned white from the sustained cannon fire. Leaves and broken branches covered the ground which looked as if it had been ploughed by the grim reaper. It took a second or two to realize that there were bodies lying everywhere.

"These are children!" John Delaney shouted.

There were four or five kids ranging from five to ten years old. They were in a group, lying in the dust half naked and mangled by gunfire, their bodies caked with sand and blood.

I glared at the scattered small, broken bodies. I pulled my eyes off them and scanned in front of me, my rifle still tight in my shoulder. In front of me and to my left, among the leaves, lay a Bushman woman. There was no mistaking the wrinkled yellow skin and small, almost square-shaped head covered with tufts of peppercorn hair. She was topless and lying on her stomach. The left side of her chest and arm were gone, cut off raggedly by a 20-millimetre round. Her ribs and sternum were exposed; the huge gaping wound looked like a side of meat hanging in a butcher's shop. In her other arm she still clutched an infant, holding him into her chest. The little tyke was naked and appeared unharmed but was dead from either shrapnel or terror. He lay with his face in the crook of his mother's elbow. A turd stuck halfway out of his little bottom, testifying pathetically to his last terrified moment. I gingerly moved through the shattered trees.

Dead SWAPO in uniform lay chopped up or whole behind almost every bush and tree. I stood next to one who had circled around and around a tree trunk, hiding in vain from the gunships' cannons. It looked like he lasted quite a long while as the tree trunk and the ground around him had taken many hits. He was cut in half. There were some more half-naked women and adolescents lying nearby. They were all dead.

Our platoon had split up, with each man on his own picking his way slowly through the carnage. Somehow our company commander had appeared on the scene. I did not know how the hell he got there. He and I stood side by side as we both surveyed the butchery.

A few yards away a SWAPO cadre who had heard our arrival groaned loudly. He tried to move but seemed mortally wounded and could only stare at us with watery eyes, like a dying animal with its head lolling in the sand. He groaned louder and louder as if asking for something but unable to say the words.

"Korff," the captain called over to me and casually pointed to the terr with his chin.

I knew what he was saying and I had no hesitation in putting the poor bastard out of his misery. I stepped over the dying SWAPO's feet, coming up behind him. I reached forward with my rifle and put the muzzle point-blank on the bump behind his ear. I looked at his ear and the back of his head for a second, then pulled the trigger. I realized too late that I should first have picked up the AK-47 that had been lying close to his head. I hesitated for a moment, then reached and grabbed it and slung it over my shoulder. It was messy, the light pinewood stock shattered by my rifle shot. Dan Pienaar put a couple of shots in the guy lying next to him as he too writhed and then lay still.

I walked through the stripped thicket. There were bodies everywhere. Thirty or forty of them. Most of the SWAPO men who lay in the sand were small, yellow Bushmen who wore an assortment of Chinese rice-pattern uniform with full kit and webbing. Some were blacks, also in SWAPO uniform. It became clear to me that we had wiped out an entire Bushman clan. The men had joined SWAPO and lived with their whole clan in or around the base, never thinking that it would be attacked being so deep in Angola. They had tried to make a break for it when the base was hit by H Company and would have made it if Commandant Lindsay hadn't spotted them.

They looked small and broken, like dolls. Some of their wrinkled, wizened-looking faces still showed the terror of being trapped like animals and slaughtered to the man. The sweet smell of blood and guts is a cliché but it was, nevertheless, a reality and clawed at the back of my throat.

I walked out of the thicket and up a little rise. At the top, Paul Greeff stood looking at an old woman who was lying on her side. She was easily in her 90s or even older. Her hair was snow-white; it covered her old head like a cap of white tufts. Her wrinkled yellow skin hung from her body like old, loose, treated leather. She lay quietly on her side, with one elbow pulled up under her head as a makeshift pillow. When I got closer I saw that her abdomen was torn open and that her entrails and liver lay in the sand next to her. She slowly moved her eyes to look at me, like a child falling asleep. Her face was calm and showed no hostility whatsoever; there even seemed to be a faint smile. Three metres away were five or six children standing in a row. They were aged from five to about ten. They stood still and looked on. Their little

327

faces were masks, ashen with fear and shock as they stood silent as statues. They had just seen their entire family wiped out; now they stood and gazed at what was probably their great-grandmother lying in front of them with her guts lying next to her. I put my rifle and the AK-47 in the sand and knelt beside the old lady. I touched her on her forehead and she smiled at me. I looked at her wound quickly, then back into her eyes.

"Its okay, its okay … you'll be all right. Don't worry, you'll be okay." I pointed up, making a whirling action with my arm over my head. "The helicopters will take you. They'll fix you … you'll be alright … you'll be okay."

She had no idea what I was saying but she turned her face up and almost smiled at me again. She looked at me with her rheumy eyes and nodded her old white head as if she knew exactly what I was saying, believing that it would all be okay. Then she lay back on her elbow and gazed at the children. I took it as just that. She knew what I was saying. She believed me. I looked back at the children, standing right there looking at the scene. They stared at me blankly, their eyes huge in their faces. One kid, who was probably around seven, had her thumb stuck deep in her mouth and was sucking as though her life depended on it. I stood up.

Dan had been standing behind me and had watched the whole scene.

"Dan, I'm going to see if I can get a medic over here to help." I shouldered my two weapons and walked down the little rise. A few metres over the rise, I heard a gunshot crack out. I turned to see Dan standing over the old lady, his rifle pointed down at her and a wisp of gunsmoke hanging around him like a shroud. The line of children stood behind him in mute terror. I stood quietly. I had really believed I was going to make an effort to save this grand old matriarch of the clan but as I'd turned my back, Dan had blown her brains out—in front of six children.

I stood looking back at the scene. I felt a detached, cold rage. I wondered what I should do. I wondered whether I should kill Dan. I knew that without a doubt I could just walk up to him, shoot him dead, not bat an eyelid and turn around and walk away. I went cold and calm as I looked at Dan standing over the shattered old lady.

I decided not to kill him and turned around and walked away.

Back in the macabre thicket I watched as the bodies were searched for documents and the area searched for stashed equipment. Nothing much was found on this scanty group that had been on the run.

We were busy loading the AK-47s in a pile when Lieutenant Doep came puffing through the trees, his face still bright red against his long blond hair. "*Valk* 3 and 4 … form up in two lines and follow me."

"What's going on, lieutenant?"

"We're going to form a stopper group. They spotted some more terrs and they're heading this way. They're going to use the gunships to drive them onto us."

We heaved ourselves farther up the little hill and walked, dripping with sweat, for about 300 metres, then spread out in a long line in the thick bush. We were able to hide pretty well in the tall dead grass and bush, each man about a dozen metres apart. I sat crouched on one buttock with one knee up and peered into the bush. I heard a gunship's 20-millimetre start hammering some distance in front of us. It had a sporadic rhythm and sounded like speculative fire.

I had the silver crucifix that hung around my neck clenched in my mouth again and was grinding away at it with my teeth. For some reason I was scared. For the first time I felt real fear sliding through my stomach and limbs like a slippery, treacherous eel. My arms felt weak and useless, like jelly, and my mind had locked into some nonsensical scared-shitless mode.

"What's going on?" It felt as if some force was in control of me. "Snap out of it, man. It's a stopper group … all you have to do is shoot them as they run toward you, fucking asshole! C'mon, c'mon!" I screamed at myself silently but got no response. A tangible fear had taken over and I felt useless. So this is what it feels like to be scared? This is what it feels like to just about shit in your pants? I couldn't understand why this was happening. I had faced many worse situations than this before.

I had been okay 20 minutes ago when we walked up the hill into the fire fight. I had not felt nearly as scared when the RPG-7s and anti-aircraft guns were flying a metre over my head or when we found ourselves in a FAPLA base with hundreds of spoor all around us. Or sneaking onto and ambushing the SWAPO at what had become known as the Breakfast Party. I had taken the forefront then. Sure, I had been scared in all of those actions but it had was controlled and buried deep down, disguised. I had felt emotionless and eager—a trained paratrooper ready to pay the ultimate price.

In seconds, I quickly tried to logic it out. If I died, I died. Why did there have to be fear in between? You live or you die. Forget getting scared in between. What's the point? I remembered what my brother had once told me. He had said that fear was the Devil's doing and had no place in a child of God. I said a prayer. I believed I was a child of God. If I died, then I died. It was in His hands, but please take this fear away.

A product of the mind or genuine Divine intervention? I did not know which but quickly the strange fear *did* subside. I felt the cold, slippery eel leave me. I was able to hold my mind steady and stay focused on the yellow and green trees in front of me, waiting for a figure to come crashing through the bush towards me. The gunships' cannons sounded closer. I pushed up my jump helmet and pulled my rifle hard into my shoulder.

"Any time now … any time now ... take in easy ..."

I heard the bush crashing somewhere in front of me but saw nothing. Then I thought I saw some yellow bush move about 30 metres ahead but saw no targets. They're right here. I can hear them! Seconds later *Valk* 3, which had formed up a few hundred metres to our right, hidden in the bush, opened up with their 5.56 rounds sounding like firecrackers popping as they sprung their trap on the fleeing SWAPOs running slap-bang into them. The whole thing didn't take long.

Within 45 minutes we were carefully walking back to the original killing zone.

I felt ashamed that I had felt so afraid. Where had it come from and how had it managed to sneak through all my intricate defences and ambush me so intensely and suddenly? Was it because I only had about three weeks left in the army before I was back in Civvy Street and my mind had loosened up too much? Was it the Bushman family we had slaughtered and that still lay here in front of me?

I pushed the thought from my mind. "You think too much, Korff."

We gathered up the AK-47s and some satchels of equipment and trudged half a click to a *chana* where four Pumas had landed. We left the grisly scene behind us. The only survivors we left were the ten or so children and a woman who had crept out of the bush. They stood in a couple of small groups and watched us silently, like mutes, as we walked out of the thicket and down the hill, leaving them to wander among and identify the over 40 corpses sprawled grotesquely among the trees.

I knew that this contact—the one where we and the gunships with their 20-millimetre cannons had wiped out a family of women, grandmas, children, babies and their menfolk in SWAPO uniform, leaving a surviving woman and a handfuul of wide-eyed children there in that carnage—would haunt me forever.

It does.

We met up with *Valk* 3 at the choppers. They said they had shot quite a few terrs who had run into them. I heard that one guy had mistakenly—or perhaps not mistakenly—shot two kids. I also heard that one terr had come forward with his hands held up in surrender and that another guy had shot him in the stomach. I did not dig for details or try to separate fact from fiction.

We flew back low over the trees in the classic Vietnam War formation— four big Pumas, a Cessna Bosbok spotter plane and two Alouette gunships, all flying side by side in a V formation barely metres above the treetops, all set against an angry red African sun that was minutes from setting.

I thought of the movie *Apocalypse Now*. We flew in this formation till we reached the airstrip at Ionde, then broke off. I sat cross-legged by the chopper door and saw all the troops looking up with contorted faces, admiring our fly-by.

Operation *Daisy* was over. It had been a fuck-up from start to finish, as far as I could tell. From what I heard, the whole huge mechanized fighting group of many hundreds of troops brought in 70 or so SWAPO kills in a period of about two weeks. I never did find out our losses but I'm sure it was a worse ratio than the our ten to their 1,000 kills of Operation *Protea*.

Valks 4 and 3 and the gunships between them had brought in 29 of those kills (not counting the families of the 29) in the last days of the doomed op. I heard that we had the largest single kill in the whole operation. Trust D Company to save the day. It was another feather in our cap. No one spoke about the

Bushman clan we had wiped out—they only bragged about the 29 AK-47s we had brought back. The families were merely casualties of war, or as the Americans would say today—collateral damage—incidental.

A few days later we arrived at the white sands of Ondangs after the long bumpy ride through the Angolan bush. Back at Ondangwa there was a festive atmosphere. We had less than three weeks left in the army and should be flying back to South Africa any day to get ready to *klaar* out and hand back all kit, uniforms and equipment.

"Oh, yeah … Civvy Street, here I come! Gonna be walking down that main road. Wake up when I want. Gonna be dancing and *jolling* all night." Delaney was on top form.

"What are you going to do? Become a bum?"

"For a while, yeah … just going to *jol* … do what I want." John was sipping a Coke, smiling from ear to ear. "What are you going to do, Gungie?"

"I don't know … my old man says I should look into being a plumber … I don't know if it's what I want to do. Bit of an anticlimax, hey?"

"Ja … that's for sure. Maybe we should sign up for short term, try for the Recces again … carry on with the war. It's still going to get hotter, I can tell you that."

I sat silently and brooded. Naawwww … fuck the army. I'd had enough of this bullshit. I had seen enough to discourage me from signing on for any extra years.

It was strange, though … no one even mentioned the Bushman family. I tried to just push it out of my mind. When I think of it now, there was no way that old lady could have survived with a wound like that and the choppers wouldn't have even attempted to take her to a hospital. What was I thinking? Maybe I just thought too much to be a good soldier.

Troops were openly drinking and horsing around in the small swimming pool, somersaulting and hurling each other in, splashing up waves that sloshed over the side of the pool. We had done our duty and given two years for the country. We had come together from rookie juniors just out of high school to become one of the two senior operational paratroop companies in the border war. We had done well. We had made a small dent in the communist threat that was infiltrating our borders and we had seen more combat than any other paratroop company before us. We had been key troops in three big cross-border operations and had, all in all, spent about three months of our operational time deep inside Angola, seeking and destroying the often elusive Boy. Our two paratroop companies, Delta and Hotel, had made a tangible difference in the outcome of this bush war we were fighting.

Just then the rowdy swimming pool group walked into our tent. They were still drunk but were in the tent grouped together with purpose.

"Hey, have you seen Baba anywhere?"

"No. Why? What's up?"

"Well, we can't find him anywhere ... he just disappeared ..."

"When did you last see him?" I asked, still leaning back in my chair.

"Naw … dunno ... we were all swimming here half an hour ago. His stuff is still at the pool."

Kurt looked up from his card hand and we exchanged looks.

"Have you checked the pool?" I said, stating the obvious.

They shook their heads. "Ja … no, we thought of that ... but no … we haven't."

Kurt and I stood up at the same time and hurried towards the pool just metres away. Kurt and I were drunk but a lot less so than the pool crowd, who followed us. Kurt quickly took up the long pool brush and started to sweep the bottom of the pool. We all watched quietly. Kurt's big frame was a dark shadow in the moonlight as he pushed the brush back and forth into the black water that still lapped the sides after the horseplay of 20 minutes before.

Suddenly he turned and looked at us, speaking in his low monotone voice. "He's here. He's right here, Gungie ... I've got the broom on him, right here."

We all looked at him for a second as he gave a few small shoves on the long broom. I was the first to react, leaping into the warm water, landing right on top of Baba. It was a sick feeling to feel him under my feet. I ducked down to grab him but could not. He was under the plastic liner of the pool. I spluttered up to the surface.

"Get me a knife, quickly ... get a knife!"

Kurt reacted quickly; it seemed like mere seconds before he returned from the tent and tossed me his bush knife. I snatched it out of the air and in one move dived down, cut the plastic liner and heaved Baba from underneath it. I pulled him up and carried his limp body to the edge of the pool where many hands reached out to grab him. I jumped out of the pool and pushed the crowd away.

"Turn him around!"

I knew little about life-saving but I did know to get the water out of him. I put him on his back and pumped his knees into his chest like a water pump. With every push gushes of water and puke shot out of his mouth like a hose. I lifted him up around his hips and held him upside down as the water streamed out of his lungs. I started to perform what little I knew of CPR. All I did was to blow as much air into his lungs as I could while Kurt Barnes pumped his chest. The air came back out at me like air escaping from a balloon and flapped through his lips. I blew and blew until my mouth was covered in his puke.

I finally stood up when a Jeep came crashing through the small pool barricade and two medics jumped out. They took over and loaded him into the back of the Jeep. I knew it was too late. I walked away across the empty tent square. Most of the tents were in blackness, their occupants asleep or passed out for the night.

I sat on a sandbag bunker outside a tent and smoked. How stupid could they have fucking been! The old swimming pool in the middle of our square of tents was just a big hole in the ground with a thick plastic liner. The liner of the pool was old and ripped. They had been playing a deadly game of crawling under the ripped plastic liner, crawling with the weight of the water on top of them and coming out the other end of the pool through another torn section.

I looked at the big three-quarter moon that hung in the late night sky, casting a milky-white sheen across the vast African horizon. The moon mesmerized me like it had done a thousand times before. I thought of Julius Caesar looking at it and pondering. I thought of Jesus Christ ... he must have looked at this same moon. I thought of every living soul over the ages who had stood and looked at this same timeless moon and asked questions of it and wondered. I shook my fist and cursed God aloud. I damned Him for letting this happen two weeks before the end. Having got through all this shit, to have Baba drown in such a cruel way, trapped under the plastic liner of the pool at the party celebrating the end of two years' national service ... coming out of it in one piece just a couple of weeks before we all went back to our families and loved ones. Emotional and drunk, I sat on the sandbags and wept tears of frustration and stared at the moon. I thought of Baba, who was the smallest guy in the company and looked as if he was a kid of fifteen.

I suddenly couldn't wait to get out.

EPILOGUE

March 2008

I never returned to live in my beautiful South Africa. The lure of a new country and life in the big bad city was hard to resist and my six-month stay in America turned into many years of ups and downs, struggles and victories.

I boxed for a couple of years and quit when I realized that I had lost the focus and dedication that was needed in the professional ring. I would take a fight because I needed the measly paycheck, doing most of my training at the 'Cat and Whistle'.

When I quit boxing, a surprise was waiting for me. As my channel and outlet for tension was now gone, I was ambushed by the past. Ambushed by dead 'freedom fighters' with their brains blown out, ambushed by the spirits of dead men, old women and children and their spilled blood on the white sands of Angola and South West Africa.

I found it hard to handle any authority and to keep a steady job at the bottom of the ladder in my new country and many a loudmouthed boss was put up against the wall. The spirits of spilled blood manifested themselves in the strangest and most perverse ways, robbing me once again of my most precious memories and happiest moments.

It would always take me by surprise. Making love to my wife I would see her as a terrorist we had left dead in the sand. In a moment of tender thought of a loved one or family member, I would see that loved one in my mind's eye shattered, broken, shot to pieces like the men we had killed. Any good and precious memory would be ambushed and drowned in the blood of headless men and mothers cut in half, still holding their dead children. These flashbacks came from nowhere. To mentally see my loved ones like

336

this was so traumatizing that I would lose my breath and have to pull the car over to the side of the road in the busy Los Angeles traffic.

I was quiet but became quieter. The quieter I became the stronger the anger grew—many's the owner of a disrespectful or sloppy Los Angeles attitude who was given an instant re-education with cruel boots and a fast, heavy fist.

For many years I couldn't handle or even watch Hollywood make-believe movies with senseless violence. I would invariably get up and leave the theatre in the middle of the film.

I was ashamed, and didn't dare tell anyone. I couldn't bring myself to even utter the words, repeat or admit the horrifying visions that took my breath away.

South Africa became a faraway place as the years went by. I had not spoken to a Parachute Battalion buddy since I had left the army in 1981. I started to doubt the stories that I told of my war in Angola. I stopped talking about it and closed the doors to it until, after many years, it felt like a dream and perhaps it hadn't even happened that way at all—maybe I'm mixed up, maybe a tank didn't come out the bush at us? Was that SWAPO ambush in the chilly dawn real or was I imagining it? All my army friends—John Delaney, Doogy, John the Fox, Kurt, Stan the Man and others who, at one time had been as close as brothers, felt like long-dead ghosts in another, faraway land.

I read about the battle of Cuito Cuanavale in Angola as a security guard one night, sitting next to an Ethiopian who claimed that he was a communist. He was the nicest person you could ever meet.

I read about Nelson Mandela being released after 27 years in prison and being elected president of the 'new South Africa'. I wrote him a letter of congratulation and to my surprise I received a letter from him enclosing a signed photo, wishing me all the best. I read how SWAPO whom we had hunted down in the Angolan bush as the sworn and hated enemy, who were the real 'red danger', had won free and fair elections in South West Africa and that not a peep had been heard out of them since. I pondered what it had all been about. Who was right and who was wrong? Were we the good guys or were we the bad guys?

I read cloak-and-dagger 'tell-tale' books on the old South African regime and realized that we might have been the ones sucked into one big lie and brainwashed for the sake of *Volk* and *Vaderland*.

In 1990, nine long years after Angola, I said 'enough' and visited a Vietnam veteran counselling centre in Los Angeles where I sat down and spoke to a counsellor. For the first time I told a living soul of my anger, torment and my debilitating visions. The moment the words left my mouth and travelled to another human being's ear, I felt the spirits' grip weaken. I walked out over the grass lawn later, elated.

It was difficult at first but I told another person, then another and each time the grip got weaker. My terrible secret was out.

I decided to write about my experiences in Angola. It took months of deep thinking, slowly bringing back the points of memory about my small war. Invited and called back, the memories all came flooding in like chickens coming home to roost but this time I was ready for them and wrote them down on paper for all to see.

The real healing had begun.

The first time I returned to South Africa to visit was in 1997, 12 years after I had left in 1985. On the second visit a few years later, I was determined to to track down some of my old 1 Parachute Battalion mates who were once my brothers.

They were difficult to find as they had bombshelled in many different directions around the world, leaving a very faint spoor to follow. Of the handful of friends I was able to find, their lives had all been affected by the bush war and changed forever.

John Delaney: one of the first to get a kill in our company, had attended a seminary and become a missionary minister, going back into Angola. He ministered at the Town of Death, Ongiva, to preach and spread the word of God. John has travelled to almost every country in Africa to minister, as well as going in to give aid among Sri Lanka's Tamil Tigers. He is married, has three children, lives in England, is a published author and still does ministry work.

Anthony Stander: hardnosed, cold-as-ice 'Stan the Man', who was raised in an orphanage and reform school and who was caught with a huge amount of money after he had robbed five banks soon after leaving 1 Parachute

Battalion, was sentenced to 30 years in prison. In prison Stan was reached by a Christian counsellor. He spent seven years in prison but is a saved man. Stan was, as he puts it, released after seven years on a 'miracle pardon'. He too is married, with three children and lives in Cape Town. He is today, and has been for many years, very active in Christian outreach and is a minister in the church. He is as hard a man for God as he was a soldier in the bush.

Aaron Green: Doogy's war still goes on. At the time of writing he has been a security contractor for an British security outfit for four years. He still sees regular action in Iraq, Algeria and Afghanistan and a year ago was the only survivor in an ambush on his motorcade in Algeria. Doogy has lived in the UK for many years, has led an interesting life owning a number of businesses—including a small factory manufacturing Mercedes gull-wing sports cars under licence. He is divorced from his second wife, has a young daughter, and when in the UK he lives on his yacht.

Michael Roberts: Mike was paralyzed from the waist down in a motorbike accident soon after leaving the army in 1981. His army mate, Anthony Stander, has stuck with him through many years and they run a roofing business together in Cape Town. Michael also stuck by Stan while in prison.

John Glover: 'The Fox', the Englishman who didn't have to do military service, and whose sharp eyes saved me from going on that never-ending patrol in the sky, is living on a farm in KwaZulu-Natal, South Africa, happily surrounded by fat cattle. He runs a construction company, is married and has three children. John tells me that his temper caused him big problems for many years, which he ascribes directly to those years when killing was something he did without the blink of an eye.

James Anders: killed himself soon after leaving the army while challenging a group of thugs to playing Russian roulette in a bar. James suggested that they put two bullets in the chamber and that he would go first.

Taina: my girlfriend, who had won so many beauty pageants and who had stuck with me for seven years, was quickly snapped up after we finally broke up a year after the army. She has been married ever since, with two children.

*****

So, many years now after the bush war in southern Africa, John Delaney, Aaron Green and I have got together over the years in different countries around the world and hoisted a few to the old days.

John Delaney and I prayed to lift any spirits and demons of death deep in our souls. I cried like a baby. I wept, too, when I burned the horrific close-up photographs of the dead SWAPO and FAPLA that I carried in my photo album and showed off for 18 years. Some of the people in those pictures I had personally shot. I burned them in Los Angeles, at John Delaney's suggestion. I dug a hole in the backyard and buried the ashes there. As I did so, I felt a burden lift instantly from my shoulders.

I wished that I had done it ten years before.

I am in contact with Stan and John Glover. And yes, since I have now visited the Old Country several times and rebuilt relations with family and old friends, military and non–military, South Africa and my past are no longer a lost misty dream, but a warm reality that stays with me and nudges me into the future.

I too am divorced now, with a beautiful young daughter of thirteen. For many years I have lived and run a successful small business in Los Angeles, California. I live an active, happy life and look forward to the future. I am finally rid of most war-related cobwebs and blockages, but when they do sneak in from across the border every now and then, this time I have an ambush waiting for them.

Other books by 30° South Publishers on the South African Border War

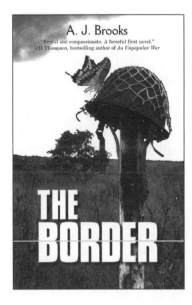

A. J. Brooks

"Brutal and compassionate. A forceful first novel."
JH Thompson, bestselling author of *An Unpopular War*

The Border

AJ Brooks

978-1-920143-10-7; R145.00; Softback;
234 x 153mm; 304pp

"There was an odd combination of anxiety and reluctant anticipation prevalent among the new troops as they made final preparations. Their dismay was evident as the section leader discarded most of the food-carrying compartments and altered the webbing to carry at least seven water bottles and as many magazine pouches. The harsh reality of Owamboland thwarted the infantry school's textbook, for this was war... war in a thirsty land."

"Inevitably, one of the insurgents found the pull ring to the cellar and shouted for support. John and some of the other men crowded around and watched as the guerrilla yanked the door up. As it was only the white woman and her young, he confidently jumped down the stairs into the darkness. John heard the dull crack of the magnum directly below him and the thump of a bullet striking the flesh of his own man. 'They're in the cellar!' he shouted, 'We'll burn her out!'"

The Border is a racy drama set against the backdrop of southern Africa's border wars in the 1980's.

This is a tale of intertwined lives; hatred, trauma and the horror of war forcing each to strangle some sense, some purity out of the world they now find themselves in while teetering on the border of their own sanity. An ordinary soldier fights for survival. A family torn apart by the brutality of war. Two women's struggle to overcome the horrors they have experienced at the hands of the terrorists. A power-hungry brigadier whose personal failures cause untold disaster for his family and for the soldiers in whose hands they place their lives. But among the death and dust Corporal Kent finds himself enigmatically drawn toward a woman recently widowed by the very insurgents he fights against.

www.30degreessouth.co.za

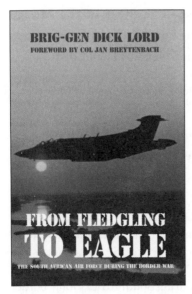

From Fledgling to Eagle—The South African Air Force during the Border War

Brigadier-General Dick Lord

978-1-920143-30-5; Cloth & dust jacket (hardback); R295.00; 544pp; 234 x 153mm; >300 colour & b/w photos, 40 maps, diagrams

From Fledgling to Eagle chronicles the evolution of the SAAF in the 'Border War' that raged in Angola and South West Africa (Namibia) from 1966 to 1989, covering all the major South African Defence Force (SADF) operations from Ongulumbashe to the 'April Fools' Day war' in 1989. Dick Lord, who writes in a 'from the cockpit' style, has drawn on his own first-hand operational reports and diaries, incorporating anecdotes from dozens of aviators from a wide variety of squadrons—Buccaneers, Canberras, Mirages, Bosboks, C-160s and -130s and helicopters. He also expands on the close relationship the SAAF had with the ground troops in a variety of operations—such units as the Parabats, Recces and Koevoet.

However, Lord studies the broader ramifications of the conflict in that it was not a simple black–white war. Angola was really just a sideshow for the Soviets who wanted to bleed the SAAF in a war of attrition before attempting total domination of South Africa—their ultimate goal. He is unafraid to admit SADF mistakes—of Operations *Hooper* and *Packer* he says: "Lines of communications were too long to ably support the battle, which is why we did not clear them off the east bank of the Cuito River and why they captured the three Oliphant tanks which was their only propaganda victory."

Although he gives credit to the enemy when they put up a stiff fight, he clearly outlines the overwhelming South African successes and dispels, in accurate detail, all enemy claims by giving an accurate account of each battle. He says: "I agree with General Geldenhuys that we thrashed them severely on the Lomba in '85 and '87 … much recent publicity has also been given to the so-called victory of the Forces of Liberation [SWAPO, MPLA, and 50,000 Cubans and Soviets] over the SADF at Cuito Cuanavale in 1988. Nothing could be further from the truth—it is blatant propaganda."

Vlamgat—The Story of the Mirage F1 in the South African Air Force

Brigadier-General Dick Lord

9781920143367; Paperback; R200.00; 368 pages; 234 x 153mm; 56 colour photos, 200 b/w photos, 12 maps, diagrams

"Their hands are shaking ever so slightly. They will be flying again in the morning"

Vlamgat, literally 'flaming hole' in Afrikaans, was the nickname the South African Air Force (SAAF) gave to the Mirage F1, its formidable frontline jet fighter during South Africa's long 'border wars' in South West Africa (Namibia) and Angola from the late 1960s to the late 1980s. Battling Soviet MiG-21s and -23s over African skies, the *Vlammies*, the Mirage pilots as they were affectionately known, acquitted themselves with distinction and honour.

Vlamgat is a gripping account of these pilots and their deeds of bravery; their experiences are authentically related with accuracy, humour and pathos—by the author, himself a *Vlammie*. As Willem Hechter, former Chief of the SAAF, says: "*Vlamgat* deserves a place of pride in the long history of this, the second oldest air force in the world."

"… Perhaps it is the early morning chill that awakens them. They are mostly young—but combat is a maturing process that can change a youth into an adult overnight.

… At last they are suited up and have completed the briefing. The weapons are loaded and the aircraft are serviceable to fly. The pilots forget the anxieties and tension of the early morning hours.

… The peace of the morning is shattered by the rising crescendo of the engine noise.

… Then they are rolling into a steep dive upon the waiting target. Their hands inside their gloves are sweating; their mouths are dry."